Vienna

H. Zdrazil /WIENER TOURISMUSVERBAND

Travel Publications

Hannay House, 39 Clarendon Road
Watford, Herts WD17 1JA, UK
☎ 01923 205 240 – Fax 01923 205 241
www.ViaMichelin.com
TheGreenGuide-uk@uk.michelin.com

Manufacture française des pneumatiques Michelin
Société en commandite par actions au capital de 304 000 000 EUR
Place des Carmes-Déchaux – 63 Clermont-Ferrand (France)
R.C.S. Clermont-Fd B 855 200 507

Typesetting: NORD COMPO, Villeneuve-d'Ascq
Printing and binding: AUBIN, Liguné

Cover design: Carré Noir, Paris 17ᵉ arr.

THE GREEN GUIDE:
The Spirit of Discovery

Leisure time spent with The Green Guide is also a time for refreshing your spirit, enjoying yourself, and taking advantage of our selection of fine restaurants, hotels and other places for relaxing: immerse yourself in the local culture, discover new horizons, experience the local lifestyle. The Green Guide opens the door for you.

Each year our writers go touring: visiting the sights, devising the driving tours, identifying the highlights, selecting the most attractive hotels and restaurants, checking the routes for the maps and plans.

Each title is compiled with great care, giving you the benefit of regular revisions and Michelin's first-hand knowledge. The Green Guide responds to changing circumstances and takes account of its readers' suggestions; all comments are welcome.

Share with us our enthusiasm for travel, which has led us to discover over 60 destinations in France and other countries. Like us, let yourself be guided by the desire to explore, which is the best motive for travel: the spirit of discovery.

Contents

Memorial to Johann Strauss the Younger in the Stadtpark

3BIS/MICHELIN

A "Heuriger"

C. Alessandri/WIENER/TOURISMUSVERBAND

Kirche am Steinhof – window by K Moser

Schloß Schönbrunn

H. Zdrazil/WIENER TOURISMUSVERBAND

P. Koller/WIENER TOURISMUSVERBAND

Maps and plans

RECOMMENDED AS A SUPPLEMENT TO THIS GUIDE:

Michelin road map 926 Austria

A road map indicating tourist sights, at a scale of 1:400 000, with an alphabetical index of towns and places, and overview plans of the Salzburg and Vienna conurbations.

...and when arriving from outside Austria:

Michelin road map 987 Germany, Austria, Benelux, Czech Republic

A road map indicating tourist sights, at a scale of 1:1 000 000

Michelin road and travel atlas Germany

Germany, at a scale of 1:300 000, Benelux, Austria, Switzerland, at a scale of 1:400 000, Czech Republic, at a scale of 1:600 000; 102 city plans, index of place names, spiral-bound, format 22.7 x 30 cm

Michelin road map 970 Europe

A road map indicating tourist sights, at a scale of 1:3 000 000, with an alphabetical index of place names

Michelin road atlas Europe

Spiral-bound with index of place names, over 40 states, 73 city plans and conurbation maps, including Vienna.

www.ViaMichelin.com

The www.ViaMichelin.com website will help you navigate your way around 43 countries with a large number of services and practical tips: online route planning, map extracts (from country maps to city plans), hotel and restaurant recommendations (selections from the Michelin Red Guide) and more.

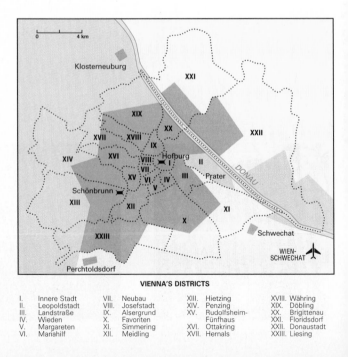

VIENNA'S DISTRICTS

I.	Innere Stadt	VII.	Neubau	XIII.	Hietzing	XVIII.	Währing
II.	Leopoldstadt	VIII.	Josefstadt	XIV.	Penzing	XIX.	Döbling
III.	Landstraße	IX.	Alsergrund	XV.	Rudolfsheim-Fünfhaus	XX.	Brigittenau
IV.	Wieden	X.	Favoriten			XXI.	Floridsdorf
V.	Margareten	XI.	Simmering	XVI.	Ottakring	XXII.	Donaustadt
VI.	Mariahilf	XII.	Meidling	XVII.	Hernals	XXIII.	Liesing

LIST OF MAPS AND PLANS

Using this guide

The Green Guide is a reliable companion for your trip, containing:

- a detailed **city plan** (with an index of streets), highlighting all the important sights.

- a **practical information** section, which gives you valuable assistance in preparing your journey (including addresses, suggested reading, calendar of events) as well as a great many **tips and addresses** (identifiable by the blue stripe along the edge of the page) to make your stay in Vienna and its environs more pleasant: hotels, youth hostels, restaurants, "Heuriger", coffee houses, information on going out, entertainment, shopping, etc.

- an **introduction** to Vienna, giving the geographical situation of the city and describing its historical development, its art, music, and literature all the way to special aspects of Viennese life and interesting background information to prepare you for a stay in the city.

- a description of the **sights and attractions**, listed by their general location in the *City Centre and the Ring*, *Outside the Ring* or *Further afield* sections respectively. Attractive destinations for excursions are described in the *Further afield* section (including Sopron in Hungary and Bratislava in Slovakia). These towns are a relatively short distance from Vienna.

- **admission times and charges** of the sights described.

- a detailed **index** at the end of the travel guide. It lets you quickly and reliably locate people or places and sights described.

We greatly appreciate comments and suggestions from our readers. Contact us at:

Michelin Travel Publications,
Hannay House,
39 Clarendon Road,
Watford, Herts,
WD 17 1JA,
England.
TheGreenGuide-uk@uk.michelin.com
www.ViaMichelin.com

Maxum/WIENER TOURISMUSVERBAND

Key

★★★ **Highly recommended**

★★ **Recommended**

★ **Interesting**

Tourism

⊙	Admission Times and Charges listed at the end of the guide	►►	Visit if time permits
	Sightseeing route with departure point indicated	AZ B	Map co-ordinates locating sights
	Ecclesiastical building		Tourist information
	Synagogue – Mosque		Historic house, castle – Ruins
	Building (with main entrance)		Dam – Factory or power station
■	Statue, small building		Fort – Cave
†	Wayside cross		Prehistoric site
◎	Fountain		Viewing table – View
	Fortified walls – Tower – Gate	▲	Miscellaneous sight

Recreation

	Racecourse		Waymarked footpath
	Skating rink	♦	Outdoor leisure park/centre
	Outdoor, indoor swimming pool		Theme/Amusement park
	Marina, moorings		Wildlife/Safari park, zoo
	Mountain refuge hut		Gardens, park, arboretum
	Overhead cable-car		Aviary, bird sanctuary
	Tourist or steam railway		

Additional symbols

	Motorway (unclassified)		Post office – Telephone centre
❶ ❶	Junction: complete, limited		Covered market
	Pedestrian street		Barracks
	Unsuitable for traffic, street subject to restrictions		Swing bridge
	Steps – Footpath		Quarry – Mine
	Railway – Coach station	B F	Ferry (river and lake crossings)
	Funicular – Rack-railway		Ferry services: Passengers and cars
	Tram – Metro, Underground		Foot passengers only
Bert (R.)...	Main shopping street	③	Access route number common to MICHELIN maps and town plans

Abbreviations and special symbols

G	Police (Gendarmerie)	U	University (Universität)
J	Law courts (Justizgebäude)		Tramway
L	Provincial government (Landhaus)		Park and Ride
M	Museum (Museum)	20	National road wit... (Vorfahrtberecht...
POL.	Police (Polizei)	128	Other feder... (Sonstige P...
R	Town hall (Rathaus)		Depar...
T	Theatre (Theater)		of h...

NB: The German letter ß (eszett) has been used throughout th...

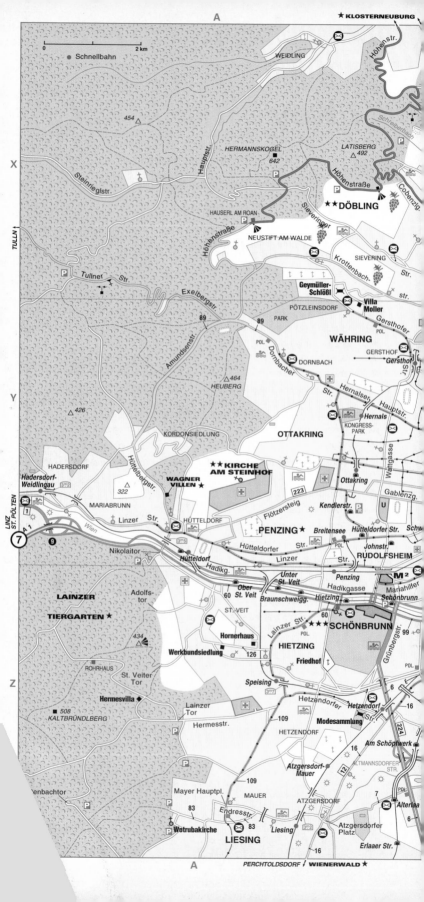

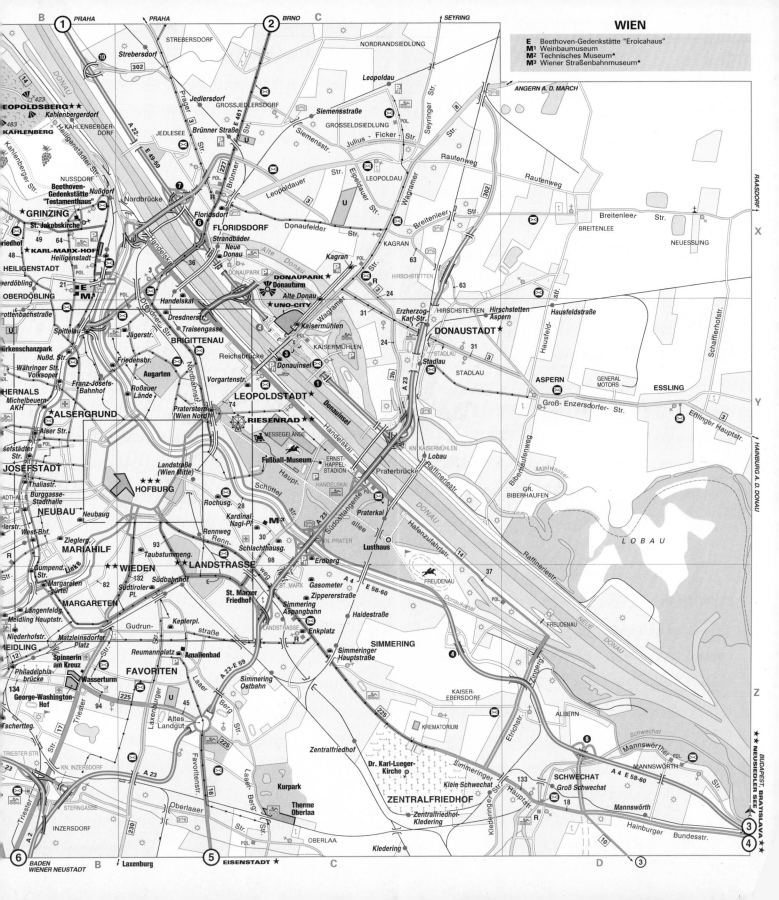

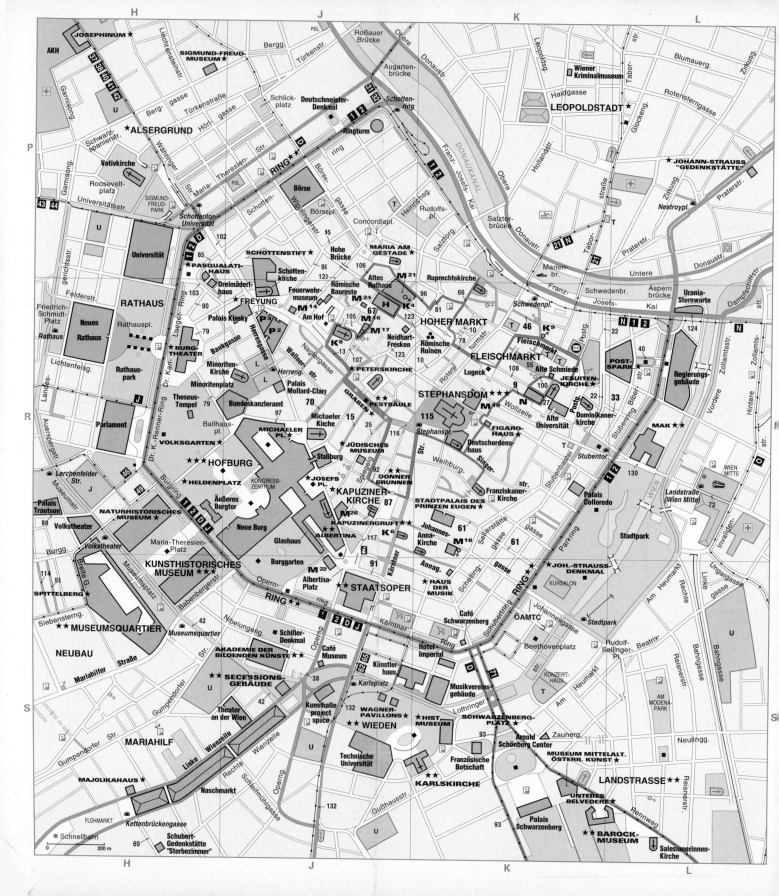

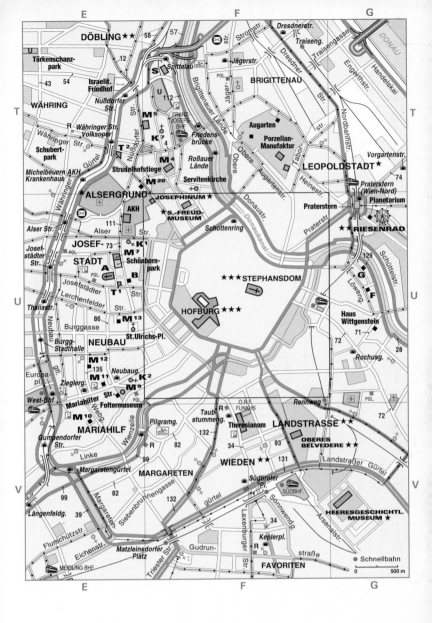

Sights indicated by a letter on maps p. 13 to 15
Street index see p. 16

A	Piaristenkirche Basilika Maria Treu
B	Alte Backstube
F	Hundertwasserhaus
G	KunstHaus Wien
H	Böhmische Hofkanzlei
K¹	Dreifaltigkeitskirche
K²	Mariahilferkirche
K⁴	Salvatorkapelle
K⁶	Malteserkirche
K⁷	Lichtentalkirche
K⁸	Kirche "Zu den neun Chören der Engel"
K⁹	Griech.-orient. Kirche zur Hl. Dreifaltigkeit
M⁴	Palais Liechtenstein
M⁵	Franz-Schubert-Gedenkstätte "Geburtshaus"*
M⁷	Österreichisches Museum für Volkskunde
M⁹	Haus des Meeres
M¹⁰	Haydn-Gedenkstätte*
M¹¹	Kaiserliches Hofmobiliendepot*
M¹²	Museum der Gold- und Silberschmiede

M¹³	Wagner-Haus
M¹⁴	Kunstforum Bank Austria
M¹⁶	Puppen- und Spielzeugmuseum
M¹⁷	Uhrenmuseum der Stadt Wien*
M¹⁸	Ursulinenkirche und-kloster
M¹⁹	Dom- und Diözesanmuseum*
M²⁰	Bezirksmuseum Alsergrund
M²¹	Ausstellung der Österreichischen Freiheitskämpfe
M²²	Gedenkräume des Österr. Theatermuseums
M²⁴	Museum Judenplatz
M²⁶	Österreichisches Theatermuseum
N	Akademie der Wissenschaften
P²	Palais Ferstel
P³	Palais Harrach
S	Müllverbrennung-Fernwärme-Heizwerk
T¹	Theater in der Josefstadt
T²	Volksoper

STREET INDEX OF VIENNA

Kärntner Durchgang – American Bar

Hüttelbergstrasse – Prima Villa

Linke Wienzeile – House with medallions

Bognergasse – Apothecary Angel

Michaelerplatz – Looshaus

The café in the Kunsthistorisches Museum

Practical information

Before leaving

USEFUL ADDRESSES

Wien-Tourismus

Internet: www.info.wien.at

Tourist information (with accommodation rentals, sightseeing and ticket service): Albertinaplatz (corner Maysedergasse/Tegetthoffstr.), 1st District, daily 9am to 7pm; ☎ 01/24 555, Fax: 01/24 555 666.

Public transport: U1, U2, U4 (to Karlsplatz or. Oper), trams 1, 2, 62, 65 (Karlsplatz or Oper), Bus 4A, 59A (to Karlsplatz or Oper), Bus 3A (to Albertinaplatz), Badner Bahn (to Karlsplatz or Oper).

Written inquiries: Wien-Tourismus, A-1025 Wien. Wien-Tourismus also distributes a **city map** for free (it's available at most hotels), indicating the most important means of public transportation and museums, as well as other tourist information.

Other tourist offices in Vienna: Westbahnhof, the main train station (Mon-Fri 8am-6.30pm, Sat 8am-noon; ☎ 01/9 30 00 31 060); Südbahnhof (Mon-Fri 8am-7pm, Sat 8am-1pm; ☎ 01/9 30 00 31 050); Airport (daily 8.30am-9pm , ☎ 01/70 07-32 828 or 32 875); Nordeinfahrt/Florisdorfer Brücke (bridge), "Donauinsel" exit (1 May-30 Sept 10am-6pm); Südeinfahrt (A 2), "Zentrum" exit (beg Apr-30 June 9am-7pm; 1 July-30 Sept 8am-10pm; 1-31 Oct 9am-7pm); Westeinfahrt, Autobahn rest stop Auhof (1 Apr-31 Oct 8am-10pm, 1 Nov-31 Mar 10am-6pm), also tourist information at Rathaus (Town Hall).

For young people (13-26 years): wienXtra jugendinfo, 1 Babenbergerstr., corner of Burgring, Mon-Sat noon-7pm, ☎ 01/17 99, Fax: 01/5 85 24 99, www.jugendinfowien.at or www.wienxtra.at

Tourist information points on the outskirts of Vienna

– **Niederösterreich (Lower Austria)**: Niederösterreich Werbung GmbH, Postfach 10 000, A-1010 Wien, ☎ 01/5 36 10 62 00, Fax: 01/5 36 10 60 60, www.niederoesterreich.at
– direct contact, catalogues, brochures and reservations at Reisebüro Intropa, 1. Bezirk, Kärtner Str. 38
– **Burgenland**: Burgenland Tourismus, Schloss Esterházy, A-7000 Eisenstadt, ☎ 0 26 82/6 33 84, Fax: 0 26 82/63 84 20, www.burgenland.at

Local tourist information points:

These points are indicated by the symbol ⏹ on the city maps of this Michelin guide.
– Baden, 3 Brusattiplatz, A-2500 Baden, ☎ 0 22 52/4 45 31-59, Fax: 0 22 52/8 07 33, www.baden.at
– Eisenstadt, Tourismusverband Eisenstadt, Schloss Esterházy, A-7000 Eisenstadt, ☎ 0 26 82/67 39-0, Fax: 0 26 82/67 39-1, www.eisenstadt.co.at
– Klosterneuburg, In der Au, A-3400 Klosterneuburg, ☎ 0 22 43/3 20 38, Fax: 0 22 43/2 58 78, www.tiscover.com/klosterneuburg
– March-Donauland: Tourismusverband March-Donauland, A-2404 Petronell-Carnuntum, 296 Hauptstr., ☎ 0 21 63/35 55-0, Fax: 0 21 63/35 55-12, www.marchdonauland.at
– Mörbisch, Mörbisch-Tourismus, 23 Hauptstr., A-7072 Mörbisch, ☎ 0 26 85/88 56, Fax: 0 26 85/8 43 09, www.moerbisch.com
– Rust, Rathaus, 1 Conradplatz, A-7071 Rust, ☎ 0 26 85/5 02-0, Fax: 0 26 85/5 02-10, www.burgenland.at/rust
– Wiener Neustadt, 1-3 Hauptplatz, A-2700 Wiener Neustadt, ☎ 0 26 22/37 34 68, Fax: 0 26 22/8 20 65, www.wiener-neustadt.at
– Wienerwald, Tourismusregion Wienerwald, 11 Hauptplatz , A-3002 Purkersdorf, ☎ 0 22 31/6 21 76, Fax: 0 22 31/6 55 10, www.tiscover.com/wienerwald

Österreich Werbung

Internet: www.austria-tourism.at

Austrian National Tourist Offices:

Vienna: 38 Kärntnerstrasse, open daily 9am-7pm.

Vienna: Rathaus, Friedrich-Schmidt-Platz, open daily 9am-7pm.

Australia: 1st Floor, 36 Carrington Street, Sydney, NSW 2000. ☎ (2) 92 99 36 21. Fax (2) 92 99 38 08.

Canada: Montreal: 1010 Sherbrooke, Suite 1410, Montréal, Québec H3A 2R7. ☎ (514) 849 37 08. Fax (514) 849 95 77, e-mail: atc.mtr@istar.ca, Toronto: 2 Bloor Street East, Suite 3330, Toronto, Ontario M4W 1A8. ☎ (416) 967 33 81. Fax: (416) 967 41 01, e-mail: anto-tor@sympatico.ca; Vancouver: Suite 1380 Granville Square, 200 Granville Street, Vancouver, B.C. V6C 1S4, e-mail: atradebc@uniserve.com

Ireland: Merrion Hall, Strand Road, Sandymount, PO Box 2506, Dublin, ☎ (01) 283 0488.

UK: 14 Cork Street, London W1X 1PF. ☏ (202) 7629 0461, Fax: (202) 7499 6036, info@anto.co.uk
USA: 500 Fifth Avenue, Suite 800, New York, N.Y. 10110. ☏ (212) 944 68 80. Fax: (212) 730 45 68, info@oewnyc.com

Diplomatic representation

Australia: 2 Mattiellistrasse, A-1040 Vienna. ☏ 01/5 12 85 80, Fax: 01/5 13 29 08.

United Kingdom: 12 Jauresgasse, A-1030 Vienna ☏ 01/71 61 30, Fax: 01/7 16 13 29 99.

Canada: 2 Laurenzerbergasse, A-1010 Vienna. ☏ 01/5 31 38 33 21, Fax: 01/5 31 38 39 05.

Ireland: 16-18 Rotenturmstrasse, A-1010 Vienna. ☏ 01/7 15 42 46, Fax: 01/7 13 60 04.

New Zealand: 28A Springsiedelgasse, A-1190 Vienna. ☏ 01/3 18 85 05, Fax: 01/3 18 67 17.

USA: 16 Boltzmanngasse, A-1090 Vienna. ☏ 01/3 13 39, Fax: 01/4 06 52 60 (embassy).

USA: 2 Gartenbaupromenade, Vienna. ☏ 01/31 33 90 (consulate).

FORMALITIES

Formalities – Holders of a valid national passport from a member state of the European Union (even citizens of countries adhering to the Schengen Agreement, like Austria, are advised to bring some form of official identification with them), from the USA or from some Commonwealth countries (Australia, Canada, New Zealand) require no visa to enter Austria, and may remain there for up to 3 months (British citizens up to 6 months). Visitors of other nationalities should check with the **Austrian Embassy** whether they need a visa.

UK
Austrian Embassy
18 Belgrave Mews West
London SW1X 8HU
UK
☏ (020) 7235 3731
Web: *www.austria.org.uk*

Ireland
Austrian Embassy
15 Ailesbury Court
93 Ailesbury Road
Dublin 4
IRELAND
☏ (01) 269 4577

USA
Austrian Embassy
3524 International Court NW
Washington DC 20008
USA
☏ 202-895-6700 or 202-895-6767
Web: www.austria.org

Australia
Austrian Embassy
12 Talbot Street
Forrest ACT 2603
Canberra NSW
AUSTRALIA
(Postal address: PO Box 3375, Manuka, ACT 2603)
☏ (26) 295 1533
Web: www.austriaemb.org.au

Health insurance – British citizens should apply to their local post office for an E111 form (application form included in the brochure *Health Advice for Travellers* available from the post office), which entitles the holder to emergency medical treatment for accidents or unexpected illness in EU countries. Non-EU residents should check that their private health insurance policy covers them for travel abroad, and if necessary take out supplementary medical insurance with specific overseas coverage. All prescription drugs should be clearly labelled, and we recommend that you carry a copy of the prescription with you.

For details or other questions, please consult with your health insurance broker directly.

Pets – House pets, such as dogs and cats, require an official vaccination pass. The vaccination has to be at least 30 days old before crossing the border, but no older than one year.

Customs – Since Austria became a full member of the European Union in January 1995, EU nationals travelling in Austria are subject to EU regulations (citizens of countries adhering to the Schengen Agreement are in principle not subject to any customs restrictions when entering Austria, also part of the Schengen Agreement since 1998). Tourists are not charged duty on items brought into the country for their personal use. The UK Customs Office produces a leaflet on customs regulations and the full range of "duty free" allowances *(A Guide for Travellers)*; for details contact HM Customs and Excise (London Central office), Berkeley House, 304 Regents Park Road, London N 3 2JY, ☎ (020) 7865 4400, Web site: *www.hmce.gov.uk*). The US Customs Service (PO Box 7407, Washington, DC 20044, ☎ 202-927-5580) offers a free publication *Know Before You Go* for US residents. Further information can be obtained from the Austrian Customs Office in Vienna: ☎ 01/79 59 09.

TRAVEL TIMES

Weather – The wind in Vienna blows from every imaginable direction, but it's the continental climate, with extensive low-pressure systems, that really marks the city's weather. For many, the climate is ideal, with well-defined seasons, hot summers, cold snowy winters and a low yearly average of precipitation (715mm/28in in the western part of town, 561mm/21in along the Danube).
Average temperature in winter is 0° C/32° F (cold snaps of up to -15° C/5° F are fairly frequent) and 25° C/77° F in summer (with highs that seldom exceed 30° C/86° F because heat waves tend to be dampened by the wind).

Recommended travel times – Vienna is good at any time of the year and is well frequented. Of course, the city is especially filled with tourists in the summer. If you have the choice, and you would like to visit Vienna in peace and quiet, then avoid the periods around Easter, Christmas, and between July and August.

Public holidays – 1 January (New Year), 6 January (Epiphany), Easter Monday, 1 May (State holiday), Ascension Day, Whit Monday, Corpus Christi, 15 August (Assumption of the BVM), 26 October (Austrian National Holiday), 1 November (All Saints' Day), 8 December (Immaculate Conception), 25 and 26 December (Christmas).

INFORMATION FOR THE DISABLED

Wien-Tourismus posts comprehensive information for the disabled on the Internet at www.info.wien.at (hotels, museums, theatre, cinemas, restaurants, public transport, special city tours, public disabled toilets, etc). From the English-language homepage you go to the link *Special Programmes* and *Vienna for Guests with Disabilities*. You can download the file from there.
The *Handicap-Redaktion* of Wien-Tourismus is available at ☎ 01/21 11 42 32, Fax: 01/2 16 84 92. The tips downloaded from the Internet can also be requested there by fax or by mail.

Arriving in Vienna

GETTING THERE

By air

Travel by air – Scheduled flights are provided by **Austrian Airlines** *(www.aua.com)* from London Heathrow (Austrian Airlines information line at Heathrow: ☎ 020 8745 7114) to Vienna; by **British Airways** *(www.british-airways.com)* from London Heathrow and London Gatwick to Vienna; by **Lauda Air** *(www.laudaair.com)* from London Gatwick and Manchester to Vienna and Salzburg; by **Aer Lingus** *(www.aerlingus.ie)* from Dublin to London for connecting flights to Vienna; and by **Lufthansa** *(www.lufthansa.com)* from Dublin to Munich (Germany). Contact your travel agent for details

Wien-Schwechat airport – ☎ 01/70 07-2 22 33, Fax: 01/70 07-2 69 21 central flight information); www.viennaairport.com

Bus stop and taxi stand is right opposite the arrivals terminal hall (☎ 01/70 07-35 910 or 32 717). Buses (one-way to town €5,09, tickets at the vending machine or from the driver) connect to the Westbahnhof and Südbahnhof and to the City Air Terminal, Hotel Hilton, in the centre of town (with connections to the underground lines U3, U4 – Haltestelle Landstrasse station). The Schnellbahn (S7) shuttles between the airport and the Südbahnhof (around 30min travel time). The Klein-Schwechat station has a connection to buses and the underground station Simmering (U3).

The following airlines offer several daily flights to and from Vienna:

Austrian Airlines – Austrian Airlines Town Office, Kärntner Ring 18, A-1010 Wien, ☎ 01/17 89 (bookings and reservations number), www.aua.com

Lufthansa – Central information and reservation offices, Wilhelmshöher Allee 254, D-34119 Kassel, ☎ 0180/3 80 38 03, www.lufthansa.com

Franz-Josef train station in Vienna

By train

The **Österreichischen Bundesbahnen (ÖBB)** provides information on schedules at ☎ 05 17 17, or on the Internet at www.oebb.at Travel by rail is from London Victoria via Dover and Ostend to Vienna (direct). The Orient Express travels from Paris (which can be reached via the Channel Tunnel on Eurostar) through Germany to Salzburg and Vienna.

Details of motorail services can be obtained from DER Travel Service in London (18 Conduit Street, London W1R 9TD, ☎ 020 7290 1111, Fax: 020 7629 7501, web site: *www.dertravel.co.uk*), and further information on rail timetables and fares from local travel agents or rail companies. Austrian rail (Österreichische Bundesbahnen) web site: *www.oebb.at*

Vorteilscard ÖBB – This rail card (€93.75) is valid for one year and entitles the holder to reductions of 50% on standard ÖBB rail fares (luggage and cycles are also up to half the price), as well as a range of additional advantages such as special discounts in hotels and car rental agencies. There are also special family rates available. The rail card *(Vorteilscard)* is on sale at Austrian railway stations and travel agencies with ticket sales facilities and some mainline stations abroad. For further details call ☎ 01/9 30 00 3 64 57 or consult the Internet *(www.oebb.at)*.

By bus

Eurolines is an international partnership of bus companies that have a Europe-wide network connecting 500 cities and 25 countries. Contact in various countries:

Austria – www.eurolines.at
Vienna: Eurolines Austria with an Internet Café, 3-5 Invalidenstr., A-1033 Wien; Mon-Fri 6.30am-9pm, Sat-Sun and holidays 6.30am-11.30am and 4pm-9pm, ☎ 01/7 12 04 53, Fax: 01/7 12 04 53-20.
Eurolines Austria – Busterminal Südbahnhof, Arsenalstraße, A-1030 Wien; daily 1pm-9pm, ☎ 01/79 68 55 20, Fax: 01/7 96 85 52-20.
Salzburg: Blaguss Internationale Buslinien, 43 Rudolf-Biebl-Str., A-5020 Salzburg; Mon-Fri 12.30pm-3.30pm, ☎/Fax: 06 62/42 10 89.

Great Britain – www.eurolines.co.uk
Eurolines UK – 4 Cardiff Road, Luton, LU1 1PP, ☎ 08705 143219 (10p per minute), Fax: 01582 400694.

By ship

DDSG Blue Danube Schifffahrt GmbH, 7 Friedrichstr., A-1010 Wien, ☎ 01/58 88 00, www.ddsg-blue-danube.at offers trips from April to October between Vienna and Bratislava (Slovakia, *see Further afield, Bratislava*) or Budapest (Hungary) as well as Dürnstein in the Wachau (Sundays only; other piers at Krems, Tulln, Korneuburg).

23

By car or motorcycle

Route planner – Michelin offers drivers and motorcyclists a convenient route planner at: www.ViaMichelin.com

Besides your starting point and destination, you can define stations on the way or establish a number of other criteria (such as time, distance, use of motorways, tolls etc). You will then receive information on distance, travel time, costs, hotels and restaurants (selection from the Michelin Red Guide) along the chosen route, and even map extracts from the tried and tested Michelin maps.

You will find further products of interest on page 6 in the *Maps and Plans* section of the Contents.

Traffic code – It is necessary to carry a valid driving licence (preferably an international driving licence), and third party insurance cover is compulsory. Drivers are advised to obtain the International Green Card from insurance companies.

Speed limits – Traffic in Austria drives on the right. Seat belts must be worn. The blood alcohol limit is 0.5ml/g. The speed limit is 130kph/80mph on motorways/highways, 100kph/62mph on other roads, and 50kph/31mph in built-up areas. Private cars towing a load in excess of 750kg/1 650lb must not exceed 100kph/62mph on motorways/highways, 80kph/50mph on other roads and 50kph/31mph in built-up areas.

Highway code – Children under the age of 12 and less than 1.5m/4ft 11in in height must travel in appropriate and approved booster seats. It is compulsory to carry a first aid kit and emergency triangle. The use of mobile telephones inside a moving vehicle is only permitted if you have a hands-free set.

The law prescribes the wearing of a helmet for all two-wheel vehicles, ie, motorcycles and bicycles. You must also keep your lights on during the day. Accidents in which any person is harmed must be reported to the police. In the event of damage to property, only report to the police if the identity of individuals involved cannot be proven.

Fuel – All petrol stations offer diesel and lead-free normal petrol (91 Octane) and Euro-Super (lead-free, 95 octane). Sale of leaded petrol is prohibited in Austria. An additive is sold at many petrol stations in 250ml bottles allowing you to run an older vehicle that might not take lead-free petrol.

A full tank and a 10-litre (2.5 gallon) reserve may be imported tax-free.

Motorway tolls (Autobahngebühren) – Since 1 January 1997, tolls have been levied on motorways, dual carriageways and urban highways in Austria. Motorists must buy a toll disc (vignette, or *Pickerl*), to be displayed in the centre or on the left of their windscreen (the discs are not valid if not displayed). Vignettes are available for one year (from December until the end of the January of the year after the following year, cost €72,60), two months (€21,80) and ten days (€7,60), valid from a day of the motorist's choice). No extra vignettes are required for trailers/caravans; camper vans are charged the same as a car. Vignettes can be bought from Austrian motoring associations (ARBÖ, ÖAMTC), larger petrol stations, post offices and tobacconists' and at the border crossing points.

Driving in winter – In snowy conditions winter tyres should be fitted, or chains if conditions are particularly severe. The ÖAMTC and ARBÖ have snow chain rental outlets in every Austrian province.

Breakdown service – This is provided *(small charge for non-members)* by two Austrian automobile clubs:

ÖAMTC (Österreichischer Automobil-, Motorrad- undTouring Club,1-3 Schubertring, A-1010 Wien, ☏ 01/71 19 97), breakdown number ☏ 120; and **ARBÖ** (Auto-, Motor-undRadfahrerbund Österreich), Mariahilfer Straße 180, A-1150 Wien, ☏ 01/89 12 10, breakdown number ☏ 123.

Other important telephone numbers are: **Police** 133, **Ambulance** 144.

Traffic reports – These are given on the hour in English after the news bulletin on radio station Blue Danube Radio, or on Ö3. If your German holds out you may try the Verkehrs- und Radar-Hotline ☏ 0 900 600 601 (approx €0.70 /min.), which gives you radar information as well. Or try the web site www.kronehit.at

GETTING AROUND VIENNA

Driving

Driving around Vienna is not recommended, simply because the public transport network is excellent. However, should you decide to use a car, note that 50kph/32mph is the speed limit within the city limits (unless otherwise signposted).

Parking – The old town of Vienna and the adjacent districts (1-9 and 20) are **fee-paying parking zones** (district 1 Mon-Fri 9am-7pm, parking duration up to 1hr 30min; in districts 2-9 and 20 9am-8pm, parking duration up to 2hr). However, these zones are only signposted at the entrance to each district concerned (no further indication is given in the streets themselves – a paid-up parking ticket is obligatory from the minute you park). In commercial streets, parking regulations (for example, concerning how long you may park) may vary, in which case these will be specifically indicated.

Pre-paid parking tickets can be bought from most authorised tobacconists (Tabaktrafiken) and banks, stations and from Vienna transport authority (Wiener Linien) ticket offices. These tickets have to be completely filled in at the beginning of your parking time: tick off the day, month, year and hour. Visitors who have booked a hotel in advance are advised to telephone before they arrive and confirm where they may leave their car (a day parking ticket may be available from reception).

The most practical solution to the difficulty of parking in the city centre is offered by numerous multi-storey or underground **car parks**, which are open daily 24hr a day. In district 1 these are the following: the car park in the Plaza-Hotel, Schottenring 11, the Parkhaus City, Wollzeile 7, the Parkgarage Am Hof, Am Hof, the Garage Freyung, Freyung, the underground car park Rathauspark, Dr.-Karl-Lueger-Ring, die Palais-Corso-Garage, Mahlerstr. 12, the Kärntnerring-Garage, Mahlerstr. 8, the Kärntner Straße underground car park, Kärntner Str. 51 (next to the Staatsoper), Garage Cobdengasse, Cobdengasse 2, the Parkring-Garage (Hotel Marriot), Coburgbastei 5, the Garage Beethovenplatz, Beethovenplatz 3, the underground car park at Franz-Josefs-Kai, Morzinplatz 1 and finally the Garage Gonzagagasse, Gonzagagasse 4.

An overview of car parks in Vienna can be requested from the tourist office or found on the Internet *(www.wkw.at/garagen)*.

Another interesting possibility to avoid the difficult parking situation of the inner city is the use of **Park & Ride parking lots**. Drop your car off in one of these car parks at the edge of town and use public transport to reach your destination. Park & Ride spots are available at the underground stations Donauinsel (U1), Ottakring and Erdberg (U3), Spittelau and Siebenhirten (U6), as well as at the Schnellbahnstation (suburban train stop) Brünner Straße (S3).

Rental cars – Most of the major car rental agencies have offices on the Ring or at the airport, including (with reference to the city offices): Avis, Opernring 5, 1. Bezirk, ☎ 01/5 87 62 41; Denzel Europcar Interrent, Erdbergstr. 202, 3. Bezirk, ☎ 01/7 99 61 76; Hertz, Kärntner Ring 17, 1. Bezirk, ☎ 01/5 12 86 77.

Taxis

Taxis in Vienna are available by telephone or at taxi stands. If you wish to flag down a cab, make sure its yellow light is on, a sign that the taxi is free. If the taxi is in some way occupied, the sign will be off. When calling a taxi by phone, the amount of time you will have to wait is generally given (☎ 01/3 13 00, 4 01 00 or 6 01 60). Rides around the inner city area are relatively low. A trip from the centre to the airport or back, however, costs a fair amount (approx €33). It is usual to round off the sum as a manner of tipping. The taxi meter displays the cost of the ride on the left and the applicable supplement on the right (weekend or night tariff). Baggage weighing over 20kg (approx 44lb) costs extra. Night tariffs are applicable weekdays from 11pm to 6am and throughout the weekend and holidays.

Public transport

Vienna has an excellent public transport system. Travelling is quick and easy, either from the city centre to the outskirts or from one district to another *(see plan in the back cover fold-out)*. The underground, trams and buses operate from 5.30am to midnight. Viennese transport authorities, Wiener Linien, operate services in the central zones of the Vienna city area (all districts) and are linked with the east Austrian transport authority (Verkehrsverbund Ost-Region, VOR). Written enquiries and requests for information by telephone can be addressed to either organisation:

Wiener Linien, Erdbergstr. 202, 1031 Wien, ☎ 01/79 09 105.

Verkehrsverbund Ost-Region, Neubaugasse 1, 1070 Wien, ☎ 05 26/60 48 0. Further details on public transport in Vienna are to be found on the Internet at the relevant web site *(www.wienerlinien.co.at* or *www.vor.at*).

Tourists in Vienna are advised to pay a visit in person to one of the **information and ticket offices** in the following U-Bahn stations: Stephansplatz, Schwedenplatz, Karlsplatz, Landstraße/Wien-Mitte, Westbahnhof, Spittelau, Schottentor, Reumannplatz, Philadelphiabrücke, Hietzing, Floridsdorf or Kagran. These outlets can also supply timetables for Vienna's transport system or the more comprehensive timetable book, as well as selling tickets (runabout or magnetic strip tickets).

Tickets – Single rides cost €1.60 (€1.38 if bought in advance). You may use any mode of transport on the Viennese network (within the Bereich 100) and change as often as you like, as long as you do not interrupt the ride and provided that you are heading in a recognisable direction. Tickets that are well-suited to individual needs of travellers include the **24-** (€4.36) and **72-** (€10.90) **hour runabout ticket** or the **8-day ticket** (€21.80; this allows the bearer unlimited travel within Vienna city centre limits per strip validated, on the date it was validated; those days do not have to be consecutive, and the ticket can be given to someone else, just validate one strip per day per person). It is valid for the Bereich 100 area, except for the night-time buses. If staying longer in Vienna, you may want to purchase the monthly **Monatskarte**. The **Wien-Karte** costs €15.26 and is valid not only for all public transport for 72hr, but also offers discounts in many museums, establishments and shops; validate it the first time you use it *(see General information, Inexpensive travel on p. 27)*. All tickets can be purchased at vending machines at the underground stations, except for the Wien-Karte. The information and sales points are open Mon-Fri. 6.30am-6.30pm.

Public transport is free for children under six. People under 15 may travel free on Sundays and public holidays, and when the schools are closed in the Vienna educational district. Travelling without a ticket incurs a fine of €40.70 plus the price of the ticket.

U-Bahn – The underground symbol is a capital U, white on a blue ground. The *U-Bahn* system consists of five lines covering the whole of the city *(see plan of the underground system)*. The five lines are colour coded: U1, red; U2, mauve; U3, orange; U4, green; U6, brown (the U5 line is still in the planning stage). There are electronic display panels on the platforms, with the name of the terminus. Locate it on the underground map in order to avoid travelling in the wrong direction. A loudspeaker system in the train calls out the stations. The underground is the best means of transport and it offers numerous connections to the Schnellbahn trains (for suburban destinations).

Viennese tramways

Trams – The *Strassenbahn* (Viennese trams) are red and white, the city's colours. In the street, the stops have oval white panels outlined in red, bearing the words "Strassenbahn-Haltestelle". Inside, a loudspeaker system calls out the names of the stops. To enter or alight from the tram, press the button near the doors.

Buses – The buses, which are also red and white, cover the city in a transverse direction to the tram routes. The stops have white semicircular panels outlined in black, bearing the words "Autobus – Haltestelle". Inside the bus, loudspeakers call out the names of the stops. To enter or alight from the bus, press the button near the doors. Buses are particularly convenient for travelling to outlying districts

Trains – There is a **Schnellbahn** and Bundesbahn service to and from several stations in Vienna and the surrounding region. A visitor to Vienna would mainly use the Schnellbahn (blue logo) from which there are numerous connections to the underground, tram or bus. Tickets for these means of transport are also valid for the Schnellbahn, but only in zone 100.

Night lines – 22 night lines operate from midnight to dawn. It is a bus system, running every 30min and displaying an N for Nachtbus or Nachtline. Lists of these lines and their routes are available from the stations mentioned above with regard to tickets. A single ticket is slightly more expensive, at €1.09, a runabout ticket with four rides costs €3.27.

On foot

In the town centre, walking is the best means of getting around. It is the only way to fully appreciate Vienna's historical centre. Many streets in the Innere Stadt are pedestrian precincts or relatively free of cars. However, beyond the 1st district, one must take extra care, for two reasons. Firstly, there is a tram line on the Ring running in the opposite direction to the cars, which could cause problems if you are not careful when alighting from the tram; secondly, people tend to drive relatively fast in Vienna. The law ordering cars to stop for pedestrians at the zebra crossing, however, is generally obeyed.

By bicycle

Cyclists in Vienna have some 700km/435mi of cycle paths at their disposal. Those arriving in Vienna by train can hire bicycles from the following stations: West- and Südbahnhof, Wien Nord and Florisdorf, and Franz-Josefs-Bahnhof. These can be returned at any station with luggage check-in facilities. Further cycle hire outlets can be found on the Donauinsel or at the Hundertwasserhaus (with some form of identification such as a passport left as a security).

The brochure entitled *Tips für Radfahrer*, available free from tourist offices, gives full details of the above.

Recommended bicycle rentals: Pedal Power, Ausstellungsstr. 3 (opposite the Ferris wheel in the Prater), 2. Bezirk, ☎ 01/7 29 72 34, Fax: 01/7 29 72 35, www.pedal power.at (April-Oct; delivery to hotel on request, tour descriptions, bicycle maps).

General information

INEXPENSIVE TRAVEL

Wien-Karte – This ticket is valid for three days and is available from many hotels, tourist information centres, various ticket sales and information offices belonging to the Viennese transport authorities (Wiener Linien; for example, Stephansplatz, Karlsplatz, Westbahnhof, Landstrasse). It can also be purchased from abroad by credit card on ☎ 00 43/1/7 98 44 00 28. The ticket gives unlimited free travel on the city's public transport (underground/subway (U-Bahn), bus, tram – but not on night buses) for 72hr (from when it is first validated), as well as discounts on the price of entry to about 150 museums, on purchases in certain department stores and in cafés, wine bars and restaurants. Full details are included in the coupon booklet that comes with the ticket. The Wien-Karte costs €15,25. Information at Wien-Tourismus *(see also Practical Information: Getting around Vienna, Public transport, Tickets)*.

GOOD TO KNOW

Money matters

Currency – Austria introduced the euro (€) on 1 January 1999. As in the other 11 EU nations, the bills and coins of the European currency have been used since 1 January 2002, finally replacing the Schilling as the official currency in Austria (1 March 2002) €1 equals 100 cents. Coins come in denominations of 1, 2, 5, 10, 20 and 50 cents and 1 and €2. Bills come in denominations of €5, 10, 20, 50, 100, 200 and 500. The design of the tails of the coins differs from one EU state to the next. Austria decided on the following designs for its coins: 1 cent: gentian, 2 cents: edelweiss, 5 cents: Alpine primrose, 10 cents: Stephansdom, 20 cents: Belvedere, 50 cents: Secession, €1: Wolfgang Amadeus Mozart, €2: Bertha von Suttner, Austrian Nobel Peace Prize-winner in 1905, author and pacifist.

Banks – Open as a rule Mon-Wed, Fri 8am-12.30pm and 13.30pm-3pm, Thur 8am-12.30pm and 13.30pm-5.30pm.

Credit cards – Widely accepted in Austria (MasterCard and Visa are the most commonly accepted). As a rule, you will have no problem using a credit card at hotels, restaurants, shops and petrol stations in Austria.

Emergencies

Ambulance **144**, police **133**, fire **122**, breakdown service **120**, **123** (the three-digit numbers may be dialled without a prefix).

Opening times

Shopping – Shops are allowed to open Mon-Fri 6am-7.30pm and Sat 6am-5pm. Obviously there is variation within these core hours. Shops in popular tourist areas and city centres often have special dispensation to remain open longer (Mon-Fri until 9pm, Sat until 6pm, in some stations and airports daily until 11pm).

Pharmacies – They have rotating night and Sunday hours. A closed pharmacy will post the address and phone for the nearest open pharmacy.

Post office

Information available on the Internet at www.post.at

The second and third digit in Viennese **post codes** denote the district (Bezirk) in question, thus 1070 denotes the 7. Bezirk, Vienna. Post offices in Vienna are generally open Mon-Fri 8am-noon and 2pm-6pm. There are post offices with longer business hours in Vienna:

Main post office of the 1. Bezirks, Fleischmarkt 19, 1. Bezirk, ☎ 01/51 50 90, rund um die Uhr geöffnet.

Post office at the Franz-Joseph-Bahnhof, Althahnstr. 10, 9. Bezirk, ☎ 01/3 19 14 70, Mon-Fri 6am-10pm, Sat, Sun and holidays 7am-10pm.

Post office at the Südbahnhof, Wiedner Gürtel 1a, 10. Bezirk, ☎ 01/50 18 10, Mon-Sat 7am-10pm.

Post office at the Westbahnhof, Europaplatz 1/Mariahilferstr. 132, 15. Bezirk, ☎ 01/89 11 50, daily 6-11pm.

Postage – Stamps are available at post offices and tobacconists *(Tabaktrafik)*. There are two types of mailing: *Priority* (or airmail alternatively) and the cheaper variant *Non Priority* with longer delivery times; there are also two delivery zones: *Europa* (Europe) and *Welt* (World).

Postal traffic within Austria is not divided between *Priority* and *Non Priority*. Standard letters (until 20 g) and postcards cost €0,51. The same postage applies to both. *Priority* is for the rest of Europe.

Post boxes – Austrian post boxes are usually yellow and those with red stripes are emptied more frequently.

Voltage

Austria runs on 220 V. On campgrounds, the amperage can vary between 4 and 16 A.

Tobacconists

Tobacco products are available at the *Tabaktrafik* for the officially set price. At hotels, restaurants and other venues you will have to pay a surcharge. The tobacconists also sell tickets for public transport, parking permits, postage stamps and telephone cards.

Telephoning

Telephoning Austria from elsewhere: 0043 + area code without the 0 + subscriber number.

From Austria:

to Great Britain: 0044;
to the USA: 001;
to Australia: 0061;
to New Zealand: 0064;
to Canada: 001;
to Hungary: 0036;
to Slovakia: 00421.
Phone cards for public phones are available at Telekom Austria, at tobacconists and at hotels.

A LOOK BEYOND THE BORDER

Bratislava in Slovakia and Sopron in Hungary are close to Vienna and have been mentioned in this travel guide.

Formalities – Citizens of EU countries may travel with personal ID or a passport, citizens from other countries require a passport to cross the border. A Class 3 EU format driving permit or an international permit are required as well, a green insurance card is also needed.

Traffic regulations

Slovakia – Your vehicle must display its country of provenance. The blood alcohol limit is a strict 0,0. A sticker is needed for use of the motorways, it is available at the border crossings. Top speeds are 60kph/38mph in built-up areas, 90kph/56mph on most other roads and 130kph/80mph on the motorways. (These speed limits are lowered in the event of rain). Motorcyclists and their passengers must wear a helmet.

Hungary – Your vehicle must display its country of provenance. The blood alcohol limit is a strict 0,0. A sticker is needed for use of the motorways, it is available at the border crossings. Top speeds are 50kph/31mph in built-up areas, 100kph/62mph on most other roads and 120kph/75mph on the motorways. (These speed limits are lowered in the event of rain). Drivers must switch on their headlamps outside built-up areas during the day as well. Motorcyclists and their passengers must wear a helmet.

Telephoning – For country codes, see above.

Currency – Slovakia has the Slovakian Crown. At the time of editing, 100 Crowns was equal to about €2,30 (€1 = 42 Crowns). Hungary has the Forint. At the time of editing, 100 Forint was equal to about €0,40 (€1 = 244 Forint).
In border areas, however, the euro is commonly used as legal tender.

Short breaks

The city centre covers the 1st district, namely Innere Stadt, encircled by the Ring and Franz-Josefs-Kai, which are also part of the city centre. To simplify the use of this guide during visits, the city centre has been divided into areas bearing the names of the best-known or most important sights. This subdivision of the city is artificial, but it has the advantage of concentrating sightseeing tours in one zone and making it easy to move from one area to another. These descriptions are summarised in the section **City Centre and the Ring**.
Many sights beyond the Ring lie within the 22 districts (not all of which require detailed description) around the Ring and Gürtel. For simplicity's sake, the chapters corresponding to these districts appear alphabetically in the section **Outside the Ring**, although there are some exceptions. The Museumsquartier (in the Neubau district), Schloss Schönbrunn (Hietzing district) and the Zentralfriedhof (Simmering district) have each been given a separate chapter because of their special importance.
The outskirts of Vienna extend as far as Mayerling and Wiener Neustadt, via the roads in the Vienna Woods, and are described in the section **Further afield** they reach as far as the Slovak and Hungarian frontiers, and even beyond them in the cases of Bratislava

and Sopron. The coverage of this guide stretches further east for two reasons: on the one hand, because up to the peace treaty of St-Germain-en-Laye in 1919 and once again nowadays, Viennese history was not limited by the present eastern frontiers of Austria; and on the other hand, the cities listed can once again be quickly and easily reached from Vienna since the fall of the Iron Curtain.

SIGHTSEEING PROGRAMMES

There is much to see in Vienna. For a first visit, it is preferable to decide on a touring programme based on the time available and your field of interests. It is also possible to follow some of the (comprehensive) suggestions below. It is a good idea to end the tour with a visit to one of the capital's coffee houses or to one of its taverns selling new wine.

A few hours in Vienna

Stephansdom★★★ (St Stephen's Cathedral) – **Graben**★ – Kohlmarkt – **Hofburg**★★★ (Palace): exterior – **Heldenplatz**★ – **Ring**★★: from the Rathaus (Town Hall) to the Staatsoper (State Opera House) – **Kunsthistorisches Museum**★★★ (Art Gallery).

A day in Vienna

Stephansdom★★★ – **Graben**★ – Kohlmarkt – **Hofburg**★★★: exterior and **Schatzkammer**★★★ (Treasury) – Heldenplatz★ – **Ring**★★: from the Rathaus to the Staatsoper – **Kunsthistorisches Museum**★★★ – **Karlskirche**★★ (St Charles Borromeo Church) – **Secession-gebäude**★★ (Secession Building).

Three days in Vienna

Day One – **Stephansdom**★★★ – **Stephansdom District**★★ – **Kapuzinergruft**★★ – **Secession-gebäude**★★ – **Karlskirche**★★ – **Das obere Belvedere**★★ (Upper Belvedere) – and its museum – and in the evening, the **Riesenrad**★★ (Giant Ferris Wheel) on the Prater.

Day Two – **Hofburg**★★★: exterior and **Schatzkammer**★★★ and (in the case of either a parade or a morning training session) **Spanische Reitschule**★★ (Spanish Riding School) or **Sammlung alter Musikinstrumente**★★ (Collection of Old Musical Instruments) – **Kunsthistorisches Museum**★★★ – walk along the **Ring**★★ in the evening.

Day Three – **Schönbrunn**★★★ and Hietzing – walk in **Grinzing**★ with an excursion up to the hillsides of **Kahlenberg and Leopoldsberg**★★ (weather permitting) – visit a tavern serving new wine in the evening.

You are interested in ...

The individual sights are listed in the index at the end of this volume.

Baroque churches – Jesuitenkirche (near Fleischmarkt), Peterskirche (near Graben), Servitenkirche (Alsergrund), Piaristenkirche Basilika Maria Treu (Josefstadt) and of course Karlskirche (Karlsplatz).

Klimt and Schiele – The Österreichische (19-20C galleries). Jahrhunderts (Oberes Belvedere), the Leopold Museum (MuseumsQuartier) Burgtheater (Dr.-Karl-Lueger-Ring), the stairwell of the Kunsthistorisches Museum (Burgring), Historisches Museum der Stadt Wien (Karlsplatz), Secessiongebäude (near Karlsplatz), Graphische Sammlung Albertina once it has reopened (Hofburg), Bezirksmuseum Hietzing (near Schönbrunn).

Furniture – The Österreichisches Museum für Angewandte Kunst (Stubenring), Schloss Schönbrunn and its apartments, Kaiserliches Hofmobiliendepot (Neubau).

Composers – Beethoven's former abode, the Pasqualatihaus (near Freyung), Beethoven "Testamenthaus" (Heiligenstadt), Eroicahaus (Oberdöbling), Beethoven-Schauräume (Baden) where Beethoven stayed, the Haydn-Museum (Mariahilf and Eisenstadt) occupying houses where Haydn lived, Schloss Esterházy (Eisenstadt) where he worked and Rohrau his birthplace, Liszts Geburtshaus (Raiding) or birthplace, Deutschordenhaus and Figarohaus (near Stephansdom) where Mozart lived, the Schubert-Museum and Schubert-Sterbewohnung where Schubert was born and died, Strausshaus (near the Prater) where Johann Strauss lived, without forgetting the Musiksammlung der Nationalbibliothek, the Sammlung alter Musikinstrumente (Hofburg) and Staatsoper (Opernring), the Haus der Musik (near the Staatsoper) and the Arnold-Schönberg Center (Schwarzenberg-Platz).

Otto Wagner – The Postsparkasse (opposite Stubenring), the Wagner-Pavillon (Karlsplatz), Linke Wienzeile (near Karlsplatz), or Wagnerhaus (Neubau), Kirche am Steinhof (Penzing) and Wagner's two villas in Penzing.

Roman excavations – The traces of the Roman camp (Am Hof at Freyung) and Roman ruins (Hoher Markt), the Archäologischer Park and the Archäologisches Museum in Petronell-Carnuntum, as well as the Ephesos-Museum collection (Hofburg).

Sissi – Imperial apartments in the Hofburg, Schloss Schönbrunn and its apartments, the Hermesvilla in the Lainzer Tiergarten, Peterskirche and Mayerling where her son Rudolf committed suicide.

Sculpted fountains – There are some fine examples in Vienna, such as the wall fountain of the Michaelertrakt (Hofburg, Michaelerplatz), Austria-Brunnen (Freyung), Donaunixen-brunnen (Palais Ferstel), Vermählungsbrunnen (Hoher Markt) Andromedabrunnen (Altes Rathaus), Donner-Brunnen (Neuer Markt and Österreichisches Barockmuseum), Pallas-Athene-Brunnen (Parlament), Mosesbrunnen (Franziskanerplatz).

Sigmund Freud – The Sigmund-Freud-Museum (Alsergrund) is in the house where he used to live and work; he was a professor at the University (Dr.-Karl-Lueger-Ring) and was an habitué of Café Landtmann (Dr.-Karl-Lueger-Ring). The Museum für Geschichte der Medizin (Josephinum) has exhibits relating to the great physician.

Animals – The Tiergarten in the park at Schloss Schönbrunn, or Lainzer Tiergarten (Hietzing) and the Naturhistorisches Museum (Burgring) which has a remarkable collection of stuffed animals.

Discovering the city

CITY TOURS

By horse-drawn carriage

A horse-drawn carriage is a delightful way of exploring the 1st district. The fee for this excursion is €40 or 65, depending on whether you are taking a small or big tour. In any event, you should agree on a price before the ride. Coachmen are easily identifiable, since they wear a bowler hat. Stops for horse-drawn carriages are fairly flexible, but there are always some in Albertinaplatz, Heldenplatz, Petersplatz, Stephansplatz and at the Burgtheater.

Bus tours

Vienna Sightseeing Tours – Stelzhamergasse 4/11, 3. Bezirk, ☎ 01/71 24 68 30. City tour with the "Vienna Line Hop on Hop off". This operates hourly between 13 stops (for example, Staatsoper, Heldenplatz, Prater) from 9.30am to 6.10pm. Commentaries in eight languages (including English, either over headphones or via tour guide). Available from any hotel in Vienna, or any travel agency in Austria as well as abroad. Cost of a ticket for one day: €13.81, for two days €18.71.

Cityrama – Börsegasse 1, 1. Bezirk, ☎ 01/53 41 30. City tours daily at 9.30am and 2.30pm with a guided tour of Schloss Schönbrunn. Takes about 3hr 30min. Tour costs €18.71 per person (including pick-up from hotel).

Horse-drawn carriage

Robin Reisen-Stattwerkstatt – Kolingasse 6, 9. Bezirk, ☏ 01/3 17 33 84. City tour entitled "Dream and Reality" focussing on Jugendstil and "Red Vienna" (1920s social-democrat housing projects). Departures: on demand. Takes about 3hr. Tour costs €24.

With the "old-timer" tram

Early May-early Oct, Sat and Sun and public holidays at 11.30am and 1pm. On Sun and public holidays the "old-timer" tram also runs at 9.30am. Departure from Karlsplatz. Takes about 1hr. Tickets available from "Wiener Linien" information office at Karlsplatz underground station. €14.53. ☏ 01/7 90 94 40 26, www.wiener-linien.co.at

By bicycle

Pedal Power – Pedal Power, Ausstellungsstr. 3 (opposite the Ferris wheel in the Prater), 2. Bezirk, ☏ 01/7 29 72 34, Fax: 01/7 29 72 35, www.pedalpower.at (May-Sept daily at 10am), duration about 3h, €23 (with your own bike €16). Also bicycle rentals from April to October; delivery to hotel on request, tour descriptions, bicycle maps. Information at www.pedalpower.at

City walks

The city of Vienna organises themed walks around town in various languages and with tour guides – for example through Baroque or Jewish Vienna, or themes such as architecture, music, culinary Vienna or erotic Vienna, as well as special tours for children. Tours take about 90min-2hr. Meeting place depends on the tour. Price €10.90 (not including tickets for museums and the like). Registration is not necessary. Monthly programme available from the tourist office at Wien-Tourismus or at your hotel. Information at ☏ 01/8 94 53 63, www.wienguide.at

"On the Trail of the Third Man"

This tour naturally takes place in part underground and revolves around the Viennese sewer system: Welcome to Orson Welles's classic film "The Third Man". The tour (which takes about 25min) leaves from opposite the Café Museum (JS) in the Esperantopark *(cross Friedrichstraße, ticket office in metal container)*. During heavy rain, tours understandably do not take place; only children older than 12 years old are admitted; sturdy closed-in footwear is recommended; tour participants should have a good command of German. If all these criteria are met, this tour is a lively and interesting experience, full of all kinds of surprises. Advance booking and information from MA 30 – WienKanal, A-1030 Wien, Friedrichstraße/Esperantopark, ☏ 01/5 85 64 55. Cost of the tour €6.54.

Boat tours

DDSG Blue Danube Schiffahrt GmbH – Friedrichstraße 7, A-1010 Wien, ☏ 01/58 88 00, Fax: 01/58 88 04 40, www.ddsg-blue-danube.at
Offers the Hundertwasser-Tour (Apr-Oct, departure 10am, 2pm, 3hr 35min) and the Große Donaurundfahrt (Big Danube Tour, May-Sept, departure 11am, 3pm, 3hr 20min). Departure from Schwedenplatz. The itinerary passes through the Nussdorf locks (on the Großen Donaurundfahrt even the Freudenau locks later on), the Reichsbrücke and the KunstHausWien. Ride from Schwedenplatz to Reichsbrücke €9.45, round trip €13.08.
Special theme tours are also offered, such as *Sound of Johann Strauss* (with supper), *Hundertwasser Total* (with coffee and cake) or *Let's swing – auf Donauwellen* (music and dance "on the Danube Wave").

From the air

Information available at Vienna Aircraft Handling, Hangar 3, A-1300 Airport Wien-Schwechat, ☏ 01/70 07 2 22 04, Fax: 01/70 07 2 24 64, vah@viennaairport.com
Flights over Vienna, over the Vienna conurbation, or over all of Austria in helicopters or two-engine plane: helicopters: €1 000 for 1hr (price regardless of number of people; max. 4 persons). In a two-engine plane, one hour costs between €400 and 500 (max. 5 persons).

LOOK-OUT POINTS

Except for the first slopes of the Wienerwald (Vienna Woods) west of the city, Vienna's topography is scarcely hilly. High-rises only came late to the city of the Habsburgs, in the past few years in fact. On the banks of the Danube, around the UNO City, the construction of the so-called Donau-City (Danube City) created an attractive skyline. Office and residential towers packed with shopping and leisure temples soar into the skies. But in the meantime, tall buildings have started sprouting in other parts of the city.

On the Danube in Vienna

It's the traditional look-outs over the city that still offer the best views, however:

The cathedral towers *(see City Centre and the Ring, Stephansdom)* lie strategically at the heart of historic Vienna. One of the towers rises 137m/449ft above the cobblestones of Stephansplatz, with a room accessible at 73m/239ft; the other tower has a platform at a height of 60m/196ft.

Kahlenberg and Leopoldsberg *(see Outside the Ring, Döbling)* are elevated sites north of the city, on the northern edge of the Vienna Woods. The first rises to an altitude of 483m/1 584ft, and the second to 423m/1 387ft. They offer a wonderful view of the city, city, weather permitting.

The Danube tower *(see Outside the Ring, Donauturm)* rises 252m/826ft in the centre of the Danube park, with a panoramic terrace at a height of 165m/541ft. It affords a sensational view.

View from Lainzer Tiergarten *(see Outside the Ring, Hietzing)* provides an unusual view of this church, and the Kahlenberg and Leopoldsberg heights.

The Ferris wheel in the Prater *(see Outside the Ring, Leopoldstadt)* raises its cabins to a height of about 65m/213ft above the merry-go-rounds and trees in this huge amusement park. There is a view of the east side of the city.

The plaza in front of the church of the Steinhof psychiatric hospital *(see Outside the Ring, Penzing, Kirche am Steinhof)* is an unusual site which offers views of the whole of the west side of Vienna and in particular Schloss Schönbrunn.

The **Gloriette in the park of Schloß Schönbrunn** *(see Outside the Ring, Schloß Schönbrunn)* overlooks the west of the city and Kahlenberg and Leopoldsberg heights

PARKS AND GARDENS

The Austrian capital possesses many parks: there are 25m²/29sq yd of green spaces open to the public per inhabitant, compared to 1m²/1sq yd in Paris and 13m²/15sq yd in Berlin. They are all easily accessible from the city centre. This limited selection intends to satisfy anyone's desire for a stroll in the greenery. Most of those mentioned below feature in the list of sights.

1st district (Innere Stadt) – There is a succession of public parks along the Ring: **Rathauspark, Volksgarten, Burggarten, Stadtpark**. All are havens of peace between museum visits. Cultural enthusiasts will no doubt enjoy studying their fine statues.

2nd district (Leopoldstadt) – The **Prater** and the **Augarten** park are now major tourist attractions, for very different reasons.

3rd district (Landstrasse) – The **Belvedere** gardens suggest another age. The site is truly superb.

4th district (Wieden) – **Resselpark** on Karlplatz is tiny, but it enjoys an ideal situation between Karlskirche and Otto Wagner's underground stations.

13th district (Hietzing) – **Schönbrunn Gardens**, steeped in history, is undeniably Vienna's finest park. Full of historical associations, it offers a variety of sights. Keen walkers and nature lovers will enjoy visiting **Lainzer Tiergarten**, Maria Theresa's former hunting ground in the Vienna Woods.

18th district (Währing) – **Schubertpark** and in particular **Türkenschanzpark** attract walkers in an old district which is now very residential. Northwest of the city on the edge of the Wienerwald, **Pötzleinsdorferpark** will be a children's paradise, because it has several play areas.

22nd district (Donaustadt) – **Donaupark** is huge and is identifiable by the Danube tower. It is very busy in summer because it lies on the edge of the Danube. Also popular is the **Donauinsel**, which teems with joggers and cyclists in fine weather. Further east, **Lobau** is a vast stretch of relatively unspoilt land where many Viennese come to swim and cycle.

UNESCO NATURAL AND WORLD CULTURAL HERITAGE

In 2001, Vienna's inner city centre (with the Belvedere, Karlskirche and Museums Quartier) and Neusiedl Lake were included in UNESCO's Natural and World Cultural Heritage list. Schloss Schönbrunn and its gardens had already been added in 1996.

Activities

BATHING

Amalienbad – Reumannplatz 23, 10. Bezirk, ☎ 01/6 07 47 47. Open 9am-6pm on Tuesday, 9am-9.30pm Wednesday and Friday, 7am-9.30pm on Thursday, 7am-8pm on Saturday, 7am-6pm on Sunday; sauna open 1pm-9.30pm on Tuesday, 9am-9.30pm Wednesday to Friday, 7am-8pm on Saturday, 7am-6pm on Sunday. This Jugendstil building is famous for its mosaics, the sauna section is especially interesting. 10m/32ft diving board, sports pool, steam bath, hot tubs, jacuzzi, sauna, "bio-sauna" *(see also Outside the Ring, Favoriten)*.

Bundesbad Alte Donau – Arbeiterstrandbadstr. 91, 22. Bezirk, ☎ 01/2 63 65 38. 2 May to mid-September, Monday to Friday 9am-7pm, Saturday and Sunday 8am-7pm. A very pleasant swimming area on the banks of the Danube with several beaches: Arbeiterstrandbad, Strandbad Alte Donau, Bundessportbad, etc. Heated open-air pool.

Diana Erlebnisbad – Lilienbrunngasse 7-9, 2. Bezirk, ☎ 01/2 19 81 81. Open 2pm-10pm Monday to Friday, Saturday 10am-10pm, Sunday 9am-10pm, during holidays noon-10pm.

Bundesbad Schönbrunn – Schloßpark Schönbrunn, 13. Bezirk, ☎ 01/81 11 30, www.schoenbrunnerbad.at. 1 May to 30 September, daily 8.30am-7pm, July to August until 10pm. Reopened May 2002. Health and fitness area with sauna, steam bath, solarium, Olympic competition pool, non-swimmer area and children's pool.

Donauinsel (Neue Donau) – Underground station on Line 1: Donauinsel. A total of 42km/26mi of beaches for bathing; all kinds of places to rent bicycles, surfboards and boats, and a complete panoply of eateries and pubs at the so-called **Copa Cagrana** (named after the local area, Kagran) all gathered along the banks of the river attract crowds on hot summer days. This is the place to really chill out.

On the Donauinsel

Freibad Gänsehäufel – Moissigasse 21, 22. Bezirk, ☎ 01/2 69 90 16. One of Vienna's most popular summer open-air pools. Beach, water games area, wave machine, competition and children's pools, water slide, nudist area with a cabin sauna, mother and child area, playgrounds. Laid out for the handicapped.

Kongreßbad – Julius-Meinl-Gasse 7a, 16. Bezirk, ☎ 01/4 86 11 63. Open-air pool, open from beginning of May to mid-September, Monday to Friday 9am-8pm, Saturday and Sunday 8am-8pm. Competition pool, fun pool, water slide, children's area with a playground. Laid out for the handicapped.

Schafbergbad – Josef-Redl-Gasse 2, 18. Bezirk, ☎ 01/4 79 15 93. Open-air pool, May 2 to September 9, Monday to Friday 9am-6pm, Saturday and Sunday 8am-6pm. The pool affords a fine view of the city. Diving tower, mother and child area, children's pool, playground. Partly laid out for the disabled.

Therme Oberlaa – Kurbadstr. 14, 10. Bezirk, ☎ 01/6 80 09, www.oberlaa.at Open daily 9am-10pm. In the large Oberlaa leisure centre, 20min from the city centre, there are swimming pools (2 indoor and 3 open-air), thermal baths, saunas, massage centre, children's world *(Kinderwelt)*, etc.

Stadthalle – Vogelweidplatz 14, 15. Bezirk, ☎ 01/98 10 04 30, www.stadthalle.com The pool is open 8am-9pm on Monday, Wednesday and Friday, from 6.30am-9pm on Tuesday and Thursday, from 7am-6pm at weekends.

ICE-SKATING

Eislaufanlage Engelmann über den Dächern der Stadt – Syringgasse 6-8, 17. Bezirk, ☎ 01/4 05 14 25. Open from the end of October to the beginning of March, daily from 9am; Monday to 6pm, Tuesday, Thursday and Friday until 9.30pm, Wednesday, Saturday and Sunday until 7pm. Friday is ice-disco day, Thursday ice dancing.

Wiener Eislaufverein – Lothringerstr. 22, 3. Bezirk, ☎ 01/7 13 63 530. Open from mid-October to March (depending on the temperature), from 9am-9pm, at weekends until 8pm, on Wednesday until 10pm. The Viennese Ice-Skating Club has an open-air ice rink. Very near Stadtpark.

Wiener Eistraum on the square in front of the Rathaus – 1. Bezirk. End of January to beginning of March, daily 9am-11pm. Ice-skating under open skies on a 2 000m²/21 000sq ft rink with the beautiful Rathaus as a backdrop and the Burgtheater in full view. Waltzes and pop music; the Rathaus is beautifully lit at night; stands offer gastronomic delight. Curling, skate rentals and special events, too.

Wiener Stadthalle – Vogelweidplatz 14, 15. Bezirk, ☎ 01/98 10 00, www. stadthalle.com Indoor rink, mid-October to end of May daily 1.30pm-5pm

SKIING

In Vienna, the first foothills of the Alps display some slopes mainly suitable for children, because of their gentle gradients. The more advanced skiers will have to go further afield, to Schneeberg or Raxalpe in Lower Austria (Niederösterreich) in order to enjoy this sport.

Himmelhofwiese – Am Himmelhof, Ghelengasse 44, access through Himmelhofgasse, 13. Bezirk, ☎ 01/8 12 12 01. The T-bars in operation from Monday to Friday, from noon till nightfall, at weekends and on public holidays from 10am, only if there is natural snow.

Hohe-Wand-Wiese – Mauerbachstr. 174, 14. Bezirk, ☎ 01/9 79 10 57. Monday to Friday 9am-9.30pm, weekends and holidays 9am-10pm. In the event of cold weather but too little snow, snow machines are used so that people can still enjoy skiing.

HIKING

Keen walkers will find plenty of footpaths in the Wienerwald, the famous Vienna woods *(see Further afield, Wienerwald)*. But it is also possible to appreciate nature in the city of Vienna. These woods encroach upon the west and north periphery of the capital. Throughout these woods forming part of the city, there are numerous waymarked footpaths. Here a few suggestions:

Beethovengang *(see Outside the Ring, Döbling, Heiligenstadt)* – This is the name of a walk which the composer of the *Eroica* favoured while living in Heiligenstadt. It runs along the Schreiberbach, west and south of Nussdorf.

Kahlenberg/Leopoldsberg *(see Outside the Ring, Döbling)* – From Grinzing, there are several footpaths through the northern part of the Vienna woods. Some run along the hilltops of Kahlenberg and Leopoldsberg to Josefsdorf, Kahlenbergerdorf and Nussdorf. The view of the city is superb in fine weather.

Lainzer Tiergarten *(see Outside the Ring, Hietzing)* – Consult the map at the entrance to this vast park to select an itinerary and preferred length of walk. Fine view of the west of the city.

Books

GENERAL

Beaumont, Antony, *Alma Mahler-Werfel: Diaries 1898-1902*, Faber & Faber, 2000, an intimate view of the turn-of-the-20C artistic life in the city.

Brook-Shepherd, Gordon, *The Austrians*, Harper & Collins, 1997, covers a great deal of ground in not so many pages.

Fodor, Pal, David, Géza, *Ottomans, Hungarians, and Habsburgs in Central Europe*, Brill, 2000, essays, thorough and academic, on the evolution of the Habsburg and Hungarian border from the 15C to the 17C.

Hasek, Jaroslav, *The Good Soldier Svejk and His Fortunes in the World War*, Penguin Books, 2000, funny, tragi-comic, sharply sarcastic view of the Dual Monarchy and its national forces.

Janik, Allan, and Toulmin Stephen, *Wittgenstein's Vienna*, 1996, Elephant Publishers, an intellectual history of the city during Wittgenstein's days.

Morton, Frederic, *A Nervous Splendour: Vienna 1888-1889*, Penguin Books, 1980, an insightful look into the Empire on the brink.

Pick, Hella, *Guilty Victim: Austria from the Holocaust to Haider*, Tauris, 2000, an uneasy look at Austria's somewhat controversial past and present.

Schorske, Carl E., *Fin-de-Siècle Vienna: Politics and Culture*, Vintage Books, 1980, one of the classics on Vienna's most dynamic, if not tragic period.

Segel, Harold B. *The Vienna Coffee House Wits, 1890-1938*, Purdue University Press, essays and short stories about Viennese society.

Taylor, AJP, *The Habsburg Monarchy, 1809-1918*, Penguin Books, 1964, a standard work, still in print and still doing well.

ARCHITECTURE, ART AND MUSIC

Anthology of *Beethoven's letters*, Dover Press, 1972.

Blau, Eve, *The Architecture of Red Vienna*, MIT Press, 1999, an illustrated look at the socialist constructions in Vienna from 1919 to 1934.

Dimster, Frank, Steele, James, *The New Austrian Architecture*, Rizzoli, 1995.

Henisch, Peter, Decker, Craig, *Stone's Paranoia: Studies in Austrian Literature, Culture, and Thought*, Ariadne, 2000, essays on various aspects of Austria's intellectual history.

Iby, Elfriede, *Schönbrunn* (photos), Verlag Christian Brandstätter, Wien 2000, in German but a good book to have on Schönbrunn.

Kallir, Jane, *Viennese Design and the Wiener Werkstätte*, 1986, George Braziller, Inc., A look at the work and impact of the Wiener Werkstätte.

Leopold, Rudolf, Schuler, Romana, *Leopold. Meisterwerke des Leopold Museums Wien*, DuMont, Köln 2001 (insight into the Leopold Museum).

Robbins-Landon, H.C., *The Mozart Compendium*, Thames and Hudson, 1996, an entertaining and educational examination of Mozart from several points of view.

Rodgers, Rick, *Kaffeehaus: Exquisite Desserts from the Classic Cafés of Vienna, Budapest and Prague*, Clarkson N. Potter, 2002, covers the art of making cake the way the world's masters do.

Wagner-Trenwitz, Christoph, *Die Wiener Staatsoper*, Styria, Graz 1999.

Winkler, Susanne, *Blickfänge einer Reise nach Wien, Fotografien 1860-1910*, ALBUM Verlag für Photographie, Vienna 2000, photographic account of a trip to Vienna *zeitgenössischen Photographien*, ALBUM Verlag für Photographie, Wien 2001, contemporary photographs.

LITERATURE

Bachmann, Ingeborg: *Malina, The Book of Franza, Requiem for Fanny Goldmann, Songs in Flight (Collected Poems)*.

Bernhard, Thomas: *The Novels of Thomas Bernhard*, Camden House, 2001.

Freud, Sigmund: *Die Traumdeutung (The Interpretation of Dreams), Das Unbehagen in der Kultur (Civilization and its Discontents)*.

Frischmuth, Barbara: *Die Schrift des Freundes* (contemporary author's whodunnit with love intrigue set in Vienna).

Grillparzer, Franz: *Das Goldene Vlieβ (The Golden Fleece), König Ottokars Glück und Ende (King Ottocar, His Rise and Fall), Ein Bruderzwist in Habsburg (Family Strife in Habsburg)*.

Handke, Peter: *Die Angst des Tormanns beim Elfmeter (The Goalie's Anxiety at the Penalty Kick), Die linkshändige Frau (The Left-Handed Woman), Publikums beschimpfung (Offending the Audience), Wunschloses Unglück (A Sorrow Beyond Dreams).*

Hofmannsthal, Hugo von: *Jedermann (Everyman), Das Salzburger große Welttheater. Der Rosenkavalier* (libretto), *Chandos-Brief* (essay), *Cristinas Heimreise (Christina's Journey Home), Der Turm (The Tower).*

Jelinek, Elfriede, *The Piano Teacher, Lust, Women as Lovers.*

Musil, Robert von: *Der Mann ohne Eigenschaften (Thè Man without Qualities), Die Verwirrungen des Zöglings Törleß.*

Rilke, Rainer Maria: *Sonette an Orpheus (Sonnets to Orpheus), Duineser Elegien (Duino Elegies).*

Roth, Joseph: *The Collected Shorter Fiction of Joseph Roth,* (transl. Michael Hofmann), Granta Books, 2001. *The Radetzky March, Weights and Measures, Flight without End.*

Schnitzler, Arthur: *Dream Story, Fräulein Else, Der Weg ins Freie (The Road to the Open).*

Stifter, Adalbert: *Der Nachsommer (Indian Summer), Bunte Steine (Colourful Stones)*

Zweig, Stefan: *Beware of Pity, Buchmendel, Royal Game, The Confusion of Sentiments, Casanova: A Study in Self-Portraiture.*

Films

Austria, and Vienna in particular, is the homeland of great film directors. However, few of them worked for their native country. Born in Vienna, **Erich von Stroheim** (1885-1957) deserted from the army, left for the United States in 1906 and became an American citizen. The creator of a masterpiece, *Greed* (1923), he was also a brilliant actor, with a career both in France and Hollywood. Born in Bohemia, **Georg Wilhelm Pabst** (1885-1967) directed in Vienna, in 1920, the Neue Wiener Bühne theatre company before making his first film, *Der Schatz* (1923). He then left for Germany where he made 19 films, including *Lulu* (1928) with Louise Brooks. Born in Vienna, **Fritz Lang** (1890-1976) started his career as a director in 1919 before leaving in 1933 for the United States, where he acquired US citizenship. He made about 50 films, including *Doctor Mabuse* (1922), *Metropolis* (1926), *M the Accursed* (1931) and *House by the River* (1949). Born in Vienna, **Josef von Sternberg** (1894-1969), who discovered Marlene Dietrich, was the creator of *The Blue Angel* (1930), *Shanghai Express* (1932) and *The Devil is a Woman* (1935). He died in Hollywood at the end of a versatile career. **Peter Handke** was joint scriptwriter in Wim Wender's German films and adapted for the screen his novel *The Left-Handed Woman*. Other contemporary filmmakers include **Niki List** *(Müllers Büro)*, **Michael Synek** *(Dead Fish)* who has recently moved to Paris, and **Wolfram Paulus** *(Holes in the Moors)*.

Only a few Austrian productions have achieved renown outside their own country, such as the *Sissi* film series (1955-57) directed by **Ernst Marischka** (1893-1963), which launched the international career of Romy Schneider (born in Vienna). The Vienna trilogy directed by **Axel Corti** (1933-93), consists of *God No Longer Believes in Us* (1981), *Santa Fe* (1985) and *Welcome in Vienna* (1986).

VIENNA IN THE MOVIES

Der Kongreß tanzt (1931) by Eric Charell.

The Third Man (1949) by Carol Reed: This classic based on a novel by Graham Greene is set in Vienna in the year 1948. The American writer Holly Martins (Joseph Cotten) arrives in Vienna, which is under the post-war rule of the victorious powers, to look for his old friend Harry Lime (Orson Welles). On arrival, however, he is just in time to witness the burial of Lime, who was allegedly mixed up in illegal dealings. Martins begins an investigation on his own, and finds out that Lime's business was to distribute cut penicillin which, sold on the black market, was making numerous people ill. His death, however, was a mere feint, performed to avoid getting caught by the police. During the grand showdown, Lime is trapped in the Viennese sewage system and shot. The soundtrack, with the famous *Harry Lime Theme*, played on a zither, is an inseparable from the film and is unforgettable *(see Practical information, Discovering the city, City tours).*

Sissi trilogy by Ernst Marischka about Empress Elisabeth, known popularly as Sissi: *Sissi* (1955), *Sissi – die junge Kaiserin* (1956) and *Sissi – Schicksalsjahre einer Kaiserin* (1957).

Rollercoaster (1977) by James Goldstone. A star-cast thriller (George Segal, Richard Widmark, Helen Hunt, etc).

Welcome in Vienna (1986) by Axel Corti.

Before Sunrise (1994) by Richard Linklater: Julie Delpy and Ethan Hawke stroll about Vienna throughout the night philosophising about life and love.

Orson Welles in *The Third Man*

Calendar of events

Vienna's monthly **calendar of events** is available at the information offices of Wien-Tourismus (on the 15th of the previous month). A regularly updated version of all events and exhibitions is also available on the Internet at www.info.wien.at

1 January
New Year's concert by the Vienna Philharmonic – at the Musikverein ☎ 01/5 05 81 90, www.musikverein.at

Mid-January to beginning of March
Wiener Eistraum – Ice-skating in front of the Rathaus 9am-11pm.

Mid-May to mid-June
Wiener Festwochen – Avant-garde festival for theatre, music and art, with fixed venues in the MuseumsQuartier, ☎ 01/5 89 22 0, www.festwochen.at

End of June
Donauinselfest – Free open-air concerts, hundreds of thousands flock to the artificial island on the Danube ☎ 01/5 35 35 35, www.donauinselfest.at

June to September
St. Margarethen (Beyond Vienna): **Passionsspiele**, Passion Plays every five years in the quarry (May 2006 is the next), ☎ 0 26 80/21 00, www.passio.at

July/August
Film festival at Rathausplatz – Free open-air projections of classical music recording videos on a giant screen. Held on the plaza in front of the Rathaus with international cuisine offered at numerous different stands. Daily at sundown.

Kino unter Sternen – Open-air films in the Augarten showing classics and rarities (almost exclusively in the original language) ☎ 01/5 85 23 24 25, www.kinounter-sternen.at

KlangBogen – Broad range of musical offerings at various venues in the city, ☎ 01/4 27 17, www.klangbogen.at

ImPulsTanz – International dance festival for viewing or participating at the MuseumsQuartier and other venues, ☎ 01/5 23 55 58, www.impuls-tanz.at

Mörbisch (Beyond Vienna): **Seefestspiele** – Operetta performances on the stage standing in Neusiedler See, ☎ 0 26 82/6 62 10, www.seefestspiele-moerbisch.at

Petronell-Carnuntum (Beyond Vienna): **Art Carnuntum** – World theatre festival in the Amphitheater II (classical drama mostly) and classic cinema film festival in the gardens of the Carnuntinum Museum, ☎ 0 21 63/34 00, www.artcarnuntum.at

St. Margarethen (Beyond Vienna): **Opera festival** in the old Roman quarry, held in the years without Passion Plays *(see above)*, ☏ 0 26 80/21 00, www.ofs.at

September

Hallamasch – "Ethnic" festival with street art, dance, performances, world music and the "parade of the cultures", ☏ 01/5 48 48 00, www.hallamasch.at

Eisenstadt (Beyond Vienna): **International Haydn festival (Haydntage) in Schloß Esterházy**, ☏ 0 26 82/6 18 66, www.haydnfestival.at

End of September/beginning of October

Jeunesse Herbstfestival – Classical music festival organised by Austria's main events organiser in this field, ☏ 01/5 05 63 56, www.jeunesse.at

October

Viennale – International film festival, ☏ 01/5 26 59 47, www.viennale.at

End of October

Kunst wien – Austria's most important art fair, held at the MAK, ☏ 01/2 16 65 62 20, www.kunstnet.at (www.kunst-wien.at during trade fairs)

November to Ash Wednesday

Viennese Ball Season – The highpoint of the "Ballsaison" is the world-famous Opera Ball, information at Wien-Tourismus.

Advent

Christmas markets – *see Practical information, Shopping, Markets.*

Accommodation

Summer season: 1 April to 31 October
Winter season: 1 November to 31 March

TIPS AND ADDRESSES IN THIS TRAVEL GUIDE

The following list of hotels and restaurants is divided into three categories: "Budget" suggests establishments that will cater to those on a limited budget. "Moderate" includes better quality establishments at commensurately higher prices. Under "Expensive" you will find the outstanding places offering the kind of luxury you might not allow yourself every day.
The Internet addresses are those available at the time of editing. Otherwise we have included any available e-mail.

HOTELS

BUDGET

Pension Franz – Währinger Str. 12, 9. Bezirk, ☎ 01/34 36 37, Fax: 01/34 36 37 23. Family guesthouse with decor in the style of the turn of the 19C-20C. 24 rooms. Single room from €57.

IBIS Wien Messe – Lassallestr. 7a 2. Bezirk, ☎ 01/2 17 70 0, Fax: 01/2 17 70 555; H2736@accor-hotels.com Hotel near the Prater, with comfortable rooms and light-coloured furniture, modern amenities. 166 rooms. Single room from €59 .

Landhaus Fuhrgassl-Huber – Rathstr. 24, 19. Bezirk, ☎ 01/4 40 30 33, Fax: 01/4 40 27 14. This country manor in the midst of the Heuriger quarter is furnished with designer and rustic furniture, rooms facing the garden are quiet. 38 rooms. Single room from €70.

Park-Villa – Hasenauerstr. 12, 19. Bezirk, ☎ 01/3 19 10 05, Fax: 01/3 19 10 05 41. Jugendstil building dating from 1888, tasteful rooms, pleasant area to stay. 21 rooms. Single room from €70.

Pension Pertschy – Habsburgergasse 5, 1. Bezirk, ☎ 01/53 44 90, Fax: 01/5 34 49 49; www.pertschy.com Family-run bed and breakfast in a 250-year-old Baroque palace with furniture in Louis XV style. 47 rooms. Single room from €72.

Zur Wiener Staatsoper – Krugerstr. 11, 1. Bezirk, ☎ 01/5 13 12 74, Fax: 01/5 13 12 74 15. Grand Viennese town house, small friendly hotel, with rooms appointed with period furniture. 22 rooms. Single room from €76.

Reither – Graumanngasse 16, 15. Bezirk, ☎ 01/8 93 68 41, Fax: 01/8 93 68 35; www.bestwestern-ce.com/reither Family-run operation with typical Austrian hospitality. Some rooms with balcony or terrace, the furnishings are functional. 50 rooms. Single room from €76.

Kaiserpark Schönbrunn – Grünbergstr. 11, 12. Bezirk, ☎ 01/81 38 61 00, Fax: 01/8 13 81 83. www.kaiserpark.at City hotel right next to Schloß Schönbrunn. 45 rooms. Single room from 80.

MODERATE

Theater-Hotel in der Josefstadt – Josefstädter Str. 22, 8. Bezirk, ☎ 01/4 05 36 48, Fax: 01/4 05 14 06. Modernised inner city hotel near the Ringstraße. 54 rooms. Single room from €95.

Mercure Nestroy – Rotensterngasse 12, 2. Bezirk, ☎ 01/4 31 21 14 00, Fax: 01/4 31 21 14 07; www.mercure.at The hotel, a former factory, has comfortable rooms with parquet floors, that give you all the well being you need far from your own four walls. 87 rooms. Single room from €104.

Am Stephansplatz – Stephansplatz 9, 1. Bezirk, ☎ 01/53 40 50, Fax: 01/53 40 57 10; www.stephansplatz.com Located directly opposite the Stephansdom; rooms at the front have a view of the cathedral. 57 rooms. Single room from €108.

König von Ungarn – Schulerstr. 10, 1. Bezirk, ☎ 01/51 58 40, Fax: 01/51 58 48; www.kvu.at Comfortable little hotel redolent of Vienna in the old days. 33 rooms. Single room from €125.

Dorint Rogner Hotel Biedermeier im Sünnhof – Landstraßer Hauptstr. 28, 3. Bezirk, ☎ 01/71 67 10, Fax: 01/71 67 15 03; www.dorint.de Biedermeier is the dominant style of the furnishings. 203 rooms. Single room from €129.

EXPENSIVE

Sacher – Philharmonikerstr. 4, 1. Bezirk, ☎ 01/5 14 56, Fax: 01/51 45 68 10; www.sacher.com. Vienna's classic Grand Hotel – and home of the world-renowned Sachertorte. The atmosphere is enhanced by a valuable collection of paintings and antiques. 108 rooms. Single room from €205.

Im Palais Schwarzenberg – Schwarzenbergplatz 9, 3. Bezirk, ☎ 01/7 98 45 15, Fax: 01/7 98 47 14. Former royal palace from the 18C, novel decor with some antiques, 7.5ha/18.5 acre private park. 44 rooms. Single room from €232.

Imperial – Kärnter Ring 16, 1. Bezirk, ☎ 01/5 01 10, Fax: 01/50 11 04 10; www.luxurycollection.com/imperial A particularly fine specimen of the Ring's romance with majestic architecture. Expensive and luxurious room design with select antiques evokes imperial Vienna. 138 rooms. Single room from €255.

The Red Guide Europe (hotel and restaurant guide), which is updated every year, offers a wider selection of hotels and restaurants in Vienna (and other major European cities) that are reviewed and evaluated by independent testers on site.

CAMPING

The Austrian tourist office and the local tourist offices provide lists of camp sites. Vienna has four camp sites (www.wiencamping.at):

Campingplatz Wien-West I – Hüttelbergstr. 40, 1140 Wien. Open from mid-July till end of Aug; Booking/check-in through camp site Wien-West II.

Campingplatz Wien-West II – Hüttelbergstr. 80, 1140 Wien, ☎ 01/9 14 23 14, Fax: 01/9 11 35 94; camping_wienwest@wigast.com Open from beginning March till end Jan. Reservations possible.

Campingplatz Wien-Süd – Breitenfurterstr. 269, 1230 Wien, ☎ 01/8 67 36 49. Fax: 01/8 67 58 43; camping_sued@wigast.com Open May to Sept. Reservations possible.

Aktiv Camping Neue Donau – Am Kleehäufel, 1220 Wien, ☎/Fax: 01/2 02 40 10; camping_neuedonau@wigast.com Open mid-May to Sept. Reservations possible.

Near Vienna, south of the city:

Campingplatz Schloßpark Laxenburg – Münchendorferstraße, 2361 Laxenburg, ☎ 0 22 36/7 13 33, Fax: 0 22 36/7 39 66; camping_laxenburg@wigast Open mid-Apr-end Oct. No reservations.

Camping elsewhere than on camp sites is only allowed with prior permission from the proprietor of the land. Sleeping in a camper outside a camp site in Vienna is considered "camping in the wild" and is punishable by a fine.

YOUTH HOSTELS

Jugendherberge Wien-Myrthengasse – Myrthengasse 7, 1070 Wien, ☎ 01/52 36 316. Overnight from €15.

Jugendgästehaus Brigittenau – Friedrich-Engels-Platz 24, 1200 Wien, ☎ 01/3 32 82 940. Overnight from €11.99 (men's dormitory), otherwise from €14.53.

Jugendgästehaus Hütteldorf – Schloßbergstr. 8, 1130 Wien, ☎ 01/8 77 02 63. Overnight from €13.90.

Hostel Ruthensteiner – Robert-Hamerling-Gasse 24, 1150 Wien, ☎ 01/8 93 42 02. Overnight from €10.10.

Schloßherberge am Wilhelminenberg – Savoyenstr. 2, 1160 Wien, ☎ 01/4 85 85 03 700. Overnight from €18.

In general you must be in possession of an international youth hostel ID. The Austrian Youth Hostel Federation (Österreichische Jugendherbergsverband) has more information: Schottenring 28, 1010 Wien, ☎ 01/5 33 53 53, www.oejhv.or.at

Eating out

VIENNESE CUISINE

Viennese cuisine is varied, reflecting the numerous traditions of the nations of the old Empire. The *Schnitzel*, a pork or veal escalope, forms the basis of many menus in the capital. Everyone has heard of *Wiener Schnitzel*, the celebrated escalope which usually comes with sautéed potatoes; a good *Wiener Schnitzel* should be golden brown. *Knödel* are another Viennese speciality; these are dumplings, which accompany several dishes, including soups, such as *Leberknödelsuppe*, a beef broth with liver-flavoured dumplings. *Rindsgulasch* is a Hungarian dish, a paprika-flavoured beef stew, with *Knödel*. There are several kinds of gulasch, including *Erdäpfelgulasch*, a potato stew served with frankfurters. *Tafelspitz mit Gröste* is a classic dish which Franz-Josef apparently ate every day and consists of boiled beef with sautéed potatoes and horseradish sauce. *Gefüllte Kalbsbrust* is breast of veal stuffed with meat and vegetables. *Bauernschmaus* was originally a peasant dish and generally comprises frankfurters, roast or smoked pork, ham and *Knödel*. *Eierspeise* consists of scrambled eggs served in a casserole. This is not a comprehensive list; there is a huge variety of poultry, game and fish dishes. Every restaurant offers a wide range of dishes such as stuffed breast of goose, capon with anchovy sauce, roast woodcock, saddle of venison, jugged hare, and also carp eggs in butter or pike-perch with paprika. Viennese recipes reflect Bohemian, Jewish, Hungarian, Croatian, Slovak and even Italian influences. Viennese cuisine is therefore varied, but not light in texture; although rich in natural ingredients, it is high in calories.

Viennese cuisine culminates in the dessert section, the *Mehlspeisen*. The highlight is *Apfelstrudel*, a flaky pastry dessert filled with apple and sultanas. There is a huge selection of cakes including *Rehrücken*, with chocolate and almonds, *Palatschinken*, thick wheat pancakes with fromage frais or jam filling, *Linzertorte*, with strawberry or redcurrant jam and enriched with almonds, *Mohr im Hemd*, a chocolate cake coated in chocolate sauce, *Kaiserschmarren*, puff pastry currant cakes browned in butter and sugar, *Topfenstrudel* with fromage frais, *Marillenknödel*, apricot dumplings, etc. The list is truly endless.

Culinary terms

Backhendl	Roast chicken
Baunzerl	Milk bread
Buchteln	Steamed dumplings (sweet)
Blunzen	Blood sausage
Erdäpfel	Potatoes
Faschiertes	Hamburger
Fisolen	String beans
Frittaten	Slivers of pancake
Gansljunges	Goose tripe
Geselchtes	Smoked pork
Golatschen	Filled short pastry
G'spritzter	Spritzer
G'spritzter Obi	Apple juice spritzer
Häuptlsalat	Lettuce
Hasenjunges	Rabbit tripe
Heuriger	Young wine (1 year old) or a wine-bar
Hupfauf	Tyrolean yeast dough
Indian gefüllt	Stuffed young turkey
Jungfernbraten	Loin of pork with caraway seeds
Kaiserfleisch	Boiled and smoked pork cutlet
Kaiserschmarrn	Dough made with eggs and raisins
Karfiol	Cauliflower
Kohlsprossen	Brussels sprouts
Kracherl	Fruit flavoured soft drink
Kren, Apfelkren	Horse radish, horse radish sauce with apple
Krügerl	A little more than a pint
Kukuruz	Corn
Marillen	Apricots
Nockerln	Dumplings of egg dough
Obi	Apple juice
Palatschinken	Crêpes with filling
Paradeiser	Tomatoes
Pfiff	Half-pint
Powidl	Plum purée
Quargel	A kind of cheese
Ribisel	Red currants
Risibisi	Rice and peas
Schill	Perch
Schlagobers	Whipped cream
Schmankerl	Delicacies

Schöberl	Fried dough for soups
Schwämme, Schwammerln	Mushrooms
Seidl	A little less than a pint
Seidl Lichtes	Small lager
Steirisches Schöpsernes	Styrian-style mutton
Strudel	Strudel dough with various fillings
Sturm	Young fermenting wine
Tafelspitz	Boiled beef
Topfen	quark (curd cheese)

RESTAURANTS

BUDGET

Kanzleramt – Schauflergasse 6, 1. Bezirk, ☎ 01/5 33 13 09, Fax: 01/5 35 39 45. One of the most famous Viennese "Beisln", very comfortable and lively, always a good crowd €5.95.

Pfudl – Bäckerstr. 22, 1. Bezirk, ☎ 01/5 12 67 05. Ranks among the inns that have become a Viennese institution. Located near the Stock Exchange. Main dishes from €6.

Figlmüller – Wollzeile 5, 1. Bezirk, ☎ 01/5 12 61 77, Fax: 01/3 20 72 97. Closed in August. One of several local eateries serving the city's largest *Wiener Schnitzel*. The place is especially popular with tourists. Main dishes from €6.20.

Haas & Haas – Stephansplatz 4, 1. Bezirk, ☎ 01/5 13 19 16. One of the most popular local restaurants in the immediate vicinity of the cathedral; in the evening the cathedral garden is a pleasant place to sit. Main dishes from €7.30.

MODERATE

Eckel – Sieveringer Str. 46, 19. Bezirk, ☎ 01/3 20 32 18, Fax: 01/3 20 66 60; www.restaurant.eckel.at Closed Sun. Cosy, rustic restaurant with elegant side rooms. The regulars enjoy the atmosphere of the terrace in summer. Classic, regional dishes are the fare at all times. Main dishes from €5.10.

Hansen – Wipplinger Str. 34, 1. Bezirk, ☎ 01/5 32 05 42; www.hansen.co.at Mon-Sat 9am-9pm. The restaurant shares the arcade in the old Vienna Stock Exchange with a high-class garden shop; modern cuisine with a faint touch of Asia. Main dishes from €6.90.

Vikerl's Lokal – Würffelgasse 4, 15. Bezirk, ☎ 01/8 94 34 30. Really comfortable little local restaurant with wooden panelling where Viennese nouvelle cuisine is on the menu. Main dishes from €7.63.

K & K Restaurant Piaristenkeller – Piaristengasse 45, 8. Bezirk *(below Piaristenkirche)*, ☎ 01/4 06 01 93, Fax: 01/4 06 41 73; www.piaristenkeller .com In a 300 year old vaulted cellar where traditional Viennese dishes are served, there is the additional option of visiting two museums – the Kaiser-Franz-Josef Hat Museum (souvenir photos are available, of visitors taking part in the "Old-style Viennese Hat Parade") and the K & K Weinschatzkammer (treasure trove of four centuries of wines from the Imperial wine cellars). Main dishes from €7.99.

Vestibül – Dr.-Karl-Lueger-Ring 2, im Burgtheater, 1. Bezirk, ☎ 01/5 32 49 99; www.vestibuel.at. Mon-Fri 11am-midnight, Sat 6pm-midnight. Light, fine cuisine is offered in the historic ambience of the Burgtheater. A terrace with a view of the Rathaus is available in summer. Main dishes from €8.36.

Fadinger – Wipplinger Str. 29, 1. Bezirk, ☎ 01/5 33 43 41, Fax: 01/5 32 44 51. The front is a bar, the back serves as a somewhat higher quality restaurant serving unusual, modern Viennese cuisine. Main dishes from €8.40.

Ofenloch – Kurrentgasse 8, 1. Bezirk, ☎ 01/5 33 88 44, Fax: 01/5 32 98 22; www.ofenloch.at Closed Sundays and Mondays. Restaurant with Viennese cuisine, known for its asparagus weeks and the special game week. Main dishes from €9.

Plachutta – Wollzeile 38, 1. Bezirk, ☎ 01/5 12 15 77, Fax: 01/5 12 15 77 20; www.plachutta.at. Restaurant dedicated to the Viennese beef tradition. Main dishes from €10.

Hedrich – Stubenring 2, 1. Bezirk, ☎ 01/5 12 95 88. Closed in August. Simple restaurant that calls itself a snack bar restaurant, but with special regional dishes for a good price. Main dishes from €11.60.

Hauswirth – Otto-Bauer-Gasse 20, 6. Bezirk, ☎ 01/5 87 12 61, Fax: 01/5 87 12 61 12; www.restaurant-hauswirth.at Typical Viennese restaurant with a pretty garden in the courtyard. Main dishes from €12.35.

Cantinetta Antinori – Jasomirgottstr. 3-5, 1. Bezirk, ☎ 01/5 33 77 22, Fax: 01/5 33 77 22 11; www.antinori.at *The* Italian restaurant in the 1. Bezirk with a large selection of excellent wines. Main dishes from €13.

Hietzinger Bräu – Auhofstr. 1, 13. Bezirk, ☏ 01/87 77 08 70, Fax: 01/87 77 08 72 2; www.plachutta.at. The classic restaurant for *Wiener Tafelspitz* and all sorts of beef dishes. Main dishes from €13.10.

Salut – Wildpretmarkt 3, 1. Bezirk, ☏ 01/5 33 13 22. In summer closed on holidays and Sat-Sun. Small friendly restaurant in several welcoming rooms in the city centre. Main dishes from €13.40.

Windows of Vienna – Wienerbergstr. 7, 10. Bezirk, ☏ 01/6 07 94 80. Restaurant on the 22nd floor of a business centre, with an excellent view of Vienna and its surroundings. Main dishes from €15.50.

Mraz & Sohn – Wallensteinstr. 59, 20. Bezirk, ☏ 01/3 30 45 94, Fax: 01/3 30 15 36. Modern restaurant, in which a father and son team produce some outstanding results. Main dishes from €16.

EXPENSIVE

Steirereck – Rasumofskygasse 2, 3. Bezirk, ☏ 01/7 13 31 68, Fax: 01/ 7 13 31 68 2; www.steirereck.at Located near the Hundertwasserhaus. Arguably the best food in Vienna, with a substantial wine cellar which it is possible to have a look round. lunchtime menu from €31.25, Evening menu from €60.30.

THE "HEURIGER"

The Heuriger is a Viennese institution that goes back to the days of Joseph II, who, at the end of the 18C, allowed winegrowers not only to sell their wines, but also to serve them. This condition exists to this day. A genuine Heuriger may only serve wine from its own cellars and from the immediate vicinity. The amount of own wine determines the opening time of the Heuriger. A pine bush hanging over the entrance portal signifies that the "Buschenschank" is currently open for business. In Vienna, this status is referred to as "ausg'steckt" (literally "hung out"). In a Heuriger, it is possible to eat. However, the meal is not served at table, but at a buffet where customers help themselves to cold or hot dishes. An establishment that buys additional wine and serves food at the table may only call itself a Heuriger-Restaurant and is not permitted to have a bush hanging outside its door. Both types of establishment must close at midnight. As far as music is concerned: the more a Heuriger is visited by locals – and the less by hoards of tourists – the less the chance it will feature musical accompaniment to the libations. This, however, is only a generalisation.

The places listed below are genuine Heuriger. If looking for a more relaxed atmosphere and music, but also quality food and drink, you will find a large selection of Heuriger-Restaurants on site.

The Heuriger district

GRINZING

19. Bezirk – Tram: Grinzing (38) from Schottentor on the Ring. Please note: the last tram to Schottentor leaves at 11.55pm (as far as the Ring) and at 12.55am to the Gürtel.

Grinzing is Vienna's most famous Heuriger district and attracts many tourists. Over twenty establishments lie along Cobenzlgasse and Sandgasse. Together with other restaurants, they form almost a gastronomic centre. It is advisable

At a Heuriger

to arrive in the district late in the afternoon, make a short exploratory tour then choose a table in one of these picturesque "houses", in the garden if it is fine. Names and addresses of establishments which are open are displayed on a board between Cobenzlgasse and Himmelstrasse, near the tram 38 terminus.

Altes Presshaus – Cobenzlgasse 15, ☎ 01/3 20 02 03, Fax: 01/3 20 02 03 23; a.p.@aon.at Closed January and February. Wine tavern-buffet with à la carte. The oldest Heuriger in Grinzing (house dates from 1527), parts of the vaulted cellar are very old, as are the winepresses it contains. Main dishes from €9.45.

Grinzinger Hauermandl – Cobenzlgasse 20, ☎ 01/3 20 89 49, Fax: 01/3 20 57 13 22; www.grinzing.net Typical Viennese cuisine, very cosy, comfortable furnishings in various rooms, small roofed garden. Heuriger buffet and à la carte; Main dishes from €6.90.

Reinprecht – Cobenzlgasse 22, ☎ 01/3 20 14 71. A huge and yet agreeable Heuriger has been arranged in this former monastery with 15 rooms in all shapes and sizes and an extensive garden. This place features traditional Viennese "Schrammelmusik" (violin, guitar and accordion).

Weingut Dr. Müller-Schmidt – Cobenzlgasse 38, ☎ 01/3 20 62 71. Very classy, typical ambience, with a wonderful garden. Not only is the wine from the owner's vineyards, the buffet also features items made on the establishment's own farm. Among the specialities are home-made grape products other than wines: sparkling wine, spirits, a house aperitif, grape vinegar, jams.

Wolf-Köller – Langackergasse 11, ☎ 01/3 20 30 02. Quintessential Viennese Heuriger run as a family operation. Remarkable Riesling, good home cooking, delightful garden, children's playground, no music.

HEILIGENSTADT

19. Bezirk – U4 to Heiligenstadt, then bus 38A to "Fernsprechamt Heiligenstadt".

Mayer am Pfarrplatz – Pfarrplatz 2, ☎ 01/3 70 33 61, from 4pm 01/3 70 12 87, Fax: 01/3 70 47 14; www.mayer.pfarrplatz.at Where Beethoven once wrote his *Heiligenstädter Testament*, modern patrons are regaled with a rich buffet, excellent wines from the best Viennese vineyards, and traditional Heuriger music.

NEUSTIFT

19. Bezirk – Tram (38) from Schottentor on the Ring to Krottenbachstraße, then bus (35A) to Neustift. Please note: The last bus for the centre leaves Neustift at midnight, the last tram for Schottentor leaves at 12.24am from the Glatzgasse stop.

Fuhrgassl-Huber – Neustift am Wald 68, ☎ 01/4 40 14 05, Fax: 01/4 40 27 30; fuhrgassl-huber@eunet.at Heurigen-Buffet. Earthy rustic atmosphere spread over several rooms. Music Wed-Sat from 7pm.

Wolff – Rathstr. 46, ☎ 01/4 40 23 35. Heuriger buffet. Typical "Buschenschank" in cosy rooms, large, superb Heuriger garden. No live music.

NUSSDORF

19. Bezirk – Tram (D) from Börse on the Ring to the terminus in Nußdorf. Please note: The last tram for Südbahnhof is at 11.47pm..

Kierlinger – Kahlenberger Str. 20, ☎ 01/3 70 22 64. Has been growing wine since 1787, specialises in Riesling, Weißburgunder and Veltliner. Jazz brunches every second Sunday in September, otherwise no music.

Schübel-Auer – Kahlenberger Str. 22, ☎ 01/3 70 22 22. Open from the end of January until Christmas, from 4pm. Closed on Sundays. Occupies a historic monument. This spacious establishment has a fine garden but no music. Several varieties of wine, even white wine for diabetics. Extensive buffet. On Sundays in June, there are *"Schrammel-Matineen"*, between 10am and 2pm, with actors from the Opera and members of the Vienna Philharmonic Orchestra playing traditional music.

Sirbu – Kahlenberger Str. 210, ☎ 01/3 20 59 28. A short walk *(approx 15min.)* from the Kahlenberg terminus *(bus 38A from the U4 station Heiligenstadt)* is rewarded with a cosy atmosphere, a delicious wine, and a superb view of the vineyards and the Danube.

SIEVERING

19. Bezirk – Underground: Heiligenstadt (U4) then bus (39A) to Sievering. The last bus to Heiligenstadt is at 11.29pm.

Haslinger – Agnesgasse 3, ☎ 01/4 40 13 47. Romantic "Buschenschank", roof terrace with a view of the vineyards. Comfortable rooms and a very good buffet, no music.

The "city Heuriger"

The Heuriger mentioned above supply wine which is strictly Viennese. They lie on the outskirts because vines cover the first foothills of the Vienna woods. The city centre does not have such open-air cafés, but it boasts some historical cellar establishments where the wine comes from vineyards outside Vienna.

Esterházykeller – Haarhof 1, 1. Bezirk, ☎ 01/5 33 34 82. Open from Monday to Friday from 11am to 11pm, and on Saturdays and Sundays from 3pm. Wines are from the estates of the celebrated Esterházy family.

Zwölf Apostelkeller – Sonnenfelsgasse 3, 1. Bezirk, ☎ 01/5 12 67 77. Open daily from 4.30pm to midnight. The medieval cellars, some 10m/32ft underground, were used as a hideout for the Viennese in the event of danger.

SNACKING

Also typical of Vienna are the ubiquitous sausage stands *(Würstel-Stände)*. You will find *Bratwürste, Frankfurter* (known as *Wiener* in Frankfurt), *Leberkäse* (a meat cheese), and other types of sausage. The crowd at these stands ranges from manager to dustman...

Recommended addresses for a snack:

Trzesniewski – Dorotheergasse 1, 1. Bezirk, ☎ 01/5 12 32 91. Stand-up snack bar with a long tradition; small inexpensive canapés with delicious spreads (to take out as well), with a *Pfiff* of beer. The waitresses wear lace bonnets, Viennese atmosphere.

Superimbiß Duran – Rotenturmstr. 11, 1. Bezirk, ☎ 01/5 33 71 15. Large selection of canapés and sandwiches or warm meals (self-service), everything for take-out as well or delivery.

Naschmarkt – Linke Wienzeile/Kettenbrückengasse, 4. and 6. Bezirk, Mon-Sat 6.30am-6pm. Many stands here also offer foreign snacks such as doner kebab, sushi, Italian or Indian snacks. Why not also enjoy a few glasses of bubbly in this oriental bazaar atmosphere?

FOR THE GOURMET

CONFECTIONERY

Altmann und Kühne – Graben 30, 1. Bezirk, ☎ 01/5 33 09 27. Magnificently packaged confectionery.

Central – Herrengasse 17, 1. Bezirk, ☎ 01/5 35 99 05. This Konditorei offers the *Imperialtorte*, the rival of the *Sachertorte*, in 5 different packagings (guaranteed to keep for four weeks)

Demel – Kohlmarkt 14, 1. Bezirk, ☎ 01/53 51 71 70. This former court supplier of patisserie sells exquisite *tortes*, cakes and chocolate products, such as the original *Demel torte*. World-wide mail-order of sweet delights at www.demel.at

Lehmann – Graben 12, 1. Bezirk, ☎ 01/5 12 18 15. Less well-known, a very good firm. The *Apfelstrudel* is almost sinful!

Sacher – Philharmonikerstraße, 1. Bezirk, ☎ 01/51 45 60. This is the home of the *Sachertorte*, the must of all Viennese cakes.

Demel's display

DELICATESSENS

Böhle – Wollzeile 30, 1. Bezirk. A wine bar with select Austrian and international wines that can be sampled in the bistro, with home-made salads and delicacies.

Julius Meinl – Am Graben, 1. Bezirk. A giant assortment of specialities spread out over two levels. The arcade bar on the ground floor has small snacks and lunch menus. Oyster and cheese bar, plus a luxury restaurant on the first floor.

Schönbichler – Wollzeile 4, 1. Bezirk. Wide range of teas (good selection of blends, also on request) and wines. Large selection of malt whiskies and international and Austrian spirits.

Zum Schwarzen Kameel – Bognergasse 5, 1. Bezirk. An old established firm (Beethoven was one of their customers) which stocks fine food and good wine.

Cafés, pubs and bars

COFFEE HOUSES

The coffee house is a Viennese institution, and visitors should therefore make sure that they try out one of the numerous speciality coffees, with perhaps an accompanying slice of cake, in at least one such establishment.

Bräunerhof – Stallburggasse 2, 1. Bezirk, ☎ 01/5 12 38 93. Mon-Fri 7.30am-8.30pm, Sat 7.30am-6.30pm, Sun 10am-6.30pm. The prototypical Viennese coffee house that has not yet metamorphosed into a café-restaurant. Serene waiters, good pastries and an international range of news media make this an agreeable place to while away some time.

Café Museum – Friedrichstr. 6, 1. Bezirk, ☎ 01/5 86 52 02. Daily 8am-midnight. This café at the corner of Karlsplatz was designed by Adolf Loos at the end of the 19C. It stands right opposite the Secession, and thus has an ideal location. It was the favourite café of Elias Canetti. Light foods, intellectual customers, chess club.

Central – Herrengasse 14, 1. Bezirk, ☎ 01/5 33 37 63 26. Open Monday to Friday from 8am to 11.30pm. 10am-6pm Sundays and holidays. This is one of Vienna's great literary cafés from the 19C, occupying the Palais Ferstel. The poet Peter Altenberg used to give this café as his address. Today, it has become a rendezvous for business men and women, the smart younger set and retired people instead of artists. Its specialities are *Mazagran* and *Pharisäer* (both rumbased). A pianist plays at the end of the afternoon until 7.30pm.

Demel – Kohlmarkt 14, 1. Bezirk, ☎ 01/5 35 17 17 39. Open daily 10am to 7pm. This is not a coffee house, but a tea and pastry shop, the oldest and most aristocratic in Vienna. People come to sip coffee and admire the interior decoration. It offers numerous specialities and varieties of tea and coffee.

Diglas – Wollzeile 10, 1. Bezirk, ☎ 01/5 12 84 01. Daily 7am-midnight. Viennese cuisine, agreeable atmosphere, tables outside in summer, a lot of young people.

The refined, elegant setting of The Café Central

Dommayer – Dommayergasse 2, 13. Bezirk, ☎ 01/8 77 54 65. Open daily from 7am to midnight. Close to Schloss Schönbrunn. Regular concerts by the "Wiener Walzermädchen", wonderful garden with a stage and theatrical productions. Café Dommayer has devoted itself to remembering Johann Strauss, who conquered Vienna with his performances at what was then called the Dommayer Casino in the 19C.

Frauenhuber – Himmelpfortgasse 6, 1. Bezirk, ☎ 01/5 12 83 83. Open Mon-Sat 8am-11.30pm. Closed on public holidays. Less select than the preceding establishments, this is the oldest café in Vienna, as it opened in 1824. There is a wide choice of dishes and the clientele includes people who long for the days of the old Empire.

Griensteidl – Michaelerplatz 2, 1. Bezirk, ☎ 01/5 35 26 92. Open daily 8am-11.30pm. The menu includes seasonal dishes and there is a good wine list. Coffee specialities are Maria-Theresia and Fiaker; they also stock six varieties of tea. Another café with a literary past, the Griensteidl has a smart and prosperous clientele and foreign papers

Hartauer – Riemergasse 9, 1. Bezirk, ☎ 01/512 89 81. Mon-Thur 8am-5pm, Fri 8am-2am, Sat 7pm-2am. A temple of the opera: the walls are hung with photographs of tenors, baritones, mezzos and sopranos.

Hawelka – Dorotheergasse 6, 1. Bezirk, ☎ 01/5 12 82 30. Open daily except Sun, 8am-2am (4pm-2am on Fri and Sun). Another institution, this small café, always packed in the evenings, cultivates a Bohemian, relaxed atmosphere. In the 1950s it was a rendezvous for intellectuals and the avant-garde. For lunch or dinner, there are only sausages on the menu. Specialities include *Buchteln*, a yeast dough filled with plum marmalade, served as of 10pm.

Imperial – Kärntner Ring 16, 1. Bezirk, ☎ 01/50 11 03 89. Daily 7am-11pm. Sigmund Freud and Anton Bruckner were regulars in this establishment, which opened in 1873.

Kleines Café – Franziskanerplatz 3, 1. Bezirk, no telephone. Daily 10am-2am. Full range of spirits. The summer terrace is especially attractive due to the backdrop of Franziskanerplatz.

Konditorei Oberlaa Stadthaus – Neuer Markt 16, 1. Bezirk, ☎ 01/5 13 29 36. In summer 8am-11pm, in winter 8am-8pm. The founders of light, modern Viennese pastry cooking. In summer the *Schanigarten* looks over the Baroque houses of the Neuer Markt.

Landtmann – Dr.-Karl-Lueger-Ring 4, 1. Bezirk, ☎ 01/5 32 06 21. Open daily from 8am to midnight. Very pleasant terrace in summer, with a view of the City Hall and Burgtheater. Good menu. Specialities are *Rüdesheimer* (mocha, brandy and whipped cream) and *Biedermeierkaffee* (mocha, liqueur and whipped cream). International newspapers are available.

Mozart – Albertinaplatz 2, 1. Bezirk, ☎ 01/5 13 08 81. Open daily from 8am to midnight. Terrace in summer and international press throughout the year. Specialities are *Maria-Theresia, Kaisermelange* and Turkish coffee.

Sacher – Philharmonikerstr. 4, 1. Bezirk, ☎ 01/5 14 56 0. Daily 8am-11.30pm. It's more a bistro than a café (in truth it is a café-hotel-restaurant), but whatever, it's a genuine institution. The summer terrace is right behind the opera-house. International newspapers are there for the benefit of the illustrious guests and the happy tourists who can find a place to sit. The legendary *Sachertorte* is also available here.

Schwarzenberg – Kärntner Ring 17, 1. Bezirk, ☎ 01/5 12 89 98. Sun-Fri 7am-midnight, Sat 9am-midnight. Piano music, except for July and August Wed, Fri, Sat 5-10pm and Sun 5-7pm. International papers. The specialities are the *Kaisermelange* and various kinds of international coffees.

Sperl – Gumpendorfer Str. 11, 6. Bezirk, ☎ 01/5 86 41 58. Open from Mon-Sat 7am-11pm, and on Sun and holidays from 11am-8pm. This old café opened in 1880 and was popular with Franz Lehár; apparently it has not changed much since then. People play cards and billiards there.

INTERNET CAFÉS

Big@Net – Hoher Markt 8-9, 1. Bezirk, daily 10am-midnight, 18 stations, €1,45/10min.; Kärtner Str. 61, 1. Bezirk, daily 10am-midnight, 34 stations, €1,45/10min.; Mariahilfer Straße 27, 6. Bezirk, daily 8am-2am, 200 stations (currently Austria's largest Internet-Café), €2.54/50min.; www.bignet.at

LM-Net InternetCafé – Taborstr. 11b, 2. Bezirk, daily 10am-midnight, 17 stations, €0.07/min.; www.lmnet.at

rhiz – Lerchenfelder Gürtel/Stadtbahnbögen 37/38, 8. Bezirk, Mon-Sat 6pm-4am, Sun 6pm-2am 5 stations, €1.09/30min., after 9pm at 2 stations free of charge. Bar in modern design, after 9pm changing DJs keep the music going; www.rhiz.org

Speednet-Café – Morzinplatz 4/Schwedenplatz, 1. Bezirk, Mon-Fri 8am-1am, Sat-Sun 10am-1am, 31 stations, €1.31/10min.; www.speednet-cafe.com

Spicecookie-Internetcafé – Arndtstraße 98/Meidlinger Hauptstr. 13, 12. Bezirk, daily 10am-midnight, 20 stations, €0.07/min., www.spicecookie.cc

Surfland Internetc@fe – Krugerstr. 10, 1. Bezirk, daily 10am-23pm, 15 stations, €1.45 basic fee + €0.07/min.; www.surfland.at

PUBS AND BARS

Vienna's so-called **Bermuda triangle** with all the pubs and bars is in the 1. Bezirk around Ruprechtskirche and Rudolfsplatz (**KPR**). That's where you will find anything to suit your fancy. Just take the plunge ...

Blaustern – Döblinger Gürtel 2, 19. Bezirk, ☎ 01/3 69 65 64. Daily 9am-2am. Formerly a famous chess café, now a designer establishment and meeting place for the in-crowd. Coffee is roasted on the premises.

Casablanca – Rabensteig 8, 1. Bezirk, ☎ 01/5 33 34 63. Open Mon-Thur from 6pm to 4am, and on Fri and Sat until 5am, Sun until 2am. This small bar in the "Bermuda triangle" has small concerts on a small stage. It is a trendy venue with plenty of atmosphere. In winter, they have an excellent *Glühwein* (mulled wine); in summer, they offer a heady fruit wine.

Cantino – Seilerstätte 30 (Haus der Musik), 1. Bezirk. ☎ 01/51 41 12 09, www.weinzirl.at Closed Sundays. Café on the ground floor (daily 9am-11pm; terrace in the inner courtyard, which is covered in a glass roof) and on the fifth floor (daily 11am-10pm), restaurant on the sixth floor (warm meals noon-3pm, 6pm-11pm). Wonderful view of the Stephansdom from the top. Mediterranean cuisine (excellent *tapas*) and wines (by the glass as well), coffee and cakes.

Fischerbräu – Billrothstr. 17, 19. Bezirk, ☎ 01/3 69 59 49. Mon-Fri 4pm-1am, Sat-Sun 11am-1am. Beer from the establishment's own brewery, nice garden, rustic atmosphere and good home cooking, a favourite meeting place.

Flanagans Irish Pub – Schwarzenbergstr. 1-3, 1. Bezirk, ☎ 01/5 13 73 78. Fri-Sat 11am-4am, Sun-Thur 11am-2am. The furnishings come from a genuine Irish pub.

Im KunstHaus – Weißgerberlände 14, 3. Bezirk, ☎ 01/7 12 04 97. Daily 10am-midnight. Designed by Friedensreich Hundertwasser. Wonderful garden, overgrown with plants on the inside. A place with a difference.

Kochwerkstatt – Spittelberggasse 8, 7. Bezirk, ☎ 01/5 23 32 91. Daily 7pm-midnight. Top cuisine in a tiny establishment in the middle of the revitalised, picturesque Spittelberg quarter.

Krah Krah – Rabensteig 8, 1. Bezirk, ☎ 01/5 33 81 93. Daily 11am-2am. Very popular establishment with over 70 types of beer.

Loos-Bar (American Bar) – Kärntner Str. 10, 1. Bezirk, ☎ 01/5 12 32 83. Daily 6pm-4am. Small, but stylish. Recommendable not only for the 1908 decor by Adolf Loos.

MAK Café – Stubenring 3-5, 1. Bezirk, ☎ 01/7 14 01 21. Tues-Sun 10am-2am. Museum café pulsating with life, Design by the star architect Hermann Czech.

Palmenhaus – Burggarten, 1. Bezirk, ☎ 01/5 33 10 33. Daily 10am-2am. Innovative bistro-type cuisine in the atmosphere of the former imperial palm tree house, terrace overlooks the garden of the Hofburg.

Panigl – Schönlaterngasse 11, 1. Bezirk, ☎ 01/5 13 17 16. Open Mon-Fri 6pm to 4am, Sat-Sun 6pm-5am The evocative words *Marienbad-Vienna-Trieste* appear below its sign. There is a wide selection of wine, mainly Austrian, Hungarian and Italian.

Loos-Bar

3BIS/MICHELIN

Planter's Club – Zelinkagasse 4, 1. Bezirk, ☎ 01/5 33 33 93. Daily 5pm-4am. The colonial feel of the name is the bar's decorative motto. From 4pm to 3.30am you can enjoy excellent food in the adjacent Thai restaurant "Livingstone".

Reiss-Bar – Marco-d'Aviano-Gasse 1, 1. Bezirk, ☎ 01/5 12 71 98. Sun-Thur 11am-2am, Fri-Sat 10am-3am. Favoured by the champagne-set, with interior design by architects' office Coop Himmelblau. This bar specialises in sparkling wines from all over the world.

Schweizerhaus – Prater, Straße des 1. Mai 116, 2. Bezirk, ☎ 01/7 28 01 52. Mid-March to end Oct daily 10am-11pm. Typical beer garden offering the most famous hocks *(Stelzen)* in all of Vienna, and original Budweiser on tap. All social strata meet here.

Skybar – Kärntner Str. 19, 1. Bezirk, ☎ 01/5 13 17 12 25. Mon-Sat 11.30am-4am, Sun and public holidays 6pm-3am. Breathtaking view from the roof of the Steffl department store onto the Stephansdom and the old town.

Zum Basilisken – Schönlaterngasse 3-5, 1. Bezirk, ☎ 01/5 13 31 23. Open daily noon to 2am, on Friday and Saturday until 4am. Well-packed bar with excellent dishes. Good for supper or just drinks.

Zum Bettelstudent – Johannesgasse 12, 1. Bezirk, ☎ 01/5 13 20 44. Daily 10am-2am, Fri-Sat until 3am. Bar with an extensive selection of beers and Austrian dishes. Youthful atmosphere and affordable prices.

Going out

CLUBS AND DISCOTHEQUES

B 72 – Hernalser Gürtel-Bogen 72, between the 8. and 17. Bezirk, ☎ 01/4 09 21 28. Live music and DJs.

Chelsea – Lerchenfelder Gürtel, Stadtbahnbögen 29-31, 8. Bezirk, ☎ 01/4 07 93 09. Daily 6pm-midnight. In-crowd meeting point in the renovated arcade of the former city train.

Havanna Club – Krugerstr. 8, 1. Bezirk, ☎ 01/5 13 32 25. Latin-American music: DJ and dance courses.

Havanna Moon – Lederergasse 11, 8. Bezirk, ☎ 01/4 02 07 86. One of those establishments in the new Latino trend, South American ambience, Salsa, Merengue, Mambo...

Papas Tapas – Schwarzenbergplatz 10, 4. Bezirk, ☎ 01/5 05 03 11. July and Aug. Thur, Fri, Sat, otherwise Mon-Sat. Daily live-music from 9pm: Blues, Country, Swing, Rock.

Rhiz-Bar Modern – Lerchenfelder Gürtel, Stadtbahnbögen No. 37/38, 8. Bezirk, ☎ 01/4 09 25 05. Avant-garde music, innovative and experimental sounds and rhythms under the former railway line (Stadtbahn). Cool crowd converges here.

Splendid – Jasomirgottgasse 3, 1. Bezirk, ☎ 01/5 35 26 21. This discotheque enjoys great popularity and is crowded on weekends.

Subzero – Siebensterngasse 27, 7. Bezirk. Tues-Thur 9pm-4am, Fri-Sun 10pm-5am. Techno-kids, hard beats.

U4 – Schönbrunner Str. 222, 12. Bezirk. The classic Viennese disco, every day has its own sound and motto.

Volksgarten Disco – Burgring 1, 1. Bezirk, ☎ 01/5 33 05 18. In 1950s style, pretty garden, the roof over the dance floor can slide back in good weather. Various events are held here, frequent reggae nights.

JAZZ

Jazzland – Franz-Josefs-Kai 29, 1. Bezirk, ☎ 01/5 33 25 75. International groups appear in this vaulted jazz cellar beneath the Ruprechtskirche. Great atmosphere. Music from 9pm.

Miles Smiles – Lange Gasse 51, 8. Bezirk, ☎ 01/5 95 17. Modern jazz of the first water, regular live acts.

Jazzclub Porgy & Bess – Riemergasse 11, 1. Bezirk, ☎ 01/50 37 009. Daily live music, concerts with Austrian and international musicians.

Otto – Altmannsdorfer Straße 101, 12. Bezirk, ☎ 01/8 04 76 50. Oct-Apr Sun at 11.30am pre-lunch drinks with jazz.

CABARET, CLUB ART, MUSICAL EVENTS

Kulisse – Rosensteingasse 39, 17. Bezirk, ☎ 01/4 85 38 70, Fax: 01/4 85 44 02; www.kulisse.at Musicals, cabaret, children's theatre, and a *Beisl* (Viennese bistro) (☎ 01/4 85 44 02).

Orpheum – Steigenteschgasse 94b, 22. Bezirk, ☎ 01/4 81 17 17, Fax: 01/2 02 61 20; www.orpheum.at Venue for events (with a *Beisl* – ☎ 01/ 2 03 12 54), cabaret and readings.

Planet Music – Adalbert-Stifter-Str. 73, 20. Bezirk, ☎ 01/3 32 46 41, Fax: 01/ 3 32 46 41 41; www. planet.at Venue for all sorts of music – from hiphop and pop, to blues, reggae, jazz, rock and metal. Also events geared towards families and children.

Szene Wien – Hauffgasse 26, 11. Bezirk, ☎ 01/ 74 93 341, Fax: 01/ 7 49 22 06; www . szenewien.com Live concerts, special acts, world music.

Vindobona – Wallenstein-platz, 20. Bezirk, ☎ 01/3 32 42 31; office@vindobona.at *The* establishment for cabaret, Sat-Sun children's theatre. Also has a restaurant so that guests are well cared for throughout the evening.

Wiener Metropol – Hernalser Hauptstr. 55, 17. Bezirk, ☎ 01/40

Street artistes on Stephansplatz

777 40, Fax: 01/4 07 77 40 10; www.wiener-metropol.at Stage for concerts (songwriter/singers, world music), cabaret and in-house musical productions.

WUK – Währinger Str. 59, 9. Bezirk, ☎ 01/4 01 21 10; info@wuk.at Cooperative **W**erkstätten **u**nd **K**ulturhaus (ateliers and cultural house): Music, dance, concerts, readings and exhibitions.

Entertainment

THEATRE

Burgtheater – Dr.-Karl-Lueger-Ring 2, 1. Bezirk. ☎ 01/5 14 44 44 40. A European theatre offering the entire range of theatrical repertoire. Tickets sold in advance from the 20th of the month preceding the month in question, for the whole calendar month. Written applications for tickets should be addressed at least 10 days in advance of the date in question to the Servicecenter Burgtheater, Hanuschgasse 3, A-1010 Wien (Fax 01/5 14 44 41 47). Tickets can be ordered by telephone (payment by credit card) daily 10am-9pm from ☎ 01/51 31 513. For performances that are not sold out, tickets can be obtained at 50% of their original price from 1hr before the performance starts from the "Abendkasse" (☎ 01/51 44 44 440). Other theatres linked with the Burgtheater are the **Akademietheater** (Lisztstraße 1, 3. Bezirk, ☎ 01/51 44 44 740) and the **Kasino** (Schwarzenbergplatz 1, 3. Bezirk, ☎ 01/51 44 44 830).

Theater in der Josefstadt – Josefstädter Str. 24, 8. Bezirk, ☎ 01/4 27 00, Fax: 01/42 70 06 0; www.josefstadt.org Venue for theatrical productions since 1788, where such famous Austrian names as Nestroy and Raimund made their debut: both classic and modern theatre. The Theater in der Josefstadt includes the smaller venue, the **Kammerspiele** (mostly comedies and light fare; Rotenturmstr. 20, 1. Bezirk).

Volkstheater – Neustiftgasse 1, 7. Bezirk, ☎ 01/5 24 72 63, Fax: 01/52 33 50 12 82; www.volkstheater.at Broad spectrum of plays from the classics to the avant-garde.

Gruppe 80 – Gumpendorfer Str. 67, 6. Bezirk, ☎ 01/5 86 52 22, Fax: 01/5 87 36 72 11; http://gruppe80.at Predominantly Austrian plays from the classics to contemporary drama.

Schauspielhaus – Porzellangasse 19, 9. Bezirk, ☎ 01/3 17 01 01, Fax: 01/3 17 01 01 22; www.schauspielhaus.at Predominantly Austrian plays from the classics to contemporary drama.

Burgtheater

Komödie am Kai – Franz-Josefs-Kai 29, 1. Bezirk, ☏ 01/5 33 24 34, Fax: 01/5 33 24 34 76; http://members.aon.at/komoedie.am.kai Popular comedies from all over the world for a pleasant evening.

Vienna's English Theatre – Josefsgasse 12, 8. Bezirk, ☏ 01/40 21 26 00, Fax: 01/4 02 12 60 40; www.englishtheatre.at English-language theatre productions from both Britain and America have been staged here since 1963 (classics, comedies, guest performances by solo artists).

Marionettentheater Schloß Schönbrunn – In the Hofratstrakt of Schloss Schönbrunn, 13. Bezirk, ☏ 01/8 17 32 47, Fax: 01/81 73 24 74, www.marionettentheater.at A puppet theatre that has earned many an international accolade.

OPERA, CONCERTS, MUSICALS

Staatsoper – (Herbert-von-Karajan-Platz, 1. Bezirk, www.wiener-staatsoper.at)

Volksoper (Währinger Straße 78, 9. Bezirk, www.volksoper.at, operas in the German language) – *The* opera venues of the Austrian capital. Tickets go on sale one month before the performance date. Written applications for tickets must be submitted at least three weeks before the performance to the Österreichischer Bundestheaterverband, Bestellbüro, Hanuschgasse 3, A-1010 Wien. Tickets can be ordered by telephone (payment by credit card) from ☏ 01/5 13 15 13. (Mon-Fri 10am-6pm, Sat-Sun and holidays 10am-noon, on the first Sat of the month and on Sat during Advent 10am-5pm). Tickets can be ordered on the Internet at www.culturall.com Tickets are also available at the following box offices: Bundestheaterkassen, Hanuschgasse 3, 1. Bezirk; Burgtheater, Dr.-Karl-Lueger-Ring 2, 1. Bezirk; Volksoper, Währinger Str. 78, 9. Bezirk (each open Mon-Fri 8am-6pm, Sat-Sun, holidays 9am-noon on the first Sat of the month and on Sat during Advent 10am-5pm) or at the daytime box office of the Staatsoper (Mon-Fri 9.30am to 1hr before curtain goes up, on the first Sat of the month and on Sat during Advent 9.30am-5pm). Evening box office 1hr before curtain goes up.

Neue Oper Wien – Herminengasse 10, 23. Bezirk, ☏/Fax: 01/2 16 27 69; www.neueoperwien.at The independent opera group, which stages only a few productions per year, has dedicated itself to premieres and 20C works that have some relevance to current affairs and that concern humanitarian and socio-political matters.

Musikverein – Vienna's Music Appreciation Society, Bösendorferstr. 12, 1010 Wien, ☏ 01/5 05 81 90, Fax: 01/5 05 81 90 94; www.musikverein-wien.at Puts on about 500 concerts of classical music every year. Tickets go on sale about three weeks before the concert date (a month for members) , Mon-Fri 9am-7.30pm, Sat 9am-5pm. For programme details call ☏ 01/5 05 13 63 (recorded message).

Konzerte der Wiener Sängerknaben – The Vienna Boys' Choir perform from Apr-June and Sept-Oct Fri at 4pm in the Brahms Room at the Musikverein. Tickets may be purchased from a number of hotels and from Reisebüro Mondial (travel agent's), Faulmanngasse 4, 1040 Wien, ☏ 01/58 80 41 41, Fax: 01/5 87 12 68; www.mondial.at

Sung Masses in the Burgkapelle at the Hofburg on Sundays and 25 Dec (with the Vienna Boys' Choir and members of the chorus and orchestra of the Vienna State Opera): These begin at 9.15am. Seats cost €5-29; there is no charge for standing room. Orders must be placed in writing (please do not enclose either cash or cheques) at least 10 weeks in advance to: Hofmusikkapelle, Hofburg, A-1010 Wien, Fax: 01/5 33 99 27 75. Collection and payment of pre-ordered tickets is on Fri 11am-1pm and 3-5pm or on Sun from 8.15-8.45am in the Burgkapelle. Availability permitting, tickets for seats for a particular Sun are sold at the Burgkapelle Tageskasse from 3-5pm on the immediately preceding Fri.

Wiener Konzerthaus – Lothringerstr. 20, 3. Bezirk, ☎ 01/7 12 12 11, Fax: 01/2 42 00 11 0; www.konzerthaus.at Orchestras and soloists from around the world, in-house events by the Konzerthaus Society.

Waltzes and operetta with the Wiener Hofburg-Orchester, in the Hofburg, the Konzerthaus or the Musikverein. ☎ 01/5 87 25 52, Fax: 01/5 87 43 79, www.wr-hofburg-orchester.at/konzerte

Schönbrunner Schloßkonzerte – In the Orangerie of Schloß Schönbrunn, 13. Bezirk, ☎ 01/8 12 50 04, www.imagevienna.com Daily 8.30pm. Music of Mozart, Strauss and others in a remarkable atmosphere.

Top-quality **musical productions** are presented by Vereinigte Bühnen Wien GmbH (Linke Wienzeile 6, A-1060 Wien, ☎ 01/58 83 02 00, *www.musicalvienna.at*), which incorporates three venues:

Theater an der Wien, Linke Wienzeile 6, 6. Bezirk;

Raimund-Theater, Wallgasse 18-20, 6. Bezirk;

Ronacher, Seilerstätte 9, 1. Bezirk.

Ticket service – For musicals and classical concerts, the main address when ordering from abroad is **Vienna Ticket Service**, Börsegasse 1, 1010 Wien, ☎ 01/5 34 17 75 (Mon-Fri 9-17 Uhr), Fax: 01/5 34 17 26, www.cityrama.at, office@viennatickets.at Pop, rock and the like is covered by **Österreich Ticket**, Kärtner Str. 19, (1. Bezirk, in Kaufhaus Steffl, 3rd floor, customer service – Kundenabteilung), 1010 Wien, ☎ 01/96 0 96 (Mon-Fri 9.30am-7pm, Sat 9.30am-5pm), www.oeticket.com

CINEMAS

The following are only a small selection, away from the mainstream, of the numerous cinemas that there are in Vienna. For the current cinema programme and additional addresses, consult *Wienside*, the weekly calendar of events available from cinemas, local "in" bars, etc or the daily press. Or check the Internet: www.film.at.

Autokino – To the east of Vienna, accessible via the B3 route, Groß-Enzersdorf, Autokinostr. 2, ☎ 0 22 49/26 60, www.autokino.at Austria's only drive-in movie is not far from the eastern city limits. A huge flea market is held in front of the drive-in on Sunday mornings.

Filmhaus Stöbergasse – Stöbergasse 11-15, 5. Bezirk, ☎ 01/54 666 30. Mainly avant-garde movies.

Gartenbau – Parkring 12, 1. Bezirk, ☎ 01/5 12 23 54, www.citycinemas.at One of Vienna's premiere movie theatres.

Imax-Filmtheater (beim Technischen Museum, AZ) – Mariahilfer Str. 212, 14. Bezirk, ☎ 01/8 94 01 01, Info hotline: 01/15 47; www.imax-wien.at Special cinema with a huge, nearly 8000sq ft, screen.

Österreichisches Filmmuseum – Augustinerstr. 1, 1. Bezirk, ☎ 01/5 33 70 54; www.filmmuseum.at Numerous retrospectives. Films are shown in their original language and not dubbed. A must for film buffs.

Schikaneder Kino – Margarethenstr. 24, 4. Bezirk, ☎ 01/5 85 28 67; www.schikaneder.at A small movie theatre that is devoted to young film art.

Votiv Kino – Währinger Str. 12, 9. Bezirk, ☎ 01/3 17 35 71; www.votivkino.at Cinema with special programming.

(Mainly English-language) films in original version:

Burg – Opernring 19, 1. Bezirk, ☎ 01/5 87 84 06; www.burgkino.at They often show Carol Reed's *The Third Man*.

English Cinema Haydn – Mariahilfer Str. 57, 6. Bezirk, ☎ 01/5 87 22 62; www.haydnkino.at

Flotten Center – Mariahilfer Str. 85-87, 6. Bezirk, ☎ 01/5 86 51 52; www.citycinemas.at

The Kino-Centers that have arisen during the past few years also offer a substantial selection of movies with new films on their programmes. They also have a wide choice of eating facilities, for example:

Cinestar im Vienna Twin Tower – Wienerbergstraße 11, 10. Bezirk, ☎ 01/918 199 00; www.cinestar.at

Hollywood Megaplex im Donauplex – Wagramer Straße 67-71, 22. Bezirk, ☎ 01/20 171 71; www.hollywood-megaplex.at

Spanish Riding School: Tickets for the presentations (gala events, 80 min, seats €21.80-145.35; standing room €14.53-25.44, except for the classical dressage with music) should be ordered as early as possible at the Spanische Hofreitschule, Michaelerplatz 1, 1010 Wien, Fax: 01/53 50 186; office@srs.at In the event of a presentation of classical dressage with music, apply to authorised Viennese theatre ticket offices or travel agents (but they do request a surcharge on the price of each ticket of at least 22%). For the Morgenarbeit (training of the Lipizzaner) you will not have to reserve. Tickets (€11.63) are available on the same day at the entrance to the Spanische Hofreitschule (Hofburg, Josefsplatz).
The Viennese tourist office has a brochure in several languages giving the exact dates and modalities. Information is available on the Internet at www.spanische-reitschule.com

Casino Wien, Palais Esterházy, Kärntner Str. 41, 1. Bezirk, ☎ 01/5 12 48 36, www.casinos.at

Shopping

Most department stores and specialist boutiques are located in the pedestrian zones in Kärntner Straße, Graben, Kohlmarkt, and Vienna's main shopping street, Mariahilfer Straße.
Since the Viennese shop in their own districts, the city centre contains mainly luxury shops. They lie around the cathedral, on the Graben, Kärntner Straße, Kohlmarkt, Neuer Markt and Tuchlauben. In the 1st District, the sumptuous Ringstraßen Gallerien (Kärtnerring 7) are a major commercial centre. The main shopping street in Vienna is Mariahilfer Straße, which separates the 6th and 7th Districts and links Westbahnhof to the Ring. It is a street featuring the large popular stores (C & A, Virgin, Billa, etc). Another major commercial street is Meidlinger Hauptstraße, in the 12th District. The city's main shopping arcade is SCS (Shopping City Sud, in Vösendorf off the Südautobahn A 2, exit SCS, www.scs.at), the largest in Austria, comprising numerous stores and restaurants. In August 2001, the **Gasometer** was opened in Simmering in the 11. Bezirk. (U3, Gasometer; exit St. Marx from the A 23 motorway, www.gasometer-wien.at). The four former gasometers, a 19C monument, were turned into apartments, student accommodation, offices and a huge shopping mall by famous architects (including Jean Nouvel, Coop Himmelblau). The shopping mall has restaurants, cafés, supermarkets, department stores, specialist shops, cinemas and other venues for events. Businesses in Vienna are generally open Mon-Fri 8am/9am –6.30pm/7pm, Sat until 5pm, many until 8pm on Thursdays.

AUCTIONS

Dorotheum – Dorotheergasse 17, 1. Bezirk, ☎ 01/51 56 02 00, Fax: 01/51 56 04 43; www.dorotheum.com The most important auction house in Central Europe (around 650 auctions per year). Auctions: Mon-Fri 2pm, Sat 10am (except in summer). Free sale Mon-Fri 10am-6pm, Sat 9am-5pm. The auctions are held at odd intervals, so it is best to inform yourself in advance.

SOUVENIRS

Specialist shops

See also Eating out and For the Gourmet

Augarten GmbH – Stock-im-Eisen-Platz 3-4, 1. Bezirk. In Schloß Augarten, 2. Bezirk. Sales outlet for the famous porcelain manufacturer, whose origins date back to 1718.

---

k. u. k.

In Vienna, shop windows or shop fronts often display the letters "K. und K. Hoflieferant". This distinction was linked to a strict selection process during the days of the Empire, and the businesses still sporting it have obliged themselves to maintain those same criteria of quality. In 1867, the creation of the dual monarchy gave rise to Austro-Hungary. Franz-Josef then became Emperor (Kaiser) of Austria and King (König) of Hungary, after his coronation at Pest. Thus, "K. und K." signifies "imperial and royal", a title to which suppliers to the Court laid claim.

Backhausen – Kärntner Str. 33, 1. Bezirk. Kärntner Straße 33, 1. Bezirk. This textile factory sells furnishing materials, curtains and silk scarves with Jugendstil designs. Good place for souvenirs.

Gunkel – Tuchlauben 11, 1. Bezirk. The company, founded in 1796, is famous for its fine sheets and linens.

J. & L. Lobmeyr – Kärntner Straße 26, 1. Bezirk. A glassware specialist which used to supply the Imperial Court, and which is famous for its extremely fragile and delicate *"Musselinglas"*.

Maria Stransky – Hofburg. Burgpassage 2, 1. Bezirk. This is the home of typical Viennese petit point embroidery.

Österreichische Werkstätten (Austrian Arts & Handcrafts) – Kärntner Str. 6, 1. Bezirk. The specialist for glass and metal design, jewellery, silverware, ceramics, and accessories, such as handbags and cloth.

Piatnik – Schottenfeldgasse 19, 7. Bezirk. This establishment founded at the end of the 19C sells such beautiful playing cards that they can almost rank as works of art.

Rasper & Söhne – Graben 15, 1. Bezirk. Porcelain, glassware, silverware.

Schau Schau Brillen – Rotenturmstraße 11, 1. Bezirk. Spectacles in the strangest shapes are the speciality here, signed by Peter Kozich. One of his clients is no less a figure than Elton John.

Thonet – Lerchenfelderstr. 77, Ecke Zieglergasse, 17. Bezirk. High-quality furniture: The world renown of this bistro chair is such that it needs no further introduction *(see Introduction, Art and architecture, Decorative arts)*.

Zum Alten Knopfkönig, Fa. Frimmel – Freisingergasse 1, 1. Bezirk. The paradise for buttons, where the Imperial Court also used to come to do business.

Fashion boutiques

Kettner – Seilergasse 12, 1. Bezirk. Comfortable clothing for all leisure occasions, from hunting to camping.

Lanz Trachten Moden – Kärntner Str. 10, 1. Bezirk. Austrian traditional fashions, the shop has subsidiaries in Salzburg and Innsbruck.

Loden Plankl – Michaelerplatz 6, 1. Bezirk. Typical Austrian fashions, especially blue, grey or green *Loden*.

Resi Hammerer – Kärntner Str. 29, 1. Bezirk. Traditional costumes *(Trachten)* and sports clothes.

Tostmann – Schottengasse 3a, 1. Bezirk. Traditional folk fashion and clothing. Large selection of *Dirndl*. Not cheap, but the quality is excellent.

MARKETS

Fruit, vegetables, flowers

Business hours are usually Mon-Fri 6am-6.30pm, Sat 6am-1pm.

Blumengroßmarkt – Laxenburger Str. 365, 23. Bezirk. The colourful sea of flowers is a delight to the eye.

Brunnenmarkt – Brunnengasse, 16. Bezirk.

Hannovermarkt – Hannovergasse/Othmargasse, 20. Bezirk.

Market at Freyung – 1. Bezirk, May-Nov Tues and Thur 10am-6.30pm.

Naschmarkt – Linke Wienzeile/Kettenbrückengasse, 4. and 6. Bezirk., Mon-Sat 6.30am-6pm.

Rochusmarkt – Landstraßer Hauptstr./Salmgasse, 3. Bezirk.

Schwendermarkt – Schwendergasse/Dadlergasse, 15. Bezirk.

Art and antique markets

Art and antique market near the Donaukanal – Donaukanalpromenade on the old town side, near the Marienbrücke, 1. Bezirk, May-Sept. Sat 2pm-8pm, Sun 10am-8pm.

Am Hof – 1. Bezirk; March to Christmas Fri-Sat 10am-8pm.

Arts and crafts market at the Heiligenkreuzerhof – Schönlaterngasse, 1. Bezirk; takes place irregularly.

Flea markets

Naschmarkt – Linke Wienzeile. 4. and 6. Bezirk. The flea market is located at the south end of the Naschmarkt: Sat 6am-6pm.

Autokino – To the east of Vienna, accessible via route B3 in Groß-Enzersdorf, Autokinostr. 2. Sunday mornings on the grounds of the drive-in cinema: a gigantic flea market.

The Naschmarkt

Christmas markets

During the Advent period, there are several Christmas markets throughout the city and its outskirts, both large and small. They are colourful, lively, noisy and friendly affairs, forming part of the Viennese heritage. Here are the main ones:

Christkindlmarkt Rathausplatz – Rathauspark, 1. Bezirk, mid-November until Christmas. Numerous stands selling pastries and sweets, hot mulled wine *(Glühwein)* are among the pleasant aspects that are part and parcel of Christmas markets.

Altwiener Christkindlmarkt Freyung – Freyung, 1. Bezirk, end of November until Christmas.

Crafts market in front of Karlskirche – Karlsplatz, 4. Bezirk, end of November until Christmas.

Christmas market at Spittelberg – Spittelberggasse, 7. Bezirk, end of November until Christmas. The young frequent this market, which is also a craft market. There is always an abundant supply of mulled wine.

Weihnachtsdorf im Uni-Campus – Formerly the Allgemeines Krankenhaus (AKH), 9. Bezirk, mid-November until Dec 24, Christmas, culture and art market.

Christmas market in front of Schloss Schönbrunn – 13. Bezirk, end of November. A calmer ambience than the one in Spittelberg, in a historic site with great tourist appeal. Concert stage.

A 10-15 % of the receipt price is standard. If you cannot pay the price plus tip exactly, then you tail your waitperson the sum you wish to pay. For example, your meal costs €12.70 and you wish to leave a tip of €1.30, then hand over a €20 bill and say €14. You will receive €6 in change.

At a Christmas market

The colourful roof tiling of Stephansdom

Introduction

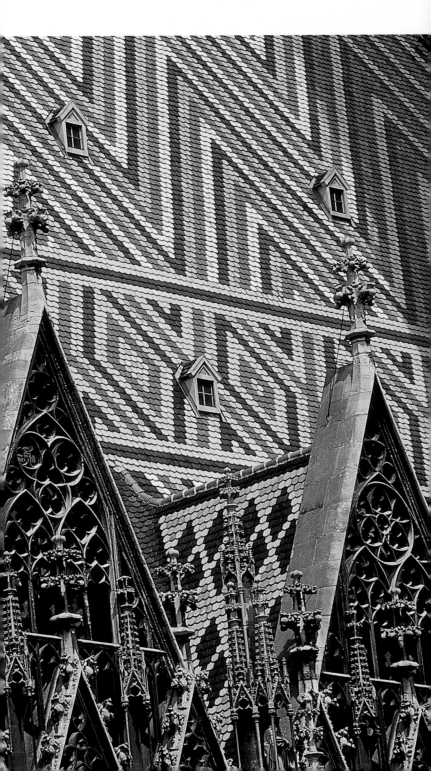

The city and its surroundings

GEOGRAPHIC LOCATION

Between the Alps and the Carpathians – Vienna lies at the base of the most easterly foothills of the Alps, in a plain opening onto the Hungarian steppes and the Little Carpathians. A Danubian city, it stands with its back to this river, which flows into the Black Sea. Initially a maze of streams and marshes, the Danube became navigable after the construction of a canal.

Vienna stands at a distance of about 60km/37mi from Hungary, the Czech Republic and Slovakia. The city is 53km/32mi from Bratislava (Slovakia), 193km/119mi from Graz (Styria), 251km/155mi from Budapest (Hungary), 300km/186mi from Salzburg (Salzburg) and Prague (Czech Republic), 440km/272mi from Munich (Germany) and 475km/294mi from Innsbruck (Tyrol).

The Vienna Basin – The Wiener Becken lies sunken amid the Weinviertel valleys to the north, the Marchfeld plain to the east, the first undulations of the Alpine Leithagebirge chain to the south and the wooded reliefs of the Wienerwald to the west. This 40km/24mi wide basin heralds the Pannonian plain of the Hungarian *puszta*, which begins with Burgenland.

Vienna is at the heart of a fertile agricultural region, which, for several decades has had to contain the development of industry and the migration of urban population. Vienna extends across a series of terraces of varying heights. The site is remarkable in that Vienna is the only European capital to produce wine, at least in such large quantities. On the slopes rising from the right bank of the Danube, 720ha/1 779 acres support 250 small winegrowing estates, giving a rural ambiance to the city outskirts. Vienna and its surroundings display vineyards and wooded hills to the north and west, and green meadows and industrial developments to the east and south.

The Danube – The second longest river in Europe after the Volga, it is the longest in Central Europe, more than 2 800km/1 736mi (its precise length has not been established). The Danube forms a natural link between southwest Germany and southeast Europe. It crosses or borders nine countries, and four capitals are built on its banks, evidence of its strategic importance as an international route.

Between Ulm (southern Germany) and Vienna, it flows through a vast and fertile alluvial plain, then takes on an alpine character, reaching flood height in summer. At the level of Leopoldsberg, north of Vienna, the last alpine foothill overlooking the Austrian capital, the river winds through the first of the alluvial plains between the Alps and the Carpathians. After Bratislava, as it flows more slowly down the gentle slope, it spreads over an exceedingly flat plain and divides into numerous arms, which silt up with sand. The Danube (360km/223mi in Austria, 20km/12mi in Vienna) is vital to the country's economy. When it reaches Vienna, it does not always display, particularly when in spate, the colour immortalised in Johann Strauss's *Blue Danube*.

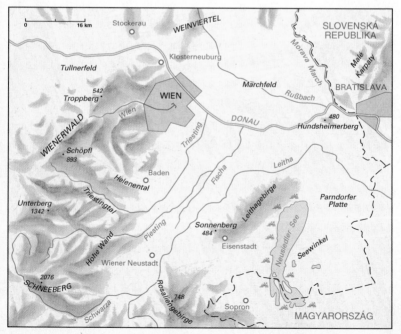

Moreover, strictly speaking, the Danube lies more than 2km/1mi from the historic centre of the city. First-time visitors to Vienna may be amazed at being able to cross the Danube four times. The eastern section of the city is crossed by the small Danube canal, the wide rectilinear Danube canal (300m/327yd), the additional New Danube canal (200m/218yd) and the meander of the Old Danube (a channel with many bathers along its banks). After the 1501 floods there was a project for flood control of the river by building a canal; this work was not completed until 1972, by which time several canals were in use.

Finally, the Danube has a small tributary, 34km/21mi long, the **Wien River**. This small river of weak and irregular flow gave its name to Vienna.

THE CITY

A federal capital since 1920, Vienna and its immediate surroundings constitute one of the provinces of the Austrian Republic. A federal state, the
country consists of nine independent *Länder*: Burgenland, Carinthia,
Lower Austria, Upper Austria, Salzburg, Styria, Tyrol, Vienna and
Vorarlberg. This is why the city also includes the departments and min-
istries of the federal government and the *Land*.

An enclave in the vast expanse of Lower Austria, the Vienna *Land* covers an area of 414km²/157sq mi and has a periphery of 133km/82mi.

Every five years, the population of the Land elects the members of the **provincial Diet**. Their number varies between 36 and 56, in proportion to the numbers of inhabitants in the province. The Vienna Diet is the only one to have 100 members. Using pro-portional representation, the Diet elects the members of the **provincial Government** that, as the administrative arm of the Diet, enjoys the confidence of the Diet and makes decisions by majority voting.

Both an urban district and a Land, Vienna's administration has a twofold purpose. The city council corresponds to the provincial Diet (elected for 5 years). The mayor, elected from the members of the Council, also acts as federal governor *(Landeshauptmann)*. The city comprises 23 districts *(see map on p. 6)*, around the historic centre that the Viennese call the "inner city" *(innere Stadt)*. The city of Vienna is not only the polit-ical, but also the economic centre of the country. It overlaps with the territory of the Vienna *Land*, which accounts for almost 30% of the country's GDP.

There is no doubt that Vienna is the political, intellectual and cultural centre of Austria. Owing to the permanent neutrality of the country, it has become the headquarters of various international organisations such as IAEO (International Atomic Energy Organisation), UNO (United Nations) and OPEC (Organisation of Petroleum Exporting Countries). The Austrian capital enjoys a strategic position between northern Europe and the Mediterranean and between Eastern and Western Europe. Since the 1815 Congress of Vienna, it also has been a major international congressional centre (1415 international conferences in 2000). In addition, it is a centre for trade fairs and a pres-tigious tourist magnet because of its rich historical heritage: 7.7 million overnight stays (about 41,000 beds) in 2000. This makes Vienna one of the most-frequently visited European cities. The annual sales figure for Viennese hotels, restaurants and cultural facilities is about €1.6 billion.

Population – The main factor in Vienna's growth through the centuries has been men and women coming from all parts of the Habsburg empire and its subsequent nations to the city. In 2000, it had 1 615 438 inhabitants, which makes Vienna a medium-sized capital among those of Europe. Around 1910, Vienna was the 4th largest city in Europe, ranking behind after London, Paris and Berlin. The number of residents had more than tripled between the mid-19C (632 127, 1869) and the First World War (2 031 498, 1910). Since 1918, the population had been steadily decreasing (1 531 346, 1981). The two main causes are a higher death rate than birth rate and a higher annual number of people emigrating from the city compared to the number of people moving into it.

However, there has been an upturn in the demographic development because of the opening of the Iron Curtain at the beginning of the 1990s and Austria's entry into the EU in 1995.

In 2000, 18.1% of Vienna's population did not have Austrian citizenship. The largest of these groups were: Yugoslavs (81 116), Turks (43 950), Bosnians (20 815), Poles (17 433), Croatians (16 863), Germans (13 715), Iranians (6 976), Macedonians (5 604), Rumanians (4 789), Egyptians (4 696), Eastern Indians (4 533) and Americans (4 052).

Religion – The majority of the Viennese are Roman Catholic (about 58%). After the Protestants, the Muslims are the third-largest religious community. About 20% of the population does not have a religious affiliation.

Industry – Because of its geographical situation, Vienna was during the Cold War a major centre of commercial exchange between the Eastern and Western blocs, an "inter-face". The disappearance of the Iron Curtain strengthened its position as a commercial staging post, which is probably why important European, American and Japanese com-panies have subsidiaries in Vienna. The Austrian capital has become a focus of commerce. Vienna, the industrial hub of the country, is particularly well represented in sectors such as food, electricity (no nuclear energy in Austria), electronics, metallurgy, chem-istry (especially the Vienna-Schwechat refinery which processes Austrian or imported crude oil), the pharmaceutical industry, precision engineering, steel construction, car manufacture (large General Motors factory in Aspern), crafts and the fashion industry. The city is also home to the head offices of the country's main banks, savings banks, insurance companies and major firms.

A historical overview

FROM THE CELTS TO THE MIGRATION OF THE PEOPLES (VÖLKERWANDERUNG)

800-400 BC	Between the Baltic and the Adriatic, between the Alps and Hungary, the Celts of Noricum settle in the Viennese basin on the Danube.
1C-2C AD	At Vindobona, "the white city", the Romans build a military camp in their defence against the Germans, near Carnuntum, headquarters of the governor of Pannonia.
180 AD	Death of the Emperor Marcus Aurelius at Vindobona, during a campaign against the Marcomanni.
212	Vindobona, with a population of 20 000, is raised to the status of *municipium*, a Roman city.
c 400	After crossing the Rhine in 376, the Goths push on to the Danube and destroy the city.
6C-8C	Fall of the Western Roman Empire in 476 followed by domination by the Avars, a nation of horsemen from central Asia.

Marcus Aurelius

S. Chirol

THE MIDDLE AGES

End of 8C	Defeat of the Avars by Charlemagne who creates the eastern March of Bavaria (Ostmark), germanises it and establishes Christianity there. Vindobona is reborn under the name of Vindomina.
881	Wenia, a fortress and trading centre on the eastward-flowing Danube, is first mentioned in the Salzburg annals.
955	With the victory of Lechfeld, Emperor Otto I the Great puts an end to the invasions of the Magyars (from the southern Urals) in Bavaria.
962	Emperor Otto I receives the new crown of the Holy Roman Empire of the German Nation from Pope John XII.
976	Bishop Leopold, ancestor of the Babenbergs, becomes first Margrave of the March, where he consolidates Christianity.
1030	The city appears under the name of Wienne.
1137	The city is granted city status *(civitas)* and acquires fortifications.
1156	Forced by **Heinrich II Jasomirgott**, Emperor Frederick Barbarossa grants the March the status of hereditary duchy with Vienna as ducal capital.
12C-13C	Several crusades pass through Vienna on their way to the Holy Land. By now, the city is the second largest in the Holy Roman Empire of the German Nation after Cologne, and is already an important centre connecting East and West.
1193	On his return from the Holy Land, Richard the Lionheart is captured in what is now the Erdberg district by Leopold V. Imprisoned in the fortress of Dürnstein in the Wachau, the King of England is freed for an enormous ransom, which is used both to build a castle on the square now known as Am Hof, and to fortify Wiener Neustadt as a citadel protecting the Hungarian border.
c 1200	The first coins are minted.
1246	Friedrich II, "the Warlike", is killed in battle against the Magyars, marking the end of the Babenberg dynasty. Vienna is left to **Ottokar II Przemysl**, the king of Bohemia.

HABSBURG RULE

Rudolf I

1278   Supported by the Pope and the German princes, **Rudolf of Habsburg** defeats Ottokar II Przemysl at the Battle of Marchfeld. With this victory, the Habsburgs acquire what is now Austria and Rudolf moves to Vienna which he elevates to the rank of Reichsstadt, a free imperial city.

1326   Great fire of Vienna.

1348   Mass outbreak of the plague throughout Europe.

1365   **Rudolf IV**, first archduke, founds the University of Vienna, the oldest German-language university after Prague.

1396   Dukes Wilhelm, Leopold IV and Albert IV grant the "Wiener Ratswahlprivileg" to tradesmen and craftsmen who may now be elected mayor or members of the town council.

1420   The Hussite heresy in Bohemia threatens to spread into the north of Lower Austria; Viennese Jews do not escape repression and are driven from the city.

1438   Albert V (of the Albertine branch) is elevated to the throne of the Holy Roman Empire of the German Nation under the title of Albert II. Vienna, where the University abandons scholasticism for humanism, becomes an imperial residence.

1462   Rebellion of the Viennese against the reduction of their privileges. For two months Emperor Frederick III is held hostage in the Hofburg.

1485   **Matthias I Corvinus**, King of Hungary, occupies Vienna for five years, abolishing privileges and concessions, which however are restored by the Habsburgs after his death.

THE TURKS AT VIENNA'S GATES

1493   Emperor **Maximilian I** moves his residence to Innsbruck in the Tyrol, to the detriment of wealthy Vienna. In the East, Ottoman expansionism continues in the direction of the Danube; the Byzantine Empire had come to an end with the fall of Constantinople in 1453.

1515   Maximilian I calls a meeting of influential figures in Vienna to decide on ways of resisting the Turkish threat, the first requirement being solidarity between Christian princes.

1521   Vienna adopts the ideas of the Reformation. The Turks seize Belgrade.

1526   Having eliminated opponents of imperial authority, Archduke Ferdinand signs a decree limiting the administrative autonomy of the city to honorary functions.

1529   **Suleyman the Magnificent**, one of the world's most powerful rulers, camps outside the city gates for three months with an army of 12 000 men. Resistance led by city leader Count Salm and the Viennese winter prompt the Turks to raise the siege.

1530-60   Erection of a massive circle of fortified ramparts, which stay in place until 1857.

1533   Ferdinand installs the centralised administration of the Austrian States in Vienna. A free city, it gradually becomes the capital of a heterogeneous and multiracial empire.

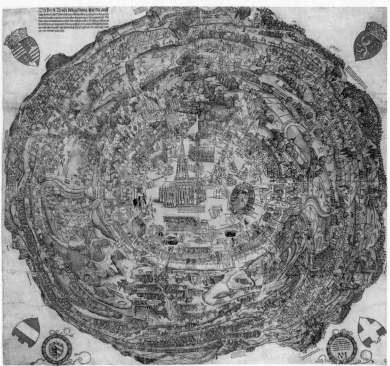

Circular map of Vienna (1545)

1550	The city's population reaches 50 000.
1556	The Jesuit Petrus Canisius is summoned to Vienna by Emperor Ferdinand I. Launch of the Counter-Reformation. Vienna recovers some of the splendour lost after the Turkish siege and becomes the permanent seat of the imperial court.
1577-1618	Protestant services are banned in Vienna (80% of the population are Protestant in 1571, including the burgomaster). The city becomes a Catholic city once again.
1618-48	The armies of the rebelling Bohemians and the Swedes threaten the capital, during the **Thirty Years War**.
1620	Triumph of the Counter-Reformation after the battle of the White Hill near Prague. Under the influence of Cardinal Melchior Khlesl, numerous religious orders establish bases for themselves in Vienna.
1629	The plague kills 30 000 people.
1648	The Treaty of Westphalia ends the Thirty Years War.
1679	A further 30 000 deaths are caused by the plague.
1683	Grand Vizier Kara Mustafa with over 200 000 men lays siege to the city, which is defended by less than 20 000 Viennese, commanded by Count Starhemberg. Vienna is delivered with the help of King John III of Poland, Jan Sobieski, in the **Battle of Kahlenberg**. However, parts of the city lie in ruins.
1699	The Peace of Carlowitz is signed, ending the Turkish war, and ceding Hungary to the Habsburgs. Vienna, which has gradually been rebuilt and embellished, is now the capital of a major European power.

"VIENNA GLORIOSA"

1700	Vienna's population reaches 80 000.
1700-40	The Baroque style, spreading from Rome and Prague, flourishes in Vienna. The city thrives, enthralled by the victories of a French nobleman disdained by the Sun King, Prince Eugène of Savoy. The "Saviour of Christendom", finally vanquishes the Ottoman menace. Vienna is a focus for intellectual and artistic activity.
1706	Founding of the Wiener Stadtbank with the support of Count Gundaker Starhemberg.
1714	Last plague epidemic.
1722	A bishopric since 1469, Vienna becomes an archbishopric.

1740-48	**War of the Austrian Succession**: France, Prussia, Bavaria, Saxony and Spain dispute the validity of Maria Theresa's claims to the imperial crown after the death of Karl VI; her claims are ultimately supported through the Peace of Aachen. Silesia falls to Prussia.
1754	First population census. Vienna has 175 000 inhabitants (including suburbs) and is now indisputably an important economic centre; its textile industry thrives.
1776	The Hofburgtheater founded by Maria Theresa in 1741 becomes a German-speaking national theatre, to break the cultural monopoly of the Italian language in the capital.
1780	Death of Empress Maria Theresa, who had elevated her son Joseph II to co-regent in 1765.
1782	Pope Pius VI visits Vienna. He asks Emperor Joseph II, eager to reform the Church and strengthen the monarchy, to be more sympathetic. Freemasonry gains many followers throughout high society.
1784	Adoption of German as the official "national" language. This seals Vienna's dominance over the Empire, despite the statutory exception of Hungary.
End of 18C	Vienna is an international capital of music, and the arts in general have shaken off the hold of transalpine influences. The city, with almost 200 000 inhabitants, has become a European metropolis owing chiefly to its cosmopolitan aristocracy and its luxury goods industry.

FROM 1789 TO 1848

1789	French Revolution, followed by the revolutionary and Napoleonic wars.
1804	Napoleon Bonaparte's assumption of the title of Emperor gives occasion for Franz II to take on the title Emperor of Austria. From then on, he rules as Franz I.
1805	Following Beethoven's composition of his *Farewell Song to the Burghers of Vienna*, first occupation of Vienna by the French (12 November 1805 to 13 January 1806) who guarantee respect for religious observances and the safety of the inhabitants.
1809	Second occupation by the French (12 May to 19 November), which leads to the financial collapse of the State. The chancellor, Count Stadion, is replaced by Prince Metternich.

1814-15	The **Congress of Vienna**, which at times resembles a Whitehall farce, unites the European monarchies to redraw the map of Europe after the fall of Napoleon.
1815-48	Prince Metternich, federal chancellor since 1821, leads a conservative regime oriented to oppose liberal and national endeavours. This period is also known as **Vormärz** (prior to the revolution of March 1848, *see below*).
1820-30	The city numbers 318 000 inhabitants. Appearance of the Biedermeier style, symbol of the 19C Viennese bourgeoisie.

Prince Metternich

1837	First railway line between Vienna (Floridsdorf) and Deutsch-Wagram.
March 1848	Following the uprising led by Kossuth in Hungary, a coalition of students and workers with the support of the lower middle classes is formed in Vienna. As barricades spread throughout the city, the army opens fire. The number of dead leads to a revolution, prompting the government to dismiss Metternich, who is forced into exile at the age of 74.
May 1848	New revolutionary movements drive the Court from Vienna to Innsbruck. A committee of public safety is formed in the capital under the leadership of Adolf Fischlo. The city has a population of 400 000.
October 1848	A popular republican uprising in which Count Baillet de la Tour, Minister of War, is hung from a lamp-post by the mob, forces the government and parliament to join the Court at Olmütz in Moravia. The Viennese middle classes and aristocracy support the policy of repression carried out by Field Marshal Prince of Windischgrätz, who storms the city and has the ringleaders of the rebellion shot.

EMPEROR FRANZ JOSEF

1848	On 2 December, Emperor Ferdinand I abdicates the throne in favour of his nephew, 18-year-old Franz Josef.
1854	Marriage of Franz Josef I with the Duchess Elisabeth of Bavaria (also known as Sissi).
1857	Vienna, with its population of 500 000, yearns for grandeur. The razing of the fortifications dating from the Turkish sieges marks the start of what is known as the "Ringstrasse era", where industrialisation combines a modern economy with a traditional society.
1867	Creation of the **Austro-Hungarian Dual Monarchy**. Arrival of numerous Jews, following their legal emancipation by Franz Josef.
1870-75	Building of the Danube Canal after the 1862 floods.
1873	Opening of the World Fair at the Prater (a failure despite 7 million visitors), against the background of a Stock Exchange crash bringing defeat for Viennese liberalism and heralding the rise of the Christian Socialist party.
1889	36km/22mi southwest of Vienna, in Mayerling, Crown Prince Rudolf commits suicide at his hunting lodge.
1890	The capital now has 800 000 inhabitants.
1897	**Karl Lueger**, founder in 1891 of the Christian Socialist party, becomes Burgomaster of the city. His talents as an administrator bring unexpected prosperity to the city.
1910	Vienna numbers just over 2 000 000 inhabitants, and is the fourth largest city in Europe after London, Paris and Berlin.
1910-14	Imperial Vienna thinks of itself as one of the most delightful cities in the world. Yet at the same time, social conflicts grow in the suburban slums. Industry is shaken by crises.
1914	After the assassination at Sarajevo, Franz Josef, sure of Germany's support, declares war on Serbia on 28 July. This spreads into the start of the First World War.
1916	Emperor Franz Josef dies on 22 November at the age of 86, after a reign lasting 68 years.

Imperial Austria about 1890 map. Labels include: RUSSIAN EMPIRE, GERMAN EMPIRE, Munich, SWITZERLAND, Milan, Po, ITALY, Venice, Trente, TYROL, AUSTRIA, CARINTHIA, Salzburg, Vienna, STYRIA, BOHEMIA, Prague, MORAVIA, SILESIA, Cracow, GALICIA, HUNGARY, Pressburg (Bratislava), Budapest, BUKOVINA, Klausenburg (Cluj), TRANSYLVANIA, Mures, Tisza, Danube, Laibach (Ljubljana), Agram (Zagreb), CARNIOLA, Trieste, CROATIA, SLAVONIA, Belgrade, Bucharest, RUMANIA, ADRIATIC, DALMATIA, BOSNIA, Sarajevo, HERZEGOVINA, NOVI-PAZAR, SERBIA, BULGARIA, Sofia, SEA, MONTENEGRO, OTTOMAN EMPIRE.

IMPERIAL AUSTRIA ABOUT 1890

0   100 km

Occupied territories
Present-day Austria

| 1918 | End of First World War. From being the head of a state with a population of 52 million, Vienna becomes overnight the capital of a country with just 6 million inhabitants. The Kaiser Karl I declines to govern the country. |

FIRST REPUBLIC AND SECOND WORLD WAR

1919	Republican Vienna, in the midst of chronic unemployment, elects the Social Democratic party to power with an absolute majority. Jakob Reumann is the new mayor (1919-23).
1920	Federal Constitution adopted. The capital has a population of 1 841 326 – a decrease from the massive urbanisation of the 19C.
1921	The city is granted the status of *Land* (a federal state).
1920-34	"Vienna the Red" launches a programme of council housing and develops a communal policy for the building of workers' housing, which revives the local tradition of housing estates around a central courtyard.
July 1927	Militia from each party confront each other in the capital. There are 89 dead and 1 057 wounded during days of fierce fighting triggered by tensions between social-democratic Vienna and the conservative provincial government.
February 1934	Tensions between the opposing camps flare up again; the capital experiences three days of what amounts to civil war. The official death toll from the fighting is 314.
July 1934	Assassination of the Chancellor Engelbert Dollfuss by a local branch of the SS during an attempted putsch in the chancellery. Dollfuss, a patriot and a Christian, was totally opposed to Marxist ideology and had also banned the Nazi party.
1938	**Adolf Hitler** completes the annexation of Austrian into the German Reich. On 15 March, he announces this "Anschluss" in Vienna's Heldenplatz. Chancellor Schuschnigg is imprisoned.
1939-45	Second World War.
1945	Owing to the Resistance movement, Vienna is not destroyed despite 52 air raids. It is liberated by the Soviet army on 13 April. Division of Vienna in September into four zones administered by the occupying powers: the USSR, the United States, Great Britain and France.

CONTEMPORARY VIENNA

1945	The constitution of 1920 is re-enacted and the **Second Republic** is founded.
1951	The mayor of Vienna, the socialist Theodor Körner, is the first president of the Republic to be elected by universal suffrage.
1955	The occupation forces leave Vienna following the Austrian State Treaty undertaking permanent neutrality. Austria joins the UN.
1956	The Austrian capital becomes the seat of the Atomic Energy Authority (AEA).

The meeting between John F Kennedy and Nikita S Khrushchev in June 1961

Dalmas/SIPA PRESS

1961	John F Kennedy and Nikita Khrushchev meet in Vienna (or more exactly, in Schönbrunn) for the first time for a "summit meeting".
1967	Vienna becomes the seat of the United Nations Industrial Development Organization (UNIDO).
1978	Opening of the first Underground railway line (U1) between Reumann-platz and Karlsplatz.
1979	Opening of United Nations City, making Vienna the third most important site of United Nations activities after New York and Geneva.
1989	Austria applies for EU membership. Death of the last Empress of Austria and Queen of Hungary, Zita of Bourbon-Parma, who had lived in exile since 1919.
1995	Austria is admitted to the EU.
1996	Celebrations of Austria's millennium.
2001	Opening of the MuseumQuartier, the eighth-largest urban cultural area in the world.
1 January 2002	Introduction of the Euro in Austria and eleven other European countries.

The Habsburg empire

FROM RUDOLF I TO RUDOLF IV

After the death of Friedrich II the Cantankerous, the last of the Babenbergs, in 1246, the duchy of Austria passed to Ottokar II Przemysl, King of Bohemia. Yet Ottokar II died fighting at the battle of Dürnkrut in 1278 against Rudolf of Habsburg. This new-comer to the Austrian scene became **Rudolf I** when he was elected King of Germany in 1273. He was of a calculating nature with far greater political acumen than the German princes had imagined. In 1282, this great statesman obtained from the prince electors the right for his sons Albrecht I and Rudolf II to share the possessions of the Babenbergs. It is thanks to Rudolf I, that the Habsburgs and Austria became nearly synonymous in terms of their shared history from this point.

History records that Albrecht I of Austria was grasping. At any rate, he brought about the Habsburgs' loss of power in Alemannic Switzerland. Furthermore, the Electors preferred Adolf of Nassau to him; the imperial crown would not become the prerogative of the Habsburgs again for another 130 years. However, this loss had one favourable consequence, in that it encouraged the Habsburgs to concentrate on their Austrian heritage. Through a policy of judicious marriages and diplomatic compromise, the Habsburgs enlarged their domains, which now extended from the Vosges to the Carpathians,

Rudolf IV, the "Founder", gained this nickname after founding Vienna University in 1365. He also responded intelligently to the menace to Trieste from the Venetian Republic. Having annexed the Tyrol to Austria, Rudolf granted his protection to the Adriatic port in 1382, thus giving *domus austriae* its famous outlet to the sea, which it was to retain until 1918. To lend more importance to his house, Rudolf assumed the title of archduke.

THE IMPERIAL CROWN

Albrecht V acceded to the throne of the Holy Roman Empire of the German Nation in 1438 under the title of Albrecht II. His was a brief reign, as he died the following year. This was immediately followed in 1440 by the coronation of Frederick V of Habsburg as King of the Romans; the seven electors did not want a strong king, and thought Frederick was a "weakling". However, the emperor persuaded the Pope

Rudolf IV

to crown him as Frederick III (a feat that even Karl V would later not be able to match), decisively strengthening his grasp on the reigns of power. Frederick III then acquired for his son Maximilian the hand of the heiress of the western archduke, Charles the Bold; when the latter died in 1477, Maximilian inherited most of the Burgundian estates (Low Countries and Franche-Comté). In his turn, **Maximilian I** married his son Philip the Fair to Joan the Mad, daughter of the King of Spain. Thus, Castille, Aragon, Sardinia and Naples became Habsburg territory. Maximilian himself then remarried, largely due to financial considerations. His second wife was Bianca Maria Sforza, who brought a dowry of 300 000 gold ducats and countless jewels to "penniless Maximilian", as the Italians nicknamed him. Upon the death of this great Renaissance prince, his grandson, Charles V, was elected as Holy Emperor in 1519 and was to reign over an empire "on which the sun never set".

Maximilian I

Austria had acquired an immense domain within just a few decades, mainly through successful marital politics. Such rapid increases generally bring about harmful consequences, however, and the domain proved ungovernable.

Emperor Charles V – His father, Philip the Fair, died in 1506 at Burgos, at the age of twenty-eight, from drinking icy water on a hot day. Charles, who was born in 1500, among other things inherited the Americas upon his maternal grandfather's death. He was elected Roman-German king in 1519, and in comparison to the brilliant, refreshing François I, was

67

of serious, cold temperament. Their rivalry was legendary. After suffering defeat at Marignan, Charles achieved a crushing victory over François at Pavia, where he even took the French monarch prisoner. In 1530 he was crowned emperor and was at the peak of his power. However, two events overshadowed his success: Martin Luther launched the Reformation in 1517; while in 1521 the Turks conquered Belgrade and threatened Vienna. Administration of the Empire, under attack on several fronts, became difficult.

Partition of the Empire – In the 1521 Treaty of Brussels, Emperor Charles V entrusted the destiny of Austria to his brother, Ferdinand. The situation was very worrying. On the one hand, Lutheranism was gaining ground; on the other hand, François I allied himself to the Turks, although, as King of France, he governed "the eldest daughter of the Church". In 1526, Ferdinand of Habsburg became King of Hungary and Bohemia after the death of the Hungarian King Lajos II at the crushing defeat of Mohàcs against the Turks in southern Hungary left that country leaderless and without a proper army. This did not impede in any way the progress of the Ottoman Empire, which was so impressive that in 1529 Suleyman the Magnificent and his troops camped outside Vienna. Count Salm's resistance and the rigours of winter forced the Turks to raise their siege, but Ferdinand ensured their absence by promising the sultan an annual tribute. The price of security was heavy, swallowing up the remainder of the American gold which Emperor Charles V had used in payment of his debts. In his contest with France for supremacy in Europe, the loss of Metz in 1552 affected him deeply. Four years later, he abdicated, leaving to his son Philip II the Low Countries, Franche-Comté, Spain, Portugal, Italy and his overseas possessions; he also renounced the hereditary Habsburg possessions and the imperial crown in favour of his brother, Ferdinand I.

TWO-HEADED EAGLE: ONE HEAD FACING WEST, THE OTHER EAST

While Spain and the Low Countries suffered under the yoke of Philip II, Ferdinand I's rule was exemplary. He endowed his kingdom with institutions that lasted until the 1848 revolution. He died in 1564. Maximilian II succeeded him and granted his subjects peace in a war-torn Europe. His successor, the morose and distrustful Rudolf II, who was passionately fond of astronomy, eventually became increasingly uninterested in politics and chose Prague as his capital. His brother Matthias became leader of a rebellion in 1612 and had himself crowned emperor. After his death in 1619, Ferdinand II took up the challenge. An uncompromising Catholic, he crushed the Czech Protestants at the battle of the White Hill in the following year.

In 1658, Leopold I became emperor. This shy man, who had wanted to enter the priesthood, was to surprise his contemporaries. The Ottoman empire revived: exploiting a rebellion of the Hungarian nobility against the Habsburgs, the Grand Vizir Kara Mustapha besieged the city in 1683. The ensuing Austrian victory over the Ottoman peril had major symbolic repercussions, which Leopold I exploited by engaging in a war for the reconquest of eastern Europe. This was a stroke of genius which set Austria back up among the major powers. The author of Leopold I's military triumph was none other than Eugène of Savoy, a French nobleman who had put himself at the service of the Habsburgs in his burning desire to win renown.

The Pragmatic Sanction – In 1711, Joseph I died without an heir. His brother, Karl VI, succeeded him just before having to renounce all rights to Spain, as a consequence of the Treaty of Rastatt in 1714, following the War of the Spanish Succession. Karl VI was an astute and very ambitious man. In Austria, he initiated the era of the enlightened despot. There was, however, a serious obstacle to his policy:

Vienna, a City that Nearly Became Turkish

14 July 1683. The grand vizier Kara Mustafa, representative of Mehmet IV, lay siege to Vienna with over 200 000 spahis and janissaries and supported by contingents from Bosnia, Serbia, Moldavia and Walachia. The sultan's energetic deputy deployed his troops in a crescent, with the tips touching the banks of the Danube. Faced with Mustafa's overwhelming army, about 16 500 Viennese, many without military training, decided to resist the enemy with a mere 312 cannon under the brave command of Count Ernst Ruediger von Starhemberg. just as the situation started becoming critical, on 10 September, Charles of Lorraine arrived, the perfect *deus ex machina*. The solidarity of the Christian nobles paid up. With him were Prince-Elector Max-Emmanuel, George Frederick of Waldeck, Ernest Augustus of Brunswick-Lüneburg and his son, the future King George I of England, under the command of Jan Sobieski, King John III of Poland, who led the relieving army. France, Austria's arch-rival, promised the Pope not to attack Austria, but French military advisers were providing assistance to the Turks. On 12 September, Mustafa was forced to retreat (and ultimately committed suicide in Belgrade after another defeat in Gran, today Esztergom in Hungary). Emperor Leopold I, who had taken refuge at Passau, returned to Vienna two days later, on 14 September.

he lacked a male heir. In Hungary, for example, the Diet recognised the succession of the House of Habsburg only through the male line. Karl VI, therefore, concentrated all his energy on persuading the European powers to recognise the Pragmatic Sanction, adopted in 1713, which declared his possessions indivisible, while at the same time appointing as his heir his daughter Maria Theresa. In the end, his death triggered the War of the Austrian Succession (1740-48). Although Silesia was to fall into Prussian hands, Maria Theresa otherwise succeeded in securing her inheritance.

MARIA THERESA

Even before her accession to the throne, this courageous woman proved her independence by marrying Francis of Lorraine, in 1736. It was a love match with a somewhat unpopular prince, to whom she gave sixteen children. Maria Theresa had to face attacks from Bavaria and Saxony (claims to the Habsburg heritage), Spain (designs on Italy), France (anti-Austrian by conviction) and Prussia whose ascension she always feared. At her coronation as Queen of Hungary at Pressburg, she guaranteed the independence of that country. Immediately, the Hungarians recognised Francis as co-regent and raised an army of 30 000 men. Thus, the queen succeeded in repelling her enemies' attacks, and in having her husband crowned as Emperor Franz I in Frankfurt, in 1747. One year later, the Treaty of Aix-la-Chapelle brought the War of the Austrian Succession to an end. Maria Theresa had largely preserved the Empire bequeathed to her by her father. She left the imprint of her personality on her long reign. She did a colossal amount of work, gave a hearing to the myriad communities in her Empire, and gained popularity by useful financial and administrative reforms, without offending Hungarian, Italian or Dutch sensibilities. Her success stemmed from this mixture of willpower and cheerfulness, which, however, declined upon the death of her husband in 1765.

ROGER-VIOLLET

Maria Theresa

ENLIGHTENED DESPOTS

After his father's death, **Joseph II** was given a share of royal authority. Granted complete power in 1780, he continued the reorganisation of the Empire. However, the head of State did not possess the skill which had benefited his mother during her 40-year reign. Instead he showed himself to be impatient, authoritarian and brusque (for instance refusing a coronation in Hungary). Still, his policies heralded a new Austria with one national language, German; one capital, Vienna; and one supreme authority, the emperor's. He also abolished serfdom and torture despite opposition from the nobility, and introduced equality in law and taxes (introducing a universal land tax). In addition, he granted freedom of religion and extended federal sovereignty over the Church. Yet it was this zeal for reform which was met with strong resistance among nobility and clergy, leading to national uprisings in the Austrian Low Countries and in Hungary, where he had to retract most of his reforms in the end. The disappointed emperor died in 1790 after having once said, "Most deeply convinced of the integrity of my actions, I have the strength to hope that after my death, the following generation may consider my deeds and test my goals more favourably, impartially and justly than my contemporaries, before judging me."

The century of the Enlightenment (Aufklärung) ended not just with the death of Joseph II the "philosopher", who contributed much to his Empire's cultural development. Pre-industrialisation occurred in an empire with a non-increasing population; and Prussia became an increasingly powerful political rival. Moreover, Joseph's brother Leopold II died too soon, in 1792. This was a tragedy for Austria, since this emperor had displayed exceptional political flair in his mere two years as head of state. His eldest son, Franz II, came to the throne with the reputation of being mediocre, and then had the misfortune to cross the path of an extraordinary man, Napoleon.

R.M.N.

Joseph II

Napoleon twice occupied Vienna, in 1805 and 1809. Between these two dates, on 6 August 1806, Franz II relinquished the imperial crown of the Holy Roman Empire of the German Nation, as he knew it to be doomed to extinction. Yet in 1804, he had proclaimed himself hereditary Emperor of Austria as Franz I.

The Congress of Vienna – With the fall of Napoleon's empire in March 1814, Vienna replaced Paris as Europe's capital. It became the seat of an international congress determining the fate of winners and losers. For an entire year, the Congress convened and "danced": the various meetings were followed by sumptuous balls and splendid feasts which are still surrounded by attendant myths today. Vienna was the meeting point for all the crowned heads of Europe: the Emperor Franz I of Austria, the young Tsar Alexander I of Russia, King Friedrich-Wilhelm of Prussia, the King of Württemberg, as well as numerous princes and archdukes. Among the diplomats representing the interests of their countries were Lord Castlereagh for Britain, Nesselrode for Russia, Humboldt for Prussia, and Talleyrand for France. These dignitaries were presided over by Austria's Foreign Secretary Metternich.

In the embassies, the salons of the Hofburg, and the Great Gallery at Schönbrunn Palace, one reception or ball was followed by the next; the old Prince de Ligne cynically remarked, "Le Congrès ne marche pas, il danse! (The Congress isn't working – it's dancing)" This comment became world-famous. No other city could have offered more diversions than the art metropolis of Vienna, including theatre, museums, chamber music and opera. Beethoven himself conducted a gala concert, and his opera *Fidelio* was received enthusiastically.

Alexander I attracted attention by his sumptuous receptions and numerous love affairs; while Talleyrand exercised astute diplomacy and was seated at the conference table as an equal, although he was the spokesman for the defeated nation. However, it was Prince Metternich, Austrian Minister of Foreign Affairs, who played the principal role in the congress. He imposed his view of a balanced, conservative Europe by developing three main themes: restoration – of the 1789 political situation; legitimacy – which entailed the return of the Bourbons to the throne of France; and solidarity – in the face of revolutionary movements.

The Metternich system – Thanks to the diplomatic ability of this arch-conservative aristocrat, Austria regained a major position in central Europe by chairing the Germanic Confederation (coalition of 39 states). 1815 saw the founding of the Holy Alliance, comprising Orthodox Russia, Protestant Prussia and Catholic Austria. These three powers undertook to govern in a "Christian" way and had the authority to "intervene against all national uprisings". Besides his native language, Metternich spoke fluent English, Italian, Latin and the Slavonic languages. An admirer of Joseph II, he established from 1815 to 1848 a "system", which was of immediate benefit to Austria, which it transformed into a bastion of the *Ancien Régime*, whereas in Europe the forces of liberalism were active. Meanwhile, Franz I died in 1835 and his successor Ferdinand I was totally incompetent, not to say somewhat feeble-minded. Metternich pursued his authoritarian regime governed by a "secret State conference" consisting of Archduke Ludwig, Count Kolowrat and Metternich. *Vormärz* denotes this period before March 1848, a curious mixture of Biedermeier ambience and an inquisition-like police repression.

THE FRANZ JOSEF ERA

The 1848 revolution – In Austria, this revolution at the same time represented a social rebellion against the police state, and nationalist uprisings in Bohemia (which belonged to the Confederation), Hungary and the Lombard-Venetian kingdom (which did not belong to it). In Vienna, there were three insurrections, forcing the government to demand Metternich's "resignation" (exile) and prompting the Court to seek refuge in Olmütz in Moravia. After the recapture of the capital by force, the army crushed the national uprisings – under Radetzky in Italy, and Windischgrätz in Prague. Russia came to the aid of Austria, causing a Hungarian surrender: 13 Hungarian leaders were executed. Ferdinand abdicated in favour of his nephew Franz, aged 18, who added Josef to his Christian name, in memory of Joseph II. By this, he wished to indicate that he wanted a centralised state open to modernisation. The age of **Franz Josef** had begun.

The reign of the status quo – Franz Josef embodied the concepts of decency and integrity. Despite innumerable family misfortunes and political upheavals throughout his reign of 68 years, he remained a sovereign who commanded the love and respect of his subjects. His mother, Archduchess Sophia, shaped the young emperor's

ROGER-VIOLLET

Emperor Franz Josef

development. It was to her that he owed his unfailing courtesy, sense of duty and talent for bureaucracy, but also his reactionary outlook. However, neo-absolutism was not a suitable formula for governing a monarchy whose subjects had just rebelled to demand closer involvement with public affairs. This combination of factors created a potentially explosive situation.

Austria-Hungary – When the Hungarians declared their independence in 1848, they suffered a crushing defeat. However, this merely reinforced their desire for national independence. After the dissolution of the German Confederation following the war against Prussia in 1866, Austria, seeking to stabilise its sprawling country, was forced to agree to the 1867 "compromise" which created the Dual Monarchy of Austria-Hungary as the union of two independent states. Franz Josef became emperor *(Kaiser)* in Austria and king *(König)* in Hungary. In practical terms, this meant that the constitution, administration and legislation were separate, while the army, finance and foreign policy were common to both. Starting from the inception of this "dualism", which was to last as long as Habsburg rule, dissension arose among the Serbs, Croats and Czechs. The French emperor Napoleon III's support of the Italian cause, Prussian hegemony in Central Europe, and the growing crisis in the Balkans further weakened the Empire. Franz Josef was not a statesman, and one defeat was followed by another. The emperor continually compromised – in general by refraining from taking any kind of action.

"I have been spared nothing" – A stunning succession of setbacks marked Franz Josef's long reign to the extent that he once declared "I have been spared nothing". In 1853, a Hungarian tailor named Libényi stabbed the sovereign in the back of his neck. In 1857, the emperor lost his first child, Princess Sophie, aged 26 months. In 1859, the Peace of Zürich deprived the Empire of Lombardy, following the defeats of Magenta and Solferino. In 1866, the Treaty of Vienna deprived the Empire of the Veneto region. In 1867, republican revolutionaries shot Maximilian, Emperor of Mexico since 1864 and brother of Franz Josef, in Querétaro. In 1868, Croatia won independence. In 1882, the kingdom of Serbia was proclaimed. In 1889, his son, Archduke Rudolf, committed suicide at Mayerling. In 1897, his sister-in-law, the Duchess of Alençon, perished in a fire in Paris. In 1898, his wife Elisabeth died, stabbed by the Italian anarchist Lucheni, in Geneva. In 1914, the heir to the Empire, Archduke Franz Ferdinand, was assassinated with his wife in Sarajevo.

THE END OF THE HABSBURG KINGDOM

The nationality problems in the Balkans and the complex European system of treaties created an explosive atmosphere in Europe. The spark which detonated this powder keg was the assassination in Sarajevo on 28 June 1914, sparking off the First World War. Franz Josef died on 22 November 1916; his grand-nephew **Karl I** succeeded him. Karl I began secret attempts at a separate peace with France, in order to attain the survival of the Austro-Hungarian Empire. However, in February 1918, French foreign secretary Clemenceau promised independence to the Czechs, Serbs and Croats, introducing the end of the Empire, particularly since the nations of the Entente Cordiale supported the separatists. On 11 November 1918, at Schloss Schönbrunn, Karl I signed the act of renunciation which ended Habsburg rule.

On 3 April 1919, the national assembly of the First Republic abolished Habsburg law, and with it, all governing rights of the Habsburgs in Austria; all the dynasty's property was also confiscated. The members of the House of Habsburg who did not wish to relinquish their privileges were expelled from the country.

Art and architecture

ABC OF ARCHITECTURE

Religious architecture

Apsidal or **axial chapel**. In churches not dedicated to the Virgin Mary, this is often the Lady Chapel. It lies along the east-west line of the building.

Ambulatory: An extension of the side aisles around the chancel. The ambulatory enabled people to file past relics in churches that were places of pilgrimage.

Chancel: Almost always east-facing.

Crossing or **transept arm:** They may or may not be projecting.

Span: Transversal division of the nave. The area between two pillars.

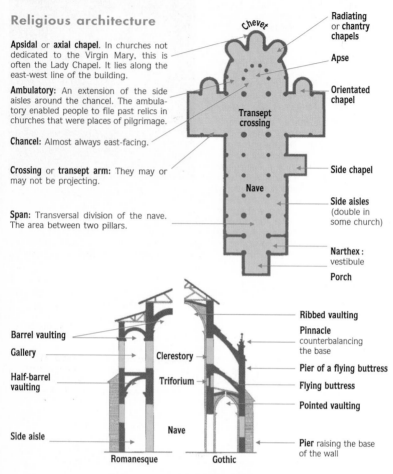

Chevet

Radiating or **chantry chapels**

Apse

Orientated chapel

Transept crossing

Side chapel

Nave

Side aisles (double in some church)

Narthex: vestibule

Porch

Barrel vaulting

Gallery

Half-barrel vaulting

Side aisle

Clerestory

Triforium

Nave

Romanesque

Ribbed vaulting

Pinnacle counterbalancing the base

Pier of a flying buttress

Flying buttress

Pointed vaulting

Pier raising the base of the wall

Gothic

Giants' Portal, Stephansdom (1230-1240)

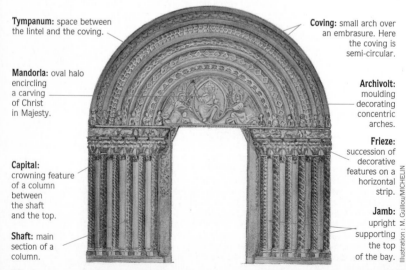

Tympanum: space between the lintel and the coving.

Mandorla: oval halo encircling a carving of Christ in Majesty.

Capital: crowning feature of a column between the shaft and the top.

Shaft: main section of a column.

Coving: small arch over an embrasure. Here the coving is semi-circular.

Archivolt: moulding decorating concentric arches.

Frieze: succession of decorative features on a horizontal strip.

Jamb: upright supporting the top of the bay.

Church of the Dominicans (1631-1634)

Spandrel: area of a wall between two arches.

Reredos: back of the altar, usually containing a painting. Also refers to the painting itself.

Sounding board: canopy over the pulpit.

Pulpit: raised platform for preaching.

Tabernacle: small cupboard in the centre of the altar, containing the ciborium.

Cherub: winged child's head symbolising an order of angels.

Culot: French term for a stucco ornament, consisting here of foliage with stems emerging from it.

Foliage: plaster ornament consisting of a stylised stem with regular undulations.

Predella: lower part of the reredos, usually divided into three panels. panneaux

High altar: main altar, on the centre line of the nave.

Church of St Charles Borromeo (1716-1737)

Belvedere: small covered shelter at the top of an edifice.

Balcony: small platform with a railing.

Arched pediment: pediment with cymas following the same curve.

Lantern turret: small construction at the top of an edifice in the shape of a lantern and with windows.

Dome: roof disposed around a centre, with continuously sloping sides and rounded form.

Triumphal pillar: monumental pillar adorned with a continuous sculpture in low relief.

Drum attic: horizontal coping.

Drum: cylindrical support for the dome.

Pavilion: wing, square in plan; in this case, included in the overall dimensions because linked to the main section.

Pronaos: in a classical temple, porch at the entrance to the sanctuary; in a church, this porch is called a galilee.

Illustrations : M. Guillou/MICHELIN

73

Schönbrunn: Gloriette (1775)

Amortizement: decorative element at the top of an edifice.

Piece of entablature: raising of the support, like a classical entablature in outline.

Arcade: open bay covered by an arch.

Pediment: triangular gable above an entablature.

Tuscan capital: differs from a Doric capital in its lack of ornamentation.

Niche: recess for a decorative object.

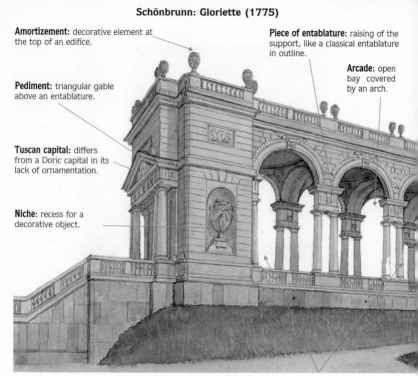

Gallery: space greater in length than width, serving as a passageway.

Upper Belvedere (1722)

Mansard roof: roof having two slopes on the same side.

Pier: the part of a wall between two adjacent openings.

Piano nobile: storey where the ceiling height is loftier than that of the other floors.

Attic storey: half storey forming the crowning feature of the façade.

Foundation floor: floor designed to compensate for a slope.

Trave: series of openings on the same vertical line.

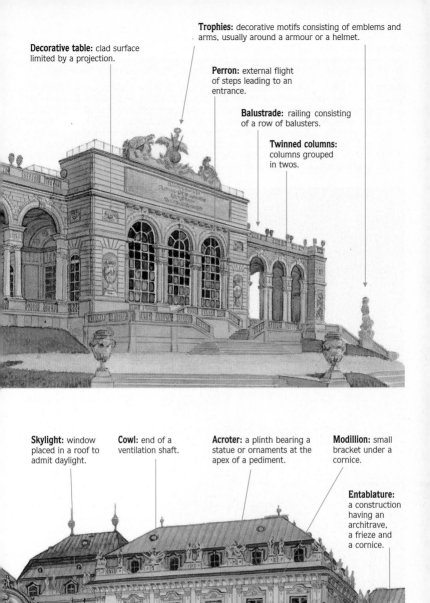

Decorative table: clad surface limited by a projection.

Trophies: decorative motifs consisting of emblems and arms, usually around a armour or a helmet.

Perron: external flight of steps leading to an entrance.

Balustrade: railing consisting of a row of balusters.

Twinned columns: columns grouped in twos.

Skylight: window placed in a roof to admit daylight.

Cowl: end of a ventilation shaft.

Acroter: a plinth bearing a statue or ornaments at the apex of a pediment.

Modillion: small bracket under a cornice.

Entablature: a construction having an architrave, a frieze and a cornice.

Portico: gallery forming an entrance to a building.

Mascaron: carved mask decorating the crown of an arch.

Pilaster: fake engaged column projecting slightly from the wall.

ARCHITECTURE

Romanesque (12C-13C) – There are few remaining examples of this style. Besides the Ruprechtskirche and Virgilkapelle, the finest Romanesque work still in existence is the west façade of Stephansdom and its superb Giants' Doorway, Riesentor.

Gothic (13C-16C) – Gothic architecture originated in Vienna with the construction of the new Stephansdom, which is of the German hall-church *(Hallenkirchen)* type. Built in late Gothic style, St Stephen's cathedral is the best illustration of Austrian Gothic; its master builders were in touch with those in Ratisbon and Strasbourg. Despite certain alterations, Annakirche, Augustinerkirche, Deutschordenskirche, Minoritenkirche and Maria am Gestade belong to the Gothic era, of which Michaelerkirche has retained some traces. Another example of this style is the Spinnerin am Kreuz, a late Gothic wayside column outside the city centre.

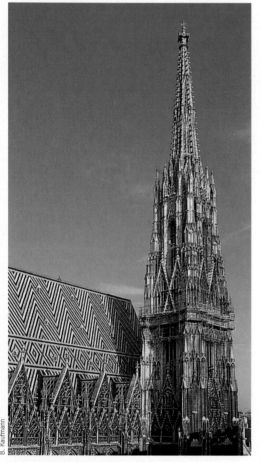

South spire of Stephansdom

B. Kaufmann

Renaissance (16C-17C) – Vienna is not the best place in which to study Renaissance architecture. Rudolf II resided mainly in Prague; this led to the emigration of some of the nobility to the new royal residence, which hardly allowed the Renaissance to unfold in Vienna. Renaissance buildings still in existence here are therefore few in number. Among them are Amalientrakt and the Schweizerhof in the Hofburg, the pediment of the Franziskanerkirche, the Salvatorkapelle entrance, and the inner courtyard of the Stallburg.

Baroque (17C-18C) – Mainly an offshoot of Italian Baroque, Austrian Baroque also combines French and German elements. Initially a religious art in essence, it enjoyed the favour of the Habsburgs, ardent supporters of the Counter-Reformation. There are two forms of this style, known as Early Baroque and High Baroque. Early Baroque, which covers the 17C, is a style of foreign origin. It is an extension of Italy's monopoly in the arts, which began to gain influence in Austria during the Renaissance. Early Baroque is contemporaneous with the establishment of a series of religious orders and is responsible for churches based on the famous model of Il Gesù in Rome: single nave with side chapels, tripartite façade with pilasters beneath a voluted pediment (Dominikanerkirche, Jesuitenkirche, Kirche "Zu den neuen Chören der Engel"). Palaces were also the work of Italian architects, such as Lodovico Burnacini, Pietro Tencala and Domenico Martinelli, who built the Liechtenstein palace. High Baroque covers a period from 1690 to 1753 and could be termed Austrian Baroque, since its great practitioners were of local origin. It gave Austria its most brilliant artistic triumphs. Architects during this second phase were Johann Bernhard Fischer von Erlach and Johann Lukas von Hildebrandt *(see below)*. One must also include **Isidore Canevale** (Allgemeines Krankenhaus), **Josef Emanuel Fischer von Erlach** (Michaelertrakt and Winterreitschule in the Hofburg), **Gabriele Montani** (Peterskirche), **Nikolaus Pacassi** (completion of Schönbrunn, Josefsplatz), **Andrea Pozzo** (interior of Jesuitenkirche).

Johann Bernhard Fischer von Erlach (1656-1723) – A native of Graz, he became Court Architect and Building Superintendent in 1687. He was a prolific architect, creating seven churches, three castles, about ten palaces, and also high altars, mausoleums and fountains in Vienna, Salzburg, Prague, Brünn, Breslau and Mariazell. In the capital, he built Karlskirche, a masterpiece still capable of amazing the most enlightened of art lovers, the Trautson palace, the world-famous Schönbrunn Palace, Prince Eugène of Savoy's Winterpalais and the Hofburg library. He also contributed to the building of the Liechtenstein and Lobkowitz palaces and Dreifaltigskeitssäule (Trinity pillar) in the Graben. Prince Schwarzenberg once described him in a letter in the following terms: "the imperial architect has no equal in Austria, yet he must have one beam too many in his head". A cutting remark, to say the least, illustrating how often geniuses are seen as nothing more than fanciful eccentrics by their contemporaries. Johann Bernard died in Vienna on 5 April 1723. One of the four children from his first marriage, Josef Emanuel, continued his work.

Johann Lukas von Hildebrandt (1668-1745) – Born in Genoa of German parents, he was the second genius of Vienna's Baroque era. He didn't come to Vienna until 1696, ten years after Fischer von Erlach; yet he brought from his studies in Italy and his stay with Carlo Fontana a less monumental architecture, which already was a precursor of neo-Classicism. He collaborated with Fischer von Erlach on Prince Eugène of Savoy's Stadtpalais and the Schwarzenberg palace. A man of great energy, he built the Kinsky, Starhemberg and Schönborn palaces, Peterskirche (which he completed), Bundeskanzleramt and his two masterpieces, also designed for Prince Eugène of Savoy the Lower and Upper Belvederes. Ennobled in 1720, he worked almost exclusively for Prince Eugène.

Classicism and **Biedermeier** (18C-19C) – The two principal architects belonging to the Classical tradition were the Frenchman Jean-Nicolas Jadot de Ville-Issey (Akademie der Wissenschaften, Maria Theresa crypt in the Kaisergruft) and Ferdinand Hetzendorf von Hohenberg (Pallavicini Palace and Gloriette). The chief representative of the Biedermeier style *(see below, Decorative arts)* was **Josef Kornhäusel** (refurbishment of Schottenstift).

Historicism (19C) – This highly eclectic style is best illustrated by a walk along the Ring. The romantic objective of this period was to create "a work of total art". This totality, however, encompasses a great variety of past styles, recreations of historical models, such as the neo-Gothic Votivkirche by **Heinrich von Ferstel**. The style fell from grace at the end of the century with the founding of the Secession *(see below)*.

Jugendstil and Secession (late 19C-early 20C) – A German version of Art Nouveau, Jugendstil acquired its name from the Munich periodical *Jugend*, founded in 1896. It was a neo-Baroque movement in evidence about 1900 but was never part of Historicism, because of its characteristic sinuous lines and lack of symmetry, in short its anti-academic attitude. Otto Wagner *(see below)*, originally an exponent of the eclectic Ring style became one of its most illustrious representatives (including Linke Wienzeile buildings).

The Secession's exact title was *Vereinigung Bildender Künstler Österreich* or Association of Austrian Artists, founded in 1897. It was a movement in opposition to official art. Unlike Jugendstil, with which it is often confused, it has a geometrical, rectilinear conception of ornamentation; this differs significantly from the organic conception of Art Nouveau. The purest expression of this movement is the Secessiongebäude by **Josef Maria Olbrich**.

Schloss Schönbrunn

Otto Wagner (1841-1918) – Born in the Biedermeier era and a product of the Classical tradition, he rose to become Imperial Architectural Advisor for Vienna and Professor at the Academy of Fine Arts. At the age of 50, he made a new start in his artistic career, and began to create the buildings which made him famous: the Karlsplatz Metro stations, Kirche am Steinhof and Postsparkasse. He changed from the sinuousness of Jugendstil to the smooth, geometric ornamentation of the Secession. He had a decisive influence on European architecture.

Adolf Loos (1870-1933) – A native of Brünn, this architect who qualified in Dresden settled in Vienna on his return from a trip to the United States. His essay *Ornament and Crime* condemns the excessive decoration of Jugendstil then at its peak. In Vienna, he built the Steiner house and Looshaus. He then left for Paris, where he built the Tzara house before returning to Vienna. A rationalist, he was a strong opponent of the Wiener Werkstätte, since, according to him, any link between art and craftsmanship was not feasible. A work of art is eternal, according to Loos; the creation of a craftsman is ephemeral.

From 1921 to the present – The Austro-Marxist municipality under Karl Seitz, Mayor of Vienna, administered the city after the fall of the Habsburg Empire. They were responsible for much public housing (known as *Höfe*) built to solve the housing shortage. The whole city became a showcase for experimental architecture in socialist functionalist style, displaying a huge programme of large housing estates which attracted the attention of the whole world. Their most spectacular achievements were Karl-Marx-Hof by Karl Ehn, Reumannhof by Franz Gessner, and Liebknecht-hof by Karl Krist. In 1932, Josef Frank headed the Werkbundsiedlung experimental project for housing in Hietzing.

Among the most significant post-war and contemporary architects in Vienna are: Hermann Czech, the "deconstructivist" duo **Coop Himmelblau** (Wolf Dieter Prix and Helmut Swiczinsky), and Friedensreich Hundertwasser (also a painter and sculptor); as well as Robert Krier, Hans Hollein and Johann Staber.

H. A. Jahr/VIENNASLIDE

House extension by Coop Himmelblau
(Falkestraße 6, 1. Bezirk)

PAINTING AND SCULPTURE

Baroque architecture is inconceivable without its natural complements of painting and sculpture. Together with the brilliantly realistic work of artists in stucco, these breathe life into the space of the buildings. A profusion of altarpieces appear in churches, legions of angels and saints people the ceilings, and armies of statues put to flight remarkable Gothic works, now considered "barbaric". Great artists contributed to the sumptuous interior decoration of palaces and churches: **Johann Michael Rottmayr** (1654-1730), Johann Bernhard Fischer von Erlach's favourite assistant and the precursor of a specifically Austrian Baroque pictorial style; **Paul Strudel** (1648-1708), founder of the Academy of Fine Arts and court sculptor; **Balthasar Permoser** (1651-1732) whose famous marble Apotheosis of Prince Eugène adorns the Österreichisches Barockmuseum; **Paul Troger** (1698-1762) was one of the first to become aware of the originality of Austrian painting and devoted his life to painting religious subjects; **Johann Martin Schmidt** ("Kremser Schmidt") whose altarpieces are visible in numerous churches; **Martino Altomonte** (1657-1745), a Neapolitan painter who entered the service of the Court in 1703 and died in Vienna; **Lorenzo Mattielli** (c 1680-1748), a great sculptor from Vicenza working in Vienna from 1714; **Balthasar Ferdinand Moll** (1717-85), the creator of the famous double sarcophagus in Kapuzinergruft; and **Georg Raphael Donner** (1693-1741), who enjoyed the flattering nickname of the "Austrian Michelangelo", best known for his fine fountain in Neuer Markt. However, it is with the highly creative **Franz Anton**

Maulbertsch (1724-96) and the German **Franz Xaver Messerschmidt** (1736-83), whose amazing grimacing heads are displayed in the Österreichisches Barockmuseum, that Austrian painting and sculpture of that period reached their peak.

In the 19C, Biedermeier *(see below, Decorative arts)* and Eclecticism (second half of the century) produced a new generation of first-rate artists. It was the age of realist painting, with an abundance of landscape painters producing small works. The great master of this genre was **Ferdinand Georg Waldmüller** (1793-1865), a master of light and colour. One must also include **Friedrich Gauermann** (1807-62), who faithfully reproduced the atmosphere of his time, and **Leopold Kupelwieser** (1796-1862) who devoted himself to religious painting after executing portraits of people in Schubert's circle. An important development in the world of sculpture occurred as a result of the large number of public commissions: for example, **Anton Dominik Fernkorn** (1813-78) created numerous war memorials.

The end of the century was a time of transition for Austrian painting. The highly successful artist **Hans Makart** (1840-84) gave his name *(Makartism)* to monumental and refined painting, while the extremely original talent of **Anton Romako** (1832-89) emerged, marking a break with the serene painting of past centuries. A profound artistic revival swept through German-speaking countries, under the name Jugendstil. In Vienna, the most brilliant exponent of this movement was Gustav Klimt. Still influenced by symbolism in the beginning of his career, Klimt was nevertheless also the forerunner of Viennese Expressionism, a stylistic direction which his students Egon Schiele and Oskar Kokoschka would further develop.

Gustav Klimt (1862-1918) – A native of Vienna and the son of a modest goldsmith, Klimt began painting in an academic style; but he reoriented himself artistically and became a co-founder of the Secession in 1897, eventually becoming the leader of this movement. This painter is surely the most famous Jugendstil artist, and his works are reproduced in huge numbers. Klimt's Beethoven frieze in the Secession testifies to the unusually expressive power of his painting.

Egon Schiele (1890-1918) – Although Klimt is the best-known Austrian painter, Schiele deserves similar appreciation. His turbulent creations convey with rare lucidity a picture of human nature and neuroses. This outstanding artist's Expressionism drew inspiration from the body; this even led to a prison sentence in 1912, as his paintings were judged to be pornographic.

Oskar Kokoschka (1886-1980) – Born in Pöchlarn (Austria), he soon joined the Viennese and Berlin avant-garde. After working as a teacher in Dresden, he settled in Vienna in 1931, before moving to Prague and London. In the tradition of Edvard Munch, his painting is characterised by a euphoric yet tortured Expressionism with violent colouring.

Egon Schiele – *Self-Portrait*

DECORATIVE ARTS

Porcelain – 1718 was the date of the founding of the second European factory producing hard paste porcelain. The founder was Claudius Innocentius du Paquier, a potter of Dutch Huguenot origin from Trier. Under the directorship of S Stölzel, the **Vienna manufacture** with its "beehive" monogram produced decorative statuettes and tableware drawing inspiration from the Meissen factories in Saxony. Late Baroque in style, the decoration was varied, displaying zoomorphic handles and spouts, scrolls, foliage and Chinese motifs. It became a state factory in 1744 during Maria Theresa's reign and produced Rococo services adorned with landscapes and animals. Starting in 1770, themes from French painting were introduced (the influence of Marie Antoinette's marriage with the future king of France, Louis XVI). The "Old Vienna" pattern of simple

Late-18C Viennese porcelain

flowers on a white ground was a great success throughout Europe, but Augarten also continued manufacturing in great numbers the porcelain statuettes, which constitute its corporate image today. The factory's golden age was between 1784 and 1805, under the leadership of Sorgenthal, who encouraged the production of neo-Classical forms and decoration. In 1805, Napoleon occupied Vienna. Count Daru, manager of the Sèvres porcelain works, became head of the imperial factory. The style of the French Empire was dominant (many items from this period are on view at the Hofsilber– und Tafelkammer), but after the 1815 Congress of Vienna it soon gave way to Biedermeier decorative styles. Among these was the "Idyll" pattern, the creation of Daffinger, a miniaturist. In 1864, the factory closed its doors, to reopen in 1923 as the **Porzellanmanufaktur Augarten** (*see Outside the Ring, Leopoldstadt*). Since that date, it has been under the administration of the municipal authorities.

Biedermeier – In Germany and Austria, the Biedermeier style applies mainly to decorative arts, but it also refers to architecture, painting and sculpture. This style belongs to the period 1815-48, namely from the Congress of Vienna to the 1848 Revolution. Most non-German speakers believe that Biedermeier was a cabinetmaker who gave his name to this style. In fact, Wieland Gottlieb Biedermeier never existed!

This fictitious character made his first appearance in the early 19C in the work of the German authors Adolf Kussmaul and Ludwig Eichrodt, as a worthy bourgeois full of fine feelings. *Bieder* means "worthy, upright"; *Meier* is a very common German name. Herr Biedermeier emerged from a literary satire to become a symbol of an age and the personification of a certain style. This style reflects the way of life and convictions of a rising social class: well-off, narrow-minded, and tending toward political apathy.

In furniture, the characteristic features of this style are: massive proportions with sober but varied lines and smooth surfaces; light wood (cherry, ash); and veneers inlaid with darker woods (mahogany or ebony). The most common pieces of furniture are writing desks, sofas, chairs, smaller items and a kind of small sideboard. The complete Biedermeier setting includes an interior with green plants, thick curtains and ornaments on

Writing desk (1825)

the mantelpiece. Finally, the backs and legs of the chairs are of varied, extravagant designs. In Vienna, the outstanding Biedermeier cabinetmaker was **Joseph Danhauser** (1805-45).

The term Biedermeier also designates a type of glassware possessing three characteristics: massive form, engraved glass and coloured subjects.

Thonet – Thonet chairs are world famous. This name belongs to a dynasty of furniture designers, starting with **Michael Thonet** (1796-1871), the creator in 1859 of the famous bentwood "chair No 14". In 1841, a year before moving to Vienna, he patented the mechanical and chemical process for bending beechwood, an invention which enabled the Thonet brothers to break new ground in the domain of quality mass production. The firm displayed great business acumen, exporting its products from Austria by distributing sales catalogues. Both commercially and aesthetically, the concept for the Wiener Werkstätte *(see below)* was complete, the forms determined by the structure and the sales addressed to all social classes. Therefore, it was not surprising when during the first quarter of the 20C, avant-garde personalities like Le Corbusier, Breuer and Mies van der Rohe were the first to test curved metallic tube furniture from the Thonet factory, which proved its capacity for innovation.

MAK

Thonet chair

At the end of the 19C and the beginning of the 20C, the great Viennese furniture designers, Adolf Loos and Josef Hoffmann, designed furniture for the **J & J Kohn** factory.

Wiener Werkstätte – 19 May 1903 was the date of the founding of the **Vienna Workshops** by the architect Josef Hoffmann, Koloman Moser and the banker Fritz Waerndorfer, who knew the Scottish designer Charles Rennie Mackintosh. The Vienna Workshops set out to make objects of artistic worth accessible to all and to put both artist and craftsman on a firm professional footing. Their full title is interesting: "Wiener Werkstätte. Association of artists and craftsmen. Unlimited company, registered in Vienna". To fulfil their mission, the founders created workshops which they equipped with modern machinery for the training of craftsmen, and decided to publicise their products by taking part in exhibitions.

The Wiener Werkstätte artists and craftsmen exercised their talent in a variety of spheres: jewellery, fabrics, wallpaper, bookbinding, utilitarian objects, glass, stained glass, posters, mosaic, fashion garments, tableware, and also architecture and interior decoration, in an attempt at producing total art. Through the Workshops, they were able to address a vast public and achieve great popularity. Their first clients were, of course, personal friends or patrons of the arts, like the Belgian Adolphe Stoclet who commissioned a mansion in Brussels entirely equipped by the Wiener Werkstätte between 1905 and 1911. Though expensive, the products soon appealed to a wealthy clientele. The novelty of these utilitarian objects lay in their beauty and purity of form, resulting both from their functionalism and the use of high-quality materials. After 1907, the early geometric style gave way to more sinuous lines. With the arrival of Dagobert Peche in 1915, this tendency became more marked and the products increasingly decorative. The Wiener Werkstätte closed in 1932, in the face of insurmountable financial difficulties due to the economic situation but also to declining standards in quality. In 1937, the Österreichisches Museum für Angewandte Kunst bought the archives and now displays numerous fine items.

Josef Hoffmann (1870-1956) – Born in Pirnitz (Moravia), died in Vienna. He was a brilliant pupil of Otto Wagner, from whom he received his diploma in 1895 before winning the Prix de Rome that same year. From 1899 to 1937, he taught at the School of Applied Arts in Vienna. A versatile artist, architect and designer, he was responsible for the interior decoration of the houses he created and he also designed the furniture and tableware. A co-founder of the Secession, he was also one of the founders of the Wiener Werkstätte, with whose co-operation he executed a major architectural project at the turn of the century, the **Palais Stoclet** in Brussels, his most spectacular and famous achievement. He worked extensively for private clients, particularly the Primavesi. He also received many commissions from Vienna city council, particularly in

the field of low-income housing in the years 1923-25. He had a considerable influence on many modern architects and designers.

Koloman Moser (1868-1918), known as Kolo Moser – Born and died in Vienna. One of the most gifted and prolific artists of the Secession movement, of which he was one of the founders, Moser was undeniably one of the most important figures of the turn of the century in the domain of applied arts. Through the activities of the Wiener Werkstätte, of which he was a co-founder, he displayed his versatility. He worked as a goldsmith, and designed wallpaper and furniture using mainly geometrical forms as a basis. One of his principal achievements in Vienna was his contribution to Otto Wagner's Am Steinhof church, for which he made magnificent stained-glass windows.

Cutlery by Josef Hoffmann

Vienna, a bastion of music

An ancient tradition – By the 12C, Vienna under the Babenbergs had become an important centre of secular music. Many German-speaking troubadours, the **Minnesänger**, came to Vienna, and by the end of the 13C they had formed guilds there. At the end of the Middle Ages, Maximilian I moved his dazzling court choir from Innsbruck to Vienna, confirming the city's status as a musical capital. The choir, now a venerable institution, was the subject of public acclaim in the 15C and still arouses the enthusiasm of modern audiences under the name of **"Hofkapelle"**.

Music-loving emperors – The most significant musical event of the Baroque era (17C-18C) was the arrival of opera which originated in Italy around 1600. It was taken up with great enthusiasm at the Viennese court. Some emperors, besides being generous patrons of music, were themselves distinguished composers. The most prolific of them, **Leopold I**, left a number of religious works which still form part of today's repertoire. The Court and the royal family sang and performed his operettas. Maria Theresa's father, Karl VI, was a talented violinist. All the Habsburgs received a solid musical education: Maria Theresa played the double bass, Joseph II the harpsichord and cello.

Gluck and the reform of the opera – Born in Erasbach (in the Upper Palatinate in Bavaria), **Christoph Willibald von Gluck** (1714-787) was one of the most important composers of the pre-Classical era. He considered opera to be an indivisible work of art, at once musical and dramatic in character; he sought above all natural effects, simplicity and a faithful portrayal of feelings. In 1754, he became Kapellmeister at the Imperial Court in Vienna and from 1774 touted the title of royal and imperial court composer. His most characteristic operas are *Orpheus and Eurydice* (1762) and *Alcestis* (1767).

The principal composers of Viennese Classicism – These include great composers, Viennese by birth or adoption, such as Haydn, Mozart, Beethoven and Schubert. Their primarily instrumental work ensured the

Joseph Haydn

82

dominance of Germanic music in Europe for over a century and made Vienna its musical capital. Italian music also played a leading role until the early 19C. An artist like **Antonio Salieri** (1750-1825), director of the imperial chapel in 1788, was arbiter of the city's musical taste. Finally, it is surprising to learn that the young **Gioacchino Rossini** (1792-1868) came to Vienna in 1820 to meet Beethoven and achieved greater success in the city than the latter.

Joseph Haydn (1732-1809) – Born in Rohrau (Lower Austria), Haydn was a choirboy in Stephansdom in Vienna. In 1761, he entered the service of the Esterházy family for thirty years, composing works which became famous throughout Europe. He defined the form of the string quartet, classical symphony and piano sonata. In 1790-92 and 1794-95 he went to London, then returned to Vienna where he wrote his two celebrated oratorios, *The Creation* (1798) and *The Seasons* (1801). He died in the imperial capital three weeks after Napoleon's occupation of Vienna.

Wolfgang Amadeus Mozart

Wolfgang Amadeus Mozart (1756-91) – Born in Salzburg, Mozart moved to Vienna in 1781 after giving up his position with the archbishop of his native city where he was director of chapel music. In the capital, his poor relations with Joseph II then Leopold II prevented him from achieving his breakthrough. He brought every form of musical expression to perfection, owing to his exceptional fluency and ever-renewed inspiration. His dramatic genius developed in the school of the German *Singspiel* and the Italian *opera buffa* and flowered in masterpieces such as *The Marriage of Figaro*, *Don Giovanni*, *Così fan Tutte* and *The Magic Flute*. He died a pauper's death in Vienna, misunderstood, leaving his *Requiem* unfinished. On his instructions, it was completed posthumously by his pupil, Franz Xaver Süßmayer.

Ludwig van Beethoven

Ludwig van Beethoven (1770-1827) – Born in Bonn (Germany), he first visited Vienna in 1787 to become Mozart's pupil. Irresistibly attracted by the capital of music, he returned at the age of 20 and found a patron in Baron Gottfried van Swieten, curator of the Court Library, who invited him to perform before the Esterházys, Kinskys, Liechtensteins, Lobkowitzes and Schwarzenbergs. They all gave the young musician their patronage. About Vienna he wrote that nobody could love the city as he did. His colleagues included Hummel, Cramer, Seyfried, Wranitzky and Eybler. Beethoven outstripped them all. He had a romantic conception of music which enabled him to compose works that revolutionised musical expression. On the point of death, the composer of *Fidelio* and the *9th Symphony* said to his friend Hummel "Applaud, my friends, the comedy is over."

Franz Schubert (1797-1828) – The great composer was born and died in Vienna, a city which he seldom left. His contemporaries did not understand his work. He sang at the Hofkapelle (Royal Chapel), studied under Salieri then rediscovered and made famous the *Lied*. Even more than his symphonies, masses, and chamber music, his *Lieder* established him as the leading lyrical composer of the 19C. 1825 saw the appearance of Schubert evenings (*"Schubertiades"*), when Schubert would present his *Lieder* to a small circle of friends before the evening more likely than not ended with a dance. The only public concert ever to be held featuring exclusively his works took place shortly before his death from typhus in November 1828. He never had time to conquer the Viennese who favoured light music.

Franz Schubert

Anton Bruckner (1824-96) – Born in Ansfleden (Upper Austria), this pious and modest man became director of music in Vienna in 1861 and organist of the imperial chapel in 1878. Compared to Johann Sebastian Bach for his talents of improvisation, he has the reputation of being the greatest 19C composer of religious music. His great symphonies reflect the influence of Beethoven and reach a high level of dramatic intensity. He died in Vienna and is buried at the foot of the great organ in St Florian Abbey in Upper Austria.

Johannes Brahms (1833-97) – Born in Hamburg (Germany), he moved to Vienna in 1862 and lived there for the rest of his life. A director of the Singakademie then of the concerts of the Gesellschaft der Musikfreunde, he attained international fame. He composed a large body of work of a lyrical nature, *Lieder*, piano quartets, striking a balance between Classicism and Romanticism: *Lieder*, piano quartets, symphonies and concertos.

Hugo Wolf (1860-1903) – Born in Windischgrätz (Styria), he came to study at the Vienna Conservatory at the age of 15. Apart from a few journeys, he never left the city. Hugo Wolf, who suffered from mental illness, had two creative phases. During the first (1878-87), he tried his hand at every form of composition. During the second (1887-97), he produced and published some magnificent *Lieder* based on poems by Goethe, Mörike and Eichendorff.

Gustav Mahler (1860-1911) – Born of a German-speaking Jewish family in Kalischt (Bohemia), this follower of Bruckner embarked in 1880 on a twofold career as conductor and composer after three years at the Vienna Conservatory. From 1897 to 1907, he conducted the orchestra of the Staatsoper. At a turning point between the Romantic and the modern era, he composed ten symphonies and five song cycles, his music combining idealism and realism.

Anton Bruckner

The New or Second Viennese School – Schönberg was at the centre of this movement which arose in 1903 and which had a crucial influence on the development of 20C music, affecting many contemporary musicians, such as the Austrian Ernst Krenek and the Frenchman Pierre Boulez.

Born in Vienna, **Arnold Schönberg** (1874-1951) revolutionised traditional music by rejecting the music theory of the past three centuries, which he assessed in his *Treatise on Harmony* dedicated to Mahler. In 1912, he gained some recognition with *Pierrot Lunaire*, a melodrama consisting of a 21-part cycle for narrator and five instruments. With his most important followers, **Anton von Webern** (1883-1945), born in Vienna, and **Alban Berg** (1885-1935), he developed a new method of atonal composition, founded on serialism. It was the theory of dodecaphonism or, in its more elaborate form, of serial music. Also born in Vienna, Alban Berg has

Gustav Mahler by Emil Orliek

been called a "mathematician-poet"; his opera *Wozzeck*, composed between 1917 and 1921, played a vital role in the history of 20C dramatic music.

THE VIENNESE WALTZ

The word waltz comes from the German *Walzer* derived from the High German *wellan* meaning "to turn". Of uncertain origin, it probably developed out of 16C and 17C country dances from South Germany. The oldest triple-time waltz is the slow waltz, or *Landler*, which villagers danced at inns in the open air. This country dance underwent a change which was slight but sufficient to revolutionise it: in a 1782 treatise on choreography, the Viennese waltz first appeared in its modern form with gliding swinging steps. A more sprightly and intoxicating dance, it found admirers everywhere.

Arnold Schönberg

The waltz earns its spurs – The waltz played a vital role in Viennese history. The greatest composers wrote waltzes: Beethoven composed eleven. Other composers included Brahms, Chopin, Ravel, Schubert and Sibelius to name but a few. They wrote concert waltzes. Kings of the genre, the masters of the ballroom waltz were the Strauss family and Lanner *(see below)*. The success of this type of waltz was so great that it found acceptance at the Austrian Imperial Court.

A Biedermeier lifestyle – To fully understand the phenomenon of the waltz in Vienna, it is necessary to bear in mind the political situation in the city at the beginning of the 19C. Metternich's system was one of repression which depended for its enforcement on the constant supervision of the omnipresent police under the command of his underling, Seldnitzky. Vienna was a city living in the shadow of implacable censorship both on the printed word and religious activity. A consequence of this was a turning towards pleasures such as the waltz. The moralists of the time, mostly foreigners, were quick to point out the unacceptable "intimacy" of couples performing this indecent dance which seemed to attract every age group. The Viennese found their comments amusing, since they had long fallen for the enchanting whirling of the waltz. Moreover, because the authorities had grasped its political advantages, the waltz reigned supreme.

The first balls – Very soon, the waltz lost its skipping steps and other characteristics of an 18C folk dance. The waltz of the *Vormärz* replaced it. This was a simpler, but more audacious dance: individual couples were free to lose themselves in the anonymity of a crowd. This development certainly accounted for the success of the new dance halls. They were so popular and so crowded that it is impossible to envisage any formation dancing.

Balls were in vogue. In the thousands, Viennese danced at the **Clair de Lune, Nouveau Monde** or **L'Apollon**, dance halls sparkling with chandeliers lit even in daytime and, most importantly, laid with parquet floors on which couples could glide into ever more intimate swirling movements.

Josef Lanner (1801-43) – He was born and died in Vienna. On the one hand, he was responsible for defining the acceleration and cadence of the Viennese waltz; on the other hand, he was the first to give titles to individual pieces of this music. At an early age, in 1819, he formed a trio with friends and played potpourris of fashionable tunes. It was a success. The trio became a quartet with the arrival of a young violist aged 15,

Johann Strauss the Younger – *The Blue Danube*

Johann Strauss, with whom Lanner soon quarrelled. Now a composer and conductor of his orchestra of 12 musicians, the latter could no longer meet the demands of the dance halls; this helped to launch his rival's newly created orchestra. In 1829, he became Court Musical Director.

He died of typhus while still young and left about 230 works, including *The Romantics*, opus 141.

The Strauss family – Only the Habsburgs stamped their name so indelibly on the history of the capital of the Austro-Hungarian Empire. The name of the Strauss dynasty evokes the enchantment of the waltz, the glorious side of 19C Vienna.

AKG Paris

Johann Strauss the Elder

Johann Strauss the Elder (1804-49) was born and died in Vienna. There he started out as a member of Lanner's orchestra, sharing with him the privilege of raising the waltz to a music form in a class of its own. Very rapidly, he created his own orchestra, playing in various dance halls. Without ever learning the rules of composition – a feature he shared with Lanner – he composed rhythmic variations to lend new lustre to his orchestra of 28 musicians. Vienna fell under his spell, as did Berlin, London and Paris where people admired this brilliant violinist who drew inspiration from gypsy music. In 1830, he managed 200 musicians, whom he divided up into various orchestras to meet demand. He played at the Sperl, Lanner at the Redoute. When the latter died, Strauss , and considered himself the one and only "Waltz King". He wrote his famous *Radetzky March* in 1848.

This triumph of Johann Strauss the Elder was short-lived, since **Johann Strauss the Younger** (1825-99) soon demonstrated that this title belonged to him. After his father died, from scarlet fever, leaving some 250 waltzes, he amalgamated the two orchestras and went on a series of tours as far as the United States. Under his direction, the waltz acquired more contrasting themes. From 1863, when he became Director of Court balls, he wrote some of his immortal works, such as *The Blue Danube* (1867), *Tales of the Vienna Woods* (1868), the operetta *Die Fledermaus* (1874) and the *Emperor Waltz* (1888).

His brother **Josef Strauss** (1827-70), an engineer by training, ultimately devoted his energies to music. He composed over 300 waltzes, including *Austrian Swallow*.

Literature

19C – In the early 19C, the German Romantic movement heralded the dawn of Austrian literature.

A poet, **Franz Grillparzer** (1791-1872) is probably Austria's greatest playwright. Withdrawing into himself in response to the sordid Metternich censorship, he produced works showing the influence of Goethe and Schiller. He is the author of several neo-Classical dramas, such as *The Golden Fleece* (*Das Goldene Vlies*, 1822), *The Waves of the Sea and of Love* (*Des Meeres und der Liebe Wellen*, 1831), and his masterpiece *Sappho* (1819).

Born in Hungary but brought up in Vienna, **Nikolaus Lenau** (1802-50) depicted characters in inner turmoil, as in his epic poem *Don Juan*. His most profound work is *The Albigensians* (*Die Albigenser*, 1842). A native of Bohemia, **Adalbert Stifter** (1805-68) came to study at Vienna University. Nietzsche and Hoffmannsthal considered him a master of German prose. A great admirer of Grillparzer, he became a writer relatively late in life and published, amongst others, *Multicoloured Stones* (*Bunte Steine*, 1853), *Indian Summer* (*Der Nachsommer*, 1857), and *My Great-Grandfather's Notebooks* (*Die Mappe meines Urgrossvaters*, 1841-42). He committed suicide.

The turn of the century – Because he portrayed the decadence of Viennese society, **Arthur Schnitzler** (1862-1931) has the unjustified reputation of being superficial. Revealing the influence of psychoanalysis, the works of this doctor delve into the subconscious of his protagonists who are often wrestling with erotic scepticism as in *Anatol* (1893), *Flirtation* (*Liebelei*, 1895), *Merry Go Round* (*Reigen*, 1900) and *Miss Else* (*Fräulein Else*, 1924).

Hugo von Hofmannsthal (1874-1929) belongs to an entirely different category. His talent, evident from an early age, displays both pathos and irony. He excelled in lyric poetry, then in metaphysical drama very different from the folk theatre of 19C Austria. A friend of Richard Strauss, he wrote the librettos for many of his operas, such as *Der Rosenkavalier* (1911). His major works include *Death and The Fool* (*Der Tor und der Tod*, 1893), *Jederman* (1911) and *The Salzburg Great Theatre of the World* (*Das Salzburger grosse Welt-theater*, 1922).

Although he was neither a dramatist nor a novelist, one cannot overlook **Sigmund Freud** (1856-1939), who founded psychoanalysis as a result of his experiences in treating perversions, analysing neuroses and studying the subconscious. He explained the theory underlying this science in his fundamental work, *The Interpretation of Dreams*, (*Die Traumdeutung*, 1900) which appeared in English in 1909. Other works include *Totem and Taboo* (1913) and *The Man Moses and the Monotheistic Religion* (1937).

Hugo von Hofmannsthal

ROGER VIOLLET

The 20C – In his first novel *The Confusions of Young Törless* (*Die Verwirrungen des Zöglings Törless*, 1906), **Robert Musil** (1880-1942) depicted the sufferings of a young boy at a military academy. This won him great renown and heralded the start of a literary career which he had embarked upon out of boredom with his profession as an engineer. Born in Klagenfurt (Carinthia), he moved to Vienna in 1910 and lived there from his meagre earnings until his death in Geneva after going into exile in 1938. An unfinished novel which remained totally unknown in his lifetime, *The Man without Qualities* (*Der Mann ohne Eigenschaften*, 1930) epitomises the essence of his work.

A man of acute psychological insight, **Stefan Zweig** (1881-1942) was a doctor of philosophy. He tried his hand at every genre, using the language of the 19C. He first became famous with his novellas, depicting mainly the eruption of violent passion into middle class lives, such as *Confusion of Feelings* (*Verwirrung der Gefühle*, 1927) and the masterful *Chess Novella* (*Schachnovelle*, 1942). He also wrote brilliant literary monographs, where under Freud's influence he analysed the inner motivation of human beings: *Fouché*, *Erasmus*, *Marie Antoinette*, etc.

Hermann Broch (1886-1951) is a difficult writer, who described the end of the Empire as a "joyous apocalypse", observed the deterioration of traditional values, as in his trilogy *The Sleepwalkers* (*Die Schlafwandler*, 1932), but believed in a new system. He is undeniably one of the 20C's greatest German-language novelists. His masterpiece is *The Death of Virgil* (*Der Tod des Virgil*, 1945).

Born in Prague of Jewish parents, **Franz Werfel** (1890-1945) was attracted to Christianity and belonged to the Expressionist movement. A liberal attitude permeates his work, including books of poetry such as *Friend of the World* (*Der Weltfreund*, 1911), and his plays and short stories such as *The Victim, Not the Assassin, is Guilty* (*Nicht der Mörder, der Ermordete ist Schuldig*, 1920).

Stefan Zweig

AKG PARIS

Born in Brody (Galicia), **Josef Roth** (1894-1939) studied philosophy in Vienna before becoming a journalist and emigrating to Paris in 1933. His thirteen novels include *Radetzky March* (*Radetzkymarsch*, 1932), which describes the defunct Austrian empire in the days of Franz Josef; and the *The Capuchin Crypt* (*Die Kapuzinergruft*, 1938) depicting characters who are the victims of their fate.

Heimito von Doderer (1896-1966) is the most Viennese writer of them all and perhaps the most brilliant. His most famous novel *Die Strudlhofstiege oder Melzer und die Tiefe der Jahre* (1951) has not yet been translated into English.

Of Hungarian, Croat, Czech and German descent, **Ödön von Horvárth** (1901-38) is the only one of these writers to avoid constantly questioning man's role and society's values. This citizen of the Austro-Hungarian Empire without a country lived in Vienna before settling in Berlin. He was killed accidentally in Paris at the age of 37 and left work of astonishing lucidity, such as *The Italian Night* (*Italienische Nacht*, 1931) and *Tales of the Vienna Woods* (*Geschichten aus dem Wienerwald*, 1931).

A novelist and dramatist of Bulgarian origin, **Elias Canetti** (1905-1994) lived for a long time in Vienna before emigrating to England. A Symbolist work, his *Comedy of Vanity* (*Komödie der Eitelkeiten*, 1934) is a precise description of mass hysteria; the author became world-famous when he received the Nobel prize in 1981.

Born in Vienna, but living in Germany, **Ilse Aichinger** (1921-) produced work expressing human anguish and solitude, first with *Greater Hope* (*Die grössere Hoffnung*, 1948) then with *The Chained Man* (*Der Gefesselte*, 1953), published in Austria under the title *Speech Beneath the Gallows* (*Rede unter dem Galgen*).

Born in Klagenfurt, **Ingeborg Bachmann** (1926-73) studied in Vienna and left two collections of lyrical poems close in style to Hoffmannsthal: *Time in Remission* (*Die gestundete Zeit*, 1953) and *Invocation to the Great Bear* (*Anrufen des grossen Bären*, 1956).

Thomas Bernhard (1931-89) first gained recognition as a lyrical poet, but he became famous for his novels and plays which were full of realism and pessimism about human nature. From *Frost* (1963) to *Extinction* (*Auslöschung*, 1986), the novels of this great writer pushed German syntax to a point which is reminiscent of serial music.

Peter Handke (1942-), who ranks as one of the best known Austrian writers, is also a filmmaker. His avant-garde work conveys the anguish of solitude and lack of communication through novels and short stories such as *The Goalkeeper's Fear of the Penalty Shot* (*Die Angst des Tormanns beim Elfmeter*, 1970) and plays like *Ride across Lake Constanz* (*Der Ritt über den Bodensee*, 1971).

There is also **Elfriede Jelinek** (1946-) whose novels such as *The Pianist* (*Die Klavierspielerin*, 1983) and *Greed* (*Gier*, 2000) have created a considerable stir.

Life in Vienna

THE "HEURIGER"

A secular tradition which Emperor Joseph II popularised but dating from the 13C, the Viennese *Heuriger* is a strange institution, typically Viennese like the Stephansdom spire, the Giant Wheel of the Prater or the Vienna Boys' Choir (*Wiener Sängerknaben*). The *Heuriger* is a kind of tavern-restaurant, with traditional rustic decor, supplying new wine, that is the current year's young wine. A true *Heuriger* offers only the wine from its own vineyards which often lie behind the building. It is, in any case, subject to regulations covering even the time of opening.

Besides red or white wine, there is also freshly pressed grape or apple juice, mineral water and lemonade. Do not ask for Coca-Cola, beer, coffee or any other drink. The waitress would almost certainly point out somewhat mockingly that you happen to be seated in a genuine *Heuriger*... Try ordering *ein Viertel Weiss* or *Rot* (a quarter litre of white or red wine), *ein Gespritztes* (wine with sparkling water) or even *ein Apfelsaft* (an apple juice).

Each *Heuriger* has its own specialities. Typically, however, they include roast pork (*Schweinsbraten*), smoked pork (*Geselchtes*), roast chicken, blood sausage, sauerkraut, dumplings (*Knödel*) and a rich selection of spreads, such as *Liptauer* (quark, a sort of cream cheese, with onions, garlic, paprika and other spices, for which each Heuriger has its own secret recipe), garlic, Gorgonzola, or egg spread. For dessert, there is a choice between *Apfelstrudel* (apple pastry slice) and *Topfenstrudel* (a strudel with a quark filling), always in generous portions.

Eating and drinking in a *Heuriger* is pleasant, but an essential part of the *Heuriger* experience is the comfortable, friendly atmosphere. However, the happiness on people's faces is not as carefree as a visitor might suppose; the typical *Schrammelmusik* of the *Heuriger* serves to remind everyone of the ephemeral side of life. A typical *Schrammel* ensemble consists of two violins, an accordion – or a clarinet – and a guitar, but a violin and an accordion alone are sufficient to create a truly Viennese atmosphere.

COFFEE HOUSES

Elegant, comfortable and traditional in character, a *Kaffeehaus* (coffee house) plays a major role in Viennese life. Even if Viennese cafés have changed over the years and are no longer a place where great authors discuss literature and politics, they have preserved some of their former glory. They are the ideal venue for peacefully reading a newspaper, writing a love letter, skimming through a favourite novel, musing on the state of the world or just watching time go by in congenial company in an elegant and tranquil setting. Ordering something to eat or drink almost becomes an afterthought.

Coffee Compendium

As there are over thirty ways of making coffee, here is a small selection of the most common versions of this delicious drink:

Grosser/kleiner Schwarzer – large/small cup of black espresso

Grosser/kleiner Brauner – large/small cup of espresso with a dash of milk

Verlängerter Schwarzer – espresso with a little more water

Verlängerter Brauner – espresso with a dash of milk and a little water

Einspänner – black coffee in a glass with whipped cream (Schlagobers)

Fiaker – black coffee in a glass with rum

Franziskaner – coffee with milk and grated chocolate

Kaffee verkehrt – more milk than coffee

Kaisermelange – coffee with a yolk of egg and brandy

Kurzer – strong black espresso

Maria Theresia – coffee with orange liqueur and whipped cream

Mazagran – cold coffee with ice cubes and rum

Melange – coffee with milk (or whipped cream)

Mokka – fairly strong black coffee

Pharisäer – rum in a cup with espresso

Türkischer Kaffee – coffee brought to the boil in small copper vessels, served very hot in small cups

A coffee house will serve breakfast, lunch and dinner, but the best time to come is undeniably late afternoon or early evening, especially after a pleasurable yet tiring visit to one of the capital's great museums. It will probably not be time for a full meal, so a cake is the obvious choice, such as the famous *Sachertorte* or *Mozarttorte*.

THE BALL SEASON

In winter, there is an endless succession of balls. On New Year's Eve, the famous **Kaiserball** (Emperor's Ball) recreates the bygone imperial era beneath the chandeliers of the Hofburg. During the Carnival, an incredible range of associations and professional groups hold about 300 balls, mostly in ceremonial halls (Rathaus, Hofburg, Musikverein). Among these are the gardeners' and florists' Flower Ball, the Rudolfina-Redoute, the Café Proprietors' Ball, the Philharmonic Orchestra's Ball, and the Technicians' Circle Ball. Doctors have their own ball, as do lawyers, messenger boys and firemen. Visitors are always welcome.

The most elegant ball is the **Opernball** or Opera Ball, which is held in February at the Staatsoper *(see City Centre and the Ring, Staatsoper District)*. It attracts Austrian and foreign celebrities and is the year's most fashionable event. It opens with the Wiener Staatsoper ballet and a select group of young men and women with fans dancing the polonaise.

Michaelertrakt in the Hofburg

City Centre
and the Ring

FLEISCHMARKT District

Local map page 14, **KLR**
Underground: Schwedenplatz (U1, U4), Stubentor (U3)
Tram: Schwedenplatz (1, 2, 21, N), Stubentor (1, 2)
Bus: Riemergasse (1A, 3A), Rotenturmstrasse (2A)

The Meat Market occupies the centre of this district, the oldest in Vienna. It is the liveliest street in this area known as "the Bermuda triangle", where young Viennese and foreign tourists gather in the evenings. This imaginary triangle lies between the church Maria am Gestade, Franziskanerplatz and the south end of Fleischmarkt. The tour starts with sights visible by daylight and continues towards Fleischmarkt, which some may enjoy more by night.

SIGHTS

Postsparkasse ⊘ – *Georg-Coch-Platz 2*. To appreciate the new concepts which **Otto Wagner**'s Post Office Savings Bank illustrated in 1906, it is best to view it from the Stubenring overlooked by the former War Ministry *(see City Centre and the Ring, The Ring, Stubenring, Regierungsgebäude)* with its giant double-headed eagle. The contrast is striking. It is difficult to believe that the neo-Baroque ministry building is more recent than the smooth-surfaced Postsparkasse. The façade of this major work by Wagner is mottled in appearance; plaques of Sterzing marble are in fact riveted to it, concealing a brick structure. Although set back from the Ring, the Postsparkasse shares the same monumental grandeur. The architect, who had also constructed neo-Renaissance buildings on the Ring, built the Postsparkasse in three years, whereas other monumental edifices on the Ring took ten years to complete. The novelty lay as much in the appearance as in the technique, one arising from the other. Indeed, Wagner's modernism consists of a functionalist approach. He left the aluminium boltheads visible, and did not wait for the plaques to bond with the mortar, which made construction faster and produced a decorative effect. Wagner's Secession functionalism was not severe; at the top of the building are Othmar Schimkowitz's winged Victories. The pomp of these triumphant symbols creates another link between the Postsparkasse and the buildings of the Ring. In this, Wagner differed from Adolf Loos, who totally opposed any ornamentation. The severe façade conceals a fine **main hall**. Its interior shows how much attention Wagner paid to detail. Light streams in, diffused through a vaulted glass roof and a glass tiled floor. Wagner turned the forced-air heating system columns into graceful tubular sculptures, and also designed the furniture, which is still in use today. *(Models based on the designs of Wagner and Kolo Moser are for sale.)*

Postsparkasse: the main hall

3 BIS/MICHELIN

Proceed past Postsparkasse along Rosenbursenstrasse and turn left up the sloping Dominikanerbastei. Stop at the level of Falkestrasse on the left.

Falkestrasse – The architects of the **Coop Himmelblau** group redesigned the roof of the classical building at No 6 in 1988. This refurbishment gives an impression of the group's avant-garde orientation and its debt to the school of deconstructivism.
Turn right into Predigergasse then left into Postgasse.

Dominikanerkirche – *Postgasse 4*. In 1226, Duke Leopold VI summoned the Dominicans to Vienna where 11 years later they consecrated their first church. The edifice was damaged by a fire and later, in 1529, by the Turks; but the architect Antonio Canevale rebuilt it from 1631 to 1634 according to Jacopo Tencala's plans. The facade and the flat cupola date from about 1670.

An interior laid out according to a basilica's ground-plan extends behind the church's towerless façade. The frescoes in the nave are by Matthias Rauchmiller (17C), the one in the cupola is by Franz Geyling (1836), and those in the high altar area by Carpoforo Tencala (1676). The view from the nave ends with the high altar by Carl Rösner (1839); above it is a painting by Leopold Kupelwieser, *Institution and Celebration of the Festival of the Rosary by Pope Pius V* (1840). Much of the decorative appeal of this church lies in its **stucco**, which is typical of the Early Baroque and which reached its height in the pilaster embellishments of the transept arms *(see also illustration in the Introduction, under Religious architecture).*

Continue along Postgasse and turn right into Bäckerstrasse which connects with Dr. Ignaz-Seipel-Platz.

★ **Jesuitenkirche** ⊙ – *Dr. Ignaz-Seipel-Platz.* After Salzburg cathedral, which was built from 1614 to 1655, this is the most famous Austrian church inspired by Il Gesù in Rome. It also bears the name of *Universitätskirche* (University church). This church was designed by an anonymous architect between 1623 and 1627 in the Early Baroque style.

Andrea Pozzo is famous for decorating the ceilings of Sant'Ignazio in Rome (1685). He redesigned the

3 BIS/MICHELIN

The pulpit in Jesuitenkirche

interior of the Jesuitenkirche between 1703 and 1707. This Jesuit father from southern Tyrol achieved a sumptuous effect with a **trompe-l'œil cupola**★ in the centre of the ceiling and a lavishly adorned **pulpit**★ encrusted with mother-of-pearl. An equally talented painter, Pozzo also created the high altar, including a painting of the *Assumption*. Another interesting detail is the altarpieces of the first chapels *(at the entrance)* depicting St Catherine embodying Philosophy on the left, and Theology on the right.

Alte Universität – *Dr. Ignaz-Seipel-Platz 1. Closed to the public.* Vienna University was founded by Rudolf IV, first archduke, in 1365 and was the earliest German-language university after Prague, founded in 1348. The first Faculty was that of Theology. The Dominicans nearby gave instruction in this subject until the Jesuits replaced them in 1623. In 1803, the Court installed there "K. und K. Stadtkonvikt", a music school recruiting the 130 children who sang on Sundays in the chapel of the imperial palace. Franz Schubert was a pupil there from 1808 to 1813, from the ages of 11 to 16 *(see wall plaque).* After the building of the Ring, the University was moved there. Today, an art gallery occupies the ground floor.

The Counter-Reformation

Ignatius of Loyola founded the Society of Jesus in 1537, and Pope Paul III approved it in 1540. Its purpose lay more in action than meditation. The Society rapidly developed and became a kind of militia defending the Church against heresy. After the Council of Trent, which took place from 1545 to 1563, a movement grew up, which the 19C termed the Counter-Reformation. Its aim was to repel the advance of Protestantism. The Jesuits were the most active participants in this Roman Catholic reformation, turning Austria and Bavaria into bastions of Roman Catholicism. In 1623, Emperor Ferdinand II guaranteed the Jesuit order a monopoly for teaching philosophy and theology at Vienna University, which accounts for the proximity of Jesuitenkirche. The Jesuits continued with this mission until 1773.

City Centre and the Ring

Akademie der Wissenschaften (N) – *Dr. Ignaz-Seipel-Platz 2. Closed to the public.*
Jean-Nicolas Jadot de Ville-Issey built the Academy of Sciences opposite the
University from 1753 to 1755 at the request of Empress Maria-Theresa. This
accounts for the note of French Classicism in this secluded quarter of old Vienna.
Before housing in 1857 the ten-year-old Academy, this palace had served as a ceremonial hall for the Alte Universität, with frescoes by Gregorio Guglielmi, who also
painted those in the Grosse Galerie at Schloss Schönbrunn. Unfortunately, these
works were completely destroyed by fire in 1961. It was possible to restore the
architecture, but new frescoes had to be painted, by Paul Reckendorfer. The
sculptor Franz Joseph Lenzbauer created the two fountains adorning the façade
(1755).

The Creation as a Musical Epitaph

The last concert which **Joseph Haydn** attended was a performance of his oratorio *The Creation* played in his honour in the university's great hall. Aged
76 and very weak, Haydn, who scarcely left the house *(see Outside the
Ring, Mariahilf, Haydn Memorial Site)*, agreed to go to this gala evening.
On 27 March 1808, Prince Esterházy's *(Further afield, Eisenstadt)* carriage
came to fetch him. As he reached the Jesuitenkirche, princes Lobkowitz and
Trauttmansdorff, as well as Beethoven and Salieri, rushed to support the
old man, who could hardly walk. At the same time, there was a drum roll
and a blare of trumpets, a great fanfare, and the Viennese aristocracy rose
to greet its national composer. Haydn advanced triumphantly in his wheel-
chair amid the cheering crowd. He was seated next to Princess Maria
Josepha Esterházy (born Lichtenstein) and despite his protests was excused
from taking off his hat. As he was still feeling chilled, the princess gave him
her shawl. A duo of poets sang in his honour. He drank some country wine,
which seemed to revive him a little. Then came the opening bars of his masterpiece. He trembled. The emotion overwhelmed him. By the end of the
first part of the oratorio, he felt obliged to return home. Beethoven, who
was equally moved, kissed the hand of his former master, who waved to
the audience as if blessing them. He left immediately, while the orchestra
continued playing his music. Many of the men in the audience could not
conceal their tears. This was Haydn's last public appearance. He died just
over a year later, on 31 May 1809, three weeks after Napoleon's troops
entered Vienna.

Return to Bäckerstrasse.

Bäckerstrasse – There is no lack of interesting façades in "Baker" Street. No 16
is a pleasant residential house built about 1712. On the right, Schwanenfeld House
(No 7) is famous in Vienna for its Renaissance courtyard with Tuscan and Ionic
columns; the arcades, now glassed-in, date from 1587. Opposite, at No 8, Count
Seilern's palace dates from 1722, then, a little further to the left, No 2 and its
tower were built in the 17C.

*The street leads to the square known as Lugeck. Notice the narrow passage leading
to Stephansplatz.*

Lugeck – In its centre is the *Gutenbergdenkmal*, a sculpture cast in bronze in 1900
by Hans Bitterlich. The invention of printing (1440) was attributed to Johann
Gutenberg of Mainz. It heralded a new era in the history of ideas, since it was then
possible to achieve the circulation of unlimited numbers of texts by means of move-
able type. In fact, the Chinese had first perfected this technique in the 7C AD.

Turn right into Sonnenfelsgasse.

Sonnenfelsgasse – This street dates from the early 12C. Hildebrandthaus (No 3)
is an elegant, impressive house built in several stages, but first constructed between
the 14C and 15C. Its Baroque façade (1721) was designed by the architect after
whom the house is named. It has fine window frames, separated at the 2nd and
3rd storeys by pilasters resting on consoles with scrolls. The *Virgin with Child* in
a small Rococo pediment is noteworthy. At present the cellars of the building house
a *Stadt-Heuriger* called *Zwölf Apostelkeller.*

Turn left into Schönlaterngasse.

Schönlaterngasse – The winding street of the Lovely Lantern is undeniably the
most charming street in the oldest quarter of the town centre. It derives its name
from the wrought-iron lantern on the façade of the 1680 house at No 6 (a 1971
replica, the 18C original being in the Historisches Museum der Stadt Wien).
Opposite, at No 5, **Heiligenkreuzerhof** is a courtyard (17C and 18C) surrounded by
buildings, most of which belong to Heiligenkreuz Foundation *(see under this
heading)* of Lower Austria. They include the residence of the abbot and

St Bernard's chapel (where society weddings take place). Its delightful Baroque interior dates from 1662 and underwent refurbishment in 1730. It houses an altarpiece by the painter Martino Altomonte. This artist, some of whose works are visible in Peterskirche *(see City Centre and the Ring, Stephansdom District)*, lived at the court of Heiligenkreuz.

At No 7 is **Wohnhaus "Zum Basilisken"** (basilisk house), mentioned as early as 1212 and therefore one of the oldest houses in the town. Its 1740 façade attracts notice, because an unknown hand added a beak and tail. There is no reason to doubt the popular Viennese legend related by Wolfgang Lazius in 1546 in his *Vienna Austriae*, according to which a basilisk – a mythical animal which came from an egg laid by a cock and incubated by a toad – poisoned with its breath the well in the house where it had its lair. The fresco on the façade describes how a fearless young master baker, Martin Garhiebl, destroyed the monster by showing it a mirror, making it die of fright at the sight of such ugliness.

Robert Schumann lived at No 7a from October 1838 to April 1839. His wife Clara was a pianist in the Habsburg capital. Being of too romantic a temperament to appreciate the frivolity of Viennese society, he did not stay long in the city. However, he spent some time there looking for an editor for his musical review *Neue Zeitschrift für Musik* and frequently met Franz Schubert's brother, Ferdinand.

Alte Schmiede (No 9) is the former smithy of Josef Schmirler, who made the street lanterns for this street. The workshop operated until 1974, after which it became a museum ⊙ and cultural centre.

Schönlaterngasse leads into Postgasse.

Postgasse – **Johannes Brahms** (1833-97), composer of the *German Requiem* among other masterpieces, lived at No 6 in 1867.

At No 10 is the **Griechische Kirche hl. Barbara**. The present façade of this church dates from 1854, but the edifice was built in the mid-17C. The church belonged to the Jesuits until 1773, then was given to the Ukrainian Catholic community two years later.

Turn left to Fleischmarkt.

Fleischmarkt – The butchers' guild established their headquarters here at the "meat market" (or "shambles") in 1220, in the heart of medieval Vienna. Today, the street is famous for the bars and nightclubs that fill the area around it.

At No 15 is the Schwindhof (1718), birthplace of the painter Moritz von Schwind on 21 January 1804 (he died in Munich in 1871).

At No 13, the **Griechisch-orientalische Kirche zur Hl. Dreifaltigkeit** ⊙ displays an ornate façade of bricks enhanced with gilding. Peter Mollner built the edifice, which also houses a school, between 1782 and 1787. In 1861, it underwent alterations, to a design by Theophil Hansen, one of the creators of the Ring, and acquired its Byzantine appearance. A corridor with frescoes by Ludwig Thiersch leads to the Greek Orthodox church of the Holy Trinity, a sanctuary noteworthy for its oblong chancel; the iconostasis dates from the second half of the 18C.

At No 11 is the **Griechenbeisl**, a tavern frequented by celebrities such as Johannes Brahms, Franz Grillparzer, Franz Schubert, Johann Strauss and Richard Wagner. Mark Twain allegedly wrote *The Millionaires' Wager* in a room with walls covered in the signatures of famous writers. The inn sign depicts a popular bagpipe player of the mid 17C. The song he wrote during an outbreak of plague in 1679 still lives in the Viennese mind:

"O du lieber Augustin,
's Geld is hin,
's Mensch is hin,
O du lieber Augustin,
Alles is hin!"
(Oh, my dear Augustin,
Money's gone,
Folks are gone,
Oh, my dear Augustin,
Everything's gone!)

In the song, Augustin gets drunk and falls into a mass grave, but he has absorbed so much alcohol that he is safe from infection. The words of this little ditty revived the courage of the inhabitants of the town devastated by plague. In his *Second Quartet*, Arnold Schönberg borrowed the melody of this legendary song, illustrating the ability of Viennese artists to turn suffering into art.

The small **Griechengasse** possesses several Gothic remains, including an old 13C Gothic tower at No 9. The façade at No 7 displays a Virgin in a niche above a wrought-iron Rococo lantern. In the courtyard, there is another Gothic tower; the Turkish inscriptions on the wooden panels date from the 1683 siege. The name of this street evokes the Greek merchants who settled in this quarter in the 18C.

Return to Fleischmarkt

Fleischmarkt – The "Lieber Augustin"

At No 9 Fleischmarkt, **Wohnhaus "Zur Mariahilf"** is a house with a late 17C façade featuring a *Virgin with Child* dating from the 16C. The plaque on the right is a reminder of the law of May 8, 1912 which required carriages to be preceded by somebody on foot to warn passers-by of the imminent arrival of a horse-drawn vehicle in the narrow Griechengasse.

At No 14, the fine green Jugendstil façade belongs to an office block built in 1899 by F. Dehm and Joseph Maria Olbrich, architect of the famous Secession pavilion. The wall plaque commemorates Johann Herbeck (1831-77), former Kapellmeister and director of opera and theatre at Court.

At No 1, "Residenzpalast", another Jugendstil building, is more austere, although elegantly set off by gold banding. Arthur Baron built it in 1910. A plaque states that this site was also the birthplace of Franz Schalk (1863-1931), a pupil of Anton Bruckner and co-director, with Richard Strauss, of the National Opera.

In addition to the last part of the Ring, the nearest sights are: Stephansdom and its surrounding area, the Hoher Markt district (in the City Centre and the Ring section), and the Landstrasse and Leopoldstadt districts (found in the Outside the Ring section).

FREYUNG District★

Local map page 13, **HJR**
Underground: Schottentor (U2), Herrengasse (U3)
Tram: Schottentor-Universität (1, 2, 37, 38, 40, 41, 42, 43, 44, D)
Bus: Teinfaltstrasse (1A), Michaelerplatz (2A), Herrengasse (3A)

One might think that the presence of the Hofburg gave rise to the numerous palaces around Freyung, but in fact the former Babenberg and Formbach residences preceded the Hofburg. The Baroque period gave birth to most of the palaces in the Innere Stadt or 1st District. However, while the Church had an archbishop's palace built near the cathedral *(see City Centre and the Ring, Stephansdom District, Dom- und Diözesanmuseum)*, and the Crown commissioned the construction of the Leopoldinischertrakt in the Hofburg, the aristocrats of the Empire built themselves palaces in the "Aristocratic District"; Herrengasse, or Lords' Street, links Freyung to Michaelerplatz, its name recalling its aristocratic past.

SIGHTS

Freyung – A "place of asylum" is the literal meaning of the name of this triangular square. It was originally a centre of festivities, surrounded by only the Scottish monastery *(see Schottenstift below)* and its church. This Benedictine monastery granted the right of asylum to any fugitive from justice, except murderers. From the 17C, the present palaces were built around Freyung: Ferstel (No 2), Harrach (No 3), Kinsky (No 4), and Schönborn-Battyány (No 4 Renngasse, *see below*).

In the centre is the **Austria-Brunnen**, a fountain by Ludwig Schwanthaler and Ferdinand Miller (1846). Its allegorical figures represent the four main rivers of the Austrian Empire: the Po, Elbe, Vistula and Danube. It is said that Alma von Goethe, the poet's granddaughter, was the model for the figure of Austria; she died at the age of 17.

Schottenkirche – *Freyung near 6.* Since its construction was begun in 1155, the church of Our Lady of the Scots *(for the origin of the name, see Schottenstift below)* has experienced several destructive episodes. The present building is the result of 15C alterations and Baroque refurbishments by Andrea d'Allio and Silvestro Carlone between 1638 and 1648. The most characteristic feature of the church is undeniably its fine onion-shaped bell tower.

Inside, the Romanesque chapel houses the much-venerated **statue of the Virgin**, the oldest of its kind in the city (c 1250). Other works of note are *The Assumption and The Martyrdom of St Sebastian* by Tobias Pock (c 1655) and *The Departure of the Apostles Peter and Paul* and *The Crucifixion* by Joachim von Sandrart (1652).

This church was the setting on 15 June 1809 for Joseph Haydn's memorial service.

★**Schottenstift** – *Freyung 6.* In the days when missionaries set sail from Ireland and the Scottish island of Iona to convert the Germans on the Continent, Ireland was still known as New Scotland. Hence, the Irish Benedictine monks who came from

Canaletto – *Freyung Seen from the Southeast*

97

City Centre and the Ring

Ratisbon to Vienna became known as Scotsmen. In 1155, in the reign of Henry II Jasomirgott, they founded the monastery which is still known today as Abbey of the Scots.

After 17C and 18C alterations, the monastery buildings underwent a complete renovation from 1826 to 1832 by Josef Kornhäusel. Among other things, they at present house a famous grammar school which has counted Victor Adler, Johann Nestroy, Johann Strauss and the last emperor of Austria, Karl I, among its students.

Museum im Schottenstift ☉ – *Entrance through the cloister store next to the church. 1st floor.* This art gallery contains Biedermeier furniture and handicrafts, some striking 17C still-lifes by Christian Luyckx, Alexander Coosemans and Nicolaas van Veerendael, and also paintings by Peter Paul Rubens *(Christ as Salvator Mundi)*, Christian Seybold *(Self-Portrait*, c 1755), Giovanni Battista Pittoni *(The Sacrifice of Abraham*, c 1720), David Vinckboons *(Alpine Landscape*, 1602), Jan Provost *(Jonah Hurled in the Waves*, 1465), Tobias Pock *(Coronation of the Virgin*, c 1655), Joachim von Sandrart *(Celestial Glory*, 1671), and many other works by important artists from the Baroque and Biedermeier eras. The star exhibit is the **Schottenaltar★★** (altarpiece of the Scots) dating from about 1470; it was created by an unknown artist who became known as the "Scottish Master". This late Gothic work occupies a room specially designed for it and comprises 19 panels (originally 24). One of its most interesting features is the way it conveys a picture of medieval Vienna. For example, in *The Flight into Egypt*, the fortified city walls, Kärntner Strasse and, in the background, the cathedral with its south tower are all clearly visible. Those who know the city well can amuse themselves by identifying silhouettes of buildings still visible today, such as the Romanesque tower of Peterskirche (St Peter's Church). Others will enjoy the perusal of scenes from the lives of Christ or the Virgin in a Viennese context, as in the first panel of the series, *Christ's Entry into Jerusalem*.

Schottenhof – Between 1869 and 1886, the Court of the Scots harboured a famous occupant at No 3: Franz Liszt, who stayed here when he gave recitals in Vienna. At No 7 of this square is "Schubladkastenhaus", the "chest-of-drawers house", a Viennese nickname due to its resemblance to Biedermeier furniture. It is the former monastery priory built in 1774 by Andreas or Franz Zach. At No 4 Renngasse is the **Schönborn-Battyány palace**, redesigned by Johann Fischer von Erlach at the end of the 17C.

Palais Kinsky – *Freyung 4.* Johann Lukas von Hildebrandt built this mansion for the Imperial Count Daun between 1713 and 1716. It is a remarkable, and probably the finest, example of Baroque civil architecture in the city. The splendid **façade★** displays a rich assortment of escutcheons, statues, huge pilasters, varied pediments and sculpted motifs. Above the monumental porch with its telamones is a pointed concave pediment.

MUSEUM IM SCHOTTENSTIFT/Wien

Vienna's Schottenaltar – *The Flight into Egypt*

A great patron of the arts, Prince Ferdinand Johann Kinsky distinguished himself at the battle of Aspern (1809) and received the Order of Maria Theresa from Archduke Karl. He died at the age of 30 after falling from his horse in his estate in Weltrus, in Bohemia. This colonel was at the height of his fame in 1809 when he decided to detain Ludwig van Beethoven in Vienna. The composer had been summoned to Kassel by Jerome of Westphalia. Together with Joseph von Lobkowitz and Archduke Rudolf, Kinsky offered the German composer a life annuity of 4 000 florins if he would remain in Austria. Unfortunately for the great composer who dedicated his *Mass in C major* to the "noble prince", the Austrian currency devalued in 1811.

Palais Harrach ⊘ (**P³**) – *Freyung 3*. Ferdinand Bonaventura Count Harrach began the building of this palace in 1689 according to plans by Domenico Martinelli; it was completed by Johann Lukas von Hildebrandt. In 1845 the palace was heavily modified through the removal of the gables on the main façade and the redesign of the courtyard. The building, which was severely damaged by aerial bombing in 1944, was restored to its original Baroque condition by 1952. Since 1994, it has been leased to the Kunsthistorisches Museum and is used for exhibitions, readings, lectures and concerts.

Palais Ferstel (**P²**) – *Freyung 2 and Herrengasse 14*. In 1860, Heinrich von Ferstel built the palace which bears his name; he was also the architect of the Votivkirche, Universität and Österreichisches Museum für Angewandte Kunst (Austrian Museum of Applied Arts) on the Ring. The building once housed the National Bank and the Stock Exchange.

Freyung Passage is a small but very elegant shopping arcade linking Herrengasse to Freyung. It has an attractive interior courtyard containing the **Donaunixenbrunnen** (fountain of the Danube sprites) by Anton Dominik Fernkorn (1861). The Palais Ferstel also houses the famous **Café Central** (*entrance at Herrengasse 14, see below*).

3 BIS/MICHELIN

The shopping arcade in Palais Ferstel

Kunstforum Bank Austria ⊘ (**M¹⁴**) – *Freyung 8*. The Arts Forum of the Bank of Austria stages large thematic exhibitions. Gustav Peihl designed the exhibition hall in 1987; the gilt metal ball above the entrance is in homage to Josef Maria Olbrich's Secession pavilion.

South of the square, turn into Heidenschuss. Before reaching Am Hof square, notice the beautiful Jugendstil façade of the Engel-Apotheke at No 9 Bognerstrasse (the latter street is an extension of Heidenschuss).

AM HOF AND THE OLD JEWISH QUARTER

Am Hof – There was once a Roman camp on the site of this square, which has always been one of the liveliest in the city – from the 12C to the 15C, it was a setting for tournaments. Its name, "At Court", refers to the fact that Henry II Jasomirgott, first Duke of Austria, settled there when he chose Vienna as his ducal capital in 1156.

Mariensäule – The Virgin Mary's Pillar in the centre of the square dates from 1647. It is crowned by the statue of the Virgin (1667) by Balthasar Herold. It stands on a pedestal flanked by armed cherubs fighting the scourges which are symbolised by animals: War (a lion), Plague (a basilisk), Famine (a dragon) and Heresy (a serpent).

Römische Baureste ⊘ – *Am Hof 9*. Traces of the Roman camp are visible here.

Feuerwehrmuseum ⊘ – *Am Hof 7*. There are about 400 exhibits in the Fire Service Museum tracing the history of firefighting (vehicles, equipment, uniforms, pictures, etc).

B. Kaufmann

Am Hof – The Fire Station

Kirche zu den neun Chören der Engel (K⁸) – *Am Hof bei 13.* A Jesuit church, the Church of the Nine Choirs of Angels has as its chief attraction a Baroque façade (1662) by the Italian architect Carlo Antonio Carlone; the façade has never undergone alterations. The remarkable design of the balcony was ahead of its time. A herald appeared on it on 6 August 1806 to proclaim Emperor Franz II's abdication of the imperial privileges, in other words, the end of the Holy Roman Empire of the German Nation. The interior of the church contains an interesting high altar executed by Johann Georg Däringer (1798); it shows the Virgin and the nine choirs of angels (according to the invocations in the Litany of the Blessed Virgin to Mary, queen of the angels).

There are other interesting sights on the square. At No 13, the Collalto palace (1671) displays its pointed pediments; supposedly, it was this palace rather than Schönbrunn which was the setting of Mozart's first concert at the age of 6. At No 12, a Baroque house (c 1730) with a façade in the style of Johan Lukas von Hildebrandt. At No 10, Bürgerliches Zeughaus or the burghers' former arsenal is now the headquarters of the Fire Brigade; above the Neoclassical pediment of the façade by Anton Ospel (1732) are **sculptures** by Lorenzo Mattielli.

Northeast of the square, take Drahtgasse.

Judenplatz – In 1783, Mozart occupied Nos 3 and 4 of this square, soon after his marriage to Constanze Weber. At No 11 is the rear façade of the former Chancellery of Bohemia *(see City Centre and the Ring, Hoher Markt).*

At No 2, the façade of the "Jordan House" has a late Gothic relief (1497) depicting the Baptism of Christ in the Jordan. The Latin diatribe below it refers to the expulsion and murder of Vienna's Jews in 1421 *(see below, Museum Judenplatz).* The pogrom is seen as atoning for alleged crimes committed by the Jews, just as sins were wiped out by the baptism in the Jordan. In the northern half of the square, the **Mahnmal für die Opfer der Shoa in Österreich** (monument for the victims of the Shoa in Austria – Shoa is the Hebrew word for Holocaust). The artist Rachel Whiteread chose a library as symbolic of the Jewish people – a people of the book, whose religious buildings are called "schools". Yet the visible pages face the observer here; the books are not clearly to be identified by their covers. The door to the library is closed, representing the irretrievable loss of lives. On the ground, the places where Austrian Jews were killed by the Nazi terror regime are listed.

Museum Judenplatz ⊙ – *Judenplatz 8.* Vienna's first Jewish community was eradicated in 1421. The Jews were persecuted due to alleged desecration of a Eucharistic Host, and many were killed. Eighty members of the Jewish community shut themselves up in the synagogue to avoid a forced baptism; when the building was surrounded, they decided to kill themselves by setting fire to the building. The Museum Judenplatz is dedicated to the memory of this medieval synagogue. In the subterranean rooms, the synagogue and the Jewish quarter looking as it did around the year 1400 are reconstructed by computer animation and shown in the form of video projections *(10 minutes each; headphones at the cashier's).* Multimedia installations present the Gesera (the Jewish chronicle of the events of 1420-21), the Jewish community, feasts and ceremonies as well as providing information about the office of Rabbi. In addition, excavations of the foundations of the original synagogue and objects from medieval times can be viewed. The hexagon of the "Bima", where the lectern used to stand, is indicated on the ground on Judenplatz, next to the monument.

A **Documentary Room** for the victims of the Shoa in Austria (1938-45) is located on the ground floor. One can get historical information or learn about victims and culprits using the computers set up here.

Take Kurrentgasse, a charming street featuring the pink and white façade of No 12, with its attractive portal (c 1730). At the end of the street, take the first on the right for Schulhof.

★ **Uhrenmuseum der Stadt Wien** ⊙ (**M**[17]) – *Schulhof 2.* Vienna's Clock Museum is housed in the Harfenhaus, one of the oldest houses in the city. It occupies three floors and traces the aesthetic and technical development of timepieces from the 15C to the 20C, using about 1 000 examples. Among the tower clocks, grill spits running on clockworks, artistic clocks, Biedermeier Laterndl and grandfather clocks on exhibit, some exceptional examples await the viewer: the clockwork (1699) from the Stephansdom, an astrological and astronomical grandfather clock by Joachim Oberkircher, and a splendid **astronomical clock★** (1769) made by Brother David a Sancto Cajetano from Vienna (Room 4). In the third floor, one may admire pocket watches from the most famous clock manufacturers, as well as seeing and hearing automatons and flute clocks.

Puppen- und Spielzeugmuseum ⊙ (**M**[16]) – *Schulhof 4, 1st floor.* The 4 rooms of the Doll and Toy Museum specialise mainly in antique porcelain dolls. Of special interest are those in the Queen Anne (c 1750), Empire (c 1800) and Biedermeier styles.

South of Schulhof, turn right into Seitzergasse then turn left into Bognergasse. At the end of it, turn right for Kohlmarkt.

HOFBURG DISTRICT

Kohlmarkt – The former coal market, now a pedestrian zone, is lined with some of the most luxurious shops in the city. At the corner of Wallnerstrasse, at No 6, is the **Thonet** furniture shop. Farther along on the same side, at No 14, is the tearoom **Demel**, one of Vienna's major institutions. Following its foundation in 1785 on Michaelerplatz by Christoph Demel, it moved to the Kohlmarkt in 1857; after just a taste of one of their pastries, it is easy to see why Demel's was supplier of confectionery to the imperial court. Still on the right at No 16 is the **Manz** bookshop which Adolf Loos designed in 1912 (it has undergone several alterations since then). On the left at No 9 is **Artariahaus** (1902) by Max Fabiani. This building is an important milestone in the history of the Viennese Secession movement, since it is a precursor of the Looshaus *(see below).* Joseph Haydn lived in **Grosses Michaelerhaus** (1720) at No 11.

Take Wallnerstrasse.

Wallnerstrasse – This street is almost as elegant as Herrengasse *(see below)* running parallel to it. It boasts fine edifices such as: the Lamberg palace (No 3), nicknamed Kaiserhaus because Emperor Franz I held audience there; the Esterházy palace (No 4), built between 1809 and 1813 to designs by the Frenchman Charles de Moreau, and the residence of Otto von Bismarck in 1892; the Caprara-Geymüller palace (No 8) built by the Italian Domenico Egidio Rossi for Enea Silvio Caprara about 1698 and purchased in 1798 by the banker Jakob Geymüller; its Pompeiian drawing room is on view at the Historisches Museum der Stadt Wien *(see Outside the Ring, Wieden).*

At the end of Wallnerstrasse, bear left for Herrengasse.

Herrengasse – The "Lords' Street", which still today is surrounded with the aristocratic flair of a past era, links Freyung to Michaelerplatz. Municipal palaces such as the Palais Ferstel (No 14, *see above*) or the Palais Mollard-Clary (No 9) are lined up one after the other. The Innenministerium (Ministry of the Interior) is housed in the former Modena palace (No 7) dating from the 16C, its façade remodelled in the early 19C by Ludwig Pichl and Giacomo Quarenghi; the Wilczek palace (No 5, 1737) was home to the poets Franz Grillparzer and Joseph von Eichendorff.

Café Central – *Herrengasse 14.* This café, located in the Palais Ferstel, reopened in 1986. It was a famous meeting place for artists and intellectuals such as the writers Peter Altenberg (immortalised in a papier maché sculpture at the entrance), Franz Werfel and Stefan Zweig, and no less a luminary than Trotsky, who founded *Pravda* in Vienna.

Palais Mollard-Clary – Herrengasse 9. This palace with its Rocaille-ornamented rooms dates from 1689 and once housed the Niederösterreichisches Landesmuseum (which is now in St Pölten, the capital of Lower Austria). The inner courtyard is graced by a fountain with an artistically pleasing wrought-iron lattice (1570).

★ **Michaelerplatz** – West of St Michael's Square is the elegant St Michael's wing of the Hofburg, at the far end of Kohlmarkt. For anyone visiting Vienna, this square is an essential tourist attraction. In the centre are the two-thousand-year-old Roman ruins uncovered during digs in 1992.

At No 2, **Café Griensteidl** is a descendant of the first great Viennese literary café of the same name. The original had been a centre for young writers such as Hugo von Hofmannsthal, who made it his intellectual home. Its patrons were so intent on remaking the world that it was nicknamed the "delusions-of-grandeur café". The new café has an unimpeded view of Michaelertrakt.

City Centre and the Ring

At No 3, Adolf Loos built the **Looshaus** from 1909 to 1911 for the firm of Goldman & Salatsch. This building, listed in 1947, is one of his best-known works. It made a considerable impact, since from its position in the Innere Stadt opposite the Hofburg, it epitomised the difference between the architecture of the old town and the new. During its construction, there was controversy both among the public and the city councillors, who wanted to clothe the "indecent nudity" of the upper section. The dispute grew so heated that the police closed the building site. Finally, the city council tired of these complications and Loos' inflexibility and allowed the architect to finish his "house without eyebrows". It seems that Franz Josef avoided looking at it by keeping the palace curtains drawn. Today, the Raiffeisenbank Wien occupies the Looshaus; the counters on the ground floor are open to the public, and the floor above opens for temporary exhibitions.

Michaelerkirche ⊙ – *Michaelerplatz 1.* St Michael's Church was the former Court parish church and dates from 1220. It has undergone many alterations. Its octagonal tower dates from 1340, the spire from 1598 and the Neoclassical façade from 1792.

During the months in which the exhibition is open, the church's interior can only be viewed in the context of the exhibition or through the grating. Access to the exhibition through the Michaeler-durchgang (passage) on the right of the church. Next to the entrance is a limestone relief depicting the *Mount of Olives* (1494).

There were additions to the church in the 14C and renovations in the 16C. The **interior** is a mixture of styles, including Gothic: the choir (1327) and remains of frescoes, particularly on the triumphal arch; Renaissance: Georg von Liechtenstein's tombstone (1548) against the last pillar of the right side-aisle; Baroque: David Sielber's great organ (1714), Michelangelo Unterberger's *Fall of the Angel* (1751) in the right arm of the

3 BIS/MICHELIN

Michaelerkirche – The high altar

transept and the high altar (1781) by Jean Baptiste d'Avrange, with carved figures by Johann Martin Fischer and Jakob Philipp Prokop and above it a remarkable **Fall of the Angel**★ by Karl Georg Merville (1782). This group is the last religious work in Baroque style of Viennese origin.

In addition to the church's interior, the **exhibition** offers the opportunity to view: a rich collection of liturgical instruments and robes (since this was the Court parish church); the splendidly fitted cloister refectory *(entrance via the courtyard)*; a presentation of the church's and cloister's history; a small gallery of paintings; funereal crowns, insignias and mourning garments honouring past emperors; and the late Romanesque transept portal. During the week, tours of the crypt (which essentially extends underneath the entire church and a little beyond) are offered several times a day.

The entrance to the crypt lies next to the north side altar with an altarpiece by Franz Anton Maulbertsch (1755). After St Michael's cemetery was closed in 1508, the various sepulchres were subsequently installed under the church. Up until 1784, parish archives reported that about 4 000 people from all social strata were interred here. As a result of the favourable climate, wooden caskets and mummies from the 17C and 18C have stayed well preserved in the crypt. An ossuary and several open coffins add to the eerie atmosphere. It is also the burial place of Pietro Trapassi (1698-1782), known as Metastasio, official Court Poet and a protégé of Maria Theresa.

Cross the square for Schauflergasse.

Bundeskanzleramt – The former Privy Court Chancellery houses the Office of the Federal Chancellor. It was built to plans by Johann Lukas von Hildebrandt and underwent several alterations. On 25 July 1934, Chancellor Engelbert Dollfuss was killed by a local SS unit.

Turn right into Bruno-Kreisky-Gasse.

Minoritenplatz – Several palaces surround the square, including the Liechtenstein palace (No 4, *see also Bankgasse, below*) and Starhemberg palace at No 5 (mid-17C).

Minoritenkirche ⊘ – The Minorite monastery and church the Holy Cross were founded under the Babenberger Duke **Leopold VI**. In the first half of the 14C, Fra Giacomo from Paris erected the present church, which received a Baroque face lift in the 17C and 18C but regained its Gothic appearance at the end of the 18C. The main portal displays a fine *Crucifixion* (1350) also accredited to Fra Giacomo. Today the church is used by Vienna's Italian community.

The interior is striking with its almost square design and its three aisles of equal height. On the left wall is a massive mosaic copy by Giacomo Raffaelli of Leonardo's *Last Supper*. Napoleon commissioned it in Milan as a replacement for the original fresco which he wished to transfer to Paris. Next to it, the bas-relief of the Virgin is by Antonio Rosselino. Against the left pillar of the nave is a 15C fresco of St Francis of Assisi, which has been taken down. Further Gothic fragments of the building are on view on the ground floor of the Historical Museum of the City of Vienna *(see Outside the Ring, Wieden).*

Take Petrarcagasse for Bankgasse.

Bankgasse – This is another street lined with splendid palaces. At No 2, the **Palais Battyány** (c 1695) is in the style of Johann Bernhard Fischer von Erlach. At Nos 4 and 6, the Hungarian Embassy, concealed behind a communal façade (1784) by Franz Anton Hillebrand, occupies the **Trautson** and **Strattmann-Windischgrätz** palaces. At No 9, **Stadtpalais Liechtenstein** was originally built for Count Kaunitz. Three architects worked on it: Domenico Martinelli, Antonio Riva and Gabriel de Gabrieli from 1694 to 1706. The façade is a magnificent creation with its monumental portal and sculptures by Giovanni Giuliani.

Continue behind Burgtheater and bear right into Oppolzergasse, at right angles to Schreyvogelgasse.

Dreimäderlhaus – *Schreyvogelgasse 10. Closed to the public.* According to one tradition, Franz Schubert gave voice and piano lessons to three young ladies here, hence the name "three maiden house".

Return up Schreyvogelgasse and turn right into Mölkerbastei.

★ **Beethoven-Gedenkstätte Pasqualatihaus** ⊘ – *Mölkerbastei 8. 4th floor, no lift.* This late 18C mansion bears the name of its owner, Josef Benedikt, Baron Pasqualati. It houses one of the three memorial sites in Vienna commemorating **Ludwig van Beethoven** *(see also Outside the Ring, Döbling, Heiligenstadt – Testamenthaus, and Oberdöbling – Eroicahaus).*

AKG PARIS

Manuscript version of the *Fifth Symphony* by Ludwig van Beethoven

In 1804 and from 1813 to 1815, the composer lived in two rooms on the 4th floor, with an unimpeded view, as the Ring had not yet been built. Among other things, he wrote the opera *Fidelio* there, first performed at the Theater an der Wien, as well as his *Fourth*, *Fifth* and *Seventh Symphonies*. The museum displays various objects and documents relating to the composer of the immortal *Ninth Symphony*. Among other mementoes such as contemporary views of Vienna and portraits of people whom Beethoven knew, there are also facsimiles of scores, including *Fidelio* (1805). In addition, Beethoven's life mask (1811-12) and several portraits including an oil painting (1804-05) by W. J. Mähler and a bust by Franz Klein (1812) are on exhibit here. It is possible to listen to extracts from his works *(earphones)*, such as excerpts from *Fidelio*, *Coriolan* or *Egmont*, which makes an agreeable way of rounding off the visit.

Besides the first part of the Ring, the nearest sights are: the Hofburg, the tour around Stephansdom, the Hoher Markt and Kapuzinerkirche Districts (to be found in the City Centre and the Ring section), as well as the Alsergrund and Josefstadt Districts (found in the Outside the Ring section).

HOFBURG★★★

Local map page 13, **JR**
Underground: Herrengasse (U3), Volkstheater (U2, U3)
Tram: Burgring (1, 2, D, J), Dr. Karl-Renner-Ring (1, 2, 46, 49, D, J)
Bus: Burgring (57A), Dr. Karl-Renner-Ring (48A), Heldenplatz (2A), Michaelerplatz (2A, 3A)

The imperial palace, favourite residence of the Habsburgs, became progressively larger over the centuries. There are no traces of the original building, a quadrilateral bristling with towers built in the second half of the 13C. This fortress had been built as a defence against the Turkish and Hungarian attacks upon Vienna, which continued until the end of the 17C. In their efforts to turn it into a palace, sovereigns continually enlarged and embellished their residence. This accounts for the juxtaposition of widely differing styles in this varied assortment of buildings.

Among the oldest are the Hofburgkapelle (chapel, mid-15C), Schweizertor (Swiss gate, mid-16C), Amalienhof (16C), and Stallburg (stables, 16C). In the 17C, Leopold I had the Leopoldinischer Trakt (Leopold wing) built. At the beginning of the 18C, Karl VI commissioned major alterations from the greatest Baroque architects in the empire, Johann Bernhard and Josef Emmanuel Fischer von Erlach and Johann Lukas von Hildebrandt. They built the Reichskanzleitrakt (Chancellery Wing), Winterreitschule (Winter Riding School) which now houses the Spanish Riding School, and Prunksaaltrakt (now the National Library); the Albertina dates from about the same period. Following the erection of Michaelertrakt (St Michael's Wing, completed in 1893), work started on Neue Burg after the construction of the Ring; its completion just before 1914 marked the end of the monumental history of the imperial palace. Despite numerous alterations, the Hofburg has retained the austerity of its military origins; put to the test in 1287, when, enraged by an unpleasant ruling by the councillors, the Viennese besieged the castle.

A TOWN WITHIN A TOWN

This is indeed a town within a town: squares, gardens and buildings lie at the very heart of the Austrian capital, covering a total area of 24 000m²/287 03sq yd.

History records in the *Continuatio vidobonensis* that in 1275, Ottokar II Przemysl, the King of Bohemia and Duke of Moravia, built an impregnable castle in Vienna on the site of the present Schweizerhof. It is probable that even in the 15C this castle included state apartments. It is known that Sigismund of Luxemburg, King of Hungary, resided there in 1422 with some church dignitaries; four years later, John I, King of Portugal also stayed there. When, in 1533, Ferdinand, the King of Bohemia and Hungary, moved the central administration of the States of Prague to Vienna, it became necessary to enlarge the palace and endow it with apartments fit for the future Emperor Ferdinand I. In fact, it became the residence of all the sovereigns thereafter. This heralded the birth of the Hofburg, a colossal creation in stone, symbolising the Austro-Hungarian empire and reminding us that the House of Austria once ruled from Castile to the West Indies.

The following section describes the Hofburg complex's exterior architecture and the squares dividing it; the next section describes the museums, galleries and other sights open to the public.

THE HOFBURG COMPLEX

The view of the Neue Burg from Volksgarten, particularly at night (see illustration), is one of the most impressive in the Hofburg. However, it is preferable to approach the palace from Michaelerplatz.

★**Michaelerplatz** – *See City Centre and the Ring. Freyung District* – This square does not form part of the Hofburg, but it leads to the imperial palace from the town centre via Kohlmarkt. This is the same route that the emperor and his family took on their way back to their apartments or audience chambers.

★**Michaelertrakt** – The semicircular façade of the M i c h a e l e r t r a k t (St Michael's Wing) faces towards Michaelerplatz. Although Josef Emanuel Fischer von Erlach had prepared plans for it, it was not built until between 1888 and 1893. This followed Emperor Franz Josef's decision to link the Reichkanzleitrakt (Chancellery Wing) and the Winterreitschule (Winter Riding School); the old Burgtheater had moved to a new building on the Ring and therefore no longer prevented the construction of the Michaelertrakt. The façade displays

J. Malbure/MICHELIN

Michaelertrakt fountain – Military might

two monumental fountains adorned by statues symbolising naval power on the left (Rudolf Weyr, 1895) and military might on the right (Edmund Helmer, 1897). **The Michaelertor**★ is a gateway flanked with groups depicting the Labours of Hercules. Its superb wrought-iron gates open into the rotunda. The outline of the **dome**★ of the Michaelertrakt is among the most elegant and famous sights in Vienna.

There is a splendid view of the steeple of St Michael's church through the wrought-iron tracery of Michaelertor. There are also niches with statues representing the imperial mottoes of Karl VI, *Constantia et fortitudine* (Perseverance and Courage), Maria Theresa, *Justitia et clementia* (Justice and Mercy), Josef II, *Virtute et exemplo* (Courage and Example), and Franz Josef, *Viribus unitis* (United Strength). The rotunda leads to the Kaiserappartements, Hofsilber- und Tafelkammer, Esperanto-Museum and Spanische Reitschule *(see below)*.

In der Burg – This courtyard, once the Franzenplatz, used to be the setting for horse races and tournaments. In its centre stands a statue of the Emperor Franz II by Pompeo Marchesi (1846). A Latin inscription on the base is a quotation from his will: "My love to my peoples".

To the south of this inner courtyard is **Schweizertor**★, the Swiss gate built in 1552 (presumably by Pietro Ferrabosco). This Renaissance gate, named after the Swiss guard manning it in 1748, replaced a drawbridge across the moat, traces of which are still visible along Alte Burg. The cartouche bears the name of Ferdinand I, ruler of Germany, Hungary, Bohemia, Spain, Austria and Burgundy.

Amalientrakt – The Amalia Wing, named after the empress who lived there in the 18C, was built in 1577 by Pietro Ferrabosco and completed in 1610 by Hans Schneider and Antonio de Moys. It was originally detached from the other buildings. Empress Elizabeth's apartments and those occupied by Tsar Alexander *(see below, Museums and Galleries, Kaiserappartements)* are open to the public. The palace surrounds Amalienhof, a trapezoid courtyard with a fine ornate gate.

Leopoldinischer Trakt – The Leopold Wing was the headquarters of Count Starhemberg who defended the city from the Turks during the 1683 siege. It was built in the reign of Leopold I to link the Amalia Wing to the rest of the Hofburg. Building work began in 1660 to designs by Filiberto Lucchese but the wing was burnt down in 1668 and was subsequently rebuilt by Giovanni Pietro Tencala. This wing, which accommodated Marie-Theresa and her husband, Franz-Stefan, now houses the department of the President of the Federal Republic of Austria. His personal office is Josef II's former study.

Reichskanzleitrakt – In 1723, Johann Bernhard Fischer von Erlach began the Chancellery Wing opposite the Leopold Wing. The architect died in April of the same year. The façade was not completed until 1730, closing off In der Burg

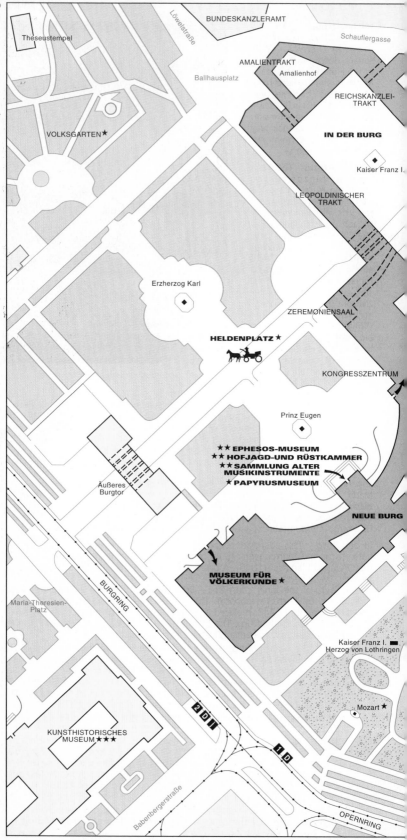

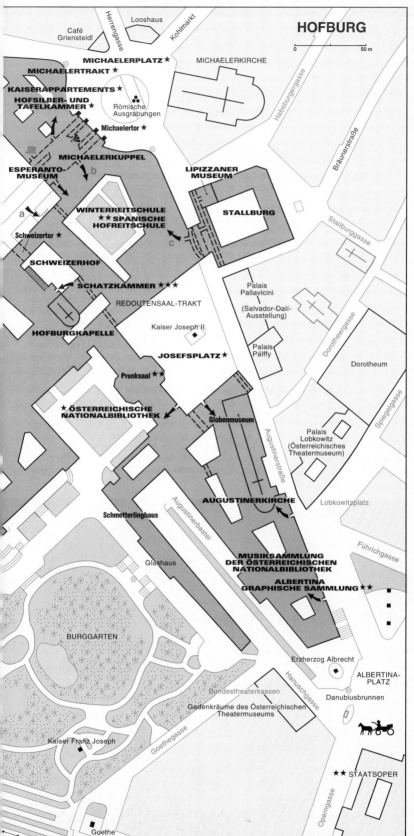

HOFBURG

0   50 m

Café Griensteidl

Herrengasse

Looshaus

Kohlmarkt

MICHAELERKIRCHE

Habsburgergasse

Bräunerstraße

MICHAELERPLATZ ★

MICHAELERTRAKT ★

KAISERAPPARTEMENTS ★

HOFSILBER- UND TAFELKAMMER ★

Römische Ausgrabungen

Michaelertor ★

MICHAELERKUPPEL

b

ESPERANTO-MUSEUM

LIPIZZANER MUSEUM

a

WINTERREITSCHULE ★★ SPANISCHE HOFREITSCHULE

STALLBURG

Stallburggasse

c

Schweizertor ★

SCHWEIZERHOF

SCHATZKAMMER ★★★

REDOUTENSAAL-TRAKT

Palais Pallavicini

(Salvador-Dalí-Ausstellung)

Dorotheergasse

HOFBURGKAPELLE

Kaiser Joseph II.

Palais Pálffy

Dorotheum

JOSEFSPLATZ ★

Spiegelgasse

Prunksaal ★★

★ ÖSTERREICHISCHE NATIONALBIBLIOTHEK

Globenmuseum

Augustinerstraße

Palais Lobkowitz (Österreichisches Theatermuseum)

AUGUSTINERKIRCHE

Lobkowitzplatz

Schmetterlinghaus

Augustinerbastei

Führichgasse

MUSIKSAMMLUNG DER ÖSTERREICHISCHEN NATIONALBIBLIOTHEK

Glashaus

ALBERTINA GRAPHISCHE SAMMLUNG ★★

BURGGARTEN

Erzherzog Albrecht

ALBERTINA-PLATZ

Bundestheaterkassen

Hanuschgasse

Danubiusbrunnen

Gedenkräume des Österreichischen Theatermuseums

Kaiser Franz Joseph

Goethegasse

★★ STAATSOPER

Operngasse

Goethe

107

courtyard. Johan Lukas von Hildebrandt designed the wing on Schauflergasse which dates from 1723. Franz Josef's apartments are open to the public *(see below, Museums and Collections, Kaiserappartements)*.

Schweizerhof – The Swiss Courtyard is the oldest part of the Hofburg, forming the very heart of the Alte Burg or old palace. In the mid-16C, Ferdinand I turned Alte Burg into a Renaissance palace. Traces of its style are still visible around the window frames on each of the four façades. The courtyard leads to Hofburgkapelle and Schatzkammer *(see below, Museums and Collections)*.

Take the arched passageway at the southeast corner of the courtyard.

★ **Josefsplatz** – This well-proportioned square is one of the finest in Vienna. It resembles a main courtyard and owes its name to the equestrian statue of Josef II in the centre (Franz Anton Zauner, 1806). During the 1848 revolution, this monument served as a rallying point for supporters of the Habsburgs.

At Nos 1 and 2 is the present Österreichisches Nationalbibliothek *(see below, Museums and Collections)*, the former Court Library, built by the Fischer von Erlach dynasty of architects (1723 to 1726). Its main façade, with alterations by Nikolaus Pacassi, is very effective; the masonry base with its splayed ridges pierced by an undecorated portal is reminiscent of the Renaissance; the Ionic order of pilasters on the upper storeys evokes the French 17C pre-Classical style. The decorative features at this level are well worth close study; a quadriga and immense golden globes borne by telamones emerge into view. Behind this façade is a magnificent hall of state, the Prunksaal.

At No 3, the Redoutensaaltrakt (Redoute Chamber Wing) was the setting for court masked balls. Its façade, also by Pacassi (1770) harmonises with that of the Nationalbibliothek. The two ballrooms, built to designs by Jean-Nicolas Jadot de Ville-Issey (about 1748) were decorated by Ferdinand Hetzendorf von Hohenberg, architect of the Schönbrunn Gloriette, in 1760. A fire entirely destroyed the small festival hall on 27 November 1992, but it has since then been entirely restored. Every year, the Kaiserball takes place in the large festival hall with its coffered ceiling resting on 24 marble Corinthian columns. The elite of Viennese society attend this ball.

The fourth side of the square is closed off by the **Pallavicini** (No 5; today housing the Salvador Dali exhibit; *see City Centre and the Ring, Kapuzinerkirche District*) and **Pálffy palaces** (No 6). Ferdinand Hetzendorf von Hohenberg built the first of these in 1784. It has a fine portal with caryatids and an attic adorned with statues, both by Franz Anton Zauner. It was the residence of a great patron of music, Count Fries. The building no longer bears his name, which however is preserved for posterity in the dedication of Beethoven's *Seventh Symphony*. The other palace, built in 1575, was the setting for Mozart's first production of *The Marriage of Figaro*.

Josefsplatz

B. Kaufmann

Stallburg – *Entrance at Reitschulgasse No 2.* A glassed-in arcade separates this palace from the Spanishe Hofreitschule (Royal Spanish Riding School). Ferdinand I had it built, between 1558 and 1565, for his son, Archduke Maximilian. When Maximilian ascended the throne, he moved to the Hofburg and the Maximilian palace was converted: the ground floor of the three storeys surrounding the Renaissance courtyard became stables for the horses of the Court. Then, from 1593 to 1766, the first floor housed the imperial pages. Since Karl VI's reign, the stables have been home to the Lipizzaner stallions of the Spanische Hofreitschule; the Lipizzaner-Museum *(see below, Museums and Collections)* offers more information on this subject.

Winterreitschule – Opposite Stallburg is the Winter Riding School, used for performances by the Spanish Riding School. It was built by Josef Emanuel Fischer von Erlach from 1729 to 1735 *(interior: see below, Museums and Collections, Spanische Hofreitschule).*

Return to In der Burg to reach Heldenplatz via the arched passageway.

3BIS/MICHELIN

★**Heldenplatz** – In 1809, the parade ground on the site of fortifications dismantled by Napoleon became the Heroes' Square after the unveiling of two equestrian statues designed by Anton Dominik Fernkorn. One depicted Prince Eugène of Savoy, the victor of the Turks in the 17C, while the other was of Archduke Karl, who defeated Napoleon at Aspern in 1809.

Standing with your back to Volksgarten, the buildings seen from left to right are: the Amalia Palace and Leopold Wing *(see above)*, the façade of the Hall of Ceremonies built by the Belgian architect Louis Montoyer in 1806, the Kongresszentrum (Congress centre) built by the same architect from 1802 to 1806, and Neue Burg *(see below)*. The fan-shaped façade of this palace overlooks the square. The view extends past the shady Volksgarten to the tower of Neues Rathaus.

Southwest of the square, Äusseres Burgtor is a monumental gateway opening onto the Ring; Luigi Cagnola began it in 1821 and Pietro Nobile completed it in 1824. In 1934, Rudolf Wondracek converted it into a Heldendenkmal, a monument commemorating the victims of the First World War. After the Second World War a memorial was erected there to members of the Austrian resistance.

Neue Burg – The new imperial palace dating from between 1881 and 1913 is in the style of the Italian Renaissance. The architects, Carl von Hasenauer and Gottfried Semper intended to complement it on the northwest side by a similar complex, but this was never built. They had in fact planned to construct a gigantic imperial forum, but Franz Josef was satisfied with this impressive wing bordering the Ring. Beneath the colonnade in the gallery, statues between the bays represent outstanding figures from Austrian history. The interior of Neue Burg was not completed until 1926; it houses the following museums: Ephesos-Museum, Hofjagd- und Rüstkammer, Sammlung Alter Musikinstrumente, Papyrusmuseum, Museum für Völkerkunde *(see below, Museums and Collections)*.

Historical fact: it was from the balcony of Neue Burg that Adolf Hitler proclaimed the annexation of Austria in 1938. Literary event: Thomas Bernhard recounted this episode in his play *Heldenplatz*, produced in Vienna in 1988; it was met by vehement reactions and controversy, both among audiences and the press.

The gardens of the "Kaiserforums" – After the departure of the French in 1809 and the dismantling of the fortified walls on Napoleon's orders, it was decided to extend the imperial city, which had already reached impressive dimensions in the city centre. The public park and imperial gardens were laid out on the sites that had been cleared by Napoleon's engineers. The imperial garden later became known as the palace garden. With these new open spaces, Vienna began to lose its defensive character. This finally disappeared, when, in December 1857, Franz Josef signed the order for the dismantling of the ramparts.

Burggarten – *see City Centre and the Ring, the Ring, Opernring.*

Volksgarten – *see City Centre and the Ring, the Ring, Dr.-Karl-Renner-Ring.*

MUSEUMS AND COLLECTIONS
For a view of the individual buildings, see Hofburg map.

★**Kaiserappartements** ⊙ – The imperial apartments are a long succession of rooms. They occupy the first floor of the Reichskanzleitrakt and Amalientrakt (Chancellery and Amalia wings). Of the 2 600 rooms in the Hofburg palace, about twenty are open to the public. Maria Theresa's rooms and those of her son Josef II (Leopoldinischer Trakt) are now used by the President of the Republic and his departments. The **Kaiserstiege** (imperial staircase) leads to the apartments.

Archduke Stefan's apartments – These are named after the Palatine of Hungary who resided there from 1848 to 1867, in the wake of the Duke of the Free City, son of Napoleon I, and Archduchess Marie-Louise. Since their renovation in 2000, these rooms have housed special exhibits.

Emperor Franz Josef's apartments – Entering through the Trabantenstube, visitors reach the **Grosser Audienzsaal** (audience hall), where people patiently gathered twice a week in the hope of petitioning or thanking the emperor. Since the beginning of the 20C, the 80 lights on the Bohemian crystal chandelier have run on electricity, illuminating Peter Krafft's mural paintings of scenes from the life of Franz I. In the smaller **Audienzzimmer** (audience room) is the lectern on which lay the list of audiences; near it, the emperor awaited his petitioners. The last portrait of Franz Josef aged 85 by Heinrich Wassmuth rests on the easel; on the walls are portraits. From left to right they represent Franz I, Ferdinand I, Franz Josef aged 43, Ferdinand II attacked by the Protestants in 1619. In the **Konferenzzimmer** or council chamber, oil paintings by Anton Adam represent the battles of Temesvár and Komorn in 1849; on the end wall is a portrait showing Franz Josef aged 20. Franz Josef learned of the tragic death of his son, Crown Prince Rudolf *(see Further afield, Mayerling)*, in his **Arbeitszimmer**, or study. This contains Elisabeth's portrait by Franz Xaver Winterhalter and, on the side walls, paintings of the battle of Custozza in 1849

Johann Strauss the Younger and his Orchestra playing for the Court Ball, by Theo Zarche

and of the popular Marshal Radetzsky, to whom Johann Strauss the Elder dedicated a famous march and whose apartments were in a wing of the Alte Burg nearby. The concealed door in the wall leads to the valet's room. Above the fireplace is a portrait of the Russian Czar Alexander II. In the **Schlafzimmer** (bedroom), with its surprisingly Spartan iron bedstead, are several interesting items: four prints of Elisabeth; an oil painting of Archduchess Sophia with her son Franz Josef aged 2; a miniature on Augarten porcelain of Franz Josef aged 23 and Sissi aged 16. Beyond the bedchamber are two drawing rooms which were never used after Sissi's death in 1898: the **Grosser Salon** and **Kleiner Salon**. In the main drawing room are two magnificent **portraits**★ of Elisabeth and Franz Josef by Franz Xaver Winterhalter, and in the small drawing room a portrait of his brother Maximilian, who was executed in Mexico in 1867 by republican revolutionaries.

Empress Elisabeth's apartments – The rooms facing the courtyard were last occupied by the Empress Elisabeth, who is affectionately known as **Sissi**. The **Schlafzimmer** served both as bedroom and drawing room (in the latter case, the bed was hidden by a screen). In the **Toilettenzimmer** (bathroom) exercise rings (at the same level as the passage into the next room) convey the amount of care the empress, an excellent horsewoman, took of her physique and her figure; a wood carving by Anton Dominik Fernkorn shows her aged 8, and four watercolours depict Achilleion Palace, which she had built on Corfu. Notable among the exhibits (Louis XIV furniture, porcelain statuettes by Herman Klotz, Sèvres porcelain vases, etc.) in the **Grosser Salon** is the famous Italian artist Antonio Canova's marble bust (1817) of Elisa Bonaparte, Napoleon I's older sister. The **Kleiner Salon** was dedicated to the memory of the Empress Elisabeth after her assassination in Geneva in 1898: the display cabinet contains a small allegorical group realised just after her death; there is also a fine **portrait**★ of her as Queen of Hungary by Georg Raab.

Elisabeth as Queen of Hungary in royal attire by Georg Raab

Finally, the **Grosses Vorzimmer**, or grand antechamber, is adorned with paintings of Maria Theresa's children; the life-size statue of Empress Elisabeth is by Herman Klotz.

Tsar Alexander's apartments – These became known as Tsar Alexander I of Russia's apartments during the Congress of Vienna in 1815. From 1916 to 1918, Karl I used them as an audience chamber and study. Today, there are two presents to Elisabeth in the **Vorzimmer** (antechamber): a majestic set of kitchen scales and a sewing machine. The **Empfangsalon** (reception room) is adorned with **Gobelin tapestries★** woven in Paris between 1772 and 1776 after cartoons by François Boucher; they and the furniture were a present to Emperor Josef II from Louis XVI and his wife Marie Antoinette, daughter of Maria Theresa. In the **Speisezimmer** (dining room), the table is beautifully laid as in Franz Josef's day. There are six glasses for white wine, champagne, red wine, liqueur, water and dessert wine respectively. The last room, the **Kleiner Salon**, is a memorial to the two unfortunate heirs to Franz Josef's throne, Prince Rudolf who committed suicide at Mayerling, and Archduke Franz-Ferdinand, assassinated at Sarajevo. Portraits and busts of the last Austrian Emperor, Karl I, and his wife, the Empress Zita of Bourbon-Parma, are also to be seen here.

★ Hofsilber- und Tafelkammer ⓥ – As the rooms are not always clearly identified, numbers referring to items in the display cases appear in brackets in italics. Objects forming part of the Court porcelain and silver collections were in use until the fall of the Habsburgs in 1918.

The imperial table services include magnificent pieces such as the gilded bronze **Mailänder Tafelausatz★★** (Milan centrepiece) *(138-142)* commissioned in 1838 from Luigi Manfredini's Milanese workshop by Archduke Rainer, viceroy of the kingdom of Lombardy-Venetia, for a table 30m/98ft long and seating 100 guests. The dancers were inspired by Canova's marble sculptures; the central decoration bears the emblems of Lombardy (the iron crown) and Venice (corno). About 1808, Eugène de Beauharnais, viceroy of Italy commissioned the **Grand Vermeil★ banqueting service** *(126-130)* designed by the Parisian Martin-Guillaume Biennais. Five goldsmiths worked on it, including Eugenio Brusa, a Milanese craftsman who made the soup tureen *(126)*. This service for 140 people formerly bore the arms of Napoleon, and now bears the monogram of Emperor Franz II.

There are also some admirable porcelain services: the "Green Ribbon" service (Vincennes and Sèvres, 1756-57) *(185-187)*; a service on a green background (Sèvres, 1777) *(188-189)*; a service decorated with golden ears of corn (Sèvres, 1778) *(190)*. There are also a Japanese-style tea service (Vienna, about 1825-50) *(46)* and a dessert service (Herbert Minton & Co, 1851) *(191-193)* by the Frenchman Joseph Arnoux, which Britain's Queen Victoria gave to Emperor Franz Josef. Its "jelly or cream stand" *(192)* is noteworthy: the two-tiered dessert dish is surmounted by a group of *putti* in biscuit ware, apparently eager to savour the jelly and cream of which the English are so fond.

Other interesting pieces on exhibit are the romantic neo-Gothic style *Habsburger service* (Vienna, 1821-24) *(194-197)* with plates adorned by castles in *grisaille* enhanced with matt gold; silverware by Mayerhofer and Klinkosch (Vienna, 1836-90) *(14-28)*; a fine soup tureen from the gold service (Vienna, 1814) *(35)* used during the Congress of Vienna; a collection assembled by Charles-Alexandre de Lorraine *(106-125)*, brother of Emperor Franz Stefan; and the Lobmeyer imperial glass service (Vienna, 1873) *(173)* engraved by Peter Eisert, who devoted three years' work to it.

Esperanto-Museum ⓥ – This small museum is devoted to Esperanto, the artificial international language developed in 1887 by the Polish optician Ludwik Zamenhof. A display of posters for various international congresses, as well as photographs and books (including the latest editions), precedes a library of about 25,000 volumes that has been administered by the National Library since 1929. This is the world's largest artificial language library. Beginners' manuals are also on sale here to those who wish to learn Esperanto.

Hofburgkapelle ⓥ – *Schweizerhof.* The chapel is the only remaining medieval building around Schweizerhof. It was built between 1447 and 1449 in Frederick III's reign, then in the 17C and 18C underwent Baroque alterations. In 1802, it regained its Gothic interior.

A.E.I.O.U.

Apart from the Emperor Frederick III who thought of this emblem without explaining it, nobody knows with complete certainty what A.E.I.O.U. signifies. It dates from the birth of the House of Habsburg, at the coronation of Frederick, Duke of Styria, in 1440. There have been several attempted interpretations, of which *Austria Est Imperare Orbi Universo* (Austria shall rule the world) is the most likely. According to another version, the letters stand for *Austria Erit In Omne Ultimum* (Austria shall survive forever). During the occupation of Vienna by the King of Hungary, Mathias Corvinus, the Viennese wryly adopted quite a different interpretation: *Aller Erst Ist Österreich verloren* (Above all, Austria is lost).

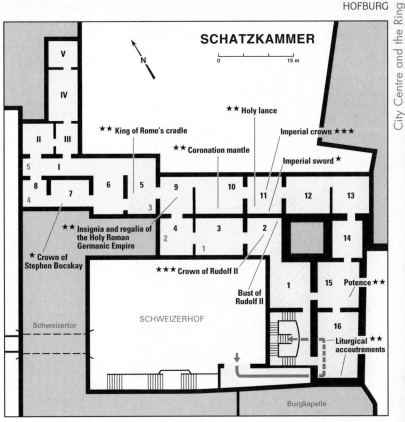

SCHATZKAMMER

The renowned *Wiener Sängerknaben* (Vienna Boys' Choir) can be heard here at Sunday mass in the Hofburgkapelle. This choral group developed out of the boys' singing school created by the Court *(see Practical information, Entertainment)*.

***Weltliche und Geistliche Schatzkammer ⊘ – *Schweizerhof No 1*. Insignia of Habsburg sovereignty, objects of sentimental value and relics which belonged to the royal house are kept here. Undeniably, a visit to the Schatzkammer is one of the highlights of a visit to Vienna.
The Weltliche Schatzkammer *(rooms 1 to 8 and 9 to 16)*, containing show-pieces from the royal jewels, is in fact also just as rich in objects of religious significance as the Geistliche Schatzkammer *(rooms I to V)*. The following summary lists the most significant exhibits, which one should take care not to pass up.

Room 1 – The insignias of the Archduchy of Austria are on exhibit here; these were employed during the coronation ceremonies of the royal lands which correspond to the Austria of today. Sceptre and orb (Prague, 14C), ducal mantle (Vienna, 1764).

Room 2 – The pièce de résistance here is the **Kaiserkrone of Rudolf II★★★**, a work by the Antwerp jeweller Jan Vermeyen in the early 17C. Sceptre and orb corresponding to the crown, by Andreas Osenbruck (Prague, 1615). The bronze **bust** of Rudolf II by Adriaen de Vries (1607) is also noteworthy.

Room 3 – Coronation mantle (1830) (1), ceremonial robes, and insignia of various orders.

Room 4 – Coronation robes of Ferdinand I (2).

Room 9 – **Insignia and regalia of the Holy Roman Empire★★**. These were used for the last time in 1792, at the coronation of Franz II.

Room 5 – **Cradle of the King of Rome★**, executed in silver-gilt. The design of the cradle came from the painter Prud'hon. The myriad golden bees that catch the eye were the personal emblem which Napoleon substituted for the monarchical Bourbon lilies. **Marie Louise's portrait★** (3) by François Gérard.

Room 6 – Baptismal garments and trimmings; keys to the coffins of the Kapuzinergruft.

Room 7 – **Crown of Stephan Bocskay★**. Precious stones and jewellery, emerald vessel (2 680 carats).

Room 8 – **Agate bowl★** (4C) (4), narwhal (sea-unicorn) tooth (243cm/8ft).

City Centre and the Ring

Kunsthistorisches Museum

Cradle of the King of Rome

Room I – **Miniature copy of the Mariensäule**★ (5), of which the original is situated on Am Hof square. It is adorned with over 3 700 precious stones.

Room II – Louis I of Hungary's reliquary cross (c 1370), purse of St Stephan (late 11C).

Room III – Small ebony temple reliquary with ivory figure of Christ, by Christoph Angermair, Florentine crucifix by Giambologna (c 1590).

Room IV – Reliquary altars (Milan, between 1660 and 1680), altar furnishings of Meissen porcelain.

Room V – Art works from the 18C and 19C, including reliquary busts (some of which are in solid silver).

Room 10 – Ceremonial garments belonging to the Norman kings, including the **coronation mantle**★★ of King Roger II of Sicily (Palermo, 1133).

Room 11 – The finest piece in the jewellery collection of the Holy Roman Empire is without doubt the **imperial crown**★★★, which was probably made in the monastery of Reichenau island (Lake Constance) or in Milan for the coronation of Otto I the Great (962). The arch is a later addition bearing the name of Konrad, who was crowned in Rome in 1027. Imperial cross (1024). The **Holy Lance**★★ (8C) was seen since the 13C as being the lance of Longinus that had pierced Christ's side; the **imperial sword**★ (11C scabbard) was once considered St Maurice's sword.

Room 12 – Reliquaries, jewellery cases.

Room 13 – Robes and coats of arms of heralds from the duchy of Burgundy.

Room 14 – Some of the treasures of the dukes of Burgundy.

Room 15 – Awards and distinctions from the Order of the Golden Fleece, armorial chains including the **potence**★★ (mid-15C).

Room 16 – Liturgical accoutrements★★ of the Order of the Golden Fleece.

★★**Spanische Hofreitschule** – *Attending Morgenarbeit (training sessions) or Vorführungen (parades) at the Spanish Riding School is the only way of visiting the Winterreitschule (Winter Riding School).*

The Spanish Riding School is one of the few places left in the world where it is possible to watch a display of *haute école* dressage, an art dating from the second half of the 16C. Beneath a coffered ceiling, two tiers of galleries surround an all-white room (57m x 19m/186ft x 62ft). This was the setting for numerous brilliant occasions, such as the banquet for the wedding by proxy of Archduchess Marie Louise and Napoleon I, the festivities of the Congress of Vienna and the debates of Austria's first constitutional assembly. The room was originally designed for

---

An Equestrian Ballet

In *haute école* dressage, riders teach their horses a repertoire of "airs" or movements. Most of them stem from Renaissance military exercises.
Piaffe: the horse trots on the spot. **Courvet**: the horse jumps several times with its front legs off the ground. **Croupade**: a jump where the horse raises its front and hind legs, folding them under its belly. **Levade**: an exercise where the horse rises on its hind legs, so that its body is at about a 45-degree angle to the ground. **Pirouette**: the horse turns on the haunches as the front legs move around the haunches in several jumps. **Capriole**: the most difficult movement of the *haute école*; during a jump, the horse kicks out its hind legs.

show-jumping competitions and tournaments that enabled the nobility to display their prowess; since 1894, it has been reserved for performances of the Spanish Riding School.

Parades – *Entrances according to the location of the seat: Reitschulgasse (a), Michaelerkuppel (b) and Josefsplatz (c) (shown on ticket).* This famous and splendid spectacle to the accompaniment of music attracts a wide and cosmopolitan audience. It is essential to reserve seats in advance (unless you buy from an agency at a higher price). The riders wear white gloves, black two-cornered hats trimmed with gold, brown double-breasted coats with brass buttons, off-white buckskin breeches and knee-high glossy black riding boots. At the start and end of each display (seven in all), the riders silently salute, slowly doffing their two-cornered hats to Karl VI's portrait hanging in the imperial box facing the doors through which they make their entrance (apart from the first display, on young stallions). It is customary not to wear a hat during the show. The performance (1hr 20min) may seem somewhat long to those who do not understand the equestrian art of dressage, since its appeal lies in the impeccable manoeuvres rather than dramatic entertainment. However, even a neophyte could not fail to respond to its highlights, the unforgettable 4th and 6th displays (*Arbeit an die Hand* and *Schools above the ground*), where traditional exercises impress by their precision and lightness. There is no music and the three chandeliers are unlit during the less formal *Morgenarbeit* (the training session).

Lipizzaner horses – The stallions of the Spanish Riding School take their name from the stud farm founded by Archduke Karl in 1580 in Lipizza (Slovenia), near Trieste. In 1920, they were brought from there to Piber castle, west of Graz (Styria), which now houses the national stud farm.

The present Lipizzaners are the descendants of six great sires: *Pluto*, born in 1765 (Danish breed); *Conversano*, born in 1767, and *Neapolitano*, born in 1790 (Neapolitan breed); *Maestoso*, born in 1773, and *Favory*, born in 1779 (Lipizzaner thoroughbreds); *Siglavy*, born in 1810 (Arab breed). All stem from an old Spanish strain, famous at the time of Caesar. They begin their training when they are three years old; they are born bay or black and do not turn white until between the ages of four and ten. Exceptionally, a horse may keep its dark colour. This earns him special consideration and the title of "brown Hofburg bay".

The Bereiter – It takes 10 to 15 years for a rider to become a Bereiter (trainer). After learning to ride without stirrups, a young rider acquires further skills by riding an older, experienced horse. After five years' practice, the novitiate Bereiter may take part in the performances. He is then entrusted with a young horse which he must bring up to the level of "school horse". Once he has successfully completed this task, the title of Bereiter is bestowed upon him. After training several horses and schooling some for jumping exercises he acquires the title of "Oberbereiter" or master trainer.

Lipizzaner-Museum ⊙ – *In the Stallburg. Genealogical tables, uniforms, harnesses and audio-visual installations give a comprehensive look into the past and present of this famous breed of horses. At the end of the tour, one can have a glimpse of the stalls through a thick pane of glass.*

Spanish Riding School

ÖNAT

City Centre and the Ring

★**Österreichische Nationalbibliothek** – *Josefsplatz*. The Austrian National Library, which had been the imperial court library until 1920, is one of the most important libraries in the world, containing 6.7 million items (of which 3 million are in printed type). Its origins stretch back to the Habsburg rule during the Middle Ages. After the War of the Spanish Succession, Emperor Karl VI (1711-40) ordered the construction of the library building (1723-26), which was executed by Johann Bernhard Fischer von Erlach and his son Josef Emanuel. The **Prunksaal**★★ with its tremendous dome is one of the finest examples of a Baroque library. The decoration is indeed worthy of the works collected here (about 200 000 volumes, primarily from the 16C and 17C). The central oval houses the approximately 16 000-volume private library of Prince Eugène of Savoy. There are two storeys of shelves concealing studies with secret entrances. In the cupola above, a fresco by Daniel Gran depicts the apotheosis of Karl VI.

By-Laws for Use of the Library of Emperor Karl VI

"Fools, lackeys, idlers, chatterers and saunterers are to stay away. Silence is to be kept; nor should one disturb others by reading out loud. When one wishes to withdraw, one should close the book and, if it is small, return it personally; or if it is large, leave it on the table and notify the attendant. The visitor need pay nothing; he is to depart enriched and return frequently".

From the Court Library to the National Library – In the course of the library's expansion into an academic institute, it was soon seen that the existing building made for this purpose would not be sufficiently large. As a result, the surrounding buildings, such as the Augustinenkloster and the Neue Burg were also included in the expansion. The latest addition was in 1988-91, when an air-conditioned subterranean storage area was installed below the Burggarten.

Today the Österreichische Nationalbibliothek is made up of a series of departments and collections, each of which has its own specialised academic library.

The manuscript, autograph and bequeathed collections contain about 50 000 manuscripts (including the *Wiener Dioskurides* and the *Tabula Peutingeriana*) and some 278 000 autographs.

The collection of incunabulae, antique and valuable publications includes about 8 000 books printed before 1501, including a 42-line Gutenberg Bible and a collection of bound editions.

The map collection and the Globe Museum *(see below)* preserve some 255 000 maps, atlases and 290 000 geographical prints, and the second-largest collection in the world of globes made before 1850.

The music collection *(see below)* contains some 49 000 music manuscripts, almost 120 000 sheet music editions, over 60 000 photographs of music manuscripts and approximately 18 000 records and tapes.

The papyrus collection here is one of the largest in the world, containing quite a variety of scrolls etc from 15C BC to 15C AD *(see below, Papyrusmuseum)*.

The portrait collection and the picture archives are home to 500 000 printed graphics, watercolours and sketches, as well as over 1.2 million photographs (positives and negatives). The former imperial family library (Fidelkommiß-Bibliothek) is composed of approximately 17 000 volumes.

In addition, the Nationalbibliothek encompasses a collection of pamphlets, posters and bookplates, the Austrian Literary Archives (since 1989, containing the bequests of important Austrian authors of the 20C), the collection for artificial languages *(see above, Esperanto-Museum)*, the anthology of Austrian Folk Songs and the Institute for Restoration.

Globenmuseum der Österreichischen Nationalbibliothek ⊘ – *Josefsplatz No 1, 3rd floor*. The Globe Museum retraces the development of growth of knowledge

National Library – Prunksaal

concerning the continents and seas since the 16C. Particularly elaborate are the celestial globes with figuratively rendered constellations. Armillary spheres and globes of the moon and mars are also on display here.

Augustinerkirche – *Augustinerstrasse No 3*. Formerly the court church. The Augustinian church was built during the first half of the 14C in the Hofburg by Dietrich Ladtner von Pirn (consecrated in 1349). It was used for great court weddings: Maria Theresa and François Étienne of Lorraine in 1736; the marriages by proxy of Marie Antoinette and Marie Louise, in 1770 and 1810 respectively (Napoleon's former opponent, Archduke Karl, represented him); Elisabeth of Bavaria and Franz Josef in 1854; Stephanie of Belgium and Crown Prince Rudolf in 1881.

In 1784, Ferdinand Hetzendorf von Hohenberg refurbished this edifice, with its austere exterior, and restored the original Gothic appearance, concealed behind Baroque decoration. It is the oldest three-aisled hall-church in the capital. One of the most impressive monuments is the **Christinendenkmal★**. Antonio Canova created the cenotaph of Maria Christina between 1805 and 1809: statues of Virtue, Felicity and Charity are shown advancing towards a 5m/16ft high pyramid of Carrara marble. At its summit, the spirit of Felicity holds a medallion portraying Maria Theresa's favourite daughter. Georgkapelle is a chapel built by Otto the Merry in the 14C for the knights of St George; it houses the remains of the imperial Count Daun who defeated the Prussians at Kollin during the Seven Years' War. Leopold II's marble tomb is empty, since his body lies in the Kapuzinergruft (the Capuchin crypt, *see City Centre and the Ring, Kapuzinerkirche District*). Near the chapel dedicated to St George is the Loretokapelle (chapel of Our Lady of Loreto) with a fine 18C wrought-iron gate leading to the Herzgruft, a crypt in which the hearts of all the Habsburgs since Emperor Matthias have been kept in 54 small silver urns; one of them contains the heart of the *Aiglon*, the son of Napoleon I. The musical organ comes from Schwarzspanierkirche (the Black Spaniard church) which was destroyed in a storm. Anton Bruckner's *Mass in F minor* was composed here.

★★Albertina: Graphische Sammlung ☉ – *Albertinaplatz No 1. Currently under renovation. Scheduled reopening Sept 2002.* The remarkable Albertina collection of graphic art owes its name to its founder, Duke Albert of Saxe-Teschen (1738-1822), son-in-law of Empress Maria Theresa through his marriage to her daughter, Maria Christina. It was founded in 1768 and since 1795 has occupied the Tarouca

G. De Laubier/FIGARO MAGAZINE

palace, a building which Louis Montoyer and Joseph Kornhäusl extended under Duke Albert and his successors, making it into the largest neo-Classical palace in Vienna. The palace and the collection it houses have been in possession of the Republic of Austria since 1918. In 1920, these works were combined with the collection of copper engravings originally assembled by Prince Eugène of Savoy. The museum now contains 60 000 drawings and watercolours and about 1 million engravings from every period, all of which constitute what is probably the world's largest collection of graphic art.

The **Dürer collection** belonged to Rudolf II who assembled it through purchases from the artist's heirs and the Cardinal Granvelle inheritance. It includes celebrated works such as *Praying Hands*, *The Hare* and *Madonna with Animals*. There are other masterpieces here, by some of the greatest names in the history of art: Hans Baldung-Grien, Brueghel the Elder, Chagall, Cranach the Elder, Fra Angelico, Gainsborough, Goya, Holbein, Klimt, Kubin, Claude Lorrain, Makart, Mantegna, Michelangelo, Nolde, Picasso, Raphael, Rembrandt, Reynolds, Rottmayr, Rubens, Schiele, Tintoretto, Titian, Van Dyck, Veronese, Leonardo da Vinci, and Watteau. This is not a comprehensive list, but it gives an idea of the exceptional quality of this museum. The public eagerly awaits its reopening.

In addition to the graphic collection, the Albertina also includes an architecture collection with bequests from influential architects, and a photographic collection.

Musiksammlung der Nationalbibliothek ⊘ – *Augustinerstrasse No 1, 4th floor*. Collection of musical instruments. Small temporary exhibitions take place in the reading room. The collection is based on musical archives of the Court and the National Opera as well as **autographed manuscripts★** by Josef Haydn, Wolfgang Amadeus Mozart *(Requiem)*, Franz Schubert, Anton Bruckner, Gustav Mahler, etc.

Schmetterlinghaus ⊘ – *Glasshouse in Burgggarten*. It is as if you have been transported into a magical kingdom when entering the Jugendstil greenhouse in the Burggarten. Innumerable multi-coloured butterflies flutter through an imitation tropical rainforest, even landing on a visitor's nose occasionally. A word of caution: it is necessary to watch your step here, since there are often quails scurrying around on the ground.

★Papyrusmuseum ⊘ – *Neue Burg*. The Papyrus Museum of the Austrian National Library is the largest collection of its kind in the world, housing about 180 000 objects. Around 400 of these (exclusively originals) are on exhibit, arranged according to topics such as school, magic, religion etc. In addition to papyruses, other exhibits include mummy portraits from antiquity. The oldest extant example of ancient Greek written music, the Euripedes score for a choral song from the tragedy *Orestes* (2C), can be listened to here as well.

★★Ephesos-Museum ⊘ – *Neue Burg*. The Ephesus Museum has been housed in Neue Burg since 1978. It possesses a series of finds made by Austrian archaeologists working on the ancient trading city on the coast of Asia Minor (1895 onwards). Only Istanbul and London have similarly magnificent collections. The architectural fragments, reliefs and sculptures are presented in exemplary fashion, and are splendidly documented with explanatory reconstructions, models and photographs. Objects from excavations on the island of Samothrace, in the Aegean Sea, are included.

On a staircase from the ground floor there are fragments of an altar of Artemis, the Artemision, from the temple of Diana of Ephesus (4C BC). This temple was destroyed by fire in 356 BC.

The mezzanine displays one of the two major works in the collection: **the frieze from the Parthian monument★★**. The senate erected this monument around 170 on the occasion of the Roman army's final victory in their war against the Parthians (161-165). It is dedicated to Emperor Lucius Aurelius Verus (d 169), who during the wars of conquest had had his headquarters in Ephesus, capital of the province of Asia since 129. This marble monument 40m/43yd long (originally 70m/76yd) probably formed the exterior decoration of a huge altar. The frieze consists of five scenes *(start at the end of the right-hand wall, from No 59)*: adoption of Verus by Antoninus Pius in 138 *(59-64)*; Verus in combat *(65-68)*; Verus as emperor with personifications of the principal cities of the empire *(69-76; Alexandria in 69, Ephesus in 70, Rome in 72, Ctesiphon in 75, capital of the Parthian empire)*; his coronation by the gods of Olympus *(77-80)*; and his apotheosis *(81-83)*. On the same floor, there is a fragment of an octagonal tomb with Corinthian columns built in the second half of the 1C for a young girl of 20, and a superb wooden model of Ephesus (1:500).

On the first floor, a collection of bronze and marble sculptures surrounds the extraordinary **Ephesian Athlete★★** *(129)*, a Roman copy of a Greek original of 340/330 BC. This 1.92m/6ft tall athlete is shown cleaning his strigil, a curved blade used to scrape the sand of the arena from the athlete's oiled body. The **Boy with a Goose★** *(147)* is a marble copy of a 3C BC Hellenistic original; during this period, artists represented children as they really were, whereas Greek archaic and classical art gave children the features of young adults. The following exhibits are also noteworthy: an Ionic capital bearing a five-branched lamp *(139)*, *Hercules Fighting* *the Centaur (141)*, a satyr's head *(143)*, fragments from the library of Celsus *(156-162)* founded by the consul Tiberius Iulius Aquila, a head which presumably represents Homer *(166)* and a portrait of Hadrian *(171)* made in 123 during one of the emperor's visits to Ephesus.

Kunsthistorisches Museum

Detail of the Parthian monument

On the same floor, on the other side of the staircase, there are finds from Samothrace. The collection comprises Victory figures, pediment sculptures, capitals and friezes. These architectural remains also include pieces *(247-268)* from the rotunda of the temple built between 289 and 281 BC by Arsinoë, wife of King Lysimachos of Macedonia.

★★ **Hofjagd- und Rüstkammer** ⊘ – *Neue Burg*. In the 19C, nearly all the Habsburg armouries in Vienna were merged, with the result that one of the most significant collections of this kind in the world is now on view here. The three primary components of the Royal Hunting and Armoury Collection are the imperial personal armoury containing pieces of equipment belonging to the Habsburgs; the royal army and hunting collection; and what is called the heroes' armoury of Archduke Ferdinand of Tyrol, who began to compile this collection in Innsbruck in 1577.

The suits of armour and weapons made for ceremonial purposes bear witness to the abilities and ingenuity of the artisans and armourers of former times; such splendour was primarily employed at the tournaments with which all noteworthy events, such as coronations, baptisms and weddings, were celebrated. As such, this finery served not just for physical protection, but also as an important means of presenting oneself. Besides the superior armoury which originated in European workshops, a Mameluke collection is on exhibit (Saal IV), demonstrating the Islamic prohibition of graven images through its greater use of luxurious materials such as precious stones. In response to this practice, Habsburg rulers sometimes imitated Turkish weapons and armour, to better illustrate the struggle between orient and occident at their tournaments. After the age of the great tournaments had passed, sovereigns did not cease to equip themselves with luxurious weaponry. Given this background, it seems only natural that crown prince Rudolf would receive a richly decorated shotgun (1866, Gallery C) as a gift at the tender age of eight.

★★ **Sammlung Alter Musikinstrumente** ⊘ – *Neue Burg*. As a musical city, Vienna needed to have a Museum of Ancient Musical Instruments. The museum has been equipped with a network of infrared headphones enabling visitors to hear sound documents relating to the period and the theme of the room they enter. This is why we recommend them to visitors, despite the fact that at present the commentaries are solely in German.

The museum's contents date back to the 16C collection of Archduke Ferdinand of Tyrol kept in Ambras Castle in Innsbruck, which was expanded with a series of instruments from Catajo Castle near Padua. This accounts for the great historical value of the Renaissance section in this wing of the Neue Burg facing Burggarten. The collection has been completed through loans from the Society of Friends of Music in Vienna. Equipped with headphones, visitors can spend just over an hour absorbing the evolution of musical instruments from the early 16C onward. The selection below concentrates on instruments of historical or aesthetic significance.

City Centre and the Ring

Further details: in the rooms, a red sticker on the label indicates that you can hear a sound recording of the instrument; a green sticker indicates that you can play the instrument; a green dotted line on the ground indicates a change of recording.

Room IX: Music in the reign of Maximilian I – A rare example of a **rebec**★ (Venice, 15C); a *lira da braccio*, a kind of viola (Verona, 1511) whose reverse is ornamented with a carving of a man's head in the middle of a woman's body; a small spinet or *spinetto* (Italy, second half of the 16C); a trumpet by Anton Schnitzer (1598), who worked in Nürnberg, a city famous in the Renaissance for its manufacturers of musical instruments; four recorders (16C); a harp (Italy, 16C); *Perseus and Andromeda*, a painting by Piero di Cosimo (after 1513).

Room X: Music in Ambras and Catajo castles – A serpent (Italy, 16C), the precursor of the ophicleide, with a zoomorphic socket for the mouthpiece; a **harpsichord**★ (Venice, 1559) with painted decoration dating from about 1580. Ferdinand of Tyrol's **cittern**★★ (Brescia, 1574). This remarkable work of art is played with a plectrum and the archduke chose the decoration: there is a portrayal of Lucretia at the top wearing real pearl earrings. The **claviorganum**★ (Central Germany, second half of the 16C) is the oldest existing example of its kind. The three *viola da gamba* by Antonio Ciciliano (Venice, towards 1600) are noteworthy, as is Kaspar von der Sitt's table (Passau, 1590), its stone top carved with musical notes and heraldic motifs; and *The Lute Player* by Annibale Carracci (c 1600).

Room XI: Musical composition in the reigns of Ferdinand III, Leopold I and Josef I – Note a lute with its case (Venice, 1626) by Vendelinus Venere, whose real name was Wendelin Tieffenbrucker. He came from Füssen, a town of lute-makers specialising in ivory. Also Leopold I's clavicytherium (Vienna, end of the 17C) by Martin Kaiser from Füssen – note the vertical lines of the case and the tortoiseshell, ivory and mother-of-pearl decoration.

Room XII: Josef Haydn – A baryton which belonged to Haydn by Daniel Achatius Stadlmann (Vienna, 1732); a harpsichord (Antwerp, 1745) by Johannes Daniel Dulcken, the principal Flemish manufacturer of harpsichords; an early kind of piano, the Tangentenflügel (Ratisbon, 1798) by Christof Friedrich Schmahl.

Room XIII: Wolfgang Amadeus Mozart – The violins from Leopold Mozart's collection; **six trumpets**★, magnificent instruments of partially gilt silver (Vienna, 1741 and 1746) by Franz and Michael Leichamschneider with interesting delicate coils on the mouthpiece; a "Glasharmonika" (first half of the 19C), an instrument invented in 1761. On the wall, *Franz-Stefan and Maria Theresa* from the studio of Martin van Meytens (about 1755) and *Marie Antoinette* probably by Franz Xaver Wagenschöm (undated), depicting the future queen of France seated at a clavichord. The 18C or early 19C pianofortes had little in common with the modern piano as regards design, if not aesthetics. They did not possess the metal frame, crossed strings and felt-covered hammer heads of modern pianos, and they differed between each manufacturer. When Johann Andreas Stein invented the "Austrian mechanism" in about 1770, the instruments acquired the sonority which was so important to Mozart.

Room XIV: Ludwig van Beethoven – A piano-organ by Franz Xaver Christoph (Vienna, about 1785). A Harmoniehammerflügel by Johann Jakob Könnicke (Vienna, 1796). A double-pedalled harp by Sébastien Érard (Paris, about 1810). Johann Nepomuk Mälzel's metronome (Paris, 1815), the first of its kind. A rosewood pianoforte by Josef Brodmann (Vienna, 1815). A pianoforte by Konrad Graf (Vienna, about 1820) with mother-of-pearl keys. *Napoleon, Emperor of the French* after François Gérard (after 1804). *Franz II* by Johann Baptist Lampi.

Room XV: Franz Schubert – Lyre-guitar by Jacques Pierre Michelot (Paris, c 1800). Guitar by Giovanni Battista Fabricatore (Naples, 1801). A pianoforte by André Stein (Vienna, 1819). The modest table piano upon which Schubert played and composed at the home of the painter Rieder. *Portrait of Schubert as a Young Man* (Vienna, c 1814).

Room XVI: Robert Schumann, Johannes Brahms, Franz Liszt, Anton Bruckner – Aluminium violin by Anton Dehmal (Vienna, last third of the 19C), whose tone was unconvincing; a Hammerflügel belonging to Robert and Clara Schumann and Johannes Brahms (C. Graf, 1839); several grand pianos by the manufacturers Graf (Vienna, 1839), Streicher (Vienna, 1840), Streicher and Son (Vienna, 1868), Bösendorfer (Vienna, 1875). *Franz Liszt at the Keyboard*, photogravure by Josef Danhäuser (second half of the 19C).

Room XVII: Dance music in Vienna – Zither (Austria, 19C). Zither by Frank Nowy (Vienna, c 1950), used by Franz Karas, composer of the score for the film *The Third Man*. The term "zither" comes from the Greek *kithara* from which guitar also derives. It covers a range of instruments with strings which are plucked or set in vibration by a plectrum; in central Europe, the resonance box is usually trapezoidal.

Room XVIII: Gustav Mahler, Richard Strauss, Hugo Wolf – A pianino by Caspar Lorenz (Vienna, c 1860). A **piano by Ludwig Bösendorfer**★ (Vienna, c 1867); the case is of ebony and is magnificently inlaid with precious woods and metals, made according to a preparatory design by A Grosser. *Richard Strauss* by the Viennese portrait painter Wilhelm Victor Krausz (Vienna, 1929), showing the German composer, aged 65, conducting at the Opera. *Hugo Wolf* by Karl Rickelt (1895).

Left side gallery: the 20C – A harpsichord by Paul de Wit (Leipzig, 1912). *Self Portrait* by Arnold Schönberg (Vienna, 1910). Grand piano by the firm of Bösendorfer (Vienna, 1958), made on the occasion of the Brussels World Fair. The tour ends with a synthesiser dating from 1913, when Jorg Mager discovered how to analyse and reconstitute sound electronically.

★ **Museum für Völkerkunde** ⊘ – *Neue Burg.* Founded in 1928 as an independent institution, the Museum for Ethnology owns about 200 000 objects, some of which had already arrived in Austria in the 16C. The actual origin of the museum traces back to an 1806 London auction at which the Emperor Franz I auctioned off ethnological objects primarily acquired during the expeditions of the Briton James Cook.

Ground floor – The ivory carvings and brass and bronze works from the kingdom of Benin (which was destroyed by the British in 1897) are of high artistic quality. The **Benin bronzes**★ document the rich royal culture which was at its height between the 15C and 19C. Two completely preserved gnomes from the beginning of the 15C are particularly splendid.

In the Japanese section is the complete armour of a samurai (17C) and a katana sabre dated 1478; the Chinese section contains a splendid red lacquer screen made in Peking about 1760.

First floor – Objects garnered by James Cook on his world voyages are kept here; they once formed the heart of the collection. Especially noteworthy among the exhibits are the ceremonial paddles from Easter Island which were probably made specially for the British explorer and a model (59cm/23in) of an oracular shrine. The antiquities of the New World comprise interesting Mexican items. After the conquest of Mexico, Hernán Cortez sent many of these to Karl V, who then gave them to his brother Ferdinand. One of the most impressive pieces here is the **feathered Aztec crown**★★ made of over 450 tail feathers of the Quetzal-bird.

Also noteworthy is the Brazilian collection of Johann Natterer (1787-1843), who spent a total of 18 years in Brazil. While there he collected mostly items relating to natural history, yet he also brought back to Vienna more than 2 000 ethnological objects from over different 60 tribes, some of which are no longer in existence.

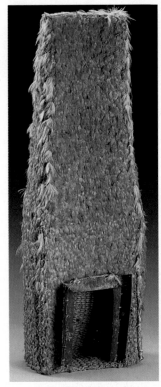

MUSEUM FÜR VOLKERKUNDE, Wien

Museum Für Völkerkunde –
Oracular Shrine

The nearest sights are: the Freyung, Kapuzinerkirche and Staatsoper, the Ring and, close to Neue Burg, the Kunsthistorisches Museum (Art History Museum, see the City Centre and the Ring section).

HOHER MARKT District

Local map pages 13/14, **JKR**
Underground: Schwedenplatz (U1, U4), Stephansplatz (U1, U3)
Tram: Schwedenplatz (1, 2, 21, N), Salztorbrücke (1, 2)
Bus: Hoher Markt (1A, 2A, 3A)

Together with the Fleischmarkt District, this forms the historic centre of the city. It features Roman and Romanesque remains, a fine Gothic church (Maria am Gestade) and some splendid creations of the Baroque period.

Hoher Markt – In the Middle Ages, the market square was the site for public executions by hanging and also for the pillory. Today, the square features the canopy over the **Vermählungsbrunnen** (the "Virgin Mary's marriage fountain", 1732) by Josef Emmanuel Fischer von Erlach with a sculpture by Antonio Corradini.

3BIS/MICHELIN

Hoher Markt: the Ankeruhr

On the archway over Bauernmarkt is the **Ankeruhr**, a magnificent clock which Franz Matsch made in 1912-14 to link the two buildings of the Anker Insurance Company. Every hour, a locally significant historical figure appears by the clock face: Marcus Aurelius at 1am and 1pm, Charlemagne at 2am and 2pm, the Babenberg Duke Leopold VI with Empress Theodora of Byzantium at 3am and 3pm, Walter van der Vogelweide at 4am and 4pm, Rudolf I and his wife Anna of Hohenberg at 5am and 5pm, Johann Puschbaum (one of the architects of the Stephansdom) at 6am and 6pm, Maximilian I at 7am and 7pm, the mayor Von Liebenberg at 8am and 8pm, Count Rüdiger von Starhemberg at 9am and 9pm, Prince Eugène of Savoy at 10am and 10pm, Maria Theresa and Franz Stephan von Lothringen at 11am and 11pm and Joseph Haydn at noon and at midnight. At noon, all the figures also file past to the accompaniment of music.

Römische Ruinen ⊘ – *Hoher Markt No 3 (entrance in the passage)*. In Roman times, Hoher Markt was the site of a forum. Excavations under the square have uncovered the remains of two houses (2C and 3C) belonging to officers (stone sculptures, pottery, tiles, paving).

North of the square, turn left into Tuchlauben and go past Schultergasse.

Neidhart-Fresken ⊘ – *Tuchlauben No 19. 1st floor*. The oldest secular frescoes (c 1400) in Vienna are on display in a building with a Baroque façade dating from 1716. These medieval frescoes were on the wall of a banqueting hall which a rich cloth merchant had decorated with scenes from the poems of the Minnesänger Neidhart von Reuental, who had performed at the Babenberger Court at the beginning of the 13C. They were rediscovered in 1979 during renovation work in a residential dwelling. Their significance and their quality prompted the city authorities to finance their restoration.

Though sometimes fragmentary, the scenes are identifiable. Starting with the first of the series opposite the entrance, there are: a wrestling match with a fortified castle in the background; a ball game and some lovers symbolising summer; the theft of a mirror, its somewhat frivolous iconography evoking the delights of court life; a snowball fight, which some see as an egg fight; and a sleigh ride, symbolise medieval Viennese winter; picking violets or spring's awakening; a circular dance, where the flower in the dancer's right hand also symbolises spring; a banquet as an allegory of autumn, a time of festivities.

Retrace your steps and turn left into Schultergasse, where Johann Berhard Fischer von Erlach died at No 5. Then turn right through Jordangasse and into Wipplinger Strasse.

Böhmische Hofkanzlei (H) – *Wipplinger Strasse No 7*. Johann Bernhard Fischer von Erlach designed the main façade of the former Bohemian Chancellery between 1708 and 1714. The telamones on the portals are the work of Lorenzo Mattielli, a specialist in this genre. In 1750, Maria Theresa commissioned Mathias Gerl to enlarge the palace; he greatly admired the work of the older master, hence, unlike the rear of the building visible from Judenplatz, today's splendid façade underwent no alterations. Today the Böhmische Hofkanzlei is the seat of the Austrian Constitutional and Administrative Court.

Altes Rathaus – *Wipplinger Strasse Nos 6 and 8*. The former town hall dates from 1316 and was the house of a burgher, Otto Heimo. The municipal authorities confiscated it, however, after he allegedly took part in a plot against the Habsburgs. The building was refurbished in the Baroque period (1699). In 1883, the municipal authorities moved into the new city hall on the Ring *(see City Centre and the Ring, Rathaus)*.

At No 8 in an interior courtyard is the **Andromeda Brunnen★**, a lead fountain of Andromeda by Georg Raphael Donner (1741). Framed by cherubs, this small masterpiece lies between the wrought-iron balustrades of the coping and the balcony.

Telamones on the facade of the Böhmische Hofkanzlei

It depicts the rescue of Cassiopeia's daughter by Perseus, the son of Zeus; she was about to fall victim to a marine monster, now harmlessly spouting water.

Continue along Wipplinger Strasse to reach Hohe Brücke.

Hohe Brücke – Spanning Tiefer Graben, the "deep ditch" where a tributary of the Danube (the Alsbach) once flowed, is a pretty Jugendstil bridge with elegant metal lampposts. Josef Hackhofer built the bridge in 1903.

Go down the staircase and take Tiefer Graben to the right. Turn right into Am Gestade for the church of the same name.

★**Maria am Gestade** – *Salvatorgasse bei 12. Entrance by the south gate.* In the mid-12C, a church known as Our Lady on the Strand stood on a terrace overlooking the main branch of the Danube. At the end of the 14C, a Gothic edifice replaced it; this is the present church. Its popular name is *Maria-Stiegen-Kirche* (Our Lady of the Steps) and it is the Czech national church in Vienna.

The late Gothic west front is tall and narrow (33m x 9.7m/108ft x 31ft). Below, the portal beneath its canopy displays sculptures (c 1410) representing St John the Evangelist and St John the Baptist; above is a pediment, flanked by pinnacles, with a wide stained-glass window between. The seven-sided tower ends in a fine pierced **spire**★; following damage during the Turkish siege of 1683, it was rebuilt in 1688. The interior is unusual in that the nave and choir are of equal length. Particularly noteworthy are the **stained-glass windows** (14C and 15C) in the choir and the statues against the pillars of the nave.

Before going into the street along the right side of the church, take a look at the fine Baroque portal (1720) of "Zu den sieben Schwertern" house at Schwertgasse 3. Go past "Stoss im Himmel" to Salvatorgasse.

Ausstellung der Österreichische Freiheitskämpfe ⊘ – *Wipplinger Strasse 8. Entrance through No 5 Salvatorgasse.* The former town hall houses the archives of the Austrian resistance. On the ground floor, an exhibition covers the period from 1934 to 1945 and commemorates those who opposed National Socialism first by a patriotic front, then by underground resistance after Hitler proclaimed the annexation of Austria.

This permanent exhibition mainly consists of photographic documents. It evokes the assassination of Chancellor Dollfuss, the reign of terror, the exile of some (including Robert Musil and Joseph Roth), the clandestine activities of the armed resistance as well as Mauthausen concentration camp in Upper Austria. Some 3 000 members of the resistance were executed during Hitler's régime, nearly 140 000 Austrians perished in the camps and 600 000 others lost their lives during World War Two, fighting in the ranks of the Wehrmacht or during air raids. The principal purpose of this museum is to act as antidote to any form of neo-Nazi propaganda.

Salvatorkapelle (**K⁴**) – *Salvatorgasse 5. Entrance through Altes Rathaus.* The Holy Saviour Chapel displays on Salvatorgasse a remarkable doorway with decoration in the Lombard Renaissance style. It dates from 1520 but is a copy, the original being in the Historisches Museum der Stadt Wien.

At the end of Salvatorgasse, take Mark-Aurel-Strasse on the left then Sterngasse on the right. Take the Salzgasse for Ruprechtsplatz.

Ruprechtskirche ⊙ – *Ruprechtsplatz.* For those that believe tradition, St Virgil, Bishop of Salzburg, founded this church in 740. This would make it the oldest building in the city. It displays some Romanesque features. The nave and foot of the tower date from between 1130 and 1170, and the choir and portal from the 2nd third of the 13C. The church was completed in the first half of the 15C. Its Romanesque bell tower and great roof lend it originality. The modern stained-glass windows are by Lydia Roppolt.

The nearest sights are: Stephansdom and its surrounding district, the Fleischmarkt and Freyung districts, the first section of the Ring (found in the City Centre and the Ring section) as well as the Leopold district with the Prater (see Outside the Ring section).

KAPUZINERKIRCHE District★

Local map page 13, **JR**
Underground: Stephansplatz (U1, U3), Karlsplatz (U1, U4)
Tram: Oper (1, 2, 62, 65, D, J)
Bus: Albertinaplatz (3A), Michaelerplatz (2A, 3A)

The Capuchin district is close to the Hofburg, the Opera and the shopping streets of Graben and Kärntner Strasse. Its dreamy, often empty streets and alleyways offer several attractions worth seeing.

SIGHTS

Start the tour at the Josefsplatz (see City Centre and the Ring, Hofburg, the Hofburg complex) and continue through the Augustinerstrasse in the direction of Albertinaplatz.

Salvador-Dalí-Ausstellung ⊙ – *This small exhibit in the Palais Pallavicini (one gallery and one room for sales) includes mainly graphics series but also several sculptures; among the former, "La Divina Comedia" is particularly noteworthy. Considering the admission price, this exhibition is primarily for dyed-in-the-wool Dalí fans.*

Lobkowitz Palace – *Lobkowitzplatz No 2.* Count Philip Sigismund Dietrichstein had this Italianate edifice built from 1685 to 1687 to plans by Giovanni Pietro Tencala. In 1709, Johann Bernhard Fischer von Erlach modified it. He added the attic and a gate showing the influence of the high altar which the architect had designed the preceding year for the Franciscan church in Salzburg. In 1753, Wenzel von Lobkowitz bought the palace; in 1804, under Franz Joseph Maximilian von Lobkowitz, its great hall called *"Eroica-Saal" (see also Eroicahaus)* saw the first performance of Ludwig van Beethoven's *Third Symphony*
It is hard to imagine now the sensation which Beethoven's symphony must have caused among the small, select audience listening to it beneath the Baroque panelling of the palace. Accustomed to Joseph Haydn's gentler and less emotive music, the audience was overwhelmed. In fact, on the day after the concert, one of the listeners wrote: "Beethoven's music will soon reach the point where nobody can enjoy it at all". A great patron of music, Franz Joseph Maximilian von Lobkowitz (at that point, 32 years old) knew better *(see inset)*.

Profile of a Patron of the Arts

Following the example of the princes of Sachsen-Hildburghausen and Prince Esterházy, who were patrons to Gluck and Haydn respectively, the Lobkowitz family played a leading role in Austrian music. Like all the aristocrats of his time, Prince Franz Joseph Maximilian von Lobkowitz was a rich man in touch with the art of music. He financed an entire orchestra and turned his palace into a veritable academy of music, bringing famous singers and piano virtuosi to perform there. Thus, Beethoven received an invitation to improvise on a quartet by Ignaz Pleyel who had travelled from Paris especially for the occasion and who was highly enthusiastic about the German genius. Beethoven was not Lobkowitz's "court musician", but he had a priority contract with him (as in the first performance of the *Eroica*). Musical evenings at the Lobkowitz Palace drew the luminaries of the empire, as the prince continuously encouraged new talent. As soon as a foreign composer came to Vienna, Lobkowitz would summon soloists and tenors so that they could play the works of his eminent guest as soon as possible.

Österreichisches Theatermuseum ⊙ – The Austrian Theatre Museum dates from 1923 and has been housed in the palace since 1991. Among other things, the permanent collection includes hand sketches, stage decor models, photographs, costumes, puppet theatre and numerous paintings. There is also a children's theatre museum with regular performances using stick puppets. Special exhibitions are organised here, drawing from the archives of one of the most extensive theatrical collections in the world. The museum has an annex nearby *(see City Centre and the Ring, Staatsoper District, Gedenkräume des Österreichischen Theatermuseums).*

Enter Führichgasse and turn left towards Neuer Markt by Tegetthoffstrasse.

Neuer Markt (**JR 87**) – This square was once the setting for tournaments, among other things. The predominance of 18C buildings means that it has retained a Baroque ambience. Particularly noteworthy are: Kupferschmiedhaus (No 13, 1796); Hatschiererhaus (No 14, 1665); Maysederhaus (No 15, second half of the 18C, former home of the violinist and composer Joseph Mayseder); Hufschmiedhaus (No 16, 1770 façade). No 2 was the site of Joseph Haydn's town residence from 1792 to 1797, where he composed the imperial Austrian national anthem in 1795-96. It begins with the famous "God save the emperor".

In the centre of "New Market" is **Donner-Brunnen**★★, a fountain which Georg Raphael Donner built between 1737 and 1739 in response to a commission from the municipal authorities. The statue of Prudence stands in the centre of a high plinth, an allegory representing the concern and wisdom of the city authorities. Cherubs and fish spouting water are grouped around it. The figures on the edge personify the tributaries of the Danube: the rivers Traun (young fisherman with harpoon), Enns (bearded old ferryman), Ybbs and March (two nymphs), symbols of the four provinces adjoining the capital. Shocked by the nude figures, Maria Theresa had them removed in 1770 – at the time, this was the first secular group to adorn a square. Franz II replaced them with bronze copies in 1801. The original lead statues are in the Barockmuseum (Museum of Baroque Art) in the Belvedere.

R. Dechamps/MICHELIN

Donner-Brunnen – The Fisherman with the Harpoon

Kapuzinerkirche – *Neuer Markt.* The church of the Capuchins was built between 1622 and 1632 and dedicated to Our Lady of the Angels. The façade recovered its original appearance in 1936. In accordance with the rules of its mendicant order, the interior decoration is very austere. In a niche on the façade, a modern statue (1935, Hans Mauer) represents the Capuchin Marco d'Aviano, papal legate to Charles de Lorraine's army. He celebrated Mass on the summit of Kahlenberg on the morning of the last battle against the Turks in 1683.

★★KAPUZINERGRUFT ⊙ *Entrance on the left of the church.*

> The crypt of the Capuchins, where my emperors lay in their stone sarcophagi, was closed.
> A friar came to me and asked:
> "What do you want?"
> "I want to see the sarcophagus of the Emperor Franz-Josef."
> "God bless you", said the Capuchin, making the sign of the Cross over me.
> "God save – !", I cried.
> "Hush!", said the monk.
>
> Joseph Roth, *The Crypt of the Capuchins.*

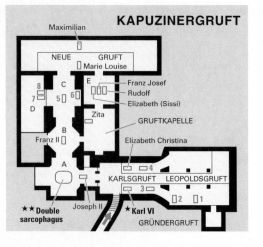

KAPUZINERGRUFT

The imperial crypt, known as both Kapuzinergruft and Kaisergruft, was founded by Empress Anna in 1618. Twelve emperors, seventeen empresses and over one hundred other members of the imperial family have found their final rest here. The coffins contain their embalmed bodies; the viscera are in the catacombs at Stephansdom and the hearts in Augustinerkirche. Two emperors were buried elsewhere since this crypt was founded: Ferdinand II (in Graz) and Karl I (in Madeira). Archduke Franz-Ferdinand and his wife, assassinated at Sarajevo on 28 June 1914, are not buried in Vienna but in Arstetten castle in Lower Austria.

Gründergruft (Founders' crypt) – The remains of Emperor Matthias and his wife Anna were brought here in 1633 from the Dorotheenkirche *(see below, Dorotheum).*

Leopoldsgruft (Leopold's crypt) – This contains the tombs of Ferdinand III (1) and Leopold I's wife, Eleonore of Pfalz-Neuburg (2) by **Balthasar Ferdinand Moll**.

Eternity through the Small Door

Accompanying the plain wooden coffin, the chamberlain would knock at the small double door of the Leopold crypt. The Capuchin, waiting in the crypt, would ask "Whom do you bring?", and the chamberlain recited a long list of titles belonging to the emperor or empress, who had ruled over the vast Austro-Hungarian empire. "We do not know this person!" came the unexpected reply. At this point, the chamberlain again enumerated the titles. Once more this met with a refusal from the Capuchin. After the third rejection, the chamberlain became humbler: "We accompany a poor sinner, who begs for eternal rest", at which the Capuchin finally said: "We recognise him as our brother and we welcome him here."

Karlsgruft (Charles' crypt) – Johann Lukas von Hildebrandt designed the sarcophagi of Leopold I (3) and Joseph I (4). Balthasar Ferdinand Moll designed the sarcophagus of **Karl VI★**, a splendid work of art displaying the coats of arms (crowning the skulls in the corner) of the Holy Roman German Empire, Bohemia, Hungary and Castile; above it is an allegory of Austria in mourning by the sculptor Johann Nikolaus Moll. Also of note are the veiled faces of the female mourners at the corners of the sarcophagus of Elizabeth-Christina, Karl VI's wife who bore the nickname of "white lily" because of her pale complexion.

Maria-Theresia-Gruft (Maria-Theresa's crypt) (A) – The Frenchman Jean-Nicolas Jadot de Ville-Issey designed this vault for François de Lorraine and Maria-Theresa. The architect conceived a domed mausoleum with an oval cupola, in the centre of which is the **double sarcophagus★★** by Balthasar Ferdinand Moll. The artist cast in lead an impressive bed of state bearing the imperial couple, symbolically face-to-face; before them an angel proclaims the triumph of faith, ready to blow his trumpet for the Last Judgment. At the corners are the crowns of the Holy Roman German Empire, Hungary, Bohemia and Jerusalem (a crown of thorns).
In front is the coffin of their son, Joseph II. A niche contains the tomb of Countess Fuchs-Mollard, Maria-Theresa's governess; although she was not of royal blood, the high esteem in which she was held by the empress accounts for her presence in the Habsburg crypt.

Franzensgruft (Franz's crypt) (B) – The last emperor of the Holy Roman Empire, Franz II, rests in a copper coffin by Pietro Nobile, with the tombs of his four wives around them.

Ferdinandsgruft (Ferdinand's crypt) (C) – Among the numerous coffins in this room are those of Ferdinand I (5) and his wife Marie-Anne of Savoy (6).

Karl's VI sarcophagus

J. Malburet/MICHELIN

Toskanagruft (Tuscan crypt) (D) – This vault contains the coffins of Leopold II (7) and his wife Maria Ludovica of Spain (8), and of members of the two collateral branches who reigned in Tuscany and Modena until 1860 (Archduke Franz-Ferdinand, born in 1863, was the heir of the last duke of Modena).

Neue Gruft (New crypt) – Below a concrete ceiling (1961), this crypt houses the sarcophagi of Maximilian, shot in Mexico by republican revolutionaries under Juárez in 1867, and of Marie Louise, Empress of the French. The coffin of her son lay in Franzensgruft until it was moved to the Invalides in Paris on 15 December 1940, precisely 100 years after his father's funeral.

Franz-Josef-Gruft (Franz Josef''s crypt) (E) – Franz Josef was the last Habsburg emperor to be buried in the Kapuzinergruft. On either side of his coffin are the tombs of Elisabeth of Bavaria (Sissi), assassinated in Geneva in 1898, and of their son Rudolf who committed suicide at a hunting lodge in Mayerling *(see the Further afield section)* in 1889. Sissi's coffin is permanently adorned with flowers, in particular a floral wreath bearing a ribbon in the national colours of Hungary (green, white, and red).

Gruftkapelle (Crypt chapel) – The last tomb in Kapuzinergruft is that of Zita of Bourbon-Parma, who died in exile in Switzerland in 1989. The chapel also contains a monument in memory of her husband Karl I, the last sovereign of the Habsburg dynasty.

> **The "Pewter Plague"**
>
> Contrary to the quotation from Joseph Roth *(see above)*, the sarcophagi are metal. Until the end of the 18C, they were made of pewter; later sarcophagi are copper. Oxidation, "the pewter plague", attacks 17C and 18C sarcophagi and necessitates expensive and regular maintenance.

OTHER SIGHTS

Near Neuer Markt fountain, enter Plankengasse.

From this little street, there are three very different views which are all interesting: opposite is the yellow façade of the Evangelische Kirche (Protestant church) built in 1784 by Gottlieb Nigelli; on the right *(near Seilergasse)*, Hans Hollein's modern Haas-Haus *(see City Centre and the Ring, Stephansdom District)*; behind, the elegant Donner-Brunnen *(see Neuer Markt above)*. Also noteworthy, at No 4, are the decorative details on the three façades of the Secession apartment house "Zum silbernen Brunnen" built of reinforced concrete in 1914.

Carry on along Plankengasse and turn right into Dorotheergasse. At the end is Café Hawelka (No 6), a Viennese institution.

★**Jüdisches Museum der Stadt Wien** ⊘ – *Dorotheergasse 11*. Since 1993, the City of Vienna Jewish Museum has been housed in the Eskeles palace (second half of the 18C), a Baroque building which has belonged to several aristocratic Austrian families over the course of time.

Jüdisches Museum, Wien

Jüdisches Museum der Stadt Wien – Hanukkah lamp

The Jewish community – The records of Upper Austria first mention the presence of Jews towards 903. 13C Vienna authorised a Jewish settlement within its walls, mainly on the site of modern Judenplatz. The first Jewish community survived until 1421 *(see City Centre and the Ring, Freyung District)*. In 1624, Ferdinand II allowed the Jews land for their exclusive use near the Danube; soon it had more than 1 000 residents. Yet already in 1670, Leopold I expelled the Jews, giving them just a few weeks to leave the city. The *Unterer Werd* then became Leopoldstadt (present-day 2nd District) and the synagogue was turned into a church.

Total emancipation was not granted to Vienna's Jewish population until 1867 and Franz Josef. This action ensured him the lasting loyalty of the Jewish community; it also resulted in a massive influx of Jews into the capital. Unfortunately, at the beginning of the 20C, they were confronted by the anti-Semitism of Karl Lueger's Christian-Democrats. According to Adolph Hitler, Lueger was "the most outstanding mayor of all time". This hostile climate lies at the root of the Zionism founded by Theodor Herzl, a Viennese by adoption. The many examples of intellectual achievement among Vienna's Jewish residents at the end of the 19C and the beginning of the 20C bear witness to the community's importance. Its members included Sigmund Freud, Joseph Roth, Arthur Schnitzler, Arnold Schönberg and Ludwig Wittgenstein, among many others. The annexation of Austria by Nazi Germany in 1938 had catastrophic consequences, especially the *Reichskristallnacht* (the Night of Broken Glass) from 9 November to 10 November 1938 and the ensuing acts of violence toward Jews. About 65 000 Austrian Jews were deported and killed during the Second World War.

Tour – The ground floor contains an auditorium in which the Jewish religion is explained according to selected objects from the collection of Max Berger. Changing exhibitions occupy the first floor. Note the interesting painted coffered ceilings. The "historical exhibition" on the second floor is an impressive holographic display of thought-provoking images relating to the Jewish community in Vienna. It features large, bare glass panels displaying their contents only if observed from the correct angle. They trace the painful recent past of the Jewish community, a nightmare which became only too real and which hopefully will never recur. Most of the documents describe the everyday life of Vienna's Jews, in particular in the former Leopoldstadt ghetto. In the centre of the room, a plinth displays the principal dates of Jewish history in Vienna, from 903 to date.

The display cases on the 3rd floor contain religious objects mainly from the modern Jewish religious community.

Take Dorotheergasse in the opposite direction.

Dorotheum – *Dorotheergasse No 17.* It is impossible to overlook the majestic façade of this institution. On the site of the church and the cloister which gave it its name, the Dorotheum is one of the largest auction houses in the world. "Tante Dorothee" occupies several neo-Baroque buildings dating from 1898 to 1901 and designed by Emil von Förster. In the courtyard *(Klosterneuburger Hof, Dorotheergasse No 15)* is a fragment of mural from the former Dorotheerkirche (16C).

Antique art, paintings, sculptures, glass and porcelain, silver objects, weapons, clocks, furniture, books, stamps, and also toys and even comic books are all auctioned in the rooms of this former pawnbroking institution which Joseph I founded in 1707 *(see Practical information, Shopping)*. Some articles are even put on free sale in the so-called Freiverkauf.

Return and turn left into Stallburggasse, then immediately to the right into Bräunerstrasse.

Bräunerstrasse – At No 3 is a house with a Rococo façade dating from 1761. **Johann Nestroy** was born there on 7 December 1801. He was an actor, opera singer, painter, moralist and theatre director.

It is possible to extend the tour by going to Graben and Peterskirche (see City Centre and the Ring, Stephansdom District).

The nearest sights are: Hofburg, the Staatsoper and the Freyung District, and the Stephansdom (to be found in the City Centre and the Ring section).

KUNSTHISTORISCHES MUSEUM★★★

Local map page 13, **HS**
Underground: MuseumsQuartier (U2)
Tram: Burgring (1, 2, D, J)
Bus: Museumsquartier (2A)

The Habsburgs assembled these collections of art, which are among the greatest and most extensive in the world. A trip to Vienna would be incomplete without a visit to this museum and its numerous masterpieces.

The Kunsthistorisches Museum comprises ten sections. The main building on the Ring houses five of these: the Ägyptisch-Orientalische Sammlung (Egyptian and Near Eastern collections), the Antikensammlung (Greek, Etruscan and Roman antiquities); the Kunstkammer (fine arts); the Gemäldegalerie (paintings); and the Münzkabinett (coins and medals). The other five collections are located in exterior annexes – primarily the Hofburg, which is home to the Weltliche und Geistliche Schatzkammer (sacred and temporal treasures), the Sammlung alter Musikinstrumente (Collection of Ancient Music Intruments), the Hofjagd-und Rüstkammer (Royal Hunting and Armoury Collection), and the Ephesos-Museum (Ephesus Museum). Last, the Wagenburg collection is found in Schönbrunn.

The main building on the Ring was opened on 17 October 1891 by Emperor Franz Josef. Construction of the exhibition building began in 1871 following plans by Viennese architect Karl Hasenauer; these were subsequently revised by Gottfried

Stairwell with Antonio Canova's *Theseus Slaying the Minotaur*

Kunsthistorisches Museum

Semper. The latter's stamp is also found on the sculptural embellishments of the façade, representing the various artistic disciplines as well as artists and thinkers from throughout the ages. Johann Bank's statue of Pallas Athene, patron of the arts and sciences, crowns the dome of the building. The building's interior furnishings are themselves works of art; thankfully, they remained largely intact despite heavy damage caused by bombing during the Second World War. Hasenaur's concept was to make the furnishings and exhibitions correspond to one another; in accordance with this, three Egyptian pillars were installed in the rooms of the Egyptian collection. The ceiling paintings frequently cite the epochs and artists displayed in these halls.

The culmination of the building's interior furnishings is undoubtedly the splendid **Stiegenhaus**★★ or stairwell, whose ceilings are graced by Mihály Munkácsy's *Apotheosis of the Renaissance*, presenting the pantheon of Italian Renaissance artists. On the left, Leonardo da Vinci converses with the young Raphael while coming down the stairs. Above them, Veronese can be seen in front of his canvas; Michelangelo is found behind the balustrade, as is Titian and a pupil in front of a female model. The twelve lunettes are furnished with Hans Makart's ten portraits of painters (including Dürer, Leonardo, Rembrandt and Velázquez), the allegorical *Law and Truth*, and a personification of profane and religious painting. The paintings between the capitals of the pillars portray the course of art's development. Among other contributors, these episodes were created by Gustav Klimt (Egypt, Grecian antiquity, ancient Italian art, Florentine Cinquecento, and Roman and Venetian Quattrocento). Canova's Theseus group, **Theseus Slaying the Minotaur**★, was created in 1820 especially for the Theseus Temple in the Volksgarten *(see City Centre and the Ring, the Ring, Dr.-Karl-Renner-Ring)*, but is now to be found here at the landing. In the middle room of the raised ground floor behind the Stiegenhaus, Julius Berger immortalised *The Patrons of the Visual Arts in the House of Habsburg* who compiled these unique collections.

THE COLLECTIONS

The following section lists only a small selection of works of art most worth seeing, as a guide to the visitor.

★★Ägyptische-orientalische Sammlung
(Egyptian and Near Eastern collection) *Ground floor mezzanine*

Old Kingdom (2660-2160 BC), Middle Kingdom (2040-1785 BC), New Kingdom 1552-1070 BC), Late Age (712-332 BC)

GALLERIES	CONTENTS	SELECTION
I	Cult of the dead	Sarcophagus of Nes-Shu-Tefnu (c 300 BC; **papyrus columns**★ (18th dynasty).
II	Ancient Orient	
III	Animal worship	Ichneumon (6C-4C BC), mongoose relief.
IV	Papyruses	Khonsu Mes' Book of the Dead (c 1 000 BC).
V	Late Age: sculptures	Walking lion (Babylon, 6C BC); sphinx of Wah Ib Re (end 4C BC).
VI	Everyday life	Necklace and bracelet (c 2290 BC, gold and faience); head of a woman (13C BC); foreign peoples represented on Tell el-Yahudiya decorated tiles (12C BC).
VI A	Old Kingdom: cult of the dead	Funeral chapel of Prince Kaninisout's mastaba (2400 BC).
VII	Middle and New Kingdoms: sculptures	Hippopotamus (faience, blue glazing, c 2000 BC); sphinx head of Sesostris III (c 1850 BC); tomb of Hori (8C BC); **Sebek Em Sauf**★★ (statue of an official, c 1700 BC); Horus and King Harembeb (4C BC); Tjenena (15C BC); Khai-Hapi (13C BC?); **head of King Thoutmosis III**★ (c 1460 BC).
VIII	Old Kingdoms: sculptures	**Substitute head**★★ (The funerary head symbolised the body of the dead person; mummification was not yet widely practised; 26C BC); Ka-Pu-Ptah and Ipep (c 2300 BC); Ba'Ef Ba (c 2300 BC); Itjef with wife and children (c 2200 BC).

KUNSTHISTORISCHES MUSEUM (Mezzanine)

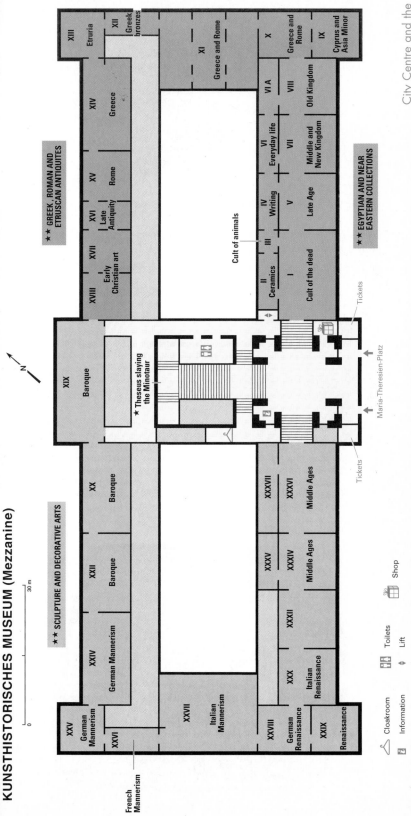

★★ SCULPTURE AND DECORATIVE ARTS

★★ GREEK, ROMAN AND ETRUSCAN ANTIQUITES

★★ EGYPTIAN AND NEAR EASTERN COLLECTIONS

French Mannerism

XXV German Mannerism
XXVI
XXIV German Mannerism
XXII Baroque
XX Baroque
XIX Baroque
XVIII Early Christian art
XVII
XVI Late Antiquity
XV Rome
XIV Greece
XIII Etruria
XII Greek bronzes

★ Theseus slaying the Minotaur

XXVII Italian Mannerism
XXVIII German Renaissance
XXIX Renaissance
XXX Italian Renaissance
XXXII Middle Ages
XXXIV Middle Ages
XXXV
XXXVI Middle Ages
XXXVII

II Ceramics
III Cult of animals
IV Writing
V Late Age
VI Everyday life
VII Middle and New Kingdom
VI A
VIII Old Kingdom
X Greece and Rome
IX Cyprus and Asia Minor
XI Greece and Rome

Cult of the dead

Tickets

Maria-Theresien-Platz

Tickets

N

30 m

◁ Cloakroom
ℹ Information
🛅 Toilets
◆ Lift
🎁 Shop

City Centre and the Ring

131

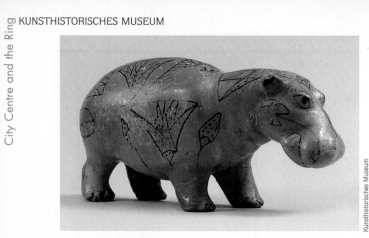

Faience hippopotamus with blue ceramic glazing

**Antikensammlung (Greek and Roman antiquities)

Ground floor mezzanine

Etruria: bronze helmets; bucchero amphoras; Athena of Rocca d'Aspromonte (5C BC).

Greek bronzes: Disc (c 500 BC); Hercules (4C BC); **Head of Zeus** (1C BC).

Greek ceramics and terracotta: **Douris cup** (c 500 BC); skyphos from Brigos (c 490 BC); series of lecythi; Tanagra figurines; **Ptolemaic cameo** (nine-layered onyx, 3C BC).

Greek and Roman sculptures: **Youth of Magdalensberg** (16C copy). This was long thought to be the original (1C BC), yet it is only a recasting of the original statue which was discovered in Carinthia in 1502; head of Artemis; (2C BC); Artemis (3C BC); **Sarcophagus of the Amazons** (second half of 4C BC); **Portrait of Aristotle** (Roman copy); fragment of Parthenon frieze (c 440 BC); relief of Mithra (second half of 2C); sphinx with four faces (2C); sarcophagus depicting lion hunt (second half of 3C).

Rome – *Cameo collection; sculpture; mosaics; glass:* **Gemma Augustea cameo** (1C). A cameo is a gem carved in relief. This art is of Egyptian and Oriental origin. The Greeks brought it to perfection with their polychrome cameos. The Romans appreciated this technique and from the 1C BC, employed valuable gems and imported artists from as far away as India. The *Gemma Augustea* enjoys world renown and commemorates the military victories of the first Roman emperor, visible at the top on his throne. Eagle cameo (1C BC); **Gemma Claudia** (1C); busts of emperors; treasure of Dolichenus (beginning of 3C).

The *Gemma Augustea* cameo

Late antiquity – *Sculpture and jewellery*: portrait of Eutropios (2nd half 5C).

Early Christian art: treasure of Szilágysomlyó (c 400, Romania); pair of fibulae (5C); golden **Treasure of Nagyszentmiklôs**★ (9C – in modern Romania). The treasure of Nagyszentmiklôs was discovered in 1799 and comprises 23 ceremonial vases belonging to a tribal chief; it amounts to nearly 10kg of pure gold. Surprisingly, several influences are evident in this find: central Asian, Persian-Sassanid, Greco-Roman and Byzantine.

★★Kunstkammer

Ground floor mezzanine

The Habsburgs' passion for collecting is legendary. Thanks to their knowledge and their artistic flair, they amassed over the years a collection which defies the imagination. It comprises the art galleries of Archduke Ferdinand II at Ambras Castle near Innsbruck, Rudolf II in Prague, Archduke Leopold-Wilhelm in Vienna and the Imperial Art Collection. Brought together in 1891, they formed a uniquely wideranging collection of outstanding quality.

This encyclopaedic collection encompasses a vast number of items. Only a few of them feature in the text, as an illustration of the extraordinarily high aesthetic worth of a collection which is almost a world of its own.

Middle Ages – The **Aquamanile in the shape of a Griffin**★★ (first third of 12C), made of nielloed bronze decorated with silver elements, is a receptacle used for hand washing in liturgical services. The griffin is a mythological creature, half eagle and half lion, and represents the twofold nature of Christ as well as the twofold power of the Church. The Wilten Chalice (Lower Saxony, c 1160-70) is a communion chalice of partly gilded, nielloed silver. The onyx cameo of Poseidon as Lord of the Isthmian games (beginning of 13C), with a gold setting dating to the early 19C, was made in southern Italy; the theme of the work is especially interesting, since it already shows characteristics of the Renaissance *(Gallery XXXVI)*. Two painted sets of playing cards: the *Ambraser Hofjagd* set (middle

Aquamanile in the shape of a griffin

Kunsthistorisches Museum

of 15C), whose 54 drawings depict the royal falconry, and the *Hofämter* set (from c 1455), whose figures mirror the social heirarchy and professions of that day. The sandstone Krumauer Madonna (c 1400) comes from Bohemia; the gracious manner of the Virgin and the swinging folds of her garment are typical of the international Gothic style *(Gallery XXXIV)*.

German Renaissance, Mannerism and Baroque – Two partially gilded silver bowls (Nuremberg, c 1510), known as the Dürer and Maximilian Trophies; illustrate the evolution in modelling of ceremonial vessels from the late Gothic period to the early Renaissance; it is evident from his studies and sketches that Albrecht Dürer played a part in this transition *(Gallery XXXIV)*. The "automaton with trumpets" (Augsburg, 1582) is a small mechanical organ with 9 pipes and 11 moving figures, made of ebony, painted silver and gold-plated brass *(Gallery XXXV)*. The *Equestrian Statue of Joseph I*★★ overcoming the forces of evil is a brilliant ivory sculpture by Matthias Steinl (Vienna, 1693). The king is portrayed at the age of fifteen; the sculpture has two matching counterparts: the equestrian statue of Leopold I as victor over the Turks, and the statue of Karl VI receiving the Spanish crown *(Gallery XX)*. The *Bust of Emperor Leopold I*★ by Paul Strudel (1695) belongs to a series of six portraits commissioned by the Elector Johann Wilhelm of Pfalz-Neuburg, brother-in-law of the emperor shown here *(Gallery XIX)*. The Bezoar vessel of enamelled gold is a delicate work by Jan Vermeyen (c 1600); bezoar is an accretion of indigestible matter

Isabella of Aragon by Francesco Laurana

in the intestines of the bezoar goat and the llama *(Gallery XXIV)*. The *Battle of the Amazons* is a cedar wood carving by Ignaz Elhafen (c 1685); it represents one of the 12 labours of Hercules *(Gallery XX)*. In Prague, Adriaen de Vries created the **Bust of Emperor Rudolf II**★★ (1603), the great Habsburg patron of the arts; the pedestal is made up of Jupiter, Mercury, and an imperial eagle *(Gallery XXIV)*. An ornamental basin and pitcher by Christoph Jamnitzer portray Cupid's triumphal procession (1604 *(Gallery XXIV)*. The **ewer**★ of Seychelles coconut (Prague, 1602) by Anton Schweinberger is a masterpiece of the goldsmith's skill, enclosing a nut which was once taken to be seafood *(Gallery XXIV)*. A jug is a fairly commonplace object; however, this example carved in amber in Königsberg in the early 17C is out of the ordinary, consisting of different transparent layers *(Gallery XXV)*. Clement Kicklinger was a craftsman from Augsburg who made some unusual objects, including an ostrich egg in a setting decorated with coral *(Gallery XXIV)*. Items from nature set in imaginative ways were very sought after for art collections.

French Mannerism – The **Bust of Archduchess Marie Antoinette**★ is by Jean Baptiste Lemoyne and represents the dauphine during the year of her marriage (at the age of 15); her husband's grandfather, Louis XV, commissioned it as a gift to Empress Maria Theresa *(Gallery XX)*. There are several Limoges enamels in a showcase: plates and dishes (mid-16C) by Pierre Reymond *(Gallery XXVI)*. The golden "Michael's goblet" was bought from an Antwerp merchant by King François I of France. The crowning figure of Michael is made up of diamonds *(Gallery XXVI)*. Both this goblet and the onyx ewer (the latter by Richard Toutain, Paris, c 1570) were gifts of Charles IX of France to Archduke Ferdinand of Tyrol. The ewer is set with enamel, emeralds, rubies and diamonds.

Salt-cellar by Benvenuto Cellini

Italian Renaissance and Mannerism – The *Bust of Isabella of Aragon*★★★ was conceived by Francesco Laurana as an idealised portrait of Petrarch's Laura (who figures prominently in his poetry) and dates from about 1488. Laurana was an itinerant artist from Dalmatia; presumably, he sculpted the portrait during a stay in Naples; the polychrome marble and subtle tones make this an outstanding work *(Gallery XXXII)*. Benvenuto Cellini made the gold and partly enamelled *salt-cellar*★★ in Paris between 1540 and 1543 for King Francis I. This masterpiece of the goldsmith's art rests on an ebony pedestal and depicts the personages of Neptune, king of the seas, holding a trident, and the goddess of Earth. The boat is to contain salt, and the triumphal arch, pepper *(Gallery XXVII)*. The handsome busts of *Emperor Karl V and Queen Maria of Hungary* (1555) were created by Leone Leoni, who also minted papal and imperial coins in Milan *(Gallery XXVII)*. His son Pompeo Leoni created the painted silver *Head of Philip II*, to which Balthasar Moll added an earthenware bust in 1753 *(Gallery XVII)*. The flying Mercury (c 1585) is a very famous work by Giambologna (Jean Boulogne), a Flemish sculptor working in Florence *(Gallery XXVII)*. The *Small Altarpiece of Christ and the Samaritan Woman*★ is a typically Florentine piece of work. It was made in the late 16C for Archduke Ferdinand I of Medici; its stone mosaic construction depicts Christ and the Woman of Samaria at Vienna's Jakobsbrunnen. The frame of rock crystal is by Gian Ambrogio Caroni, and the goldsmith work by Jacques Byliveldt *(Gallery XXIX)*. The *Flagellation of Christ* by Alessandro Algardi, a Roman work dating from about 1630, is fire-gilt with bronze, agate, lapis lazuli and marble *(Gallery XXII)*.

★★★Gemäldegalerie

First floor

Special exhibitions are mounted in Gallery VIII; entry to these is included in the museum's price of admission.

In the following, we have limited ourselves to a selection of especially noteworthy works of art, together with a few biographical details of some of the artists. This approach offers the advantage of highlighting the major features of this extensive art gallery; as such, it also takes into account the preferences of the individual Habsburg art patrons who created this princely collection.

Gallery IX – Michiel Coxcie (1499-1592), *The Expulsion from Paradise* (c 1550), also works of Hans Vredeman de Vries (1527-c 1605), Frans Floris (1516-70) and Lucas Valckenborch (c 1530-97).

Side gallery 14 – Jan van Eyck, *Cardinal Nicolo Albergati*★★ (c 1435), a dignified realistic portrait, and *The Goldsmith Jan de Leeuw* (1436). Jean Fouquet, *The Ferrara Court Jester Gonella*★ (c 1440-50). Hugo van der Goes *Diptych: The Fall of Man and Redemption*★★ (c 1470-75). Rogier van der Weyden, *Triptych: the Crucifixion*★ (c 1440). Hieronymus Bosch (c 1450-1516), by whom the Gemäldegalerie der Akademie der bildenden Künste has a further masterpiece *(see City Centre and the Ring, the Ring, Opernring)*, *Christ Carrying the Cross* (c 1480-90). Gerard David (c 1460-1523), *The Archangel Michael's Altar* (c 1510). Joos van Cleve, *Virgin with Child* (c 1530) and *Lucretia*★ (1520-25).

Jan van Eyck (c 1390-1441) – With his brother Hubert, he further developed the technique of oil painting. The two were the founders of the new style of painting which evolved out of the Gothic tradition into the art of early Dutch masters.

Jean Fouquet (c 1420-c 1480) – During his stay in Italy, his talent attracted the attention of Pope Eugenius IV who commissioned him to paint his portrait. According to a contemporary Italian artist, he was "a good master, especially in his portrayal from life".

Hugo van der Goes (c 1440-82) – This artist of melancholy temperament assimilated the achievements of Jan van Eyck. He suffered mental illness and retired to an Augustinian monastery near Brussels as a lay brother. More than any other artist, he knew how to express the personality of his subjects.

Rogier van der Weyden (c 1400-64) – After Jan van Eyck's death, he was the leading representative of Flemish painting, although he was born in Tournai, which was French at the time. He was official painter to the city of Brussels, hence the translation of his name which was originally Rogier de la Pasture ("of the meadow" in French).

Joos van Cleve (c 1485-1540) – He travelled to Germany, France and probably Italy, integrating these experiences with Flemish tradition. His portraits earned him lasting fame.

Side gallery 15 – Joachim Patenier (c 1485-1524), *The Baptism of Christ* (c 1515). Herri met de Bles (c 1510-c 1550), *Landscape with St John the Baptist Preaching* (1535-40). Jan Gossaert (c 1478-1532), called Mabuse because he was born in Maubeuge, *St Luke Painting the Virgin* (c 1520).

City Centre and the Ring

Kunsthistorisches Museum

Hunters in the Snow by Pieter Bruegel the Elder

Gallery X – This room undeniably holds a unique assembly of paintings, including 14 paintings by **Pieter Bruegel the Elder** – out of a total of 45 throughout the world: *The Tower of Babel*★★, *The Battle of Carnival and Lent*★★ (1559), *Children's Games*★★ (1560), *The Ascent to Calvary*★ (1564), *Peasant Dance*★ (1568-69) and *Peasant Wedding*★ (1568-69). One of the most remarkable features in many of the paintings is the near absence of a sky. *Hunters in the Snow*★★★ (1565) is indisputably a masterpiece, part of a series of six seasonal paintings of which five are still extant, including three in this museum. The cycle began with the first days of spring and ended with this scene showing the peasants returning home after hunting. Even more than the subject itself, it is the pictorial composition and coldness of the colours that convey the chilly wintry atmosphere.

Bruegel the Elder (c 1527-69) – Pieter Bruegel probably came from a village called Brueghel, in Dutch Brabant or in the Limburg Kempen (in modern Belgium). He soon signed his name Bruegel, a spelling to which he adhered to the end of his life. *Bruegel de Oude*, i.e. the Elder, served his apprenticeship in Antwerp, then travelled as far as Messina before returning in 1554 to Flanders, which was then the richest country in Europe. In 1563, he settled in Brussels and married Marie Coecke, daughter of Pieter Coecke, court painter to Charles V. He founded a family which produced 26 painters. His eldest son was Pieter Brueghel the Younger (1564-1638), his youngest son was Jan Brueghel (1568-1625) who in the 18C acquired the nickname of "Velvet" Brueghel or "Flowers" Brueghel.

Gallery XI – Jacob Jordaens (1593-1678), *The Feast of the Bean King* (before 1656). Frans Snyders, (1579-1657), *Fish Market* (c 1618).

Side gallery 16 – Albrecht Dürer, *Madonna and Child with Pear* (1512), **Portrait of a Young Venetian Woman**★ (1505), *The Martyrdom of the Ten Thousand Christians* (1508), and **The Adoration of the Holy Trinity**★★ (1511). This altar has an unusual feature: there is a self-portrait of the painter in the lower right-hand corner and he is the only person in the painting with his feet on the ground; the inscription he is holding makes it clear he is the artist.

Albrecht Dürer (1471-1528) – Germany's most illustrious artist already enjoyed great renown during his lifetime, especially as an engraver. He had learned how to use an engraver's chisel in the studio used by his father, a Nürnberg goldsmith of Hungarian descent. The German Romantics considered him to be the supreme example of German artistic genius.

Side gallery 17 – Albrecht Dürer, **Portrait of Emperor Maximilian I**★ (1519) and *Portrait of Johann Kleberger* (1526). Martin Schongauer, **The Holy Family**★ (c 1480). Lucas Cranach the Elder, **The Crucifixion**★★ (1500-01), **Judith with the Head of Holofernes**★ (c 1530). Hans Baldung-Grien (c 1485-1545), *The Three Ages and Death* (1509-10). Leonhard Beck (c 1480-1542), *St George and the Dragon* (c 1515). Bernhard Strigel (c 1460-1528), *Emperor Maximilian I and his Family* (1515). Albrecht Altdorfer, **The Nativity**★ (c 1520). Wolf Huber (c 1485-1553), *The Humanist Jakob Ziegler* (after 1544).

KUNSTHISTORISCHES MUSEUM (1st floor)

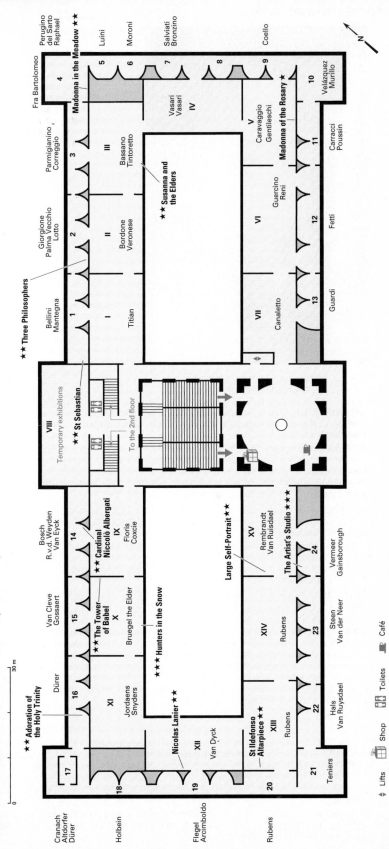

City Centre and the Ring

★★ Three Philosophers

★★ Madonna in the Meadow

Perugino
del Sarto
Raphael ★★

Fra Bartolomeo

Luini

Moroni

Salviati
Bronzino

Coello

Velázquez
Murillo

Parmigianino
Correggio

Giorgione
Palma Vecchio
Lotto

Bellini
Mantegna

★★ Susanna and
the Elders

Bassano
Tintoretto

Vasari
Vasari

Bordone
Veronese

Titian

Caravaggio
Gentileschi

Madonna of the Rosary ★

Guercino
Reni

Canaletto

Carracci
Poussin

Fetti

Guardi

★★ St Sebastian

VIII
Temporary exhibitions

To the 2nd floor

Bosch
R.v.d. Weyden
Van Eyck

★★ Cardinal
Niccolò Albergati

Floris
Coxcie

Large Self-Portrait ★★

The Artist's Studio ★★★

Van Cleve
Gossaert

★★ The Tower
of Babel

Bruegel the Elder

★★★ Hunters in the Snow

Rembrandt
Van Ruisdael

Vermeer
Gainsborough

Dürer

Steen
Van der Neer

★★ Adoration of
the Holy Trinity

Jordaens
Snyders

Nicolas Lanier ★★

Rubens

Rubens

Cranach
Altdorfer
Dürer

Holbein

Flegel
Arcimboldo

Rubens

St Ildefonso
Altarpiece ★★

Van Dyck

Hals
Van Ruysdael

Teniers

Lifts   Shop   Toilets   Café

30 m

137

City Centre and the Ring

Kunsthistorisches Museum

Judith with the Head of Holofernes
by Lucas Cranach the Elder

Martin Schongauer (c 1450-91) – The son of an Augsburg goldsmith, he trained in Colmar, where he was born, in a milieu rich with Flemish influences. His work comprises engraving on copper, a technique in which he excelled, and painting. His painting is notable for great attention to detail.

Lucas Cranach the Elder (1472-1553) – This friend of Luther produced his first paintings in Vienna. His work has been considered by some to be over-emotive or too demanding. He also worked at the Court of Wittenberg and painted portraits of Protestant princes. It is sometimes difficult to distinguish his work from that of his assistants.

Albrecht Altdorfer (c 1480-1538) – A member of the Danube School, this citizen of Regensburg specialised in scenes from the Passion and landscapes, which increasingly became void of any human representations. The Romantics prized his works.

Side gallery 18 – Hans Holbein the Younger, *Jane Seymour*★ (1536) and *Dr John Chambers, Physician to King Henry VIII* (1543). Jakob Seisenegger (1505-67), *Emperor Charles V* (1532).

Hans Holbein the Younger (1497-1543) – Born in Augsburg and died in London. His first patron was the burgomaster of Basle, Jakob Meyer. In England, he became famous among the aristocracy at court for his portraits which combine total objectivity in his reproduction of human features with minutely observed detail in his representation of sumptuous court dress.

Side gallery 19 – Giuseppe Arcimboldo, *The Fire*★★ (1566). Roelant Savery (1576-1639), *Landscape with Animals* (c 1618). Georg Flegel (1566-1638), *Still Life Dessert with Bouquet of Flowers*★ (1632), an unusually refined composition.

Giuseppe Arcimboldo (c 1527-93) – The museum has four allegorical paintings by this artist *(Fire, Water, Summer, Winter)* who attained the rank of Count Palatine. His technical brilliance is unusual in Mannerist art but his style found great favour in the German Empire.

Gallery XII – This room is devoted to Sir Anthony van Dyck, and contains some exceptionally fine portraits and religious works: *Study of a Female Head* (c 1620), *Portrait of a Young General* (c 1624), *Nicolas Lanier*★★ (1628), *Samson and Delilah* (1628-30), *Venus at Vulcan's Forge*★ (1630-32), *Prince Rupert of the Palatinate* (1631-32) and *Jacomo de Cachiopin* (1634).

Sir Anthony van Dyck (1599-1641) – It may well be true that Rubens' former assistant enjoyed luxury and that his behaviour was apt to be capricious; however, the secret of his success depended on the principles of study and discipline. He was a portrait painter who tried to delve into the soul of his models rather than flatter them, even if they were kings or princes.

Side gallery 20 – This and the two following galleries concentrate on Peter Paul Rubens. *The Lamentation* (1614) and *St Jerome Dressed as a Cardinal* (c 1625).

Gallery XIII – *The Triumph of Venus* (1635-37); *Self-Portrait*★ (1638-40); and *The Little Fur*★★ (1635-40), which depicts Helen Fourment, Rubens' wife. The *Ildefonso Altar*★★ (1630-32) dates from the time when Rubens was Court painter in the Netherlands. Coudenberg Abbey sold it for 15 000 livres to build a church in Brussels, which gives an indication of how much the Viennese Court appreciated Rubens.

Gallery XIV – *Vincent II Gonzaga, Prince of Mantua* (1604/05), *The Annunciation* (1609), *The Assumption* (1611-14), *The Miracles of St Francis Xavier* (1617-19) and *Young Girl with Fan* (1612-14).

Peter Paul Rubens (1577-1640) – A dominant figure in Baroque art, he was a prolific painter, famous during his lifetime, and worked also as a diplomat. His lasting prestige rests upon his powerful style and his designs in warm colours, both precise and monumental. Some modern viewers might find his paintings pompous, however they should remember that his grandiose style heralded the Baroque era in the northern countries and that his influence was decisive there.

Side gallery 21 – David Teniers the Younger, *Archduke Leopold Wilhelm in his Gallery in Brussels*★ (c 1651).

David Teniers the Younger (1610-90) – This member of St Luke's Freemasons' Lodge in Antwerp was an eclectic painter who settled in Brussels. There, Archduke Leopold Wilhelm made him the director of his art gallery.

Side gallery 22 – Frans Hals (c 1585-1666), *Portrait of a Man* (1654-55). Salomon van Ruysdael (c 1600-70), *Landscape with Fence* (1631).

Side gallery 23 – Jacob van Ruisdael (c 1628-82), *River Landscape with Cellar Entrance* (1649). Aert van der Neer (c 1603-77), *Fishing by Moonlight* (c 1669).

Side gallery 24 – Thomas Gainsborough (1727-88), *Suffolk Landscape* (c 1750). Jan Vermeer, *The Artist's Studio*★★★ (1665-66). To achieve this view of his studio where we see him from behind, the artist used a camera obscura. This is his most ambitious painting, bathed in an exceptional light through the use of an almost Pointillist painting technique.

Jan Vermeer (1632-75) – This Dutch painter's reputation rests upon a relatively small number of paintings. His work often depicts scenes of everyday life, to which he added a timeless dimension. His work did not revolutionise painting. However, his masterful use of light and his subtle palette make Vermeer one of the most remarkable masters of the 17C and in the whole of art history.

The Artist's Studio by Jan Vermeer

Gallery XV – Jacob van Ruisdael, *The Great Forest* (1655-60). Ludolf Bakuizen (1631-1708),*The Swedish Yacht "Lejonet" on the Ij off Amsterdam* (1674). Rembrandt is represented by the portraits *Prophetess Hannah* (1639), *Titus van Rijn, the Artist's Son, Reading* (1656-57); and a very interesting series, including: *Small Self-Portrait*★ (c 1657) and *Large Self-Portrait*★★ (1652). The latter dates from a period of financial difficulties and does not depict the artist in the splendid attire of his youth. He wears a simple, dark painter's smock; the light primarily illuminates his face, as if to stress the ravages of time.

Rembrandt (1606-69) – Few painters have achieved such universal appeal as Rembrandt, the son of a Dutch miller. This highly successful artist is intriguing, nevertheless, because of the disparity between his life and his art. He painted his most serene pictures soon after his wife's death, and his happiest self-portrait was his last, now in Cologne.

Cross the hall to Gallery I.

Gallery I – The museum possesses numerous paintings by the Venetian School. This room is devoted to Titian and contains many of his masterpieces, including *The Virgin of the Gypsies (1510), The Virgin with Cherries* (1516-18), *Bravo* (c 1520), *Woman in Furs*★★ (c 1535) and *Ecce Homo*★ (1543, dated and signed on the palace steps).

Titian (c 1490-1576) – This Venetian painter enjoys universal renown. His work is among the greatest achievements of the Renaissance, displaying vivacity, energy, psychological insight in portraits, and grandeur. He was exceptionally long-lived for the time. His earlier naturalistic vision developed into a Mannerist technique which gave free reign to his almost dramatic expressiveness. At sixty, he was still innovative, executing commissions from princes and producing work which was increasingly occupied with the spiritual.

Side gallery 1 – Andrea Mantegna, *St Sebastian*★★ (1457-59).

Andrea Mantegna (1431-1506) – His work is of particular significance in the history of art. It combines Tuscan perspective, Venetian dramatic flair and Roman echoes of classical mythology. Anyone wishing to understand Italian Renaissance painting should study the work of this painter from Padua.

Side gallery 2 – Palma the Elder, *Virgin with Child Surrounded by Saints* (1520-25). Giorgione, *Young Woman* (1506) and **The Three Philosophers**★★ (1508-09), a major contribution to the history of Venetian painting. According to Giorgio Vasari, his "new manner" was to paint without a preliminary sketch on paper, a technical change of the utmost importance. Lorenzo Lotto, **Portrait of A Young Man against a White Curtain**★ (c 1508), *Gentleman with Lion's Paw* (1524-25) and *Triple Portrait of a Goldsmith* (1525-35).

Giorgione (c 1477-1510) – Few details of his life are known, but his fame is great, owing mainly to the celebrated *Tempest* in the Galleria dell'Accademia in Venice.

Lorenzo Lotto (c 1480-1557) – Although not much is known about this Venetian painter, we can say that he was an independent spirit of daring temperament and a very active artist. His greatest ambition was to develop a highly eclectic style, without drifting into Mannerism. Therein lies the great power of his work.

Gallery II – Veronese, *The Anointing of David* (c 1555), *The Raising of the Youth of Nain* (1565-70) and *The Adoration of the Magi* (c 1580).

Gallery III – Tintoretto, *Lorenzo Soranzo* (1553), *Sebastiano Venier* (1571-72), *St Jerome*★ (1571-75) and **Susannah and the Elders**★★ (1555-56). The latter typically Mannerist painting displays various influences and represents the peak of Venetian art. The composition is full of contrasts (light-dark, youth-age, proximity-distance) and takes as its subject a scene from the Old Testament.

Tintoretto (1518-94) – Jacopo Robusti was the son of a dyer, and he was small, hence his nickname. He was of affable temperament and transmitted this name to his descendants. It is said that his studio displayed a sign saying: "Michelangelo's drawing, Titian's colours".

Side gallery 3 – Correggio, *Ganymede* (1530) and *Jupiter and Io* (1530). Moretto (c 1498-1554), *Portrait of a Young Woman* (c 1540). Parmigianino, **Self-Portrait in a Convex Mirror**★ (1523-24) and *Portrait of a Man* (1525-30).

Parmigianino (1503-40) – **Francesco Mazzola** was born in Parma and came under the influence of Correggio. He was very precocious, producing mature works at the age of sixteen. The self-portrait in Vienna is part of a whole series tracing the psychological development of this artist.

Side gallery 4 – Perugino (c 1450-1523), *The Baptism of Christ* (c 1500). Fra Bartolomeo, *Presentation in the Temple* (1516). Andrea del Sarto (1486-1530), *Lamentation* (1519-20). Raphael, **Virgin in the Meadow**★★ (1505), a painting typical of the Florentine High Renaissance, in its balance and harmony. It is also known as *Madonna of the Belvedere*.

Raphael (1483-1520) – For a long time, Raffaello Sanzio enjoyed a reputation as the greatest painter of all time. He is certainly the spiritual master of those who prized form above colour. Although his appeal waned after the birth of Impressionism, his powerful and lasting influence must be the envy of any creative artist. His paintings of the Virgin assured his immortal popularity.

Side gallery 5 – Giovanni Battista Moroni (c 1529-78), *The Sculptor Alessandro Vittoria* (1552).

Side gallery 6 – Bronzino (1503-72), *The Holy Family with St Anne and the Young John the Baptist* (1545/46).

Side gallery 9 – Alonso Sanchez Coello (c 1531-88), *The Infant Don Carlos* (1564). François Clouet (c 1510-72), *Charles IX of France* (1569).

Side gallery 10 – The department of Spanish painting is famous for its portraits of infantes and infantas by Velázquez: **The Infanta Margarita Teresa in a Pink Dress**★ (1653-54), **The Infanta Margarita Teresa in a Blue Dress**★ (1659) and *The Infante Philip Prosper* (1659). Bartolomé Esteban Murillo (c 1617-1682), *The Archangel St Michael*. Juan Bautista del Mazo (c 1612-1667), *Portrait of the Artist's Family* (1664-65).

Diego Rodríguez de Silva y Velázquez (1599-1660) – The creator of *Las Meninas* (1656; Prado, Madrid) became in 1633 Chief Marshal of the palace in Madrid. He painted portraits of the royal family before travelling to Italy on "in the service of the king". His encounter with the Venetian Cinquecento in c 1650 transformed his painting.

Side gallery 11 – Annibale Carracci, **The Lamentation**★ (1603-04) and *Christ and the Samaritan Woman* (c 1605).

Annibale Carracci (1560-1609) – Brother of Agostino and cousin of Lodovico, Annibale belonged to a leading family of painters. In 1595, Cardinal Farnese summoned the Bolognese artist to Rome. After 1605, mental illness prevented him from working.

Gallery V – Orazio Gentileschi (1563-1639), *Rest during the Flight into Egypt* (1626/28). Mattia Preti (1613-99), *The Incredulity of St Thomas* (1660-65). Caravaggio, **David Holding the Head of Goliath★** (1606-07) and **The Virgin with a Rosary★★** (1606-07). Here is artistic composition perfected: the realism and intensity of the scene almost make viewers feel they are taking part in the distribution of rosaries by St Dominic on the left.

Caravaggio (1573-1610) – Michelangelo Merisi, who became known as Caravaggio, had a tempestuous personality. Brawls and periods in prison punctuated his life in Milan until he fled to Genoa. In 1606, he killed his opponent in a game. He had to flee to Rome, then Naples, from where he left for Sicily. He died on the beach at Porto Ercole, completely exhausted and in a fever. Yet despite all this, he ranks among the greatest Italian painters, and many consider him the greatest of all Baroque painters.

Gallery VI – Guercino, **The Return of the Prodigal Son★** (c 1619). Guido Reni (1575-1642), *The Baptism of Christ* (1622/23). Giovanni Lanfranco (1582-1647), *The Virgin Appearing to St James and St Anthony* (c 1624). Francesco Solimena (1657-1747), *Descent from the Cross* (1730-31). Luca Giordano, **St Michael casts the Rebel Angels into the Abyss★** (c 1655).

Guercino (1591-1666) – His real name was Giovanni Francesco Barbieri. His career as a painter dates from his meeting with Lodovico Carracci. The latter encouraged him to develop his original naturalistic style and produce grand, luminous paintings.

Luca Giordano (1634-1705) – At the age of twenty, this Neapolitan artist conquered Rome with his virtuosity. He was in such a hurry to do everything that people nicknamed him *Luca fa presto*. He travelled throughout Italy then left for Spain in answer to Carlos II's summons. He was a prolific artist and is of great significance to anyone wishing to understand early 18C painting.

Side gallery 12 – Domenico Fetti (c 1588-1623), *The Return of the Prodigal Son* (1620-23). Jacopo Chimenti called Empoli (c 1551-1640), *Susannah Bathing* (1600). Bernardo Strozzi (1581-1644), *The Lute Player* (1640-44) and *The Prophet Elijah and the Widow of Zarephath* (c 1640).

Side gallery 13 – Francesco Guardi (1712-93), *The Miracle of St Dominic* (1763).

Gallery VII – Hyacinthe Rigaud (1659-1743), *Philipp Wenzel, Count Sinzendorf* (1728). Joseph-Sifrède Duplessis (1725-1802), *Christoph Willibald von Gluck* (1775). Canaletto, **View of Vienna from the Belvedere★** (1758-61), *Freyung from the Southeast* (1758-61) *(for illustration, see City Centre and the Ring, Freyung District)*.

Bernardo Bellotto (1720-80) – Bellotto was the nephew of the great Canaletto and is known under the same name as his uncle in Germany and Austria. He ranks among the greatest vedutisti, or painters of identifiable town- or landscapes. He worked in Dresden, Vienna, Munich and Warsaw.

Münzkabinett
Second floor

The coins and medals collection contains about 700 000 items spanning 3 millennia: coins, paper money, medals and awarded decorations etc. Two rooms of the collection give an outline of the evolution of money and of medals; special exhibitions are shown in the third room.

Kunsthistorisches Museum

A florin bearing the effigy of Maximilian I

The nearest sights are the Burgring and Hofburg, the Staatsoper District (see the City Centre and the Ring section), the MuseumsQuartier, and the Mariahilf, Neubau and Wieden Districts (in the Outside the Ring section).

RATHAUS

Local map page 13, **HR**
Underground: Rathaus (U2)
Tram: Rathausplatz/Burgtheater (1, 2, D), Rathaus (J)
Bus: Teinfaltstrasse (1A)

Neues Rathaus ⊘ – *Rathausplatz 1.* Facing Burgtheater, the "New City Hall" was constructed from 1872 to 1883 by Friedrich von Schmidt to replace the old one (called the Altes Rathaus, *see City Centre and the Ring, Hoher Markt District*), still visible in Wipplingerstrasse. The architect decided upon a neo-Gothic style evocative of the Middle Ages when most of the large cities acquired their borough charters. Brussels City Hall (1402-55) on the magnificent Grand-Place was his inspiration.

The building is the seat of the administrative and legislative authorities of the Land (the Regional Assembly) and the City of Vienna; these functions have been amalgamated under the same administration since 1921 when Vienna acquired the twin status of federal capital and independent state within Austria. Simply walking along one of the streets bordering it *(Felderstrasse or Lichtenfelsgasse)* makes the visitor aware of the colossal bureaucracy behind the majestic and impressive walls of this monumental building. The figures speak for themselves: an area of 14 000m²/ 16 744sq yd, seven interior courtyards, a central tower 98m/321ft high, two lateral towers "only" 61m/200ft high. At nightfall, the middle tower lights up; it is surmounted by the *Ratshausmann*, a copper figure of a knight carrying the town banner (which weighs 1 800kg/4 000lb and measures 3.40m/11ft).

The tour starts with the Stadtbureau *(entrance through Friedrich-Schmidt-Platz)* in the former foyer and continues through the reception rooms. These include the great Festsaal (assembly hall), 71m/77yd long and 17m/55ft high, where the Book Fair takes place in November. The Gemeinderatssitzungssaal (debating chamber) is lavishly decorated with rare woods and a large chandelier designed by the architect. The Roter Salon (red room) with its Venetian chandeliers is the mayor's reception room.

In July, the central courtyard of the Rathaus is the setting for the **Jazzfest**.

The spire of the Rathaus (Town Hall) from Heldenplatz

Rathauspark – Rudolf Sieböck, director of the city's gardens, laid out the attractive City Hall park in 1872-73. It features statues of people who left their mark on the history of the city. The following **eight sculptures★** stand on either side of the avenue dividing the park in two. Starting at the southern end of the park, on the Ringstrasse side, there are monuments to: *Henry II Jasomirgott* (by Franz Melnitzky) who chose Vienna as his ducal capital, *Rudolf IV the Founder* (by Josef Gasser) who founded Vienna University, *Ernst Rüdiger Count of Starhemberg* (by Johann Fessler) who bravely resisted the Turks in 1683, *Johann Bernhard Fischer von Erlach* (by Josef Cesar), the most brilliant court architect, *Leopold VI the Glorious* (by Johann Preleuthner) who granted Vienna its first authenticated city charter in 1221, *Niklas Count Salm* (by Matthias Purkartshofer) who defeated Suleyman the Magnificent in 1529, *Leopold Count Kollonitsch* (by Vinzenz Pilz), the bishop of Wiener Neustadt who gave moral support to Vienna's inhabitants in 1683, and *Josef von Sonnenfels* (by Hanns Gasser), Maria Theresa's counsellor who abolished torture.

The park also contains several other monuments: To the south, the *Johann Strauss und Josef Lanner Denkmal* (by Franz Seifert and Robert Oerley, 1905) which reconciles the famous rivals of the Viennese waltz; the *Ratshausmann*, a recent copy (1986) of the knight's statue above the immense belfry of the City Hall and the *Karl Renner Denkmal* (by Alfred Hrdlicka and Josef Krawina, 1967), in memory of the father of the Second Austrian Republic, of which he was president from 1945 to 1950. To the north, there is the *Ferdinand Georg Waldmüller Denkmal* (by Josef Engelhart, 1913), a memorial to a Biedermeier painter who frequently depicted the countryside around Vienna, and the *Karl Seitz Denkmal* (by Gottfried Buchberger, 1962), the popular Social-Democrat mayor of Vienna from 1923 to 1934.

A large projection screen is set up in front of the Town Hall in July and August, on which classical music video clips can be viewed free of charge in this open-air setting. During Advent, a large Christmas market occupies the central avenue in the park and the trees are adorned by red fairy lights, creating a magical festive atmosphere.

The closest sights to the Rathaus are the Freyung District, the Kunsthistorisches Museum and the Hofburg (to be found in the City Centre and the Ring section), as well as the Alsergrund, Josefstadt and Neubau Districts (found in the Outside the Ring section).

The RING★★

Local map pages 13/14
Ring Tram: Lines 1 and 2

The Ring is more than a street; it is the symbol that took Vienna into the modern world in the mid-19C. On 20 December 1857, Franz Josef signed a letter ordering the demolition of the ramparts around the town centre, in order to make way for a peripheric throroughfare lined with public buildings and rented accommodations.

The Ring represented a new Vienna with a neo-Absolutist regime gradually giving way to constitutional monarchy. It was a city in the process of throwing off the shackles of its old fortifications and opening up to growing industry and a "second society" of newly rich industrialists. It had economic hegemony and a programme of urbanisation comparable in Europe only to Haussmann's Paris.

Ringstrasse is 4km/2mi long and nearly 60m/196ft wide, and is lined with ailanthuses, lindens and plane trees. The buildings vary in style, but all fall under the category of "historicism". It was this grandiose historicism which, later, became anathema to the Secession movement. The architects erected a prestigious and fantastic façade of neo-Gothic towers, neo-Classical pediments, neo-Renaissance attics and neo-Baroque ornamentation. However, social contrasts in the city were as acute as in modern New York, then in its infancy. Slums abounded. This accounts for the large housing estates built after the proclamation of the Austrian Republic. These, together with the Ring, contributed to the reputation of Vienna.

The Ring is the last heritage of imperial Vienna. Although it took over three decades to carry out, this boulevard has since remained unchanged. Exploring it is a form of time travel.

Exploring the Ring by car is not recommended, because of the heavy traffic. The best method is on foot or by bicycle – unless you prefer to go by tram (circular lines Nos 1 or 2), an especially good choice in bad weather. An evening stroll along the floodlit Ring is undoubtedly one of the most outstanding memories anybody can carry away from Vienna.

SCHOTTENRING (HJP)

For the origin of the name, see City Centre and the Ring, Freyung District, Schottenstift. Anton Bruckner lived at No 5 from 1877 to 1895. No 14 was the birthplace of Stefan Zweig, on 28 November 1881. No 23 (façade with nail-head ornamentation) is one of Otto Wagner's first achievements (1877).

City Centre and the Ring

Building the Ringstrasse

Fotostudio Otto/Museen der Stadt Wien

Ringturm – *Schottenring 30.* Built between 1953 and 1955, Erich Boltenstern's Ring Tower is a typical example of Vienna's sober post-war architecture.

Deutschmeisterdenkmal – *Schlickplatz.* This building commemorates the Hoch- and Deutschmeister, the legendary regiment of the city of Vienna. Behind it is Rossauerkaserne (1869) barracks, built in the Windsor style.

Börse – *Schottenring 16.* Theophil von Hansen was one of the Ring's most pro-lific architects (Parliament, Academy of Fine Arts). With the assistance of Carl Tietz, he built the Stock Exchange in a neo-Renaissance style from 1874 to 1877. So this building was not the site of the famous "Black Friday" stock market crash which marked the end of Viennese Liberalism in 1873. The main hall underwent restoration after a large fire in 1956.

Votivkirche ⊘ – *Rooseveltplatz.* Although part of the Ring, the votive church is set back from the line of buildings. Its name commemorates Franz Josef's escape from an assassination attempt. On 18 February 1853, a Hungarian tailor named Libényi stabbed the emperor in the throat, but a metal collar stud saved his life.

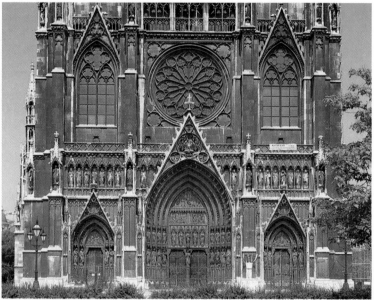

3 BIS/MICHELIN

Votivkirche

The idea of building this church came from Archduke Maximilian, Franz Josef's brother and later Emperor of Mexico. Architect Heinrich von Ferstel (who also built Vienna's university) erected it between 1856 and 1879.

With the Prater Ferris wheel and the cathedral spires, the two traceried spires (99m/324ft) of this neo-Gothic church are among the architectural landmarks on the Viennese horizon. The Viennese architect sought inspiration for his design in the 14C German Gothic style and particularly from the Cologne cathedral. Inside, in the Taufkapelle, is the tomb and **recumbent figure**★ of Count Salm, who successfully resisted the siege of Vienna by Suleyman the Magnificent in 1529. The tomb dates from 1530 and is from the studio of Loy Hering. The stained-glass windows illustrate the history of the Austrian Catholic church; they date mainly from 1966. The **Antwerpener Altar** in the Votivkirche Museum (in the oratory) is a fine late Gothic woodcarving by the 15C Flemish School.

DR.-KARL-LUEGER-RING (HPR)

Universität – *Dr.-Karl-Lueger-Ring 1*. Next to the neo-Gothic Votivkirche, Heinrich von Ferstel designed a building in a style reminiscent of the Italian Renaissance, the period seen as the Golden Age of Knowledge. Founded by Rudolf IV on 12 March 1365, this is one of the oldest German-speaking universities, second only to the one in Prague. It once stood on Dr.-Ignaz-Seipel-Platz *(see City Centre and the Ring, Fleischmarkt District, Alte Universität)*. The building (1884) comprises eight inner courtyards surrounding a central courtyard, "Arkadenhof" (3 300m²/3 946sq yd). In the centre is Kastaliabrunnen, a fountain by Edmund Hellmer (1904). Originally, the University entrance displayed frescoes by Gustav Klimt. People disliked his work because of the nude figures on some panels (the frescoes disappeared during the Second World War).

Beneath the arcades of the central courtyard are busts of famous University professors, including: Anton Bruckner, Theodor von Billroth, Sigmund Freud, Karl Landsteiner (1930 Nobel prize for medicine) and Gerhard van Swieten.

Opposite, behind the memorial to the mayor Johannes Andreas von Liebenberg (1890) is the **Pasqualatihaus** *(see City Centre and the Ring, Freyung District)*.

Rathaus – *See under this heading in the City Centre and the Ring section.*

Café Landtmann – *Dr.-Karl-Lueger-Ring 4*. Franz Landtmann launched this famous Viennese café in 1873. Besides the cream of Viennese society, the clientele consists of politicians from the neighbouring parliament and actors from the Burgtheater. Sigmund Freud enjoyed smoking cigars in this comfortable setting.

★**Burgtheater** ◎ – *Dr.-Karl-Lueger-Ring 2. Guided tour only (in German)*. The Burgtheater opposite the City Hall opened in 1888, replacing the court theatre on Michaelerplatz, which Maria Theresa had founded in 1741. In 1776, Joseph II made it a national theatre, and for many decades it remained the leading German-speaking theatre in the world. Even since then, to play in the Burgtheater has remained the crowning achievement of any actor's career. Numerous actors played there, including: Ewald Balser, Hedwig Bleibtreu, Klaus Maria Brandauer, Annemarie Düringer, Käthe Gold, Werner Kraus, Adolf Rott and Hugo Thimig.

The theatre's construction was begun in 1874 and completed in 1879. Gottfried Semper created the neo-Renaissance façade, while Carl von Hasenauer designed the interior with its neo-Baroque elements. It is of respectable size: 136m/446ft long, 95m/311ft deep and 27m/88ft high. On the convex façade of the central section, there is a statue of Apollo flanked by the muses Melpomene and Thalia (by Carl Kundmann), over a frieze depicting Bacchus and Ariadne (by Rudolf Weyr). The first floor windows display nine colossal busts by Viktor Tilgner: in the centre, Goethe, Schiller, Lessing (all representing Germany); on the right, Halm, Grillparzer, Hebbel (Austria); on the left, Calderon, Shakespeare, Molière (other European countries). The two wings contain monumental staircases. One was for the Court, the other for the public.

The tour *(60min)* of the interior *(entrance via the box-office hall)* is less interesting than the Staatsoper tour. Nevertheless, it gives an opportunity of appreciating the early works of Gustav Klimt. With his brother Ernst and Franz Matsch, he produced the ceiling **frescoes**★ above the staircases *(lit by night, therefore partially visible from outside)*. He painted two scenes: *Romeo and Juliet (right staircase)*, and *Theatre at Taormina (left staircase)* in which a performance of Salome is obviously taking place. The semicircular foyer is 60m/196ft long and provides a fine **view** of the City Hall *(particularly at night)*. On its walls hang portraits of famous actors and actresses. The auditorium was rebuilt to designs by Michael Engelhart following Second World War air raids and can now accommodate about 1 300 people.

There is an interesting anecdote concerning the fire which gutted the auditorium in 1945: in 1888, soon after the opening of the theatre, Gottfried Semper was showered with heavy criticism, directed mainly at the deplorable acoustics. He dismissed these by saying that "every theatre requires reconstruction after 60 years, unless it burns down before then." He was wrong by only three years!

DR.-KARL-RENNER-RING (HR)

Parliament ⊘ – *Dr.-Karl-Renner-Ring 3*. Theophil Hansen designed this rather pompous edifice with its large dimensions and its strict academic resemblance to a Greek temple. Although the architect spent some time in Athens, this does not really explain why he chose this style as a setting for meetings attended by delegates from the various countries in the Austro-Hungarian empire. However, Hansen wished to allude to ancient Greece, the country which gave birth to democracy.

Two long wings ending with small neo-Classical pavilions stand on either side of the projecting part of the building. The latter ends with eight Corinthian columns bearing a triangular pediment. Its richly decorated tympanum displays Franz Josef granting the Constitution to the 17 peoples of his empire (by Edmund Hellmer). The double flight of steps leading to the building features statues of historians from Classical Antiquity. On the left, Greeks: *Herodotus* (by Karl Schwerzek), *Polybius* (by Alois Düll), *Thucydides* (by Richard Kauffungen) and *Xenophon* (by Hugo Haerdt). On the right, Romans: *Sallust* (by Wilhelm Seib), *Caesar* (by Josef Beyer), *Tacitus* (by Karl Sterrer) and *Livy* (by Josef Lax). In front of Parliament, almost on the Ring, is Carl Kundmann's **Pallas-Athene-Brunnen★**, dating from 1902. This fountain represents the Greek Pallas Athena or Roman Minerva, goddess of wisdom and intelligence. With gilded helmet, the daughter of Zeus stands above four figures symbolising the rivers Danube, Inn, Elbe and Moldau.

The legislative assembly – "Austria is a democratic republic. Its laws emanate from the people". This is Article 1 of the 1920 federal constitution. On 27 April 1945, the Declaration of Independence stipulated in Article 1: "The Austrian Democratic Republic is restored and must function in the spirit of the 1920 constitution." Article 2 continued: "The annexation imposed on the Austrian people in 1938 is

null and void." The 1920 federal Constitution was mainly the work of Hans Kelsen, an American jurist of Austrian descent, who also defined democracy as "the most precise approximation of the idea of liberty within a real social context."

The Austrian Parliament has two chambers: the Nationalrat and the Bundesrat (national Council and federal Council). The **Nationalrat** passes federal laws and has the power to dismiss the federal government or one of its members; it has 183 deputies elected by secret ballot (proportional representation). Like the Diets of the Länder and the governments of the nine federal Länder, the **Bundesrat** represents the federal states. It is made up of 64 deputies who are delegated to represent the Diets of the Länder. Nearly every draft law must also be passed by this body – although it can only veto by postponement, and the Nationalrat can eventually have its way by filibuster. The two chambers come together to form the **Bundesversammlung** or federal Assembly. Its most important task is to accept the oath of the incoming federal president, who is elected by popular vote.

Volksgarten – Louis de Rémy designed the city's first public garden, which was built from 1819 to 1823 on the site of the fortifications which Napoleon destroyed in 1809 before leaving the city. The "People's Garden", so-called because it was open to the public, was designed as a counterpart to the Burggarten *(see below, Opernring)*. It offers fine views of the neighbourhood and has benches where it is pleasant to sit between museum visits.

The gardens enclose two monuments: one commemorates Empress Elisabeth (by Friedrich Ohmann), the other is a memorial to the poet Franz Grillparzer (by Carl Kundmann).

Theseustempel – In the middle of the rose gardens stands a small temple with Doric columns, built in 1823 by Pietro Nobile. Its original purpose was to contain the sculpture group *Theseus Slaying the Centaur* by Antonio Canova, which now stands in the stairwell of the Kunsthistorisches Museum *(see City Centre and the Ring)*.

3 BIS/MICHELIN

BURGRING (HR)

On the right is the vast Maria-Theresien-Platz with its two gigantic symmetrical and identical buildings housing the Naturhistorisches Museum (architects Gottfried Semper and Carl von Hasenauer) and the Kunsthistorisches Museum (architect, Carl Hasenauer).

★**Naturhistorisches Museum** ⊙ – *Entrance at Maria-Theresien-Platz.* The collections in the Natural History Museum originate from the reign of François-Étienne of Lorraine, husband of Maria Theresa, and thus predate the opening of the museum in 1889, during Franz Josef's reign. The original ordering of the 39 exhibition rooms has been largely retained until the present, although the presentation of the objects has been adapted to the demands of a modern museum.

On Wednesday evenings the museum offers a tour on the subject of the history and architecture of the museum itself; the tour goes right up to the roof with a view of Vienna. Details available from the Naturhistorisches Museum.

Ground floor mezzanine – The **mineralogical-petrographic collection**★★ (Galleries 1 to 5) with its expecially rich collections of minerals and meteorites contains about 30 000 objects. Among other things, the precious stones hall houses a gold nugget weighing more than 8kg/17lb and a topaz weighing 117kg/258lb. The famous **bouquet of precious stones**★ (1760) which Maria Theresa gave to her husband François-Étienne of Lorraine is also on exhibit here.

The **paleontological collection** (Galleries 7 to 10) documents the Mesozoic and Neozoic eras with plant and animal fossils. Dioramas give a look back at tropical coral reefs 210 million and 16 million years ago. The complete skeleton of a 17-million-year old mammoth, a collection of amber fossils, and the largest known skeleton of a tortoise (more than 4.5m/14.5ft long), as well as numerous casts of dinosaur skeletons are only a few of the many impressive specimens on exhibit.

The Hallstatt period is given emphasis in the **Prehistorical section** (Galleries 11 to 15); the period was named after the town in Upper Austria in which excavations turned up extensive finds from the 8C BC to the 5C BC. Finds from the salt-mine and nearby graveyard there illustrate a human culture of more than 2 500 years ago. Yet the most important pieces in the collection are the **Willendorf Venus**★ (about 25 000 years old), and the so-called **Fanny from Galgenberg**★, the oldest sculpted representation of a human form, dating to about 32 000 years ago.

The **anthropological collection** (Galleries 16 and 17) is devoted to the evolution of the human race.

With its aquariums, terrariums, a small pond and a beehive with live bees, the **children's section** doesn't only attract small visitors.

1st floor – In Galleries 22 to 24 the visitor is reminded of the endless variety of invertebrate animals; some of these are so small that they are not visible to the naked eye. Galleries 25 to 39 present preserved specimens of about 5 000 vertebrates. Among the mammals, birds, fish and reptiles, some species threatened by extinction – and some already extinct (such as the famoous dodo bird and the great auk, and their mammal cousins the Tasmanian tiger and Javan rhinoceros) – are also represented here.

In Gallery 21, the **Mikrotheater** shows projections which provide a view into the world of the microcosmos, for example, the life in a drop of water.

Maria-Theresien-Denkmal – *Maria-Theresien-Platz.* The sculptor Kaspar Zumbusch made this monument in 1888; it is nearly 20m/65ft high. It represents Empress Maria Theresa holding the Pragmatic Sanction in her left hand. The four allegories at the upper corners of the plinth symbolise Power, Wisdom, Justice and Mercy.

★★★**Kunsthistorisches Museum** – *See under City Centre and the Ring.*

★★★**Hofburg** – *See under City Centre and the Ring.*

OPERNRING (JS)

Burggarten – Like Volksgarten *(see above, Dr.-Karl-Renner-Ring)*, the palace garden stands on the site of the fortifications which Napoleon destroyed in 1809 before leaving the city. Franz I had it laid out between 1816 and 1819. Courtiers at the imperial palace soon called it the "promenade". It has been open to the public since 1919 (apart from the lawns). There are several statues in this little park: the **Mozart-Denkmal**★ (1896 by Viktor Tilgner), a memorial to the composer with reliefs showing a scene from *Don Giovanni* and *Mozart with his Family*; the equestrian statue of Franz I (1781, by Balthasar Ferdinand Moll); the Franz Josef monument (1903, by Josef Tuch); and a bronze originally from Wiener Neustadt, installed here in 1957.

Glashaus – This imperial glasshouse consists of glass and steel set in a stone structure; it is quite enchanting with its beautiful sweeping lines. Built by Friedrich Ohmann between 1901 and 1907, it now houses the Schmetterlinghaus *(see City Centre and the Ring, Hofburg)* and the café-restaurant **Palmenhaus**.

At the south corner of Burggarten is the Goethe memorial (1900, by Edmund Hellmer).

Schiller-Denkmal – Robert-Stolz-Platz opens into Schillerplatz, a former market which in 1876 was named after the great German dramatist. His statue by the Dresden sculptor Johann Schilling shows him standing next to Goethe, surrounded by allegorical figures representing the four ages of man.

Theophil Hansen built the neo-Renaissance edifice housing the Academy of Fine Arts in 1876. Adolf Hitler sat, and failed, the entrance examination for this institution in 1907. It offers training for painters, sculptors, interior decorators, architects, restorers and curators. Friedensreich Hundertwasser and Fritz Wotruba taught here.

★★ **Akademie der Bildenden Künste – Gemäldegalerie** ⊘ – *Schillerplatz 3*. The first room contains many treasures, including works by the masters of the German Renaissance such as Lucas Cranach the Elder. It is easy to see why this painter is so famous, looking at one of his early paintings, such as *St Francis Receiving the Stigmata*, or the admirable and enigmatic **Lucretia**★★ (1532), Tarquin's legendary wife who stabbed herself rather than bear the shame of rape. There are representatives of various schools (German, Danube, Flemish, Dutch, Swiss) here: *The Coronation of the Virgin Mary* (between 1450 and 1460) by Dirk Bouts, *The Holy Family* (c 1512) by Hans Baldung-Grien, *The Holy Family* (c 1515) by Joos van Cleve, *Death of the Virgin* (c 1518) by Ambrosius Holbein, and *Portrait of Moritz Weltzer von Eberstein* (1524) by Hans Maler.

Hieronymus Bosch's great **Triptych of the Last Judgment**★★★ (1504-08) is a true masterpiece. The Last Judgment is the only theme in Christian art to be depicted as a series of levels. This is why the triptych is the most suitable representational form for it. This one illustrates *The Last Judgment* and *The Seven Deadly Sins (central panel)*; *The Fall of the Angels, The Creation of Eve, The Temptation, The Expulsion from Paradise (left wing)*; and *Hell and its Laws (right wing)*. There are *grisaille* representations of St Bavo and St James on the outer parts of the wings. Paradise is seen here as a cool welcoming place for the blessed and elect who have resisted the Devil's temptations. They stand naked, because they are clothed in light and will no longer know disease, ageing or death. Hell, on the other hand, is the kingdom of eternal darkness, a furnace of blazing flames which nevertheless do not completely destroy the damned, who will never escape their torments. It is the destination of those who have become slaves of pride, greed, unchastity, envy, gluttony, rage, or sloth (the seven deadly sins).

Some especially prominent examples of Italian painting in the academy's collection are *Virgin with Child and Angels* (c 1480) from Sandro Botticelli's studio, and *Tarquin and Lucretia* (c 1575), one of Titian's last pictures. Among the works from

The *Last Judgment* triptych by Hieronymus Bosch (detail)

the Spanish School are **Boys Playing Dice**★ by Bartolomé Esteban Murillo. Illustrious examples of Baroque painting from the southern Netherlands are in evidence: Sir Anthony van Dyck, **Self-Portrait**★ (c 1614), Jacob Jordaens, *Portrait of the Artist's Daughter* (c 1640), and Peter Paul Rubens' six oil studies for the frescoes (destroyed by fire in 1618) in the Jesuit church in Antwerp.

The 17C Dutch School produced predominantly genre painting, but was also responsible for some fine landscapes and splendid portraits. This collection features: **Portrait of a Young Woman**★★ (1632) which Rembrandt painted at the age of 26, *A Social Gathering* (1635) by Pieter Codde, **Portrait of a Delft Family**★ (c 1660) by Pieter de Hooch, and *Small Still Life* (1671) by Willem van Aelst. The Dutch School also included painters in the Italian manner who – well ahead of their contemporaries – painted in the open air. Among them were Jan Both, *Utrecht about 1615*, and Thomas Wijck with his *Harbour Scene in Southern Climes* (1650).

One of the highlights of the collection of 18C painting is the cycle of eight **Views of Venice**★ (between 1742 and 1780) by the famous Francesco Guardi. These should nonetheless not completely overshadow the two paintings by Pierre Subleyras: *Portrait of Virginia Parker Hunt* (after 1746), and *The Artist's Studio* (c 1747), which bears on the back a self-portrait, discovered after restoration in 1968.

Also worth mentioning are the *Bouquet of Flowers* (c 1720) by Jan van Huysum, the *Cupboard Panel: Trompe-l'œil* (1655) by Samuel van Hoogstraten, and the *Mourning Mother* by Rogier van der Weyden. Last, it would be a pity to leave the exhibit without having seen **Still Life with Flowers and Fruit**★ (1703) by Rachel Ruysch, a Dutch painter who was a pupil of Willem van Aelst.

★★**Staatsoper** – *See City Centre and the Ring, Staatsoper District.*

KARNTNER RING (JKS)

Hotel Imperial – *Kärntner Ring 16.* This is one of the best hotels in the Austrian capital. Since 1873, it has occupied the palace of the Duke of Württemberg who had the edifice built in 1865 (upper storey added in 1928). Richard Wagner stayed here when he conducted *Tannhäuser* and *Lohengrin* in 1875 and 1876.

Café Schwarzenberg – *Kärntner Ring 17.* This is one of the city's pleasantest cafés; its Belle Epoque decor is in the style of the great Viennese tradition.

PARKRING (KRS)

Stadtpark – This vast public garden (114 000m²/135 660sq yd) opened in 1862. Rudolf Sieböck, architect of the imperial gardens, laid it out and Josef Selleny designed it. There are two bridges over the River Wien which flows through the middle. At night, illuminated fountains light up the central lake.

The park contains several statues of the city's famous painters and musicians, such as Friedrich von Amerling (1902, by Johannes Benk), Hans Makart (1898, by Viktor Tilgner), Anton Bruckner (1899, by V Tilgner), Franz Lehár (1980, by Franz Coufal), Franz Schubert (1872, by Carl Kundmann) and Robert Stolz (1980, by Rudolf Friedl). However, it is the famous **Johann-Strauss-Sohn-Denkmal**★, the monument to Johann Strauss the Younger, which most often appears in tourist brochures of Vienna. It is the work of Edmund Hellmer (1921) and consists of a marble arch adorned by nymphs framing the gilded bronze figure of the celebrated violinist.

In the late 19C, the **Kursalon** was one of the cafés famous for music-hall performances. Now, it is the setting for waltz recitals, between Easter and October.

Palais Colloredo – *Parkring 6.* This palace once belonged to the Colloredo family. This family is descended from the prince-archbishop whose employment Wolfgang Amadeus Mozart decided to leave in 1781 *(see City Centre and the Ring, Stephansdom District, insert: "My happiness starts today.").*

STUBENRING (LR)

★★**MAK (Österreichisches Museum für Angewandte Kunst)** ⊙ – *Stubenring 5.* When it was founded in 1864, the Austrian Museum of Applied and Decorative Arts was unusual in that it had no permanent collections. Its purpose was primarily educational: to develop the aesthetic sensibilities of the public without having recourse solely to the heritage of the past. In 1868, drawing inspiration from the Victoria and Albert Museum in London, the Museum für Angewandte Kunst began working closely with the *Kunstgewerbeschule* (School of Arts and Crafts). This reflected the trend of the time, which tried to encourage a close relationship between art and industry, as in the English Arts and Crafts movement. Thus, the museum has always favoured projects in the field of design, notably those of the *Wiener Werkstätte*.

Since 1871, it has occupied a neo-Renaissance building by Heinrich von Ferstel, which was extended in 1909 by Ludwig Baumann. Following restoration work begun in 1989, the museum reopened its doors in 1993. In keeping with its educational aims, the museum developed a remarkable **museology**★★. Famous contemporary artists have created settings to show the splendid collections to their advantage *(numbers in brackets refer to the numbers of the galleries)*.

Romanesque, Gothic, and Renaissance (1) – Designer: Günther Förg, German painter. The bold cobalt blue on the walls sets off the exhibits splendidly. The pearwood folding stool (Salzburg, early 13C), a maple cabinet (south Germany, late 16C) and the Urbino majolica ware (16C) are especially of note here. The room contains some further edifying objects, starting with the *sacerdotal ornaments*★ (embroidered linen and silk vestments and antependium, c 1260) from the Benedictine convent of Göss in Styria, which form the oldest collection in existence. Then, there is a painted cherrywood *table top*★★ (Swabia, late 15C), which is one of ten existing examples and allegedly from a convent in Ulm; it depicts scenes from the Passion and the legend of St Ursula.

Baroque, Rococo and Classical (2) – Designer: Donald Judd, American minimalist artist. The sobriety of the decor suits the exhibits, notably furniture including a cabinet signed Haberstumpf (Eger, 1723) which belonged to Karl VI. In the centre is a reconstruction of the porcelain room of the Dubsky palace at Brno (porcelain from the Viennese Du Paquier factory, before 1730). On one of the walls hang two *inlaid panels*★ (Neuwied, 1719) by David Roentgen for the palace of Charles of Lorraine in Brussels. Also noteworthy is the **centrepiece** from Zwettl monastery (Viennese porcelain, 1768) consisting of 60 figurines and vases made for the abbot's jubilee festivities.

Renaissance, Baroque and Rococo (3) – Designer: Franz Graf, Austrian painter. In one of the two cases displaying glass there is some 16C Venetian glass. The extensive lace collections include a *chasuble*, also from Venice (late 17C).

Empire and Biedermeier (4) – Designer: Jenny Holzer, American artist. A long column of chairs precedes a striking cherrywood *writing desk*★ (Vienna, towards 1825). The display cases contain silver, china and glass, in particular a travelling service (1811) which Napoleon ordered upon the birth of his son, the future Duke of Reichstadt. The stemless glasses (c 1830), with enamelled decoration depicting the capital's most prestigious sites, are especially noteworthy.

Historicism, Jugendstil and Art Deco (5) – Designer: Barbara Bloom, American artist. A superb shadow show traces the evolution of the Viennese **chair**, with special emphasis on the *Thonet*★ dynasty. The retrospective ends with other masters of the genre: Loos, Hoffmann, and Frank.

Orient (6) – Designers: Gang Art, a group of Viennese artists. The MAK **carpet**★★ collection is one of the most famous in the world, mainly because of its Egyptian, Persian and Turkish exhibits. Particularly noteworthy are the hunting carpet (first half of the 16C) from Kashan in central Persia, and the unique silk Mameluke carpet (early 16C); all of these objects belonged to the imperial family.

20C design and architecture (3) – Designer: Manfred Wakolbinger, Viennese sculptor. This room on the first floor concentrates on art applied to architecture, or the relation between art and function through the designs of Nils Landberg, Walter Pichler, Philippe Starck or Frank Gehry.

Evolution of the Viennese chair – Museum of Applied Arts

MAK, Wien

Jugendstil and Art Deco (1) – Designers: "Eichinger oder Knechtl", Viennese designers. This is a fine and varied collection of **glass** and **furniture** bearing the signature of masters such as Hoffmann, Mackintosh, Moser, van der Velde and Wagner. One of the most impressive exhibits is the series of **drawings**★★ (1905-09) by Gustav Klimt for the dining room of Stoclet House in Brussels: 9 tempera cartoons for the mosaic decoration of the famous mansion which Josef Hoffmann built for the engineer and businessman Adolphe Stoclet. The materials alone for this mosaic by the *Wiener Werkstätte* cost 100 000 crowns, an absolute fortune at the time.

★★**Wiener Werkstätte (2)** – Designer: Heimo Zobernig, Austrian sculptor. Anyone fond of Art Deco should visit this room, if only because it contains the archives of the **Wiener Werkstätte**: a collection of sketches by all the artists in the association, as well as factory marks, cartoons, photographs, etc. In the display cases are numerous items of silverware, jewellery and bookbinding, most of them signed by Hoffmann or Peche.

Contemporary art – Designer: Peter Noever, Austrian designer and curator of the department. The purpose of this section is to display, through a collection begun in 1986, the links uniting "fine art" and "applied art", despite the differences between them.

In the museum basement, there is a study collection divided into sections: furniture, textiles, metalwork, ceramics. This apparent jumble should not confuse the visitor. It features objects of high quality. The presentation is designed to highlight the contrast between exhibits.

In the centre, the Far East room has a superb display of items originating from European collections, when orientalism was so fashionable as to influence continental art, or imported from Asia in the early 20C to illustrate the evolution of art in that part of the world.

Regierungsgebäude – *Stubenring 1*. Formerly the War Ministry, this huge government building is 250m/272yd long. At the top, its bronze eagle has a wingspan of 16m/17yd. The building (1912) by Franz Neumann looks all the more massive in comparison to the Post Office Savings Bank opposite *(see City Centre and the Ring, Fleischmarkt District)*.

The Radetzky monument in front of the façade commemorates the famous field marshal and war minister. As a mark of his admiration, Franz Josef wanted him to be buried in the Kapuzinergruft (crypt of the Capuchins). This monument (1892) by Caspar Zumbusch once graced Am Hof square.

Urania-Sternwarte ◔ – *Uraniastrasse 1*. This building (1909) by Max Fabiani is located on the Danube canal. It was originally conceived as a "people's" or adult education institution, so it is no surprise that it contains, among other things, the first "people's" or public observatory in Austria. The observatory was equipped with some new equipment in the 1980s, including a new telescope.

Franz-Josefs-Kai, which closes off the loop of the Ring, runs along the Danube canal. The nearest sights in the area of the Ring include: the Fleischmarkt District in the city centre, and the Alsergrund, Josefstadt, Neubau, Mariahilf, Wieden, Landstrasse and Leopoldstadt Districts (found in the Outside the Ring section). See also Kunsthistorisches Museum and Hofburg (City Centre and the Ring, as well as MuseumsQuartier (Outside the Ring).

STAATSOPER District★★

Local map pages 13/14, **JKRS**
Underground: Karlsplatz (U1, U2, U4)
Tram: Oper (1, 2, 62, 65, D, J)
Bus: Oper (59A), Karlsplatz (4A)

★★THE STAATSOPER, THE OLDEST BUILDING ON THE RING

Emperor Franz Josef opened the Vienna State Opera House, then known as Hofoper, on 25 May 1869. The inaugural performance was Wolfgang Amadeus Mozart's *Don Giovanni*. Very soon, from its position at the Kärntner Ring, it attracted people of fashion and right until the eve of the First World War was one of Viennese society's favourite venues. In June 1944, Joseph Goebbels, the Third Reich's Minister of Propaganda, ordered German theatres to be closed. The ironies of history are often appreciated with hindsight: the final performance at the Vienna Opera House before enforced closure was *The Twilight of the Gods* by Richard Wagner. This took place less than a year before the air raid of 12 March 1945, when fire gutted the building, completely destroying the auditorium and stage. After reconstruction, it reopened on 5 November 1955 with a performance of *Fidelio* by Ludwig van Beethoven.

An institution heavy with symbolism – With its undisputed international reputation, Austria's most illustrious theatre, so dear to the heart of the Viennese, has numbered outstanding figures among its directors: Gustav Mahler (1897-1907), appointed despite Cosima Wagner's reluctance, and who began his directorship with a performance of *Lohengrin*; Felix Weingartner, Richard Strauss (1919-24), Clemens Krauss, Karl Böhm (1943-45 then from 1954-56), Herbert von Karajan (1956-64), Lorin Maazel (1982-84) and Claudio Abbado (1986-91). Bruno Walter was assistant artistic director in the years preceding the Anschluss. During his decade as director, Gustav Mahler influenced the Opera in ways which can still be felt in the present. Under his direction 184 operas were staged, and he systematically carried out a thorough reform of the staging of the most renowned opera series (Mozart, Wagner), raising Vienna's Opera House to an eminence which was the envy of the musical world. Many a Viennese singer has forgone an international career to remain with the Staatsoper and its music-loving public.

The Vienna State Opera has a permanent company of singers, as well as its own orchestra training school, from which the Viennese Philharmonic recruits. It is one of the few opera houses in the world able to show a different work every night, almost the whole year round. The season starts on 1 September and ends on 30 June. There are no operas or ballets on Christmas Day, Good Friday, on the day of or preceding the debutantes' ball *(see below, Die "Opernball")*, or on 18 May (the date of the Mahler concert). During the musical season, some sixty operas are staged, all of them performed in the original language of the libretto (unlike the Volksoper). There are three price categories: A, for operas starring world-famous singers; B, for all other operas; and C, for ballets. Seats are on sale a month before the performance *(see Practical information)*. An unchanging Staatsoper tradition allows standing spectators to buy tickets for as little as €1.45 or €2.18. These tickets, which are restricted in number, are on sale on the evening of the performance and often require a long wait, at the end of which only the first in the queue or those keen to watch an opera such as Richard Wagner's *Die Meistersinger von Nürnberg (5hr 15min)* on their feet, will be rewarded.

Decisive influences of Mahler and Karajan – After being conductor of the Hamburg Stadttheater, Gustav Mahler became director of the Viennese Imperial Opera in May 1897, one year after Bruckner's death and a month after Brahms' death on the day of the creation of the Secession. Under his guidance, orchestration gradually abandoned austerity in favour of expressionism, and he took a particular interest in the way the works were directed. This development, unusual for the time, modified an essential aspect of opera: thereafter, singers also concentrated on acting. When Karajan became director in 1956, he also made his personality felt by instilling new life into the dramatic style, which had lost all spontaneity over the years. He introduced a policy of co-production with La Scala in Milan to the Opera and left behind him an organisation based on the repertory system.

Gustav Mahler by Auguste Rodin

Fotostudio Otto/Museen der Stadt, Wien

The building ⊙ – *Entrance under the arcades, Kärtner Strasse.* A rumour that eventually passed into folklore had it that one of the architects hanged himself in 1868, driven to suicide by criticisms and Franz Josef's alleged remark that the opera "looked about to sink into the ground". According to the same rumour, the other architect died of grief following his friend's death. In fact, Eduard van der Null suffered from depression and August Siccard von Siccardsburg died following an operation two months after his colleague's suicide. The former was in charge of decorating the edifice, while the latter directed the construction. Nonetheless it is true that in artistic matters the emperor usually restricted himself to making bland generalised compliments. The building, begun in 1861, has a stone façade in the French Renaissance style (left intact after the air raid and subsequent fire in 1945) facing the Ring. It represents the peak of what is known as Romantic Historicism. Its loggia features five bronze statues by Ernst Julius Hähnel: Heroism, Drama, Fantasy, Humour and Love.

The tour of the interior *(45min)* starts with the interval rooms. The Gobelins room features modern tapestries by Rudolf Eisenmenger depicting Mozart's *Magic Flute*. The **Schwind Foyer★** (spared in 1945) takes its name from the painter Moritz von Schwind whose frescoes represent scenes from operas; among the busts of composers and conductors, that of Gustav Mahler by Auguste Rodin (1909) is of special interest. Otto Prosinger decorated the marble room. Once exclusively reserved for the Court during the intervals, the tea room (undamaged in 1945) is adorned by silk draperies stamped with the imperial initials. Nowadays, this room is only used for press conferences, interviews with famous singers or receptions paid for by the few spectators willing to pay out a substantial sum *(about € 1 450, champagne and tickets not included)* in order to await the start of a performance or pass the time during the interval in luxurious surroundings. From it, the superb **grand staircase★** (undamaged in 1945) leads opera-goers down to the auditorium. The lunettes are decorated with allegorical reliefs (Light Opera, Ballet, Opera) painted by Johann Preleuthner, and with statues of the seven liberal arts by Josef Gasser. Erich Boltenstern, in charge of its reconstruction, did not restore the rich Italianate decoration of the theatre designed by the two original architects. Abandoning all ornamentation and discarding the ribs of the last balcony and the columns which obstructed the view, he designed a horseshoe-shaped auditorium for over 2 200 spectators and 110 musicians.

Recently, a "Children's Opera Tent" with 140 seats was set up on the roof terrace of the Staatsoper, offering performances for children aged 6 to 14.

Opernball – In Vienna the ball season starts on 31 December with the *Kaiserball* which takes place in the Hofburg. However, the most prestigious of them all is undoubtedly the *Opernball* or **Debütantinnenball** (debutantes' ball), created in 1877 to celebrate the entry of aristocratic young girls into high society. It takes place on the last Thursday of carnival *(Fasching)* in February. For this occasion, the auditorium of the Opera converts into a ballroom by means of a fitted floor; thousands of flowers are specially flown in from the Riviera to adorn the boxes for this, the most fashionable night (until 5am) of the year. Anyone may attend provided they have a ticket... which will cost about €210 (no seat), to which they should add €870 for a table for six, and about €14 500 for a box *(see also Introduction, Life in Vienna)*.

An Impressive Technological Achievement

The lighting, air conditioning and machinery of the opera uses the same amount of electricity as a town of 30 000 inhabitants. A total of almost 2 000 people work in shifts at the Opera House; some 100 of them are employed as stagehands and dressers. Due to space restrictions, the scenery has to be stored at the Arsenal depot, 4km/2.5mi away. The vans transporting it have their own entrance at the back of the building and the scenery is moved automatically on stage by means of lifts 22m/72ft long. The huge ultra-modern stage (1 500m²/16 145sq ft, 50m/164ft deep, 45m/147ft high) is able to cope with the needs of today's productions with its 45 tonnes of machinery, including an array of hydraulic jacks, lifts, cranes and a turntable. Every day, the scenery from the previous night is replaced by the sets required for the current day's performance. Before this, the scenery for a rehearsal is often introduced to accustom the singers to the dimensions of the stage. In a way, the Staatsoper is a permanent building site.

ADDITIONAL SIGHTS

Albertinaplatz – Behind the Opera is this large square dominated by the Erzherzog-Albrecht-Denkmal by Kaspar Zumbusch, an equestrian statue of Archduke Albert, who defeated the Italians at Custozza in 1886. The foundation wall consists of the remains of a former bastion of the city fortifications. Backing on to it is the Danubiusbrunnen, or Danube fountain (1869). It was designed by Moritz Löhr, while its allegorical sculptures were by Johann Meixner; the central group represents the rivers Danube and Wien.

The **Mahnmal gegen Krieg und Faschismus** on the north side of the square was dedicated in 1988. This four-piece monument decrying war and fascism was created by the Austrian sculptor Alfred Hrdlicka. The viewer can actually walk around this work of art; in the shadow of its "gate of violence" an elderly Jewish man is pressed to the ground under barbed wire. In the background is a block of marble from which emerge some male figures. Under them is the inscription "Orpheus enters Hades". Chiselled in this "Stone of the Republic" are excerpts from the declaration of 27 April 1945, made by the provisional national government that took over after democracy was restored in Austria.

This square leads to the Burggarten or imperial gardens *(see City Centre and the Ring, The Ring, Opernring)*.

Gedenkräume des Österreichischen Theatermuseums (**M²²**) ⊘ – *Hanuschgasse 3; take the entrance on the left and go up to the first floor*. These rooms commemorate ten personalities who left their mark on Austrian theatre *(documentary in German, 20min)*. Some of the most well-known are the sculptor Fritz Wotruba (1907-75) and the impresario Max Reinhardt (1873-1943), born in Baden as Max Goldmann, who had to emigrate to New York in 1938.

Philharmonikerstrasse – In this street is the **Hotel Sacher** (No 4), a real institution frequented by diplomats and opera singers. Built between 1874 and 1876 by Wilhelm Frankel for the restaurateur Eduard Sacher, on the site of the former court theatre, it evokes the memory of Anna Sacher who was almost as famous as the hotel. Towards the end of the 19C, she served her illustrious guests while smoking a cigar. The tea room with its red velvet decor once attracted men of letters such as Arthur Schnitzler who alluded to the hotel's private dining rooms in his *Farewell Supper*. Today, gourmets come to savour the famous *Sachertorte*.

> **The "Sacherbuben"**
>
> Anna, Eduard Sacher's widow, was not just the promoter of the family *torte*; she acted as financial sponsor for the impoverished sons of good Viennese families who frequented the hotel. This was so well known that these young people awaiting their inheritance acquired the nickname of *Sacherbuben*, or "Sacher's rascals".

Kärntner Strasse – *See also City Centre and the Ring, Stephansdom District.* Below the junction of Kärntner Strasse and the Ring is Operngasse, a passage with several shops. At No 51, opposite the right side of the Staatsoper, is the imposing façade of the Palais Todesco, built between 1861 and 1864 in a neo-Renaissance style by Ludwig Förster and Theophil Hansen for the banker Eduard Todesco. Eminent politicians such as Anton Schmerling viewed works by playwrights such as Hugo von Hoffmannsthal (as the palace had its own theatre).

Malteserkirche (K⁶) – In about 1200, Leopold VI summoned the Knights of the Order of St John (known as the Knights Hospitaller of Malta as of 1530) to Vienna and built a chapel for them. The present church goes back to the middle of the 14C. Inside the church are 40 coats of arms of those connected with the Order. On the left is the memorial (1806) to Jean de la Valette, Grand Master of the Order. He distinguished himself on the island of Malta during the Turkish attacks of 1565. In 1530, Charles V granted the island to the Order, which retained its seat there until 1798. The *St John the Baptist* on the high altar is by Johann Georg Schmidt (c 1730). The church's Gothic choir can be seen from the courtyard of the building at Johannesgasse 2.

Opposite the church is the famous **Glashaus Lobmeyr** (No 26) founded in the 19C. Its crystal chandeliers are for luxurious display in public places (Staatsoper, the Kremlin, etc). During business hours, the **Wiener Glasmuseum** is open to the public on the second floor, exhibiting 18C chandeliers and various objects of glass. At No 41, the **Palais Esterházy** (mid-17C, refurbished in the 18C) first belonged to the imperial counsellor Adam Antonius Grundemann von Falkenberg before passing to Count Moritz Esterházy-Galantha-Forchtenstein in 1871. Since 1968, it has housed the **Casino Wien**.

Annagasse – This delightful, narrow street at the corner of the Esterházy palace is bordered by attractive buildings: at No 4, the fine façade of Kremsmünsterhof (17C); at No 6, Herzogenburgerhof, its Baroque façade dating from the 1730s; at No 8, Täubelhof, also known as Deybelhof, built about 1730 to a design by Johann Lukas von Hildebrandt and modified in 1789 by Andreas Zach; at No 14, "Zum blauen Karpfen", a house which owes its name to the blue carp, still visible, that was the inn sign on Georg Kärpf's tavern c 1700 (the façade was refurbished in 1824 by Karl Ehmann who added a frieze of *putti*); at No 18, the building known as "the Roman Emperor".

Annakirche – *Annagasse 3b.* Built in Gothic style in the 15C and remodelled in Baroque style between 1629 and 1634 by Christian Tausch, a pupil of Andrea Pozzo, the little church of St Anne houses several interesting works: the ceiling frescoes (1748) and the altarpiece on the high altar *(The Holy Family)* by Daniel Gran, as well as the delicately carved wooden statue **St Anne with Mary and the Child Jesus** (representing the Holy Parenthood (c 1510) attributed to Veit Stoss (a Nuremberg artist) or to the Master of the Mauer altar, near Melk. Although the Madonna occupies the place of honour everywhere in Austria, there is also a special devotion to St Anne. She is frequently depicted as one of the three generations of the Holy Family: the grandmother holds the Virgin Mary on one arm and the infant Jesus on the other.

Turn left into Seilerstätte.

★**Haus der Musik** ⊙ – *Seilerstätte 30. The late opening hours make this an interesting and entertaining way to spend an evening.* The former palace of Archduke Carl, the victor at the battle of Aspern, is now ruled by music. Both a music store and a violin maker have taken up residence on the ground floor. The first floor houses the **Museum der Wiener Philharmoniker** whose founder, composer and conductor Otto Nicolai, lived here in 1842. In addition to its founding decree and the first photograph of the orchestra, one may see here the batons of the famous conductors Strauss, Furtwängler and Karajan and others. The picture gallery and the projection room provide many insights into the work and everyday routine of this famous orchestra.

Haus der Musik – The virtual conductor

The second, third and fourth floors are occupied by the Haus der Musik itself.
On the second floor, visitors are transported into the **world of sounds**. For example, they can duplicate the sound perception of an embryo in its mother's womb, experiment with pitch, volume and spatial perception using interactive terminals, or experience the creation of sound on four gigantic instruments (including a walk-in organ pipe). Other sound experiments include the intensifying of natural sounds using frequencies beyond levels of human perception; and visitors have the opportunity to use pre-recorded material to burn their own CD (and then buy it at the museum's shop).

The **great masters of Viennese music** come alive on in the third floor. Recordings are combined with installations and interactive terminals, bringing to life again the worlds of Haydn, Mozart and Beethoven (whose increasing deafness is duplicated in a very interesting installation), Schubert, Strauss, Mahler and the Second Viennese School (Schönberg, Webern, Berg). The tour's culmination is the moment in which you can swing the baton yourself as a **virtual conductor**, standing in front of a screen on which the Wiener Philharmoniker follows its serendipitous leader's movements. A word of warning: these sophisticated yet demanding gentlemen will not hesitate to "sound a retreat" for the maestro who can't keep the beat.

Besides watching or listening to TV or radio productions of the Österreichischer Rundfunk in the ORF room on the fourth floor, visitors can take part in the **Brain Opera** made by the Massachusetts Institute of Technology. Interactive sounds can be created and music composed in sometimes rather amusing ways; we recommend taking the time to simply allow your imagination free reign. Before going to the shop, stop at the *Sensor Chair*. This unusual piece of furniture creates music as soon as someone sits on it.

The café-restaurant is located partly on the ground floor and partly on the fifth and sixth floors. (The fifth floor also contains a venue room.) There is a very good view of the Stephansdom from the upper two floors.

Turn left into the Johannesgasse.

Ursulinenkirche und -kloster (**M**¹⁸) – *Johannesgasse 8*. Empress Éléonore summoned the Ursuline nuns from Liège in 1660. They commissioned an architect now unknown to build their convent and their church between 1665 and 1675. The barrel-vaulted sanctuary contains an altarpiece by Johann Spillenberger, *The Martyrdom of St Ursula* (1675).

Sammlung Religiöse Volkskunst ⊘ – The core of the collection at the museum of religious folk art is the original 18C Ursuline apothecary's shop with the painting, *Christ the Apothecary* (1747). The Saviour is also represented in various other forms here, and there are some examples of the veneration of Mary and other saints.

Johannesgasse – At No 15 nearly opposite the church stands the Savoyisches Damenstift (1688), the Ladies of Savoy foundation. In a niche of the façade there is a lead statue of the Virgin Mary by Franz Xaver Messerschmidt (1768) better known for his grimacing heads *(see Outside the Ring, Landstrasse,*

Barockmuseum). At No 6, the Hofkammerarchiv (Archives of the Court treasury) had dramatist Franz Grillparzer as its director from 1832 to 1856 (his study on the 4th floor is open to the public). A little further away, at No 5, is the fine Questenberg-Kaunitz palace (1701), after a design by Johann Lukas von Hildebrandt; Talleyrand stayed there during the Congress of Vienna.

It is possible to extend this tour by going to Himmelpfortgasse via Kärntnergasse (see City Centre and the Ring, Stephansdom District).

The nearest sights are: the Hofburg, Kapuzinerkirche District, Stephansdom, and the Ring (to be found in the City Centre and the Ring section), as well as the Wieden (in the Outside the Ring section).

STEPHANSDOM★★★

Local map page 14, **KR**
Underground: Stephansplatz (U1, U3)
Bus: Graben-Petersplatz (1A, 2A, 3A)

THE SYMBOL OF THE CITY

Stephansdom (St Stephen's Cathedral) is unique. With its vast roof of glittering polychrome tiles, it emerges from the compact old city, an elegant silhouette with its narrow south tower soaring majestically to the skies. Despite its Gothic style, the cathedral lies at the heart of this Baroque city. This stone edifice has shared the vicissitudes of Viennese life for over eight centuries.

An incomplete masterpiece – The first building on this site was probably erected before 1137; yet records confirm that a simple three-aisled Romanesque basilica was built between 1137 and 1147, the date of its consecration by the Bishop of Passau, who administered the city. In accordance with the wishes of Friedrich II the Warrior, another basilica soon replaced it, c 1230. In 1258, a fire destroyed a large part of it, although it left intact the present west front, the Riesentor (giants' portal), and the Heiden (pagan) towers. After swift reconstruction, the church was again consecrated in 1263 in the reign of Ottokar II Przemysl.
In 1359, Duke Rudolf IV of Habsburg wished to refurbish the cathedral in the Gothic manner, a style first seen in 1140 in the ambulatory of St Denis cathedral north of Paris. He laid the foundation stone of the present three-aisled nave. The vaulting was not completed until the first half of the 15C. The following date from this period: the Bischofstor (bishops' doorway) (north) and Singertor (singer's doorway) (south), and the south tower, the famous *Steffl* so dear to the Viennese, completed in 1433. In 1469, at the request of Emperor Frederick III, the pope raised Vienna to the status of an episcopal city. St Stephen's then became a cathedral.
After the completion of the work carried out under **Anton Pilgram**, head of the guild of stonemasons of St Stephen's cathedral from 1510 to 1515, the Baroque style made its appearance in 1647 with the construction of a high altar by the brothers Johann and Tobias Pock. The cathedral was damaged during the Turkish siege in 1683 and again by Napoleon's troops in 1809, but experienced its worst destruction at the end of the Second World War. After restoration work from 1945 to 1952, the cathedral regained its incontrovertible brilliance.
Despite all this history, the Stephansdom is still incomplete: construction of the north tower began in 1467, was interrupted in 1511 and was never finished.

EXTERIOR

West front – Framing the Romanesque façade are the 66m/216ft high octagonal Heidentürme or towers of the Pagans. Its chief artistic attraction is the **Riesentor★★** (or Giants' Doorway, *see illustration in the Introduction, ABC of Architecture*). It acquired its name after the discovery during construction work in 1230 of an enormous bone. According to tradition, the bone belonged to a giant drowned during the Flood; in the 18C people realised that it was in fact the shin bone of a mammoth, and the relic was removed from its position hanging in the doorway. The tympanum displays a Christ in Majesty between two angels; wearing a philosopher's tunic, he holds the Gospels in His left hand and with the right blesses those entering the cathedral. In the past, this doorway was opened only for ceremonial occasions; it was at this entrance that the Babenbergs meted out justice. On the left of the doorway, two metal bars are embedded in the wall. They served as measures; the shorter one was an ell and the other a two-foot rule (the standard measures in Vienna of yore).

North façade – The left pillar of the Adlertor (Eagle Doorway) includes an iron handle which once bore the name of "asylum ring"; anyone grasping it automatically came under ecclesiastical jurisdiction. Master builder **Johann Puchsbaum** began the Adlerturm (Eagle Tower) in 1467; it should have reached the same height as

B. Kaufmann

Stephansdom – Detail of roof

the south tower but was never completed. Since 1957 it has housed the **Pummerin**, an impressive bell weighing 21t. Nobody knows why work on the Adlerturm came to a stop. Possibly, the troubles of the Reformation were a factor. However, a legend offers another explanation: Puchsbaum fell in love with the daughter of the cathedral's architect, Johann von Prachatitz. The architect promised to give his daughter to Puchsbaum, provided he managed to finish the tower in one year. Aware of the impossibility of the task, Puchsbaum asked the devil for help. The devil agreed, on the condition that the master builder should never say the name of God or the Holy Virgin. One day while Puchsbaum was working on the scaffolding, he caught sight of his betrothed and could not refrain from attracting her attention by calling out her name, "Mary! Mary!" The devil immediately caused the scaffolding to collapse, hurling the builder to his death. After this disaster, the workmen refused to continue building the accursed tower.

At the corner of the chevet is the Capistrano pulpit (1738), in memory of St John Capistrano, an Italian Franciscan monk canonised for his part in the evangelisation of Central Europe. It was here that the remains of **Wolfgang Amadeus Mozart** received absolution on 6 December 1791.

Bischofstor (Bishop's Doorway) was the women's entrance, hence its nickname of "Brides' Doorway". It was the work of Gregor Hauser.

Chancel apse – This features a bust of Christ with the nickname of *"Zahnwehherrgott"*, or "Lord God with toothache", dating from about 1440. The sandstone relief *Christ on the Mount of Olives* (1502) is also to be found here.

South façade – St Stephen's Tower★★★ also bears the name of **Steffl**, a diminutive of Stephan. It was begun in 1359 and completed in 1433. Soaring to a height of 137m/449ft, it is a masterpiece of the German Gothic School, and undeniably one of the two finest spires in the German-speaking world, the other being that on the Minster in Freiburg, Germany. The master builder's triumph lies in the way he completed the transition from the square section of the tower to the octagonal section of the spire. He achieved this by increasing the number of gables, pinnacles, finials and crockets in a filigree which lightens the potentially heavy superstructure. The Singertor (Singer's Doorway) was the men's entrance to the cathedral.

The roof – The cathedral roof features a magnificent expanse of glazed tiles with zigzag motifs, always a delight to tourist photographers. It is a tapestry of about 250 000 tiles, with the imperial two-headed eagle on the southeast. Beneath the roof are metal rafters dating from 1945; previously, the roof was supported by 1 000 five-layered larch beam trusses.

INTERIOR ⊙

On entering the late Gothic nave of this hall-church (170m/552ft long and 39m/127ft wide), visitors can sense peace and serenity despite the never-ending stream of tourists. The Secession architect Adolf Loos, who favoured functionality above the more usual ornamentation of his day, considered that Vienna was home to the most majestic church nave in the whole world.

The lierned cathedral vaulting looks down on some fine works of art and interesting monuments. In the Kreuzkapelle (Holy Cross chapel) is the tomb of **Prince Eugène of Savoy** *(see Outside the Ring, Landstrasse)*, a simple sword blade embedded in the ground. On the third pillar in the north aisle is the splendid **pulpit★★** (c 1515). The famous watcher at the window at the foot of the pulpit is reputedly a self-portrait of the sculptor himself. This Late Gothic masterpiece features busts carved in the round of the Fathers of the Church: from right to left are St Ambrose, St Jerome, St Gregory the Great and St Augustine. Carved details illustrate the symbolic significance always

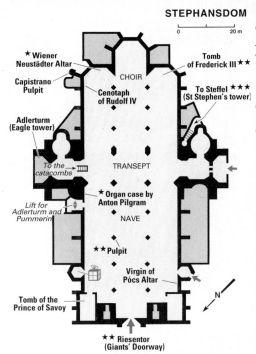

STEPHANSDOM

★ **Wiener Neustädter Altar**
Capistrano Pulpit
CHOIR
Cenotaph of Rudolf IV
Adlerturm (Eagle tower)
To the catacombs
TRANSEPT
★ **Organ case by Anton Pilgram**
Lift for Adlerturm and Pummerin
NAVE
★★ **Pulpit**
Virgin of Pócs Altar
Tomb of the Prince of Savoy
★★ **Riesentor (Giants' Doorway)**

Tomb of Frederick III ★★
To Steffel ★★★ (St Stephen's tower)

N

present in medieval religious art. Creeping up the banister, toads and frogs represent evil thoughts, while the lizards pursuing them symbolise good thoughts. A remarkable work by Anton Pilgram, who clearly adopted an anthropocentric tendency in the Renaissance style, is his self-portrait at the foot of the **organ case★** (1513) by the north wall; the organ itself was removed in 1720. The artist holds a master builder's set square and compass.

At the end of the north aisle is Rudolf IV the Founder's cenotaph, with an angel from the Annunciation, and on the Wiener-Neustädter Altar in the apsidal chapel known as the "Virgin's choir" is the **Wiener Neustädter altarpiece★**. It dates from 1447 and displays figures carved in the round. When the altarpiece is open, *The Coronation of the Virgin* is visible on the upper level, and on the lower level a *Virgin with Child* with St Barbara and St Catherine; when its wings are closed, the panels illustrate scenes from the Passion. The brothers Johann and Tobias Pock made the black marble high altar in 1647; the altarpiece, executed on pewter, depicts the Stoning of St Stephen. The right apsidal chapel, the "Apostles' choir" contains **Frederick III's tomb★★** carved from red Salzburg marble, first by Niclaus Gerhaert van Leyden in 1467, then by his pupils *(see Outside the Ring, Wiener Neustadt, Neuklosterkirche)*. The artist represents the struggle between good and evil represented by animals: dangerous beasts try to enter the emperor's tomb and disturb his final rest, while on the surround, creatures symbolising good restrain them.

At the other end of the south aisle is a canopy housing the Mariapócs altarpiece, which takes its name from a village in eastern Hungary. This naive painting on two maple panels is an object of great veneration. In 1696, a peasant saw real tears in its eyes and the emperor had the miraculous icon brought to Vienna. It was held responsible for Prince Eugène's victory over the Osman armies (1697).

Cathedral towers ⊙ – It is possible to climb the south tower *(343 steps)* to the watchman's room, at a height of 73m/239ft. Access to the 60m/196ft high platform on the north tower is by lift. On a clear day, it offers an enchanting panoramic **view★★** over Vienna, the Kahlenberg Heights and the Danube plain to the east.

The north tower, or Adlerturm (eagles' tower), contains the **Pummerin**, the free-swinging bell which among other occasions rings in the New Year. Originally cast in 1711 from 180 bronze canons captured from the Turks in 1683, this monumental bell used to be in the south tower. After its destruction in 1945, it was recast in 1951 as a present from the state of Upper Austria; yet its remounting was in the north tower in 1957, because the south tower had suffered damage from the vibrations caused by the pealing of the original *Pummerin*.

Catacombs ⊙ – *Guided tour only; ask the guide to translate his commentary into English*. This vast network extends beneath the choir and Stephansplatz, occupying several levels and comprising an old (14C) and a new (18C) section.

Frederick III's tomb

The Cardinals' crypt is still in use. The **ducal crypt** dates from 1363 in the reign of Rudolf IV, who was buried there at the age of 26 after his death in Milan. His wife Catherine of Bohemia lies at his side. Niches display urns containing the entrails of the imperial family. In accordance with Viennese Court ceremonial, the embalmed bodies are entombed in the Kapuzinergruft, while the hearts are interred in the Augustinerkirche.

After passing the cathedral foundations (6m/19ft thick in places), you reach the former city cemetery containing some 16 000 graves. This extends into the area of the mass grave for victims of the 1713 plague, whose bodies were simply thrown down shafts with openings that could be sealed to avoid contamination. Later, prisoners were given the task of bringing order to this putrid necropolis.

For sights around the Stephansdom, see the following chapter, Stephansdom District.

STEPHANSDOM District★★

Underground: Stephansplatz (U1, U3), Herrengasse (U3)
Bus: Graben-Petersplatz (1A, 2A)

The following tour through historic Vienna starting from Peterskirche (St Peter's church) can be enjoyed as a leisurely stroll through the heart of the city.

★**Peterskirche** ⊘ – *Petersplatz.* St Peter's church was built from 1702 to 1733 by Gabriele Montani and Johann Lukas von Hildebrandt, on the site of what was thought to be a Carolingian church as well as Vienna's first ecclesiastical building (first documentary evidence: 1137). The present church lies near the imperial apartments in the Hofburg; Empress Elisabeth often used to come and pray here in complete privacy, when the doors were locked to the public.

Exterior – The restricted site of this building (narrow and without an adjoining square) is typically Baroque. Its façade has sweeping lines and relatively austere decoration; the west front features two towers obliquely framing a central concave section. In front of this stands Andrea Altomonte's porch, built between 1751 and 1753, surmounted with lead figures by Franz Kohl (pupil of Georg Raphael Donner): allegories of Faith, Hope and Charity. The east end is adorned by statues by Lorenzo Mattielli, a sculptor from Vicenza (very active in Dresden in the last ten years of his life): *St Peter* and *St Michael* (below).

Interior – The **interior decoration**★ is sumptuous down to the last detail, for example the pews in the short nave which follow the oval line of the dome. The dome gives visitors the illusion of entering a much larger building. It is adorned with a fresco of the Assumption by Johann Michael Rottmayr (1714), a brilliant artist famous in Austria for the decorated dome of St Charles Borromeo church *(see Outside the Ring, Wieden).* Under this imposing structure lit by eight windows lie the side chapels, their altarpieces made by the most eminent artists of the period. Starting from the left, there are chapels dedicated to St Barbara (Franz Karl Remp), St Sebastian (Anton Schoonjans), and the Holy Family (Martino Altomonte); on the right are chapels dedicated to St Anthony (M Altomonte), St Francis de Sales (Rottmayr), and St Michael (M Altomonte). On the left of the chancel, the gilded pulpit designed by Matthias Steindl (c 1719) matches the monumental altar by Lorenzo Mattielli on which a gilded wood group (c 1729) depicts St John of Nepomuk being cast into the Moldau. The saint was a canon of Prague cathedral; he was confessor to the Queen of Bohemia. He was martyred by drowning in 1393 for refusing to betray the secret of the confessional to King Wenceslas IV (and is now called upon to ward off the dangers of false testimony). Finally, the chancel is adorned by a *trompe-l'œil* dome by Antonio Galli-Bibiena and stuccowork by Santiono Bussi (c 1730); the

Peterskirche

B. Kaufmann

splendid high altar is also by Galli-Bibiena, while the altarpiece is by Altomonte.

GRABEN AND KÄRNTNER STRASSE

After viewing the church with the finest Baroque interior in Vienna's inner city, the tour starts in the historic town centre with these two streets which now serve as pedestrianized shopping streets with elegant stores. In summer they teem with musicians and singers; in winter, they are dotted with groups of carol singers and kiosks selling mulled wine.

★**Graben** – Graben, once a Roman moat in front of the city wall, is now a lively pedestrianized street lined with smart shops. After the moat was filled in c 1200, it became the flour and vegetable market until the 17C. In the 18C it became a haunt for the "nymphs of Graben", whose fame has often been sung, and who plied "the oldest trade in the world". From the 1870s – when the Ring began to attract industrialists and bankers – this road assumed its present commercial role. Wider than a street, Graben is more of a long square leading to Stock-im-Eisen-Platz and Stephansplatz, where the cathedral suddenly comes into view. When strolling along past the boutiques, it is worth dragging your gaze away from the enticing shop windows once in a while to appreciate the elegant architecture. At No 21, Alois Pichl created the Postsparkassenamt in a neoclassical style (1838); at No 17, Ernst von Gotthilf built a Jugendstil façade (1906) on the site of a house where Mozart lived from September 1781 to July 1782 and where he composed *Die Entführung aus dem Serail (The Abduction from the Seraglio)* in "a beautifully furnished room"; at No 13 (beyond Bräunerstrasse), is the little shop **Knize** designed by Adolf Loos between 1910 and 1913; at No 11 is Graben's last remaining Baroque building, the Bartolotti-Partenfeld palace (1720); at No 10 (between Dorotheergasse and Spiegelgasse) is the Ankerhaus, built by Otto Wagner in 1894. Adolf Loos designed the stylish public toilets in 1905.

Since the 15C, two fountains have adorned Graben. They are generally attributed to Lorenzo Mattielli. However, the lead figures are certainly by Johann Martin Fischer (1804): *The Flight into Egypt* on the Josefsbrunnen, and *The Discovery of St Agnes' Veil (see Further afield, Klosterneuburg)* on the Leopoldsbrunnen.

The **Pestsäule**★★, or Plague Pillar, also known as *Dreifaltigkeitssäule* (Trinity Pillar), dates from 1693. Emperor Leopold I built it to fulfill a vow made during the plague of 1679. Matthias Rauchmiller (1645-86) began this Baroque monument in 1682; Johann Bernhard Fischer von Erlach and Paul Strudel continued the work after his death, and Lodovico Burnacini completed it. The figure of Emperor Leopold I kneeling in prayer crowns the complex iconography of this column.

H. A. Jahn/VIENNASLIDE

The Graben

Stock-im-Eisen-Platz – The "trunk set in iron" square owes its name to the tree trunk standing in a niche at the corner of Graben and Kärntner Strasse. According to a mid-16C tradition, apprentice locksmiths hammered a nail into the tree trunk before setting off on their journey round Austria.

From this square there is a striking view of the architectural contrast between the glass, post-modern Haas Haus (1990, *see below, Stephansplatz*) and the venerable walls of Stephansdom.

Kärntner Strasse – *See also City Centre and the Ring, Staatsoper District.* In the mid-13C, *strata Carinthianorum* marked the start of the road to Carinthia (Kärnten) via Styria (Steiermark). During the Middle Ages this road went as far as Trieste and Venice. However, the buildings on this street date from the 18C or later, except for some fragments of the Malteserkirche (church of the Knights of Malta). The street's architectural unity suffered its final damage through Second World War bombings. The street was reduced in size about 1860. Since 1973 most of it has become a pedestrian precinct, filled with a lively crowd of busy Viennese and tourists ambling under the lime trees, window-shopping.

In 1896, the façade of No 16 was decorated with pre-Secession Venetian-style mosaics (restored in 1959), the work of Eduard Veith; they represent the five continents.

American Bar (Loos-Bar) – *Kärntner Strasse 10.* Adolf Loos built this small bar (4.45m x 6.15m/14ft x 20ft) in 1908. A listed monument since 1959, it is one of the artist's major works, notable for its meticulously designed interior (mahogany, leather, brass, marble, onyx and mirrors). In it is a copy of the portrait of Peter Altenberg (by Gustav Jagerspacher), a friend of Loos who put the painting there himself. In 1985, Hermann Czech constructed an imitation of this bar for the exhibition "Traum und Wirklichkeit" (Dream and Reality) in the Wiener Künstlerhaus. When the bar was renovated in 1989, Loos's original idea for the upholstery of the seats was finally implemented: green automobile leather, unavailable in 1908, was finally used.

THE "SAVIOUR OF CHRISTENDOM"

When in 1683, the Christian princes came to the aid of the Viennese besieged by the Turks, the King of Poland's army included a French nobleman who was to become justly famous, **Eugène of Savoy**. This great military leader finally overcame the Ottoman menace with the Peace of Karlowitz (1699), then the Treaty of Passarowitz (1718). He subsequently acquired two magnificent Viennese residences, one for winter *(see below)* and one for summer *(see Outside the Ring, Landstrasse, Belvedere).*

Himmelpfortgasse – In this narrow street, named "Heaven's Gate" after an old convent, is **Ronacher**, a recently restored building from the end of the 1880s. This theatre once featured Josephine Baker; it boasts one of the finest auditoriums in the city and was the first to stage variety shows in German. As well as Prince Eugène's winter palace *(see below)*, the fine Baroque Erdödy-Fürstenberg palace also stands on this street (No 13). Its 1720s façade and magnificent portal adorned by telamones is reminiscent of the entrance to the former Bohemian Court Chancellery *(see City Centre and the Ring, Hoher Markt District)*, designed by Johann Bernhard Fischer von Erlach more or less during the same period.

★**Stadtpalais des Prinzen Eugen von Savoyen** – *Himmelpfortgasse 8 (the palace now houses the Ministry of Finance; it is only accessible to the public on certain occasions)*. Construction of this winter palace for Prince Eugène of Savoy, who defeated the Turks several times between 1697 and 1716, was begun by Johann Bernhard Fischer von Erlach (from 1695 to 1698) and completed by Johann Lukas von Hildebrandt (from 1702 to 1724). The prince had his apartments decorated with a magnificence equal to that of Schönbrunn. He died there in April 1736, in a room with panelling and blue ceilings adorned by gold arabesques. However, with apparent indifference, Emperor Karl VI was not present at his funeral; he spent the day in Laxenburg. Eugène of Savoy's embalmed body rests in the Stephansdom. His heiress, Anna Victoria of Savoy-Soissons, rapidly squandered the fortune of her illustrious relative.

Unfortunately, the view of the long palace façade is rather restricted by the narrowness of the street. Its unadorned façade is lined by an order of Ionic pillars bearing an entablature adorned by statues. The portal features bas-reliefs, attributed to Mattielli, since the narrow street does not allow for the traditional telamones or caryatids adorning the Erdödy-Fürstenberg palace. A look behind the double doors *(ask permission from the porter)* reveals the interior courtyard with a fountain as well as Fischer von Erlach's **Grand Staircase**★★. The latter is often mentioned as one of the finest examples of Baroque art, owing to the four telamones by Giovanni Giuliani exuding an impressive sense of physical strength, beneath the absent-minded gaze of a nonchalant Hercules in his alcove. The general lack of space only magnifies this effect.

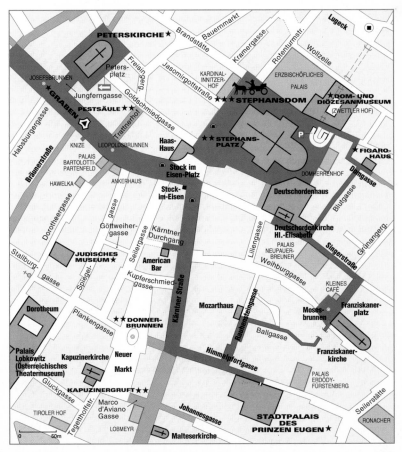

> ### Celestial Palaces Supported by Human Hands
>
> There are numerous palaces in Vienna from the Baroque period. This style favoured eloquent decoration. The highly expressive telamon, or atlante, was often used to lend strength and power to the architecture of aristocratic residences.
>
> This architectural element is a colossal statue of a man designed for support. The word "atlante" comes from the Greek **Atlas**, a god of the archaic theogeny and brother of Prometheus. Atlas sided with the Titans and rebelled against Zeus. After their defeat, he was condemned to support the sky on his shoulders.

MOZART IN VIENNA

Wolfgang Amadeus Mozart arrived in Vienna in 1781. Like Ludwig van Beethoven, he lived in various residences – 18 in the present first district. This tour ends near the cathedral where he married Constance Weber on 4 August 1782; this area includes notable dwellings where the musical genius from Salzburg stayed: his first and last address, and the house which is now a Memorial Museum.

Rauhensteingasse – This street has the dubious honour of being the address of Mozart's final residence. On 30 September 1790, he moved into No 8, in the house known as *Kleines Kaiserhaus* (Small Imperial House).

He composed several famous works here, including *The Magic Flute* and *La Clemenza di Tito*. He died on 5 December 1791 at five minutes to one in the morning while in the process of writing the *Requiem*, commissioned by Count Walsegg-Stuppach via the memorable "messenger in grey"; Franz Xaver Süssmayr completed the work at the composer's request.

Franziskanerplatz – In the centre of this attractive square is the **Mosesbrunnen**, the Moses Fountain, by the sculptor Johann Martin Fischer (1798). At No 3 is the tiny, nostalgically decorated **Kleines Café**.

Franziskanerkirche – The church of the Order of St Francis (1603-14), or church of St Jerome, boasts a curious façade inspired by south German architecture: a Renaissance pediment adorned with statues crowns the typically Gothic lancets. A Renaissance portal was added in 1742.

The Baroque interior guards a fine canopied high altar by Andrea Pozzo *(Miraculous Image of Mary with Axe, 1707)*, a *Crucifixion* by Carlo Carlone (4th chapel on the right, mid-18C), a painting by Johann Georg Schmidt (who was known as "Wiener Schmidt") depicting St Francis (4th chapel on the left, 1722) and an organ carved by Johann Wöckerl (1643), which is Vienna's oldest organ.

Singerstrasse – There is much to see in this street leading to Stock-im-Eisen-Platz and lined with many Baroque palaces. These include Neupauer-Breuner palace (1715-16) displaying a fine doorway at No 16 and the House of the Order of the Teutonic Knights, or"Deutsches Haus" (German House), with its particularly valuable collection of treasures.

Deutschordenshaus – *Singerstrasse 7*. The House of the Order of the Teutonic Knights contains the treasures of its knights. Founded by the burghers of Bremen and Lübeck during the siege of Acre in 1191, this order of hospitallers became a military order in 1198. In 1244, it acquired a definitive set of by-laws distinguishing between three categories of members: knights, priests and domestics. Under the leadership of its Grand Master, it prospered until the defeat of its knights at Tannenberg in 1410. After a period of decline, it once again earned renown fighting

"My Happiness Starts Today"

Following his return from Munich to Vienna on 16 March 1781, Wolfgang Amadeus Mozart decided on 9 May to leave the employment of Prince-Archbishop Colloredo in Salzburg. This event, which took place in Deutschordenshaus in Singerstrasse, is significant in musical history because it was the first time a composer had withdrawn from his position of dependency on a benefactor. Some 60 years earlier, Johann Sebastian Bach had been imprisoned after seeking to leave the employ of the Duke of Sachsen-Weimar.

That evening, at the age of 26, Mozart wrote: *"My happiness starts today"*. Thereafter, he had to ensure financial independence by giving lessons to Countesses Rumbeck, Zichy and Pálffy, as well as Frau von Trattner. This previously inconceivable emancipation paved the way for Beethoven, Schubert and Liszt, who all followed Mozart's example.

the Turks in 17C Hungary. Napoleon dissolved the Order in 1809, but it was revived in 1834 under Franz I as the "Grand and German Masters" The spiritual branch of the Order, which survived the end of the Habsburg Monarchy, was suppressed during the Nazi era but restored in both Austria and Germany after 1945.

★**Schatzkammer des Deutschen Ordens** ⊙ –*Stairwell 1, second floor. A small guidebook is supplied to English-speaking tourists free of charge.* Assembled by the Grand Masters, the collection in this treasure chamber is varied and comprises unusual items such as the *Tigermuscheln* (tiger's shell) spoons (17C, Room 2) or the "grass snake's tongue" salt-cellar (1556, Room 2) supposedly capable of detecting poisoned food. The following exhibits are of particular interest: a ceremonial ring in solid gold and a ruby set with diamonds (Room 1), the **chain of the Order**★ (c 1500, Room 1) with sword-shaped links joining 12 shields, Grand Master Westernach's coconut goblet (16C, Room 2), a **clock**★ (c 1620, Room 3) supported by Hercules and indicating the position of the sun and moon, and a series of weapons including a Persian sabre (c 1600, Room 3) adorned by 30 rubies and 13 turquoises.

Deutschordenskirche Hl. Elisabeth – *Singerstrasse 7.* Built between 1326 and 1395, St Elizabeth's church is almost totally surrounded by the buildings of the order. It is a Gothic edifice with alterations in the Baroque style dating from between 1720 and 1722. The interior features a fine southern Dutch **altarpiece**★ *(Crucifixion, Flagellation and Ecce Homo, 1520)* by the sculptor Nicolas van Wavere, which was until 1864 in the church of Our Lady of Gdansk. About 1722, the walls were hung with coats of arms of the knights of the order.

On the ground floor of Deutschordenshaus is the **Sala Terrena**, a delightful little concert hall featuring Venetian style Baroque frescoes from the second half of the 18C. *(If the hall is closed, go to the interior courtyard to view it through the windows).*

R. Dechamps/MICHELIN

Deutschordenshaus – Fresco in the Sala Terrena

Domgasse – Since 1862, Kleine Schülerstrasse has been known as "Domgasse" or "Cathedral Street". Vienna's first café opened there in 1683, at No 8. The sign *Zum roten Kreuz* ("at the Red Cross") recalls this; it is on the building constructed on the site in the 18C. However, the street owes its current fame to the fact that Mozart stayed in the Camesinahaus, which since then is known as the Figaro-Haus.

★ **Mozart-Gedenkstätte "Figaro-Haus"** ⊘" – *Domgasse 5*. The great Mozart lived in this house from 29 September 1784 to 23 April 1787, namely less than three years during a period which could be qualified as "happy". It was one of his most productive periods. He composed *The Marriage of Figaro*, an opera which gave its name to the building, a good address at the time, attracting numerous visitors such as Josef Haydn, Lorenzo da Ponte and his pupil Johann Nepomuk Hummel.

In addition to musical extracts *(earphones)*, several objects and documents are of interest *(numbers in brackets are those used on the exhibits)*. Room 1: after joining a Masonic lodge in December 1784, Mozart composed the cantata *Die Maurerfreude* (Masonic Joy) (frontispiece of first edition, *4*); contrary to the common view, Antonio Salieri greatly respected his rival's music (lithography by K. T. Riedel, *9*). Room 2: fine map of Vienna showing the location of Mozart's 18 residences *(10)*; his father, Leopold Mozart (engraving by J. A. Friedrich, *15*); Joseph Haydn (engraving by J. E. Mansfeld, *16*) to whom Mozart dedicated six string quartets in 1785 *(18)*; on the ground, two coins found between the floorboards during restoration work (Nuremberg Rechenpfennig and Bavarian Kreuzer, *25*). Room 3: Pierre-Augustin Caron de Beaumarchais who wrote *La Folle Journée* or *the Marriage of Figaro* (anonymous engraving, *26*); Michaelerplatz with the Burgtheater where three of Mozart's operas were first performed (engraving by Schütz, *33*). Room 4: Leopold Mozart and his children Wolfgang and Maria Anna with whom he went on a European tour (engraving by J. B. Delafosse, *37*).

> ### The Viennese Marriage of Figaro
>
> In 1785, Emperor Joseph II forbade the performance of Beaumarchais' *The Marriage of Figaro*, because he thought the contents dangerous. Only a few years before the French Revolution, the play promoted the abolition of the aristocracy's privileges. Still, in October of that same year, Mozart started composing an *opera buffa* in four acts after Beaumarchais' example, which he completed in April 1786 and which was produced a month later with an Italian libretto by Lorenzo da Ponte, court poet. Although the librettist toned down some of the political edge of the original, this version still had considerable impact on the Viennese public.

Room 5: portrait of Constanze Mozart (anonymous pastel, *70*); portraits of Mozart's sons, Karl Thomas and Franz Xaver Wolfgang (engraving after a painting by Hansen in Salzburg, *69*). Room 6: facsimile of the letter Mozart sent his father informing him of his marriage to Constanze *(48)*; 6 scenes from *The Magic Flute* (coloured engravings by J. and P. Schaffer, *66*); facsimile of a page from the handwritten score of the *Requiem* *(67)*. Room 7: Mozart was small in height and apparently had a pale complexion, his blue eyes were framed by thick blond hair (six portraits, *73-78*).

Stephansdom (St Stephen's cathedral) is nearby. Anyone who has not yet visited it should walk back up Domgasse and turn left into Schülergasse. After reaching the chevet of the cathedral, you may feel like the visitor to whom the great writer Adalbert Stifter alluded: " ...as he went round a corner, the cathedral came suddenly into view. Like a mountain, it was simple and wonderful; his spirits rose and were strengthened at the sight."

In addition to Stephansdom, the nearest sights are the districts in the city centre: Fleischmarkt, Freyung, Hofburg, Hoher Markt, Kapuzinerkirche, Staatsoper.

★★ STEPHANSPLATZ

Time has preserved the small dimensions of St Stephen's Square which contrast with the vast cathedral and its soaring 137m/449ft spire. Now almost exclusively a pedestrian zone, it features pale red paving stones on the west side; these indicate the site of St Mary Magdalene chapel, where funeral Masses were once celebrated. Fire destroyed this building in 1781.

Virgilkapelle ⊘ – Below the site of the former St Mary Magdalene chapel is the Virgil chapel. It was discovered during construction of the Stephansplatz underground station, and unearthed in 1973. There is a view of it through a window from the underground passage (Museum in der Station Stephansplatz).

★ **Dom- und Diözesanmuseum** ⊘ – *Stephansplatz 6 or Wollzeile 4. Entrance though Zwettler Hof*. Giovanni Coccaponi was probably the architect of the archbishop's palace (1640). Adjacent to it is the cathedral museum, the creation of Cardinal Theodor Innitzer in 1933, in the former courtyard of Zwettl abbey dating from the 14C. Besides a fine picture and sculpture collection, it has a display of the most precious items in the cathedral treasury, and constitutes an ideal ending to a visit to Stephansdom. In a succession of rooms, the museum features exhibits ranging from the Baroque period to the early Middle Ages *(numbers in brackets correspond to the numbering of the exhibits)*.

Bartl/ÖSTERREICH WERBUNG

Stephansdom and Haas-Haus

In the first rooms are numerous paintings and a few sculptures from the Baroque period: *Christ Bound to a Pillar* (mid-17C) *(126)*, an unusual *St Mary Magdalene* carrying a skull (c 1670) *(128)*, *God the Father and the Holy Ghost* (1724) *(134)* and *Glory of St Charles Borromeo* (1728) *(135)* by Johann Michael Rottmayr, *Virgin with Child* (c 1725) *(139)* by Martino Altomonte, *Virgin with Child Appearing to St Anthony of Padua* (1744) *(142)* by Michelangelo Unterberger, *The Holy Family* (1775-80) *(151)* by Martin Johann "Kremser" Schmidt, *St Catherine of Sienna* (late 17C) *(155)* by Tanzio de Varallo.

Then there are many Gothic works, including a superb fragment from a stained-glass cathedral window, the **Thurifer Angel**★ or incense-bearing angel (c 1340) *(59)*, a fine *Virgin with Milk* (post 1537) *(73)*, a painting from Lucas Cranach the Elder's studio, a *Virgin with Child* (c 1320) *(76)* and an *Entombment* (early 17C) *(121)* both from Thernberg church in Lower Austria. In the end room are the **Ober St Veit altarpiece**★ (c 1507) *(69)* by one of Dürer's pupils, Hans Schäufelein, *The Mocking of Christ* (c 1505) *(70)*, **Ecce Homo**★ (1537) *(72)* by Lucas Cranach the Elder, depicting Christ's presentation at the temple with Pilate saying to the crowd "Here is the man", and a carved group, *The Birth of Christ* (c 1500) *(100)*. Before leaving the room, one may note the two series of seven painted panels, one dating from the end of the 14C *(60)* and the other from the beginning of the 15C *(62)*.

The two rooms of the treasury contain old and rare items, including in particular **Rudolf IV's shroud**★ *(3)*, of gold silk brocade made in Persia (first third of 14C), and **Duke Rudolf IV's portrait**★ (c 1360) *(2, see illustration in the Introduction, the Habsburg empire)*. Rudolf IV was the founder of the cathedral and Vienna University. Like the portrait of the King of France, John the Good (1319-64) in the Louvre, this tempera portrait is one of the earliest in the history of western art. There is also a sardonyx cameo (3C, the cross and stole being later additions, c 1365) *(1)*, six enamelled plaques (1160-70) *(5)* from a reliquary, two glass **Syrian vases**★ (c 1280 and 1310) *(6)*, a reliquary of St Andrew's cross (1440) *(8)*, a reliquary containing St Stephen's skull (1741) *(12)*, a Carolingian Gospel (late 9C) *(13)* depicting the four Evangelists, a monstrance from Stephansdom (1482) *(17)*, two monstrances in the shape of a tower (1508 and 1515) *(18 and 19)*, a **chasuble shroud**★ (c 1400) *(24)*, its Latin cross embroidered in high relief with the *Crucifixion* in the centre.

After going through a room containing liturgical accessories including the Mariapócs monstrance (Hungary, c 1680) *(44)*, you reach the old chapel. On its walls hangs *The Immaculate Virgin with St Elizabeth, St Joseph, and St Francis of Assisi (1856) (174)* by Leopold Kupelwieser.

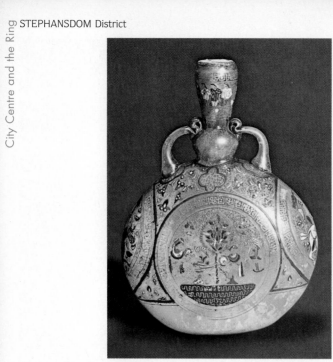

Erzbischöfliches Dom- und Diözesanmuseum

A Syrian vase

Haas Haus – *Stephansplatz 12.* Opposite such a historic site, the architect **Hans Hollein** had no qualms about building a structure of blue-grey marble and glass, which reflects the Gothic arches of the cathedral. Since its opening in 1990, this building has been the source of much heated discussion. It houses shops, cafés, a restaurant and offices, and symbolizes the rebirth of architectural creativity in a city where practitioners of this art a hundred years ago were the best in their field. The building's critics fail to understand that by his bold treatment of form, Hollein has restored the full broad dimension to the Stephansplatz and Stock-im-Eisen-Platz intersection. By following the old curving lines of the area, he has opened up the view of the Gothic cathedral, which is now visible when coming from the Graben.

In addition to Stephansdom, the nearest sights in the city centre are the Fleischmarkt, Freyung, Hofburg, Hoher Markt, Kapuzinerkirche and Staatsoper (in the City Centre and the Ring section).

The Giant Ferris Wheel in the Prater

Outside the Ring

ALSERGRUND★

9th District

Local map page 15, **EFTU**

Underground: Schottentor (U2), Schottenring (U2)

Tram: Schottentor-Universität (1, 2, 37, 38, 40, 41, 42)

Bus: Schottentor (40A)

With its numerous hospitals and convalescent homes, this district north of the town centre is a focus of the healing arts. France, too, however, is well represented, with the French Lycée (Liechtensteinstrasse 37a) and the French Cultural Institute (Währingerstrasse 32). Many famous people have lived here, including Ludwig van Beethoven, Anton Bruckner, Sigmund Freud, Franz Schubert and the writer Heimito von Doderer.

SIGMUND FREUD

Biographical notes – 1856: birth in Freiberg, Moravia to Jakob and Amalia Freud. 1859: settles in Vienna. 1873: student at the Faculty of Medicine. 1881: doctor of medicine. 1882: marriage to Martha Bernays, in Hamburg. 1883: doctor at Vienna General Hospital. 1885: lecturer in nervous diseases; internship with Charcot in Paris. 1886: Marries in Hamburg. 1910: founding of the Association of the Society of Psychoanalysts, C. G. Jung is named president. 1924: becomes "honorary citizen of the City of Vienna". 1933: in Berlin, the Nazis burn Freud's books. 1939: death of Freud in London; his ashes are placed in a Greek wine bowl from his collection of antiques.

The Freudian revolution – Before Freud, people viewed the unconscious as a negative force, a chaotic disorder clouding reason and disrupting conscience. Starting from research on the aetiology of neuroses, Freud evolved a revolutionary theory. Its impact on the history of ideas was as dramatic as that of the discoveries of the astronomer, Copernicus, who revolutionised thinking with the theory that the planets moved round the sun. Freudian theory describes the psyche and develops a technique for the interpretation of dreams. This theory is the subject of a cult book, *The Interpretation of Dreams*, published in German in 1900 (in 1909 in English). For the first time, dreams had a coded meaning, which concealed the unconscious desires of the dreamer. The language and syntax of dreams were that of the neuroses which begged analysis. Briefly, psychoanalysis was seen as a means of communicating with the patient's unconscious and restructuring his or her personal history.

M. Halberstadt/Sigmund Freud Museum

Freud had to face the opposition and incomprehension of most of his contemporaries. However, with the support of students such as A Adler or Carl Gustav Jung, he was able to have his theories recognised by the scientific community. The modern view of the human psyche originated here, at No 19 Berggasse, in an unprepossessing townhouse.

★**Sigmund-Freud-Museum** ⊘ (HP) – *Berggasse 19. Underground: Schottentor (U2); tram: Schlickgasse (D); bus: Berggasse (40A)*. This address has almost become a place of pilgrimage, since the founding father of psychoanalysis lived there from 1891 to 1938, that is for nearly half a century before leaving the Austrian capital for London, to escape the Nazis.

Sigmund Freud by Max Halberstadt

The apartment – *1st floor*. Dating from 1971, this museum occupies the apartment where Freud wrote his works; his study was on the ground floor. The famous couch is in the Freud Museum, in the London suburb of Hampstead. On the other hand, the furniture in the waiting room is back in Vienna, thanks to his youngest daughter Anna Freud, herself a psychoanalyst.

> **A Great Collector**
>
> Sigmund Freud possessed a remarkable collection of antiques. Thanks to the cooperation of Hans Demel, the director of the Kunsthistorisches Museum at the time, who deliberately undervalued them, Freud was able to take them with him into his London exile. These objects literally filled his Berggasse chambers. The eminent psychoanalyst found them instructive both for himself and his patients.
>
> On his desk, he kept significant items, such as the bronze head of Osiris, ruler of the underworld, and a bronze statuette of Imhotep, architect of the Sakkara pyramid.

Most of the collection consists of photographic documents *(explanatory leaflets are available in English)*. There is a veritable panorama of photographs tracing Freud's life, from the Freiberg house to his departure to London and including family photographs, such as the snap of Freud with his daughter Sophia. An audio-visual documentary with a commentary by Anna Freud shows her father with his family, during rare moments of leisure in the Viennese suburbs. It is a touching and somewhat unexpected scene.

THE MANY FACES OF ALSERGRUND

Der alte Jüdische Friedhof in der Rossau – The old Jewish cemetery of Rossau was founded in the 16C and is now only indirectly accessible *(Seegasse 11)* through the *Kuratorium Wiener Pensionistenheime Zentrale* or the administrative offices of the Viennese retirement homes. Samuel Oppenheimer and Samson Wertheimer are buried there *(see Further afield, Eisenstadt, inset "Court Jews")*. However, if it is sunny, a walk along the embankments of the Danube is an attractive option. Of particular interest is the *Rossauer Lände* (U4), the underground station which Otto Wagner designed on the quay at the turn of the 20C.

Servitenkirche – *Servitengasse 9. Tram: Schlickgasse (D); bus: Berggasse (40A)*. Construction on the "Servants of our Lady" church, also called Annunciation church, was begun in 1651 and completed in 1677 by Carlo Canevale. The two towers were added between 1754 and 1756. It is the earliest edifice in Vienna to possess a central space of oval shape. It provides valuable evidence for foreign artistic influence in the early Baroque style in the Austro-Hungarian capital. One may reasonably suppose that it inspired the architects of Karlskirche and Peterskirche.

Its rich interior attracts visitors. The stuccowork was by Johann Baptist Barberino and Johann Baptist Bussi. On the left, the fine Baroque **pulpit**★ (1739) displays carved figures by Balthasar Moll. Some of his masterpieces can be viewed in the Capuchin Crypt *(see City Centre and the Ring, Kapuzinerkirche District)*. Here, he created the Four Evangelists *(lower level)* and the Three Divine Virtues *(on the sound board)*.

On the right of the church is St Peregrine's chapel, added in 1727, a year after the canonisation of the Servite Peregrine. The frescoes in the cupola are the work of the Tyrolian artist Josef Adam Mölk (1766).

Palais Liechtenstein (M⁴) – *Fürstengasse 1. Tram: Fürstengasse (D); bus: Bauernfeldplatz (40A)*. Domenico Martinelli designed this Baroque building, which is inspired by Italian models. He began it c 1700 and completed it in 1711. The Hall of State on the first floor has frescoes by Andrea Pozzo depicting the *Apotheosis of Hercules*. As of 2003, the palace will be exhibiting the substantial collection of Prince Liechtenstein.

Strudelhofstiege – *Between Strudlhofgasse and Liechtensteinstrasse. Tram: Sensengasse (37, 38, 40, 41, 42); bus: Bauernfeldplatz (40A)*. The architect Johann Theodor Jager designed these picturesque steps with several flights in 1910. A fine example of urban art, it boasts Jugendstil balustrades and candelabras. It was the setting of a famous novel by Heimito von Doderer, *Die Strudlhofstiege oder Melzer und die Tiefe der Jahren* (1951, not yet translated into English).

Bezirksmuseum Alsergrund ⊙ **(M²⁰)** – *Währingerstrasse 43. Tram: Sensengasse (37, 38, 40, 41, 42)*. This museum has a commemorative exhibition to **Heimito von Doderer** (1896-1966), author of *Die Strudlhofstiege*, who is practically unknown outside Austria. For a time he flirted with National Socialist ideology, but abandoned this after Hitler's annexation of Austria. He lived in Währingerstrasse. The Jewish poet **Erich Fried**, who emigrated to London in 1938 is also remembered here by a reconstruction of his study in London. The rest of the museum is devoted to the crafts and professions in old Vienna and the history of the district of Alsergrund.

3 BIS/MICHELIN

Waste incineration and heating plant

Volksoper (**T²**) – *Währinger-strasse 78. Tram: Währinger-strasse/Volksoper (40, 41, 42). Währingerstrasse/Volksoper (40A)*. The People's Opera was built in 1898 to mark Franz Josef's fiftieth jubilee celebrations.

The company dates from 1903. At the Volksoper, unlike at the National Opera, the works are always sung in German. It is often young singers or conductors who perform in this opera house and the operas or operettas sometimes display an avant-garde spirit. The Volksoper also stages musical comedies such as *My Fair Lady*. It is the opera of the people, in the best sense of the word.

Müllverbrennung-Fern-wärme-Heizwerk (**S**) – *Heiligenstädter Lände. Underground: Spittelau (U4); tram: Spittelau (D)* – This is the name, difficult for a foreigner to pronounce, of the waste incinerator that **Friedensreich Hundertwasser** decorated, north of Franz-Josef station. The gold-tipped chimney of this building is a landmark in

the Viennese urban landscape. The incinerator is part of the new university complex which Kurt Hlawenicka and Company built between 1972 and 1990 (Economics Department, Institutes of Zoology, Biology and Botany).

THE MASTER OF LIEDER – FRANZ SCHUBERT

"When I wanted to sing about love, I became sad; when I wanted to sing about sadness, it led me to love". Franz Schubert wrote this famous sentence in 1822. It sums up the attitude of this composer, underrated in his time, who wrote over 1 200 pieces of music in a mere twenty years.

★**Franz-Schubert-Gedenkstätte Geburtshaus** ⊙ (**M⁵**) – *Nussdorferstrasse 54. Tram: Canisiusgasse (37, 38). Althanstrasse (D)*. This museum commemorating Franz Schubert was opened in 1912 in a house formerly called *Zum roten Krebs* ("At the Red Crayfish"). Franz Peter Schubert was born there on 31 January 1797; his family lived in the rooms overlooking the inner courtyard. The future composer spent the first four years of his life there, before moving to No 3 Säulengasse.

The Historisches Museum der Stadt Wien (Historical Museum of the City of Vienna) had the excellent idea of equipping the "great musician memorials" under its administration with a sound system enabling visitors to hear musical extracts. Using headphones, you can listen to Schubert and select the music of your choice.

The museum possesses numerous documents and mementoes. It displays the famous spectacles of the composer of *Der Tod und das Mädchen* (*Death and the Maiden*, Room 1), extracts from his diary (Room 1) and a lock of his hair in a medallion with an authentication certificate. Among the portraits, there are a signed zincograph by Leopold Kupelwieser (1821), a lithograph by Josef Teltscher (about 1825) and a Carrara marble bust (1893) by Carl Kundmann (Room 2). His guitar is also on view, dating from about 1820 and made by the Viennese craftsman Bernard Enzensperger (Room 4).

A prolific composer – Schubert was born and died in Vienna, a city which he rarely left. He composed almost ceaselessly, allowing himself only the occasional break. He took his first lessons in counterpoint a few weeks before his death. He was a great friend of Franz Grillparzer and an admirer of Johann Wolfgang von Goethe and Friedrich von Schiller. By 1818, he had already composed nearly 600 pieces, having achieved in 1815 and 1816 an output greater than many composers produced in a lifetime. Surprisingly, he rarely met Beethoven, who lived in the city during the same period and died a year before him. From the depths of his solitude, Schubert composed five masses, 10 symphonies, 15 operas and over 600 *Lieder*.

Schubert's piano

It was during his adolescence that Schubert began writing *Lieder*, a musical form present throughout his work. His childhood as a choirboy *(see Lichtentalkirche, below)* probably led him to explore this new genre which can be defined as a musical setting of a poem for one or more voices. His masterpiece is probably *Der Doppelgänger (The Double)*, which he composed at the age of 31 for a text by Heinrich Heine.

After leaving the museum, bear left and cross Nussdorferstrasse, then turn right into Säulengasse.

Schubert lived at No 3, *Zum Schwarzen Rössel* ("The Black Horse") house, from 1803 to 1808. He moved back in 1813, spending 17 years of his short life there. It was where he composed, among other works, *Erlkönig* in 1815. The house is now a garage, formerly *Schubertgarage*.

Cross Nussdorferstrasse again and take the steps up to Liechtensteinstrasse. Cross it and enter Lichtentalergasse. Marktgasse is the second street on the left.

Lichtentalkirche (K⁷) – *Marktgasse 40*. This small church was the setting for Schubert's christening on 1 February 1797. It was also here that he played the violin and sang in public for the first time, before becoming a pupil at the choir school "K. und K. Stadtkonvikt". This comprised 130 pupils who sang on Sundays at the imperial chapel. Finally, the first public performance of one of his works, the *Mass in F Major*, was given in this church on 16 October 1814.

A CENTRE OF THE HEALING ARTS

★**Josephinum (HP)** – *Währingerstrasse 25*. Tram: Sensengasse *(37, 38, 40, 41, 42)*. Joseph II founded the former Military Academy of Surgery and Medicine known as the "Josephinum". Isidor Canevale built it between 1783 and 1785. In the main courtyard is a fountain by Johann Martin Fischer dating from 1787. Since 1920, the Josephinum has housed the Museum of the Institute of the History of Medicine.

Museum des Institutes für Geschichte der Medizin ⊙ – *First floor*. This museum devoted to the history of medicine is in two sections. First, there are two rooms displaying 19C instruments (including Karl Zeiss's first magnifying glass) and documents (photographs, engravings, etc). Of interest is the display case dedicated to S Freud, A Adler and J Preuer (manuscript of a letter by Freud). Then, there are three rooms containing life-size **anatomical preparations**★ modelled in wax under the supervision of Felice Fontana and Paolo Mascagni. Joseph II commissioned this collection of figures, the "Anatomia Plastica", to make the study of anatomy easier for future military surgeons. A visitor will marvel at the astonishing precision of this unusual series of flayed wax torsos, incorporating muscles, nerves, ligaments and blood vessels, by the two Tuscan sculptors. The model of the Lunatics' Tower *(see Narrenturm below)* will be of interest to anyone who does not have time for a visit to the General Hospital.

AKH (Allgemeines Krankenhaus) – *Alserstrasse 4*. At the end of the 18C, Joseph II had the old hospital for the poor expanded into the Vienna General Hospital. The task was completed in 1784. During the following century new wings were added to form a large complex with 13 inner courtyards. Today it serves the University, whereas a huge new General Hospital was erected on the Gürtel.

Narrenturm – *Follow the signs in the hospital precinct in the sixth yard*. The architect Isidore Canevale constructed the tower here as the asylum for the mental patients. Behind these narrow windows like arrow slits with bars, the patients inhabited (until 1866) cells opening onto a corridor skirting a really sinister inner courtyard. People nicknamed it "Emperor Joseph's Gugelhupf", a kind of cake with a hole in the middle.

Pathologisch-Anatomisches Bundesmuseum ⊘ – The Museum of Pathology and Anatomy occupies several storeys of Narrenturm *(only the ground floor is open to the public; the rest is for use by medical students)*. It contains an impressive display of preparations and casts of ill or deformed organs and limbs.

After leaving the General Hospital by Alserstrasse, the visitor will be nearly opposite the Church of the Holy Trinity *(see Outside the Ring, Josefstadt)*.

The nearest sights are: the Freyung District in the city centre, and the districts of Döbling, Währing, Josefstadt and Leopoldstadt (in the Outside the Ring section) .

DÖBLING★★

19th District

Local map pages 10-11, **ABX**

The Döbling area is extensive, but little known to those who do not live in Vienna. It includes two districts with internationally famous names: Heiligenstadt, immortalized by Ludwig van Beethoven's testament of the same name, and Grinzing, famous for its vineyards.

The district has been divided into three, with directions indicating modes of transport for visiting each section from the centre of the town. It is however possible to visit all three sections successively by following the directions printed in italics. In this case, it is advisable to begin the itinerary with the diverse sights in Heiligenstadt, then go to Grinzing, the hillsides of Kahlenberg and Leopoldsberg and back to the city via Oberdöbling.

★HEILIGENSTADT

Underground: Heiligenstadt (U4); Train: Heiligenstadt (S40); Tram: Halteraugasse (D)

This old wine-growing village has been part of Döbling since 1892. One hundred years earlier, it had only three streets. Today, it consists of a lower urbanised section and an upper residential quarter, which follows the banks of the Danube Canal and is pleasantly remote from the bustle of downtown Vienna.

If the weather is fine, visitors in light-hearted mood may deviate from the tour and explore the **Nussdorf** vineyards, a region less popular with tourists than Grinzing. It is a good opportunity for walking the **Beethovengang** alongside a brook, past the Lehár-Schikaneder Villa *(Hackhofergasse 18)*. As its name suggests, past owners included Emanuel Schikaneder, German librettist of *The Magic Flute* and director of the Theater An der Wien, then from 1932 the Hungarian composer Franz Lehár.

★**Karl-Marx-Hof** – *Heiligenstädterstrasse 82 to 92*. Facing the exit from the underground is the immense "red fortress". Vienna's Austro-Marxist council in power from 1919 to 1934 opened it on 12 October 1930. This monumental ensemble is the most famous *Hof* of this period in the capital, and it is known to architectural students throughout the world. It was built between 1927 and 1930 by Karl Ehn, a pupil of Otto Wagner, who was director of planning services in 1922. This "stronghold" numbers about 1 400 apartments for approximately 5 000 people. It comprised cooperative groceries, central laundries, kindergartens, a dental clinic, an infirmary and a workers' library. The complex lies on a long narrow stretch of land with an area of 156 000m²/186 574sq yd; buildings occupy 20% of it, while the rest is for garden areas. It is a striking display of archways over passages between courtyards and gardens, sculptures (Joseph Riedl) over the arches, blue flagpoles from which banners fluttered, and the red and ochre contrasting colour scheme of the roughcast. The whole effect has led people to define it as proletarian *Ringstil*. Such critics may be correct from the point of view of form. However, they forget to mention that in Karl-Marx-Hof, just as in the similar Karl-Seitz-Hof (built by Hubert Gessner in Floridsdorf), there is no lift. Moreover, the largest 3 room apartments measure 60m²/71sq yd in total. This is a far cry from the apartments on the Ringstrasse.

Karl-Marx-Hof

During the three-day civil war that broke out in Vienna in 1934, militants from the Republikanischer Schutzbund retreated to communal dwellings, including Karl-Marx-Hof, 1km/0.5mi long. Chancellor Engelbert Dollfuss ordered the army to dislodge them by force. According to official figures, there were 314 dead; the Social-Democrats, on the other hand, stated there were 1 500 victims and over 5 000 wounded. Bloodshed confirmed the nickname Red Vienna, which the city had gained because of its ideology. In 1938, the Austro-Fascist regime renamed the site Heiligenstädter-Hof, added a chapel and doubled the rent. In 1977, Karl-Marx-Hof became a historic monument. It is now a cultural tourist attraction, of artistic and historical interest.

Take bus 38A to Februar Platz (opposite the underground station) and get off at the Fernsprechamt Heiligenstadt stop. Walk back up Grinzingerstrasse and turn right into Nestelbachgasse to reach Pfarrplatz.

St. Jakobs Kirche – *Pfarrplatz 3.* This church has been rebuilt a number of times on Roman and early Christian foundations. It has a simple façade of brick and rubble stone. In 1952, excavations revealed 2C Roman remains as well as a burial place with a baptismal font dating from the 5C under the simple Romanesque structure. It is presumed that this is the original burial place of St Severin. This *locus sanctus* or "Heilige Stätte" ("the holy place") is what gave the quarter its current name. Inside the church, a relic reminds visitors of this saint; above it is glass painting from 16C.

Outside the church, there is on the right a map listing and locating Beethoven's various residences in Heiligenstadt. In 1817, he lived at No 2 on the square, in a 17C house with its corner adorned by a wooden statue of St Florian on one corner; it is now a Heuriger **Mayer am Pfarrplatz**.

Probusgasse leads off opposite the church.

Beethoven-Gedenkstätte Testamenthaus ⊘ – *Probusgasse 6.* At the age of 27, the composer noticed the onset of deafness, which gradually grew worse. At 30, he mentioned it for the first time in a letter to his friend Karl Amenda: "*I cannot hear the high notes of the instruments*". When he was 31, his doctor sent him for treatment at Heiligenstadt spa, but he soon realized that there was no cure. At 32, he drew up the harrowing **"Heiligenstadt Testament,"** in which the first lines describe his sense of desperation: "*Oh you people, who consider me hostile or inflexible, even a misanthrope, you misjudge me profoundly! You do not know the hidden cause of all these symptoms ...*" The letter was addressed to his brothers, but he never sent it.

Beethoven lived in this house (mid-18C) in 1802. In 1970, it was turned into a museum (engravings, facsimiles, Streicher piano). Today, this residence where he composed the *Second Symphony* now houses the Viennese Beethoven Society's exhibition. In one of the eight glass cases there is a facsimile of the famous "Testament" that has been in Hamburg National University Library since 1888. On the end wall are five attractive engravings on wood by the Viennese painter Karl

---

Beethoven the Nature-Lover

Following in the footsteps of Haydn and Mozart, Beethoven worked tire-lessly to create works of genius. He frequently changed accommodation, so there are numerous places dedicated to him in and around Vienna (as far as Baden). Beethoven loved the countryside. In the summer, he stayed north of Vienna. It was there that he composed most of the *Eroica (Third Symphony)*. In 1808, its rustic character inspired him to create the *Pastoral (Sixth Symphony)*. Between Heiligenstadt and Nussdorf lies Beethovengang (Beethoven's promenade) along the banks of the Schreiberbach *(go down Eroicagasse from Pfarrplatz, the square including St. Jakobs Kirche)*. This serves as a reminder of the extent to which the composer enjoyed immersing himself in nature. *"Because he lost contact with the outside world, they called him hostile. And because he avoided feelings, they called him callous. He withdrew from other people after he had given them everything and received nothing from them in return..."* (Franz Grillparzer).

Moll (1907) showing the places where Beethoven lived in the region. Just in front is a plaster bust that the sculptor Josef Danhauser made (1827) after completing the composer's death mask *(the original mask is in the Historisches Museum der Stadt Wien)*.

The street takes its name from the Roman emperor Probus (276-282) who allowed his Vindobona legionaries to plant the first vines in the region.

In Grinzinger Strasse, take bus 38A at the Armbrustergasse stop and get off at Grinzing.

★GRINZING

Tram: Grinzing (38)

The first mention of Grinzing occurs in 1114. It is a delightful village on the out-skirts of Vienna with low-roofed, brightly coloured houses; it is famous for its wine and Heuriger. As part of Döbling District, Grinzing now has to contend with the urban development that is gradually spreading towards the lower slopes of the Viennese forest. To remedy the situation, the village has been practising a pleasant subterfuge for some years: Anyone may buy 1m²/1.25sq yd with a single vine, just like Leonard Bernstein, Jimmy Carter or Sophia Loren.

In Grinzing

Situated at the foot of verdant, vine-clad slopes, Grinzing attracts many Viennese and tourists, who come to taste the new wine sold by the winegrowers, mainly on Sandgasse. The village comes to life in the evening, recovering its usual calm with twelve strokes of the clock from the onion-shaped dome of Grinzinger Pfarrkirche (early 15C); this heavily restored church lies on Himmelstrasse. No 25 features a plaque in honour of Franz Schubert, "prince of *Lieder* who enjoyed staying in Grinzing". At No 29, another plaque evokes the memory of the Schrammelmusik player Sepp Fellner, the "Schubert of Grinzing". The celebrated conductor Böhm occupied the elegant white Jugendstil building at No 41. He was a friend of Richard Strauss and director of the Vienna Philharmonic. Viennese music lovers held him in great respect and he became famous for his interpretations of German compositions (Mozart, Wagner etc.).

Return to the chevet of the church; bear right into Mannagettagasse, which soon becomes Mannagettasteig, then turn right into the street An den langen Lüssen.

The cemetery – *Consult the map on the right just beyond the entrance.* Gustav Mahler (block 6, row 7) is buried here next to his daughter Maria, who died at the age of five. Josef Hoffmann designed the austere tombstone. Some yards away is the grave of his wife Alma (block 6, row 6), buried under his name despite two later marriages. In an anonymous grave lies the great writer Thomas Bernhard who died in 1989.

The Loveliest Girl in Vienna

Alma Mahler: a legend. Born in the imperial capital in August 1879, Alma Mahler was the daughter of Jakob Emil Schindler, a famous landscape painter, and Anna von Bergen who, after her husband's death, married Karl Moll, a founder member of the Secession.

Towards the end of the century, the Habsburg regime was approaching its demise, but the city was a focus of European cultural life. At the end of the century, the twenty-year-old Alma was to become the muse of the greatest artists of the time. Gustav Klimt and the musician Alexander von Zemlinsky fell in love with her before her marriage in 1902 with Gustav Mahler, then director of the imperial Opera. After the composer's death in 1911, she had a stormy relationship with Oskar Kokoschka. She married the architect Walter Gropius in 1915, then the poet Franz Werfel in 1929. The woman once known as the most beautiful girl in Vienna died in New York in December 1964.

EXCURSIONS TO KAHLENBERG AND LEOPOLDSBERG

By car: From Grinzing via Cobenzlgasse and Höhenstrasse. Or take bus 38A to the stops at Kahlenberg or Leopoldsberg.

From the Cobenzl café and restaurant at the foot of Latisberg, there is an interesting **view** of Vienna, particularly by night. It was on the way to this restaurant that, on 24 July 1895, Sigmund Freud suddenly realised the importance of dreams in the study of mental illness. Follow Höhenstrasse to the Gasthaus Häuserl am Roan on Dreimarktstein (alt. 454m/1 489ft). There is a fine view from the car park of the whole of Vienna and the Wienerwald.

★**Kahlenberg** – The roof terrace (alt 483m/1 584ft) of the restaurant provides a **view**★ of Vienna alive with the soaring spires of Stephansdom and Ringturm. In the foreground stretch the Grinzing vineyards, to the right are the slopes of the Wienerwald. On a clear day, there is a distinct view of the Gloriette over Schönbrunn Park, and, in the distance, of the massive black and white Alt-Erlaa tower blocks. Kahlenbergkirche dates from 1629. This church contains a replica of the Black Virgin of Czestochowa, which is greatly venerated in Poland and attracts the Polish community of Vienna. The façade displays a plaque in honour of John III Sobieski. In 1809, many Viennese climbed "the bald hill" to watch the troop movements against Napoleon during the battles of Wagram (east of the city) and Essling (on the site of modern Donaustadt, 22nd District).

★★**Leopoldsberg** – Leopold III of Babenberg built a castle for his wife Agnes on this promontory at the tip of Wienerwald (alt 423m/1 387ft). The Turks destroyed the stronghold in 1529, during Suleyman the Magnificent's unsuccessful siege of Vienna. Opposite the small Leopoldskirche (1679-93), a church that has often been rebuilt, there is a restaurant with a courtyard terrace. From a platform (relief map of Vienna in 1683), featuring the Heimkehrerdenkmal in memory of victims of the Nazis, there is an extensive **view**★★. In the foreground is the multicoloured tower built by Friedensreich Hundertwasser for the incineration plant Müllverbrennung-Fernwärme-Heizwerk. There is a view of the Prater, the Danube canal, UNO-City and the Donauturm, the meander of the Old Danube, the Wagram plain and, on the horizon, the Little Carpathians in Slovakia as well as the alpine profile of Leithagebirge at the edge of Neusiedlersee.

An Observation Post for the Christian Army

In 1683, when Grand Vizier **Kara Mustafa** was about to capture Vienna, John Sobieski, King John III of Poland, responded to Pope Innocent XI's appeal. With 65 000 men under his command, he joined the remains of the imperial army under Charles of Lorraine. On 12 September, the morning of the last battle, Marco d'Aviano, a Capuchin friar and papal legate, celebrated Mass on the top of Kahlenberg. Strengthened by the papal blessing, the army left this observation post and marched to attack the forces of *Babi Ali*. At noon, the enemy began to give way. By nightfall, the Turks were defeated. In accordance with custom during periods of conflict, John III Sobieski's men were authorised to loot their opponents' camp.

People travelling by car can continue driving along Höhenstrasse to Klosterneuburg (see the Further afield section). From the slopes on the other side of the valley, the winding road offers fine views. Otherwise, return through Grinzing and on to Oberdöbling.
Or return to Grinzing with bus 38A and take tram 38 to the Silbergasse stop. Walk from there and turn into Hofzeile, which leads to the Döblinger Hauptstrasse.

OBERDÖBLING

Tram: Pokornystrasse (37)

Weinbaumuseum ⊙ (**M¹**) – *Döblinger Hauptstrasse 96*. This small museum in a medieval cellar contains documentation and objects relating to the history and traditions of the Döbling District that includes Grinzing, Nussdorf and Sievering and is the wine-growing region of Vienna. Among the wine-growing equipment are a large winepress known as *Winzerkrone* (winegrower's crown) and a winepress that dates from Maria-Theresa's time.

Beethoven-Gedenkstätte Eroicahaus ⊙ (**E**) – *Döblinger Hauptstrasse 92*. Beethoven liked to spend the summer months in the suburbs of Vienna and in the countryside. In the summer of 1803, he is generally believed to have lived in Oberdöbling and worked on several compositions at the same time, as was his habit. Within its three rooms, the Beethoven-Gedenkstätte "Eroicahaus" houses some engravings and etchings relating to his work here on the *Eroica (Third Symphony)*. It also displays other works from this time such as the famous *Triple Concerto* for piano, violin and cello (opus 56), as well as illustrations of other places where Beethoven lived in the Viennese suburbs of his day.

The neighbouring districts (with sights described in this guide) are: Alsergrund and Währing (in the Outside the Ring section).

DONAUSTADT★

22nd District
Local map page 11, **CXY**

Donaustadt and Floridsdorf (21st District), both suburbs located east of Vienna on the other bank of the Danube, are sometimes slightly disparagingly nicknamed "Transdanubia". Donaustadt is still alive with the memory of the conflict between Napoleon and Archduke Karl. The silhouette of UNO-City dominates this part of town, a modern urban landscape that has nevertheless retained many areas of greenery.

SIGHTS

Donauinsel – *Underground – Donauinsel (U1); tram: Floridsdorfer Brücke/ Donauinsel (31, 33). The Tourist Information Centres have a leaflet describing the tourist attractions on the island.* Danube Island was created during construction of the supplementary New Danube canal. Straddling the 21st and 22nd Districts, it is a narrow strip of land covering 700ha/1 729 acres and 21km/13mi long. It specialises solely in **recreation activities**, except when the river is in spate. Because of its proximity to the Kagran section of the city, it is also jokingly called **Copa Cagrana**. The north end is a paradise for walkers, as well as swimmers (beaches), devotees of water sports (pedalos, motor boats, windsurfing schools, yachting), cyclists *(access by the cycle path on Floridsdorf bridge)* and joggers (fitness course).
The central and the southern sections also boast numerous beaches; however, they are more popular with keen cyclists *(access by Reichsbrücke and Praterbrücke, mountain bike trails and cycle race track)*, roller skaters and even divers (one school) or anglers *(permit compulsory)*. There is also water skiing and canoeing. The southern part of the island is a conservation area and has a nature reserve harbouring fauna in the reeds on the riverbanks.

★**Donaupark** – In 1964, a former rubbish dump became the site for the international flower show. Next to UNO-City, the Danube park is today the second largest public park in the city, covering 100ha/247 acres; it is also one of the most attractive in Vienna. A small train carries visitors round the gardens and the artificial lake.

The park's main attraction is the **Donauturm** (Danube Tower), which at 252m/826ft is the tallest building in Vienna. There are two fast lifts to the panoramic platform 165m/541ft from the ground and to two restaurants. From this revolving terrace it is possible to enjoy a magnificent 360° panoramic **view**★★ of Vienna and the surrounding area.

★**UNO-City** ⊘ – *Underground: Kaisermühlen-Vienna International Centre (U1).* Since August 1979, Vienna has been one of the four cities of the United Nations, in addition to New York, Geneva and Nairobi. More than 4 000 people from over 100 different countries work for the international organisations located here. Generally known as UNO-City, the **Vienna International Centre** was built according to plans designed by the Austria architect Johann Staber on the grounds of the Donaupark. It belongs to the Austrian state, which rents it to the organisations for 99 years for the symbolic sum of 1 schilling (€0.07) a year.

UNO (United Nations Organisation) – The official founding date for the United Nations is 24 October 1945, the day that the UN Charter was ratified by China, France, Great Britain, the Soviet Union and the USA, as well as most of the other signatory nations (51 charter members). Membership of the UN, founded to promote world peace and international co-operation, is open to all nations that accept the provisions of the Charter (189 members in 2002). The six main organs of the United Nations are the General Assembly, the Security Council, the Economic and Social Council, the Trusteeship Council, the International Court of Justice and the Secretariat, which is headed by the Secretary-General. The former president of the Austrian Republic (1986-92), Kurt Waldheim, was previously the Secretary-General of the UNO from 1972 to 1981. Since January 1997, the Ghanian Kofi Annan has been the 7th Secretary-General of the UNO.

The UNO in Vienna – In the Vienna International Centre, there are the offices of the United Nations Organisation in Vienna (UNOV), the Office for Outer Space Affairs (OOSA), the Office for Drug Control and Crime Prevention (ODCCP), the International Atomic Energy Authority (IAEO), United Nations Industrial Development Organisation (UNIDO), the Preparatory Commission for the Comprehensive Nuclear-Test-Ban Treaty Organisation (CTBTO Prep Comm) and the United Nations Commission on International Trade Law (UNCITL). In addition, other UN agencies like the World Health Organisation (WHO) and the United Nations High Commissioner for Refugees (UNHCR) are represented with offices in Vienna. The International Commission for the Protection of the Danube River (ICPDR), which also has its headquarters in the Vienna International Centre, coordinates environmental protection projects for the Danubian States.

The nearest sights are in Leopoldstadt (see Outside the Ring)

UNO-City

B. Kaufmann

Napoleon's First Defeat

There is no doubt that Emperor Franz wished to erase the humiliations of Austerlitz in 1805. Without declaring war, the Austrian armies mobilised in April 1809 against Bavaria, Italy and Poland. When he became aware of the situation, Napoleon marched on Germany, then Vienna, from the Rhine to the Danube.

Four years after the first occupation of Vienna by the French, Napoleon entered the Habsburg capital once again in 1809 to suppress the Austrian uprising on 12 May. On 20 May, after the construction of numerous pontoon bridges, since the Austrians had destroyed every means of crossing the Danube, 24 000 French soldiers positioned themselves on Lobau island, between the villages of **Aspern** and **Essling**. However, with his army of 95 000 men, Archduke Carl staged a surprise attack on the much smaller French army (a total of 32 000 soldiers), which had to admit defeat on 22 May. The Austrians lost 23 000 men, while the French lost 21 000.

The *Aspern Lion* has stood opposite Aspern church since 1859. This sculpture by Anton Dominik Fernkorn commemorates the 50th anniversary of an Austrian victory, which represented a check to Napoleon's advance. Incidentally, French speakers call Napoleon's first setback the Battle of Essling. This defeat was psychological rather than military. In addition, failure was of short duration, since Archduke Carl and Napoleon met again on 5 and 6 July at **Wagram**, 4km/2.5mi northeast of modern Vienna, on the borders of the Marchfeld area where Napoleon inflicted a severe defeat on the Austrians. He also imposed draconian terms on them: loss of Istria, Carinthia, Carniola and Trieste.

FAVORITEN⚓

10th District

Local map page 11, **BCZ**

The 10th District lies south of the urban area, beyond Wieden coming from the city centre. Like its neighbouring districts of Simmering and Meidling, it is mainly a working class area.

SIGHTS

Amalienbad – *Reumannplatz 23. Underground: Reumannplatz (U1); tram: Quellenstrasse/Favoritenstrassse (6, 67); bus: Reumannplatz (14A, 66A, 67A, 68A), Davidgasse/Reumannplatz (7A, 65A).* This public bath complex can accommodate over 1 000 people. It forms part of the extensive programme of social architectural development of "Red Vienna" in the 1920s. The Viennese architects Otto Nadel and Karl Schmalhofer built it between 1923 and 1926. At the time, it set new standards in European bathing culture. A visitor could, and still can, enjoy saunas, steam baths, warm-water pools, whirlpools, therapeutic baths and a swimming pool with a 30m/32yd long glass roof. The show-piece of the complex is the hot-water pool of the women's sauna decorated with ceramics, the sight of which transports the viewer straight back into the Jugendstil era.

After suffering damage at the end of the Second World War, the establishment underwent restoration and acquired an additional training hall for schools and clubs in 1986.

Spinnerin am Kreuz – *Triesterstrasse. Tram: Windtenstrasse (65).* This late Gothic medieval column (1452) is the work of Johann Puschbaum, the architect of the cathedral's Adlerturm. It marked the city's southern boundary, and therefore the end of the safe area of the city, at a point where, according to legend, a woman spent years waiting for her husband's return from the Crusades. This woman spent her time at her spinning wheel, spinning wool, hence the name of the column: "of the spinner by the Cross". The reality was less romantic; it was the site for public executions.

The Historisches Museum der Stadt Wien (Historical Museum of the City of Vienna) contains a painting of the site at the beginning of the 19C. This provides a good opportunity to observe to what extent urbanisation has encroached upon the surrounding countryside.

George-Washington-Hof – *Unter Meidlingerstrasse 1 – 12.* Next to Spinnerin am Kreuz is a housing estate typical of 1920s and 1930s Vienna. Karl Krist and Robert Oerley built it between 1927 and 1930. It comprises 1 085 apartments divided between five blocks of buildings set in gardens. At the time of their completion, these buildings bore the name of "neighbourhood units", a concept that has to be seen in the historical context of working-class Vienna after the dissolution of the Empire.

3 BIS/MICHELIN

The Amalienbad swimming pool

Wasserturm – *Windtenstrasse 3*. In the street at right angles to Triesterstrasse, near Spinnerin am Kreuz, this 19C red brick water tower with a strongly defensive character has a richly corbelled silhouette with a roof of polychrome tiles. Its purpose was to supply the capital with drinking water from the Alps. It closed in 1910. In addition to housing temporary exhibitions, it also enables visitors to see the pumps still in place.

Oberlaa Spa ⊘ – *Kurbadstrasse 14. Tram: Kurzentrum Oberlaa (67)*. The Oberlaa thermal centre is a reminder that Vienna is also a spa. It lies at the southern tip of the district, not far from Zentralfriedhof. In 1934, oil prospectors found sulphurous waters on the site. The water is harnessed at a depth of 418m/1 371ft and reaches the surface at a temperature of 54°C/138°F. Sulphur treatment is mainly for people with arthrosis, spinal disorders and rheumatic complaints. Two thermal indoor and two thermal outdoor pools, three whirlpools, a Kneipp installation, as well as a sauna landscape, are available to visitors. There is also a "Kid's World" section for children, the main attraction of which is an 80m/260ft -long slide.

Kurpark – This vast park to the north of the establishment is a pleasant place for walks, with about 25km/15mi of footpaths, playgrounds and sports facilities. In the 1920s, this park was a location for filming the monumental film productions of Austria.

The nearest sights are in the districts of Landstrasse, Wieden, Hietzing, Liesing and the Zentralfriedhof (see Outside the Ring section).

HIETZING

13th District
Local map page 10, **AZ**
Underground: Schönbrunn (U4), Hietzing (U4)
Tram: Hietzing (58, from Westbahnhof)

Schloß Schönbrunn★★★ *(see separate entry in Outside the Ring)*, one of the Austrian capital's principal sights, stands in Hietzing. That was indeed one of the reasons that in the late 19C, the 13th District became fashionable and attracted many industrialists, artists and intellectuals, such as Egon Schiele and Gustav Klimt. The latter was born there and his last studio was in Feldmühlgasse. The Austrian television (O.R.F.) buildings overlook Hietzing. Once the abode of the aristocracy, it is now the smartest district in the capital. It is the residential area par excellence, bathed in a timeless atmosphere that is particularly discernible in the streets separating Lainzerstrasse from Maxingstrasse.

The tour described below offers a concise overview of Vienna's residential architecture between 1912 and 1932. The houses that are a little further beyond Am Platz have been listed along with their nearest tram stop.

The Stormy Launch of Johann Strauss the Younger

Johann Strauss, the Elder began his musical career in the Pramer orchestra and in the quartet conducted by the famous Josef Lanner. Rivalry soon developed between them and it was to prove of lasting benefit to Viennese music. In the 1830s, Lanner played at the Redoutensaal, Strauss at the Café Sperl. He was already internationally famous, when he learned that his son, a mere twenty-year old, intended to form his own orchestra. Their rivalry came to a head with Johann Strauss the Younger defying his father's ban and performing his first concert on 15 October 1844 at Hietzing, at Dommayer's. Its resounding success sealed the antagonism between father and son: in 1848, the year of the revolution, the father supported the Habsburgs and composed the immortal *Radetzky March*, while the son favoured the rebels and incorporated *La Marseillaise* in his works. **Café Dommayer** still exists, not far from Am Platz *(Dommayergasse 1)*.

A LITTLE TOUR OF HIETZING

The tour begins at the Hietzinger Tor (gate) of Schönbrunnpark. Map see Outside the Ring, Schloss Schönbrunn.

Immediately on the right there is a post office (opposite Park Hotel) which was once the Kaiserstöckl (1770) or summer residence of Maria Theresa's Ministers of Foreign Affairs.

On **Am Platz** stands Pfarrkirche Maria Hietzing, better known as Maria Geburt, dating from the 13C. Refurbished in the 17C, the interior displays decoration in the Baroque style; the ceiling frescoes are by Georg Greiner, the stucco work by Dominicus Piazzol and the altars by Matthias Steindl. Other interesting features about the square include: a Marian column (1772) and a statue of Maximilian, brother of Emperor Franz Josef and Emperor of Mexico. The **Bezirksmuseum Hietzing** ⊘, a building which dates from the Gründerzeit, documents local history and focuses on famous local people such as the actress Katharina Schratt *(see Gloriettegasse below)*, the composer Alban Berg and the painter Egon Schiele.

Hofpavillon Hietzing ⊘ – *Schönbrunner Schlossstrasse.*This former underground station spanning the present line was for the sole use of the imperial family and the Court. Otto Wagner designed the capital's overhead railway between 1893 and 1902 (stations and bridges); he built this pavilion in 1899 with the assistance of Leopold Bauer (his pupil) and Josef Maria Olbrich, the creator of the famous Secession pavilion near Karlsplatz.

This building underwent restoration between 1986 and 1989 and boasts a fine central octagonal room: the **emperor's waiting room**. The sober decoration combines the rigour of imperial protocol with the principles of the Secession (the carpet is a recent copy of the original).

Return to Am Platz and turn into Altgasse, where No 16 is a Biedermeier period Heuriger, and bear left into Fasholdgasse. Turn right into Trauttmannsdorffgasse.

Trauttmannsdorffgasse – In this street are several Biedermeier houses which form an interesting group, typical of its period. Alban Berg lived at No 27.

Turn left into **Gloriettegasse** *to No 9, home of the actress Katharina Schratt, friend and confidante of Emperor Franz Josef. Retrace your steps and bear right into Wattmanngasse.*

Lebkuchenhaus – *Wattmanngasse 29.* Built in 1914 by a pupil of Otto Wagner, the "gingerbread" *(Lebkuchen)* house displays a remarkable façade decorated with dark majolica at the level of the windows and the entablature.

Retrace your steps and turn right into Gloriettegasse.

Villa Primavesi – *Gloriettegasse 14-16. From Hietzing terminus, take tram 60 and alight at Gloriettegasse.* This building, by **Josef Hoffmann** (1913-15), now houses the *Kulturamt der Stadt Wien* (Vienna council cultural department). Also known as the Villa Skywa, it was built for Robert Primavesi, representative at the Diet of Moravia and Member of Parliament. The architect came from the same region.

Turn left into Alois-Kraus Promenade. At the end bear left into Lainzerstrasse before taking the first street on the right, Veitingergasse. Walk up the street and turn right into Nothartgasse.

Hornerhaus (**AZ**) – *Nothartgasse 3. From Hietzing terminus, take tram 60 and alight at Jagdschlossgasse.* The barrel-shaped roof of the Horner house (1912) is somewhat startling. Forced by regulations not to build more than one storey on the street or garden side, **Adolf Loos** resorted to this shape to gain an extra storey. Partly modified, the house became a listed building in 1972.

Return to Veitingerstrasse. Walk up the street and turn left into Jagicgasse.

Werkbundsiedlung (AZ) – Fans of 20C architecture will be interested by this housing development greatly ahead of its time. Founded in Germany in 1907, the Werkbund was an artistic movement embodying most of the principles of the English Arts and Crafts movement, except that it did not oppose mass production. The period of *Werkbundsiedlungen*, or Werkbund-settlements, began in 1927 with the Stuttgart *Weissenhof*. Under the direction of Mies van der Rohe, this included prototypes of residential buildings incorporating research on new construction methods. There followed the Breslau *Wohnung und Werkraum*, in 1929, and the Vienna *Werkbundsiedlung*, in 1932. In a city such as Vienna, where the socialist administration had begun its urban development projects with compact blocks of flats in 1922, including the famous Karl-Marx-Hof *(see Outside the Ring, Döbling, Heiligenstadt)*, the construction of the Werkbund housing estate with 70 social housing units under Joseph Frank's direction was an extremely innovative project. The City of Vienna bought back most of the houses in this architectural "laboratory" between 1983 and 1985 and restored them. There were some famous names among the architects involved in the original project *(see map at the entrance to Jagicgasse)*: the Viennese Adolf Loos, Josef Hoffmann, Oscar Strand; the Frenchmen André Lurçat and Gabriel Guévrékian (former pupil of Strand); the Dutchman Gerrit Rietveld; the American Richard Neutra (former pupil of Loos); etc. There is a small **museum** ⊙ in the district, which is part of the Bezirksmuseum Hietzing *(Woinovichgasse 32)*.

ADDITIONAL SIGHTS

Friedhof Hietzing ⊙ – *Maxingstrasse. From the Hietzing stop, take bus 56B or 58B and alight at Montecuccoliplatz. Numbers in italics in brackets specify the location (see plan at the entrance).* South of the Tiroler Garten (Tyrolean Garden) at Schönbrunn is the cemetery of the 13th District of Vienna. Many famous people are buried here: the composer Alban Berg (1885-1935) *(group 49-tomb 24F)*; Chancellor Engelbert Dollfuss (1892-1934) *(27-11/12)*, murdered during an attempted putsch in the chancellery; Franz Grillparzer (1791-1872) *(13-107)*, the greatest Austrian playwright; Gustav Klimt (1862-1918) *(5-194/195)*, "academic" painter; Koloman Moser (1868-1918) *(16-14)*, very active in the Wiener Werkstätte; Anton Schmerling (1805-93) *(5-47)*, statesman; and Jean-Baptiste Cléry (1759-1809) *(3-6)*, Louis XVI's last servant, who served the king until his encounter with the guillotine.

★**Lainzer Tiergarten** ⊙ (AZ) – *From Hietzing terminus, take tram 60 and alight at Hermesstrasse. Take bus 60B to Lainzer Tor terminus. Enter through Lainzer Tor (car park outside, map of park at the entrance).* West of Hietzing is Maria Theresa's hunting ground covering 25km²/9sq mi, which was converted into a forest park. Most of the trees are oak or beech. In 1782, the empress decided to enclose the estate with a stone wall 24km/14mi long with six gates: Gütenbachtor, Lainzer Tor, St Veiter Tor, Adolfstor, Nikolaitor and Pulverstampftor. Open to the public since 1921, this vast domain has footpaths covering 80km/49mi making it an excellent venue for open air walks, if visitors tire of the city's museums.

Hermesvilla ⊙ – *15min by the main avenue.* Karl von Hasenauer built this residence as a retreat for the empress between 1882 and 1886 at the request of Franz Josef. The villa now regularly hosts temporary exhibitions organised by the Historisches Museum der Stadt Wien. These offer the chance of admiring in particular the bedroom and the murals inspired by *A Midsummer Night's Dream* designed by Hans Makart.

Even during construction of Hermesvilla, the unhappiness in the marriage of Elisabeth and Franz Josef was public knowledge. There is a certain noticeable melancholy in the decor of the interior. The decoration of the walls, designed by Makart and executed by his successors (including Georg and Gustav Klimt), reflects, almost certainly involuntarily, the disillusion and increasing solitude of the sensuous yet ascetic Empress Elisabeth ("Sissi"), who withdrew completely into herself following her son's death at Mayerling in 1889.

Straight through the woods to the viewpoint – *90min.* Coming either from Lainzer Tor or the villa, head first for "St Veiter Tor". After this gate *(open Sundays and public holidays)*, follow the wall, turning left after 50m/54yd up a fairly steep path climbing beneath the trees. The path runs alongside an animal preserve, which is entered through a gate with wire netting *(signpost: "Nikolai-Tor-über-Wienerblick")*, and climb the hill on the right. Go straight on (it is not always easy to pick out the path at this point) to the top of the hill (alt 434m/1 423ft). From here there is a fine view of west Vienna including the Kirche am Steinhof (Otto Wagner's church) and further to the right the two towers of Votivkirche and the spire of Stephansdom. After a short pause, skirt the forest to the left towards "Rohrhaus" and its café with a children's play area.

J. Malburet/MICHELIN

The Hermesvilla in its verdant setting

EXCURSIONS

Modesammlung ⊘ (**AZ**) – *Hetzendorfer Straße 79 in Meidling, 12th District. From Hietzing terminus, take tram 60 and alight at Hofwiesengasse. Take tram 62 and alight at Schloss Hetzendorf.* One of Maria Theresa's former palaces, Hetzendorf (late 17C, refurbished in the mid 18C) houses the **fashion section** from the Historisches Museum der Stadt Wien, which was founded at the end of the Second World War. The collection comprises no less than 20 000 costumes and accessories, making it one of Europe's largest costume collections. Its main focus is on women's costumes from the 19C and 20C (mainly society, evening and ballroom wear). A public library contains 12 000 volumes on fashion, art and cultural history, photos, fashion magazines from 1786 to the present, as well as around 3 000 copperplate prints on the subject of fashion. Changing **topical exhibitions** display various parts of the collection.

During the summer of 1876, Hugo Wolf, the famous composer of *Lieder*, lived at the corner of Schönbrunner Allee (No 53) and Hetzendorferstrasse, opposite the palace entrance.

From Hietzing you can quickly reach the sights in the districts of Mariahilf, Penzing and Liesing (see Outside the Ring).

Those travelling by car can easily follow the itinerary described under Wienerwald in the Further afield section.

JOSEFSTADT

8th District
Local map page 15, **EU**
Underground: Lerchenfelderstrasse (U2), Rathaus (U2)
Tram: Rathaus (J), Lange Gasse (43, 44)
Bus: Theater i.d. Josefstadt (13A)

This small district lies northwest of the town centre, very close to Ringstrasse. It takes its name from Emperor Joseph II and its attractive streets display many 18C façades. The presence of the University and the Law Courts makes itself felt by the number of students and lawyers in the local restaurants. The English Theatre with productions in English is also in this district *(Josefsgasse 12)*. In the course of his frequent changes of lodgings, Beethoven stayed in Josefstadt in 1819-20 *(Auerspergstrasse)*. Another famous resident was Stefan Zweig .

A good starting point for a tour of the district is Josefstädter Strasse *(see the plaque at No 12 relating the history of the district)*; this street lies on the site of an old Roman road and affords delightful views of the Vienna woods and the outline of Stephansdom.

SIGHTS

Theater in der Josefstadt (T[1]) – *Josefstädter Strasse 26*. This theatre so dear to Viennese hearts dates from 1788 and is still putting on productions. In 1822, it was rebuilt by Josef Kornhäusel, an architect responsible for the finest buildings in Baden *(see Further afield)*. For its reopening, Beethoven composed the *Consecration of the House*, and conducted it himself. This old theatre's reputation is due largely to the writer Hugo von Hoffmannsthal and to the producer Max Reinhardt, whose portrait appears in a medallion on the façade.

Turn right into Piaristengasse.

Piaristenkirche Basilika Maria Treu ⊘ (**A**) – *Jodok-Fink-Platz*. The Church of Mary the Faithful belongs to the "Patres scholarum piarum" (Fathers of the Pious Schools). This clerical order was founded in 1597 and settled in Vienna in the 17C. Its calling was to educate poor children in religious schools. Construction of the church began in 1716 and continued until 1777. The architect was Johann Lukas Hildebrandt, whose reputation stemmed mainly from the many palaces he built. The fine façade is a blend of the Baroque and classical styles. A pediment rises above the central section with two belltowers on either side, which were not completed until c 1860. As a whole it makes a fine composition.

Inside, two large domes feature Rococo frescoes by the celebrated Franz Anton Maulbertsch; they were the master's first major work (1753). He is also the creator of the *Crucifixion* (1772) in the altar-room on the left of the choir. However, the church's focal point of interest is the picture of the Mother of God on the high altar. It was created by the painter as a fulfilment of his vow after he had been miraculously healed of the plague. This is reflected in the name of the church, "Faithful to Mary". A small detail may interest fans of classical music: The list of famous musicians who played in the organ loft of the Piaristenkirche ranges from Joseph Haydn to Franz Liszt and from Anton Bruckner to Paul Hindemith.

The monastic buildings surround the square. In the centre stands a votive column crowned by a statue of the Virgin, one of the numerous

Piaristenkirche

Pestsäulen or plague columns in Vienna and the surrounding area. This one commemorates the end of the 1714 epidemic, but is not as fine as those of the Graben *(see under City Centre and the Ring, Stephansdom District)*, Mödling or Perchtoldsdorf *(see under Further afield)*. At the corner of the square, the **Piaristenkeller** (Piaristengasse 45) occupies the former monastery wine cellar. The 300-year-old vaulted cellar offers Viennese cuisine based on old "K-und-K" recipes, i.e., dating to the days of the Austro-Hungarian empire. It also has two museums – the *Kaiser-Franz-Josef-Hutmuseum* (Emperor Franz Josef Hat Museum), where visitors can participate in the *Alt-Wiener Hutparade* (Old Vienna Hat Parade) for souvenir photographs, and the *k. u. k. Weinschatzkammer* (K & K Wine Treasure-Vault), which contains four centuries of the imperial family's royal table wines *(see also Practical information, Restaurants)*.

Opposite Jodok-Fink-Platz, go down Maria-Treugasse and bear right into Lange Gasse.

Alte Backstube ⊘ (**B**) – *Lange Gasse 34*. Behind the attractive façade of this residential house, dating from 1697 – easily identifiable by the sandstone group *Zur Hl. Dreifaltigkeit* (Holy Trinity) over the entrance – is one of Vienna's oldest baker's shops, which was transformed into a café and museum in 1965. The old bakery, which produced bread from 1701 to 1963 is still visible with its original baking oven, as well as many implements of former trades in the district.

Retrace your steps up Lange Gasse.

Schönborn-Park – *Corner of Lange Gasse and Florianigasse. See also Schönborn Palace below.* The name of this park commemorates Count Friedrich Karl Schönborn-Buchheim. It is shady in summer and features two magnificent Jugendstil wrought-iron gates on Lange Gasse. It offers play areas for children and numerous chairs for the benefit of sightseers, who are invariably weary after exploring a cultural capital such as Vienna especially in summer. A bust (1974) by Leo Gruber represents the composer Edmund Eysler. On the other side of the park is Kochgasse where the writer Stefan Zweig lived at No 8 from 1907 to 1919.

Continue along Lange Gasse and turn left into Laudongasse.

Österreichisches Museum für Volkskunde ⊘ **(M⁷)** – *Laudongasse 15-19. Tram: Lange Gasse (43, 44), Laudongasse (5); bus: Laudongasse (13A).* The Austrian Folklore Museum is the only Viennese museum devoted to the folk arts and customs of Austria and of the former provinces of the Empire, apart from the Sammlung Religiöse Volkskunst (Museum of Religious Folk Art) that is under the same administration *(see City Centre and the Ring, Staatsoper District).* The varied exhibits illustrate everyday life in the Austrian provinces from the 17C to the 19C. Among them are woodcarvings, tools, models of rural housing, reconstructed rooms, furniture (sometimes painted), costumes, pottery, etc. Some items are of particular interest *(numbers in brackets correspond to the numbering of the exhibits),* including: the strange **"the bird's self-recognition"**★, a wood carving from the Tyrol dating from the mid 18C *(1/0)*; an impressive Tyrolean mask dating from about 1900 *(1/61)*; a raincoat made of rushes from Slovenia or Croatia dating from about 1900 *(2/2)*; a painted cupboard from Upper Austria made in 1791 by Mathias Huember who decorated it with allegories of the seasons *(12/1)*; a mechanical theatre from Vienna dating from about 1850 *(14/14).*

Schönborn Palace – The museum occupies what was once an opulent country home refurbished from 1706 to 1711 by Johann Lukas von Hildebrandt and Franz Jänggl to turn it into a summer palace for Friedrich Karl Schönborn-Buchheim. He was assistant chancellor of the Empire, soon to become Hildebrandt's patron.

Return to Lange Gasse and turn right into Alserstrasse.

Dreifaltigkeitskirche ⊘ **(K¹)** – *Alserstrasse 17. Tram: Lange Gasse (43, 44).* Opposite the General Hospital *(see Outside the Ring, Alsergrund)* is the Church of the Holy Trinity, often known as Alserkirche, dating from between 1687 and 1727. More than 4 500 votive tablets illustrate the Viennese veneration for St Anthony *(in the cloister gallery and the chapel, right side).* The north aisle houses an altarpiece by Martino Altomonte (1708); In the south aisle is a wooden crucifix (early 16C) from the studio of Veit Stoss, an artist from Nuremberg.

Ludwig van Beethoven died on 26 March 1827. On 29 March, he was laid in state in the Dreifaltigkeitskirche before the funeral service, which Franz Grillparzer and Franz Schubert attended. Schubert declared later, "A great deal more water will flow into the Danube before people fully understand this man's achievements." Thirty-thousand Viennese accompanied the lonely genius to his grave in Währing cemetery to pay him a last tribute.

Besides the Rathaus (see City Centre and the Ring), opposite the Ring, the nearest sights are: the Alsergrund, Hernals, Neubau and Währing Districts (see Outside the Ring).

LANDSTRASSE★★

3rd District

Local map page 14, **KLS**; page 15, **FGUV**
Underground: Stadtpark (U4)
Tram: Schwarzenbergplatz (1, 2, 71, D, J), Unteres Belvederes (71)
Bus: Schwarzenbergplatz (3A), Gusshausstrasse (4D)

"Asia begins in Landstrasse", Metternich once said. Yet the third district, which lies southeast of the inner city, is known today as both the city's embassy row and the most varied neighbourhood in the whole of Vienna. Famous former residents include Beethoven *(Untergasse 5)*, Anton Bruckner *(Oberes Belvedere)*, Gustav Mahler *(Auenbruggergasse 2)*, Robert Musil *(Rasumofskygasse 20)*, Adalbert Stifter *(Beatrixgasse 18 and 48)* and Richard Strauss *(Jacquingasse 8 and 10)*.

★SCHWARZENBERGPLATZ

This vast square bears the name of Prince Schwarzenberg, supreme commander of the combined Austrian, Prussian and Russian armies during the campaigns of 1813 and 1814. His bronze equestrian statue (1857) by Ernst Julius Hähnel stands in the centre of the square.

French Embassy – Dating from between 1901 and 1909, this edifice was built to plans by the architect George Chedanne. The building is a beautiful example of Art Nouveau architecture and is immediately recognisable by its French tricolour flag.

Arnold Schönberg Center ⊘ – *Schwarzenbergplatz 6; entrance at Zaurnergasse, first floor, access via stairwell 1.* This institution, in which a private foundation has administered Schönberg's inheritance since 1998, produces rotating exhibitions concerning the life, work, and influence of this Viennese composer. A permanent exhibit is his last workroom from Los Angeles (complete with original furniture and tools of his trade); it was in this city that he died in 1951. In addition, a reference library and a media library, both open to the public, offer opportunities to learn more about Schönberg. The foundation's archives and a meeting room (for concerts, *Lieder* recitals and readings) complete the offering here.

Sowjetisches Kriegerdenkmal – Schwarzenbergplatz was once renamed Stalinplatz by the Soviets; they inaugurated this monument on 19 August 1945 to honour the soldiers of their army who died while liberating Austria from Fascism. However, the Viennese resented it and nicknamed the soldier above the fountain "the unknown looter".

Palais Schwarzenberg – This is the work of two great Viennese architects of the Baroque period, Johann Lukas von Hildebrandt and Johann Bernhard Fischer von Erlach (1697-1723). In its time, the palace was among the foremost summer residences outside the city walls. Almost entirely destroyed in 1945, it now houses a hotel.
On the side of the main courtyard, the Schwarzenbergplatz side, the building displays a façade with colossal pilasters.
The palace gardens are by Josef Emmanuel Fischer von Erlach. As is the case with many Baroque gardens, their sumptuousness is an extension of the reception rooms and conforms to a geometrical design.

★★THE BELVEDERE

Prince Eugène of Savoy, the "little Capuchin" – This is the nickname given to Eugène of Savoy-Carignan (Paris, 1663-Vienna, 1736) by his soldiers, because he wore a simple brown tunic, instead of the magnificent military attire befitting his rank. Moreover, before Eugène became a brilliant army commander, his parents had intended him for the Church.
The son of the Count of Soissons and Olympe Mancini, Cardinal Mazarin's niece, who lived the life of a "merry widow" in Brussels after her husband's death, Eugène started his career by joining Louis XIV's army. Yet following a refusal to give him command of a regiment, he proudly enlisted in the service of Leopold I. At the age of 20 he joined the King of Poland's army, which the Pope had entrusted with the relief of the siege of Vienna by Kara Mustapha in 1683.
Despite his rejection by the Sun King, the French nobleman nevertheless became highly respected when as supreme commander of the Austrian imperial armies he defeated the Turks at the battle of Zenta (1697). He then imposed on them the Peace of Karlowitz (1699) and the Treaty of Passarowitz (1718), which defined the furthest eastward expansion of the Habsburg Empire.
A field marshal at 25, Prince Eugène became counsellor to Joseph I, then prime minister under Karl VI. Eugène of Savoy had the satisfaction of imposing the Treaty of Rastadt on Louis XIV. The military commander was by now a true statesman. Wealthy and successful, he built two magnificent residences, a winter *(see City Centre and the Ring, Stephansdom District)* and a summer palace, the Belvedere.

Outside the Ring

F. Simak/© ÖSTERREICHISCHE GALERIE BELVEDERE

Southern façade of the Oberes Belvedere with palatial garden

A man of culture – A lover of art and a great collector, Eugène of Savoy was largely responsible for the acquisition of the art treasures which Vienna gained during the 18C. A testimony to his influence is the fact that the philosopher Gottfried Wilhelm Leibniz dedicated to him two of his works written in Vienna, *Principles of Nature and Grace* and *Principles of Philosophy*; and it is the 15 000 volumes from Eugène of Savoy's collection that form the nucleus of the majestic Prunksaal (Grand Hall) in the National Library.

The prince was just over fifty when he signed the Treaty of Rastadt in 1714. He decided to stop fighting against Louis XIV and enjoy the fruits of his labours. He commissioned Johann Lukas von Hildebrandt to build two palaces linked to one another by a garden, on the gentle slope of a hill not far from the Carinthian gate *(near the present Staatsoper)*. Some years later, as he was passing through Vienna, Montesquieu declared on seeing the Hofburg and the Belvedere: "It is pleasant to be in a country where subjects live in finer lodgings than their sovereigns."

Today, this magnificent example of late Baroque architecture is one of the loveliest, most coherent and best preserved in Europe.

The three museums of the Österreichische Galerie Belvedere which are housed in the two parts of Belvedere can be visited with a single admission ticket.

★UNTERES BELVEDERE

Tram: Unteres-Belvedere (71)

At an angle to Rennweg, the Lower Belvedere stands at the end of a great courtyard with an imposing gate displaying the Cross of Savoy on its pediment. This wide palace reached completion in 1716. Of greater interest than the façade overlooking the courtyard, the façade facing the garden is a superb harmonious ensemble of pilasters and decorative sculptures, extending from the central building to the two wings with pavilions.

★★**Österreichische Galerie Belvedere: Barockmuseum** ⊙ – The prince's summer residence is a majestic setting for the Museum of Austrian Baroque Art, which gives an excellent idea of painting and sculpture in 18C Austria.

Three rooms make an outstanding impact during a visit to this museum, putting many of the works described here very much in the shade. First, the magnificent **Marmorsaal★** or great Marble Hall (Great Hall) which houses the originals of the sculptures on the **Neuer Markt fountain★★** *(see City Centre and the Ring, Kapuzinerkirche District).* The ceiling frescoes (1716) by Martino Altomonte glorify Prince Eugène's Triumph; the trompe-l'œil architectural paintings are by the Bolognese painters Gaetano Fanti and Marcantonio Chiarini, who also painted the bedroom frescoes. The second gem in this museum is the **Groteskensaal★** or "antechamber with grotesque paintings" and its series of *grimacing faces★★* which Franz Xaver Messerschmidt fashioned from 1770 in an amazingly avant-garde spirit. This German sculptor created precisely 69 *Heads of Characters* (in lead or stone). There are 49 in the museum's possession, of which seven are to be found in this room. Legend has it that the artist drew inspiration for these studies in physiognomy by grimacing in front of a mirror. According to another version, Messerschmidt avenged himself on people who mocked him at Court by depicting them with eccentric expressions. Another German artist, Jonas Drentwett, is responsible for the decoration of the room, which shows the influence of frescoes from ancient Rome and Pompeii (with allegories of the Four Seasons and Four Elements). Finally, the **Goldkabinett**★★ or "Conversation Chamber" contains the **Apotheosis of Prince Eugène**★ (1718-22) by Balthasar Permoser, who painted himself at the feet of his model, who himself appears as Hercules treading on Envy.

Many of the exhibits in the museum's other rooms also deserve full attention. In room 1, *The Wrath of Samson* (c 1740) by Johann Georg Platzer. In room 2, *Empress Maria Theresa* and *Emperor Franz Stefan* (c 1760) by Franz Xaver Messerschmidt. In room 4, *Mourning for Abel* (1692) by Johann Michael Rottmayr, the pair to this painting *The Sacrifice of Isaac* is in the Landesmuseum in Graz; *The Lamentation* (c 1692) by Peter Strudel; *Susannah and the Elders* (1709) by Martino Altomonte. In room 5 or the "dining room", **Christ on the Mount of Olives**★ (c 1750) by Paul Troger, with typically Baroque sharp contrasts between light and shade; *Venus at Vulcan's Forge* (1768) and the *Judgment of King Midas* (1768) by Johann Martin Schmidt. In an adjoining room, the marble statue of François Étienne of Lorraine as Emperor Franz I (between 1770 and 1780) by Balthasar Moll. In the small drawing room, bronze reliefs with classical themes by Georg Raphael Donner: *Venus at Vulcan's Forge* and *The Judgment of Paris* (c 1735).

In the former military bedroom are sculptures by Donner: *Apotheosis of Emperor Karl VI* (1734), *Hagar in the Desert* (1739), *Jesus and the Samaritan Woman* (1739). On the walls of the gallery hang *The Family of Count Nikolaus Pálffy* (1753) by Martin van Meytens, *Emperor Ferdinand I* (c 1750) by Franz Anton Palko and the imposing **Napoleon's Passage over the St Bernard Pass**★ (1801) by Jacques-Louis David. In the passage is a *Self-Portrait* (c 1767) by Franz Anton Maulbertsch. The second gallery displays works, including his **View of Laxenburg**★ (1758), by Johann Christian Brand, an important Austrian landscape painter of great influence on Martin von Molitor and Michael Wutky. The seven niches in the "Marmorgalerie" used to contain the statues of three women from Herculaneum, a gift to the prince in 1713 from the general in command of the imperial troops in Naples, as well as four Baroque statues by Domenico Parodi. The antique statues were sold to a buyer in Dresden the day after the prince's death, and Parodi replaced them by three other sculptures.

Grimacing Head by Franz Xaver Messerschmidt

Fotostudio Otto/Österreichische Galerie Belvedere

★**Österreichische Galerie Belvedere: Museum mittelalterlicher Kunst** ⓥ –
Entrance through the Barockmuseum – The Museum of Austrian Medieval Art occupies the Orangerie next to the Unteres Belvedere, and offers a nearly seamless overview of Austrian painting from 1370 to 1520. The following merely presents a selection of the numerous highly acclaimed works which can be seen here.

The Stummerberg crucifix, carved in oak at Stummerberg in the Tyrol (about 1160), is the museum's only example of Romanesque art. The High Gothic is represented by two statues of Mary and a relief portraying her birth, whereas the remaining works belong to the late Gothic period: four sculptures from the Master of Grosslobming (c 1375-85); the altarpiece "of Znaim", made in Vienna by woodcarvers there (c 1427); a **Crucifixion**★ by Konrad Laib (1449), which he painted to attain citizenship in the city of Salzburg; seven large panel paintings with scenes from the life of the Virgin and the Passion by Rueland Frueauf, who created them as the altarpiece for the St. Peters-Stiftskirche in Salzburg (1490-91); two altar-panels from the town of St. Lorenzen in the Pustertal as well as fragments of the last important work by Michael Pacher; *The Adoration of the Magi* and **The Lamentation**★ by the Master of the Viennese altarpiece of the Schottenkirche (c 1469); and **The Legend of Susannah**★ by the Carinthian artist Urban Görtschacher.

Bundesgarten Belvedere ⓥ – The Parisian Dominique Girard designed this French-style garden at the beginning of the 18C. This pupil of André Le Nôtre was a landscape architect, specialising in hydraulics. To link the two palaces, he laid down ramps and terraces adorned by sculptures, flower beds, groves, pools, fountains and waterfalls. As was usual at the time, the composition of the Belvedere gardens featured some esoteric symbols. The lower section is dedicated to the Four

Elements, the middle evokes Parnassus, and the upper part is an allegory of Olympus. In the upper part, there are sphinxes, mythical creatures with the head and breasts of a woman and the body of a lion. Those familiar with classical literature will recall that this animal challenged travellers on the road from Delphi to Thebes to solve a riddle. Those who did not know the answer were thrown into the sea. Oedipus' correct answer sent the sphinx itself hurtling into the deep.

At the top of the garden, there is a splendid **view**★ reminiscent of a Canaletto. It is obvious why the prince named the edifice "Belvedere".

★★OBERES BELVEDERE

Tram: Schloss Belvedere (D)

The Masterpiece of Johann Lukas von Hildebrandt's Masterpiece – *See illustration in the Introduction, ABC of Architecture.* The Upper Belvedere is of a later date (1722) than the Lower Belvedere (1716). It was the setting for celebrations given by the prince and consists of seven buildings under one roof; those who have travelled beyond the Bosphorus will recognise the Oriental touch. The main façade stands south, and is therefore not the first one visible from the terraced gardens, arriving from the Lower Belvedere. The south side displays accentuated divisions, and a central building; the carriages of the prince of Savoy's guests used to pass through its three-arched gateway. They had to drive through the south gateway, which today faces Landstrasse Gürtel, and round the vast pool reflecting the palace. The wrought-iron **gate** is a sumptuous Baroque work by Arnold and Konrad Küffner. Attentive visitors will be able to decipher the "S" of the House of Savoy and the cross of its blazon.

Interior decor – Visitors enter through the basement on the north side, since Ferdinand Hetzendorf von Hohenberg sealed the windows of the porch on the south façade, when Archduke Franz Ferdinand, Franz Josef's brother, moved into the Belvedere in 1897. With its four Telamones (Lorenzo Mattielli) and its stucco-clad vaults (Santino Bussi), the **Sala Terrena**★ opens on the right into a room displaying **frescoes** by Carlo Carlone *(The Triumph of Aurora)*. Above the sweeping staircase is the *piano nobile* where the Grosser Marmorsaal, a vast red marble ballroom occupies the whole height of the central building. Its ceiling features a fresco by Carlo Leone representing the Glory of Prince Eugène. This immense room was the scene, on 15 May 1955, of the signing of the State Treaty which brought to an end the Allied occupation of Austria. The room contains a facsimile bearing the signatures of Figl, Dulles, McMillan, Molotov, Pinay, etc. From one of the rooms on the first floor, the chapel is visible with frescoes also by Carlone; the altarpiece by Francesco Solimena (1723) depicts the Resurrection.

★★Österreichische Galerie Belvedere – 19-20C Collections ⊙ – *Prinz-Eugen Strasse 27.* This gallery contains a large number of major works illustrating the principal trends in 19C and 20C Austrian and international painting. Lovers of Klimt, Makart, Romako or Schiele will be in their element here.

Ground floor – Special exhibitions are held here; the museum shop and café are also located on this floor.

First floor – After coming up the staircase and entering the red marble hall, the "**Historicism, Realism, Impressionism**" section is on the left , and the "**Kunst der Jahrhundertwende**" section on the right. In chronological order, the tour begins with the section on the left. The first room contains the synthesis of the arts *The Judgment of Paris* (1885-87) by Max Klinger, which manifests both painting and sculpture in the painting and its frame; *The Bad Mothers* (1894) by Giovanni Segantini; Carl Moll's *The Naschmarkt in Vienna* (1894); and French landscape paintings by Daubigny, Millet and Courbet.

Born in Salzburg in 1840, **Hans Makart** died at the height of his fame 44 years later. His historical paintings ensured him rapid fame. However it is his portraits and monumental compositions that linger in the memory, conveying the society of the Ringstrasse. He organised on this street the famous silver wedding procession of the imperial couple, riding at its head on a white horse and wearing a wide-brimmed plumed hat.

Makart's works in the Oberes Belvedere include *The Triumph of Ariadne* (1873); the ceiling painting *The Four Parts of the World* (1870-71); successfully executed portraits such as *Clothilde Beer* (c 1880); and **The Five Senses**★ (1872-79), a series of which four paintings remain.

After a start as a historical painter, **Anton Romako** (1832-89) worked in the shadow of Makart's success and developed a highly personal style, without any imitators or pupils. His work has often failed to be appreciated.

In the case of *Empress Elisabeth*★★ (1883), nobody can say for sure whether this is an example of Mannerism, irony, or dreamlike projection. On the other hand, the portrait of *Mathilda Stern* (1889) is enchanting because of its charm (or perhaps hers). With *Admiral Tegetthof at the Naval Battle of Lissa I* (1878-80), an oil painting on wood, the painter broke with 19C historical painting and its heroic focus.

Some further outstanding works in this section of the museum are *Early Mass* (1852) by Adolph von Menzel; the *Puddler* (1890) by Constantin Meunier; *The Final Reserves* (1874) by Franz Defregger. The paintings of Leopold Carl Müller, who travelled to Egypt nine times, reflect the artist's enthusiasm for the Orient typical of the 19C.

Return to the red marble hall to reach the section **Kunst der Jahrhundertwende**, featuring works in the Impressionist and Expressionist styles. Among other examples, French Impressionism is represented here with works by Renoir, Degas and Monet. Also to be seen are *The Plain at Auvers* (1890) by Vincent van Gogh, and *The Ducal Residence on Walchensee, in the Snow* (1922) by Lovis Corinth.

Empress Elisabeth by Anton Romako

Fotostudio Otto/Österreich Galerie Belvedere

The Viennese **Gustav Klimt** (1862-1918) has acquired a reputation as a "painter of women" or as the "Messiah of the Secession". The characters he paints in a naturalistic manner often display angular bodies on an abstract surface.

Youthful works such as the pastel portrait **Emilie Flöge**★ (1891) and *Portrait of Sonia Knips* (1898) give way to the creations of maturity. *Adele Bloch-Bauer I* and *II* (1907 and 1912): portrait I is reminiscent of the mosaics of Ravenna which Klimt first saw in 1903; the second portrait is of the frontal type typical of this painter. **The Kiss**★★★ (1907-08): even if there is little left to say about this work and

The Kiss by Gustav Klimt

BILDAGENTUR BUENOS DIAS

although reproductions of it are arguably too numerous (leaflets, posters, post-cards), it still retains the intensity of desire communicated both through the drawing and the contrast in the decoration. *The Bride* (1918) is an unfinished work on which the underlying sketch is still recognisable.

The series of square landscape paintings is interesting in that it represents an entirely different aspect of Klimt's work.

The Schlosskapelle, or Palace Chapel, can be seen from the southern corner room.

Born in 1890 in Tulln, in south Austria, **Egon Schiele** died in Vienna in 1918. After a period inspired by Klimt, he soon found his own style, depicting bodies swamped in elaborate decoration which in Klimt's work was marginal to his figures. His work consists mainly of studies of models and self-portraits (about a hundred), hence his label as a "narcissistic" painter.

Rainerbub★★ (1910) conveys the uncomplicated freshness of an evidently happy child. *Death and the Maiden*★★ (1915) is at the other end of the spectrum: this extraordinary painting expresses his pain of separation from Wally Neuzil, his favourite model and companion for many years, from whom he parted to marry Edith Harms (who died of scarlet fever two years later). The darkly clad figure portrays Schiele himself, and the young woman's hands close the embrace holding on by only one finger. *Four Trees* (1917) is one of his typical desolate and Expressionist landscapes (one of the four trees has shed all its leaves), but this late work displays a warmer range of colours. *The Family* (1918): this last major painting is surprisingly realist in comparison to its predecessors, taking the por-trayal of motherhood as its theme.

Among other examples, the scope of Expressionism is illustrated by works by Kokoschka, Lehmbruck, Kirchner, Léger and Beckmann. *Laughing Self-Portrait*★ (1908) was painted by Richard Gerstl, a solitary figure who committed suicide at 25 without ever having exhibited his works.

Second floor – From the top of the staircase, the "Classicism and Romanticism" section is on the right, while the "Biedermeier" section is on the left.

Classicism and Romanticism: Noteworthy among the portraits are *Countess Meerfeld* (c 1790) by Angelika Kaufmann and *The Family of Count Moritz Christian Fries* (c 1805) by François Gérard. *The Great Waterfall of Tivoli near Rome* (1790) by Jakob Philip Hackert provides an example of a heroic landscape; other outstanding landscapes are: *The Königssee with the Watzmann Peak* (1837) by Adalbert Stifter; *The Halstättersee* (1834) by Franz Steinfeld; *Seaside in the Mist*★★ (c 1807) and *Rocky Landscape in Elbsandsteingebirge* (c 1822-23) by Caspar David Friedrich. The Nazarenes are represented here with Ludwig Ferdinand Schnorr von Carolsfeld's *Rudolf von Habsburg and the Priest* (1828).

Biedermeier: The collection is divided into four parts, from each of which we have chosen a representative example. Portraits: *The Fisherman's Son*★ (1830) by Friedrich von Amerling; still lifes: *Tribute to Jacquin* (1821-22) by Johann Knapp; land-scapes: *Stephansdom* (1832) by Rudolf von Alt; genre painting: *Peasant Wedding in Lower Austria* (1843) by Ferdinand Georg Waldmüller.

BELVEDERE DISTRICT

Besides the Salesianerinnenkirche there are several interesting sights on Rennweg.

Palais Hoyos (No 3), the present Yugoslav embassy, is the work of Otto Wagner (1891). It is easy to recognize the Historicism, typical of this famous architect's early career, and the decorative Rococo elements. At the corner of Rennweg and Auenbruggergasse (No 2) is the house where Gustav Mahler lived from 1898 to 1909, opposite the **Gardekirche** (1763) by Nikolaus Pacassi, the former church of the Polish guard; this is now the parish church for the Polish community, attracting a large congregation every Sunday beneath its flat ribbed cupola.

Salesianerinnenkirche (LS) – *Rennweg. Tram: Unteres-Belvedere (71)*. There is a splendid gateway in front of the church of the Salesian Convent by the Italian archi-tect Donato Felice d'Allio (1717-30), and a dome soaring to 48m/157 ft. The church's proportions are harmonious, particularly those of the façade completed by Josef Emmanuel Fischer von Erlach. However, it lacks the Baroque force of many of the city's churches.

Botanischer Garten – *Rennweg 14. Tram: Rennweg (71)*. Empress Maria Theresa founded the Botanic Gardens in 1754 with the assistance of her physician Gerhard van Swieten, to create a reserve of medicinal plants for Vienna University. Disappointed in herbal medicine, she had it turned into a botanical garden by Nikolaus von Jacquin. It now contains 9 000 species of plant and is a pleasant setting for a stroll.

In the upper section, a small gate links it to a garden dedicated to the cultivation of rare alpine species *(Alpengarten)*.

★**Heeresgeschichtliches Museum** ⊘ **(GV)** – *Arsenalstrasse. Tram: Südbahnhof (18, D); bus: Südbahnhof (13A, 69A); train: Südbahnhof (S1, S2, S3, S15)*. The Museum of Military History lies at the heart of the Arsenal, a pseudo-medieval fortress (1852-56) by Theophil Hansen, one of the future pioneers of the Ring, and Ludwig Förster. Franz Joseph commissioned the building one year after the 1848 revolution, when Metternich went into exile and the Court took refuge in Innsbruck. Of a Gothic-Byzantine-Moorish style, the museum is only one of 31 edifices in this Babylonian barracks; the building is undeniably the precursor of the Historicism which dominated the Ring. The museum traces the military history of the Habsburgs, from the end of the 16C until 1918.

To view the exhibits in chronological order, enter through the **Generals' Room** leading up to the first floor. This three-nave neo-Gothic room houses statues of the most famous generals of the Empire.

From the Thirty Years' War (1618-48) to Prince Eugène of Savoy – *First floor, left of the Hall of Fame*. In this section are numerous weapons (halberds, lances, muskets, armour), documents signed by Wallenstein and Tilly, 12 battle scenes by the painter Pieter Snayers, the **seal of Sultan Mustafa II**, the red standard of Prince Eugène of Savoy's 13th Dragoon regiment, as well as his breastplate, **Marshal's baton** and the funeral altar cloth for his Requiem Mass, in St Stephen's cathedral (Stephansdom).

The 18C (until 1790) – The room consists of three sections. The first covers the period from 1700 to 1740: on display are numerous standards and a pen-and-ink drawing (1700) by the future Karl VI and a full-sized cannon barrel *(below the window)*, the **tent of an Ottoman prince★** and the **Belgrade mortar bomb** which caused the explosion of the powder magazine of that city during the Turkish siege of 1717. Section two covers Maria Theresa's reign, the time of the War of Austrian Succession and the Seven Years' War (1756-63): a showcase contains the "Albertina Manuscript", with a series of watercolour drawings (copies) from it illustrating the uniforms of the imperial and royal army from 1762; an oil painting depicts Marshal Count Daun who defeated the Prussians at Kolin in 1757. The third section deals with the reign of Joseph II: *Field Marshal Gideon Ernst Freiherr von Laudon* is a major work (1878) by Sigmund L'Allemand representing the man who defeated Friedrich II at Kunersdorf and captured many standards.

Return to the Hall of Fame and cross the whole of the other wing on the first floor.

The Austro-French Wars (1789-1815) – There are many exhibits of interest, including flags, paintings by Johann Peter Krafft, the original model of the *Aspern Lion* by Anton Dominik Fernkorn *(see City Centre and the Ring, Donaustadt, insert "Napoleon's First Defeat")*, the Russian general Schuwalow's greatcoat which Napoleon wore to conceal his identity when he left Fontainebleau for exile on the island of Elba in 1814, the **Hercules balloon★** captured at the battle of Würzburg on 3 September 1796; this Montgolfière or hot-air balloon belonged to the first French aeronautical company and served for reconnaissance missions.

Archduke Karl Room – Anton Dominik Fernkorn is the sculptor of the statue of Napoleon's famous adversary; it is a replica of another statue of the victor of Aspern (1809), which is in Heldenplatz. The room also contains some family portraits (Johann Ender).

Radetzky Room – Marshal von Radetzky was governor of Lombardy and Minister of War. He distinguished himself by fighting the nationalist movements in Italy. Johann Strauss the Elder dedicated a famous march to him which bears his name. There are many mementos of him in this room.

Franz-Josef Room – His equestrian portrait (1856) by Franz Adam dominates this section.

Go down to the ground floor and bear left after the Generals' Room.

Franz Josef and Sarajevo – Uniforms and objects from all nationalities of the Empire precede the Sarajevo Room. This Bosnian city was the scene of the assassination of Archduke Franz Ferdinand and his wife Sophia Chotek. The **car** in the tragedy is on display (one can see the impact of the bullet through the bodywork of the Graef & Stift vehicle), together with the archduke's bloodstained uniform. A photographic report of the tragic event is visible in a corner of the room. The assassin, Gavrilo Princip, died in a Bohemian cell on 28 April 1918. He had been kept in chains throughout the First World War – which he had precipitated by pressing the trigger of his revolver.

First World War and the end of the Habsburg Monarchy – The most interesting items are pieces of heavy artillery, particularly a 38cm/15in canon. An Albatross aeroplane (1914) is also on display.

Return to the Generals' Room and continue into the other wing.

Republic and Dictatorship, Austria from 1918 to 1945 – Using objects from these times as well as photographic and audio documentation, twelve sections trace scenes in Austria's political development (in parliament, barricades and battlefields). After the fall of the monarchy, Austria moved through the forms of republic and corporative state, was included in the Greater German Reich, took part in the Second World War and finally arrived at the Second Republic.

Heeresgeschichtliches Museum

The car in which the royal couple were assassinated in Sarajevo

The Assassination at Sarajevo

While on a state visit to Sarajevo, the successor to the throne of the Austro-Hungarian Empire was assassinated by Serbian nationalists on 28 June 1914. **Franz Ferdinand** and his wife Sophie died of the gunshot wounds they suffered in the attack. As soon as they received news of the archduke's death, General Chief of Staff Count Conrad von Hötzendorf and the Foreign Secretary, Count Berchtold, pushed to attack Serbia in a localised military operation; their intention was to conquer and dismantle the young state of Serbia, which had become a threat to Austro-Hungarian interests since the Balkan wars of 1912-13. Assured of German support, Franz Josef approved their decision. Serbia was given an ultimatum with the purpose of explaining the circumstances surrounding the case – and among other things, an Austrian official was to be allowed to investigate in Serbia. Serbia balked at this point, despite showing willingness to compromise in response to other demands.

Austria-Hungary thus declared war on Serbia on 28 July, triggering the First World War (1914-18) and resulting in the loss of eight million lives. The hope of a localised conflict proved to be an illusion.

The Navy Room – It may surprise some to learn that Austria was once a great naval power. Since the end of the 14C, Trieste and its port had belonged to the Empire, which extended to the Venetian and Dalmatian coasts at the beginning of the 19C. Of special interest is the 1:25 **cutaway model of the Viribus Unitis**★ (7m/23 ft), the Austro-Hungarian flagship during the First World War; and the coning tower of the imperial submarine U20. Two hundred years of Austrian marine history are documented here, including rescue, research and discovery voyages and the development of the navy (which among other things had warships on the Danube), until the fleet's demise in 1918.

St. Marxer Friedhof (**CZ**) – *Leberstrasse 6-8. Tram: Litfassstrasse (71, 72); bus: Hofmannsthalgasse (74A).* On 6 December 1791, Mozart's remains were moved from the Rauhensteingasse house in which he died *(see City Centre and the Ring, Stephansdom District)* to the cathedral *(see City Centre and the Ring, Stephansdom)* where the coffin received benediction. Owing to severe weather, the sad cortège then entered the modest St Mark's cemetery unaccompanied by Salieri or van Swietens, and Mozart was buried in a common grave.

Today, Mozart's cenotaph is in the Zentralfriedhof *(see entry in the Outside the Ring section)*, but St Mark's cemetery is also interesting because of the supposed site of Mozart's grave.

★**Wiener Strassenbahnmuseum** ⊘ (**CY M³**) – *Erdbergstrasse 109. Entrance: Ludwig-Koessler-Platz. Underground: Schlachthausgasse (U3); tram: Schlachthausgasse (18); bus: Erdbergstrasse (79A); Ludwig-Koessler-Platz (80B); Schlachthausgasse (79A, 80B, 83A, 84A).* This Tram Museum, which opened in 1986, is the largest of its kind in the world. Its main exhibit is of course the Viennese tram, with its red and white livery representing the city. The museum fully documents the development of public transport in Vienna (technical information, photographs, etc.), and houses about one hundred trams and buses, restored and in excellent condition.

Outside the Ring

Haus Wittgenstein ⊘ (**GU**) – *Kundmanngasse 19. Entrance: Parkgasse 18. Underground: Rochusgasse (U3); bus: Geusaugasse (4A).* The philosopher built this house in 1929 for his sister, Gretl, with the assistance of Paul Engelmann. Drawing direct inspiration from Adolf Loos' theories, the building is of a somewhat dry modernistic style. This exercise in minimalism was a reaction to Biedermeier neoclassicism. Since 1975 the building has been the home of the Bulgarian Embassy, but temporary exhibitions are nevertheless held here.

Ludwig Wittgenstein – Born in Vienna in 1889, he studied in Berlin, Manchester and Cambridge where he became Professor of Philosophy in 1929. He had a large following in English-speaking countries and influenced philosophers of the Vienna Circle and the analytical School. He died of cancer in Cambridge in 1951.

Hundertwasserhaus

(**GU F**) – *Kegelgasse 36-38, at the corner of Löwengasse. Closed to the public.* A painter and a cosmopolitan engraver, **Friedensreich Hundertwasser** started work in Paris. However, it was in Vienna that he expressed his conception of housing in a creation repudiating any form of architectural conformity. The city of Vienna sponsored this residential complex commissioned by the former mayor, Leopold Gratz; it was completed in 1985.

Hundertwasserhaus

It avoids the monotony of conventional housing estates through the use of varied motifs, a wide range of materials (glass, brick, ceramic, roughcast of a different colour for each apartment), and sloping terraces laid out as hanging gardens. This example of low-income housing met with criticism in Vienna and praise abroad. It comprises 50 apartments and always attracts a large number of visitors and lovers of architecture. According to Hundertwasser, its design encourages a creative spirit and enables the individual to live in harmony with his environment. Two golden onion domes surmount the edifice, because "a Byzantine bell-tower on a house raises its occupant to the status of a king".

KunstHaus Wien ⊘ (**GU G**) – *Untere Weissgerberstrasse 13.* Also by Hundertwasser, this building consists of two sections, one of which houses a collection of works of art illustrating the diversity and originality of the artist: paintings, engravings, plans and models. Temporary exhibitions are staged in the other half of the museum. The typical Hundertwasser architecture in the building's café offers a somewhat different setting for getting to know Vienna's coffee-house culture.

The nearest sights are the Fleischmarkt District, in the city centre, and the districts of Wieden and Leopoldstadt (to be found in the Outside the Ring section).

LEOPOLDSTADT★

2nd District

Local map page 15, **FGTU**
Underground: Praterstern/Wien Nord (U1)
Tram: Praterstern/Wien Nord (O)
Bus: Praterstrasse (5A)

Just as the Eiffel Tower symbolises Paris or the Atomium represents Brussels, the Riesenrad or Giant Ferris Wheel is an emblem of Vienna. Since 1897, this monumental steel construction situated in the 2nd District has enabled sightseers to view the Prater and further afield while suspended in mid-air in a cabin. Carol Reed immortalised this site as the location of the famous Ferris Wheel scene in his 1949 film, *The Third Man*. Historically, the district's name derives from Leopold I's expulsion in 1670 of the resident Jews originally from Poland and the Balkans, less than half a century after Ferdinand II allowed them to settle here. The "*Untere Werd*", as people used to call this Jewish district, became "Leopoldstadt".

★THE PRATER

From imperial hunting ground to public amusement park – The first mention of the Prater dates from 1403. In 1560, Maximilian II transformed the wide island between the Danube canal and the river into a walled imperial hunting ground. Joseph II, a liberal emperor, opened the Prater to the public in 1766. Within ten years, stalls and circus tents had made their appearance. From then on, the Prater became an amusement park. In 1771, it was the site of a fireworks display; in 1791, Jean-Pierre Blanchard flew from here for the first time in his hot-air balloon; in 1815, sovereigns descended from sumptuous carriages for the Congress of Vienna. It was a place for riding or promenading and was extremely popular in the heyday of the Viennese waltz, the late 19C. At that time, the Prater was filled with cafés where people could sing or dance. Until the end of the Empire, this park was a fashionable and smart centre, where the crinoline skirts only stopped twirling long enough for the ladies to change dance partners.

Prater today – Nowadays, this huge public park has become a focus of attraction for tourists with children. With its area of 1 287ha/3 180 acres, it exists for the amusement of all, children and also adults if they are fond of football or harness racing. The park consists of two sections: one is a fairground, while the other is a setting for trade fairs and sporting facilities. The first section is known as **Wurstelprater** ("Mr Punch's Prater") and **Volksprater** ("People's Prater"). It is a vast fun fair, colourful and noisy, with rifle ranges, roller coasters, dodgem cars, roundabouts and sticky candy-floss.

5km/3mi long with chestnut trees on either side, Hauptallee starts near Praterstern (Prater Star). It runs through the second part of the Prater from end to end. Although tarred, the avenue is closed to traffic. This former bridle path leads to a roundabout on which stands the **Lusthaus**, a leisure pavilion once belonging to Karl VI which underwent alterations by the French architect Isidore Canavale in 1785. Today, it is a café and restaurant. Trade fairs take place in the exhibition grounds of the Messegelände, and various parts of the park are a setting for numerous sporting events: the Krieau harness racing track dating from 1913 (September to June), the Ernst Happel football stadium, the Freudenau flat racing track (spring to autumn), a swimming pool, a tennis club, a golf links, and a large number of joggers' paths.

Behind the Giant Wheel, the **Liliputbahn** is a little train reaching the Stadion (football stadium) and swimming pool after a tour of 4km/2mi.

★★**Riesenrad** ⊙ – An English engineer, Walter B Basset took eight months to build the Giant Ferris Wheel which started functioning on 21 June 1897. It was to be an advertisement for the British metallurgical industry. Basset built other Ferris wheels in Chicago, London and Paris, but only the Viennese one is still in operation. During the First World War, it served as an observation post. After fire and bomb damage in 1944, it was rebuilt in 1947 with half as many cabins. It was a spectacular setting for the meeting of Harry Lime (played by Orson Welles) and Holly Martins (Joseph Cotten) in Carol Reed's film *The Third Man* (1949). The fifteenth *James Bond* film (The Living Daylights, 1986) used some shots featuring it. It provides an interesting **view**★ of Vienna.

> **Riesenrad facts and figures:** 64.75m/212ft high, 61m/200ft diameter, 430 tonnes, eight pylons of steel girders, 120 wire cables, one complete rotation every 20 minutes, as the cabins move at a rate of 75cm/29in per second.

Planetarium ⊙ – *Hauptallee; next to the Riesenrad.* In 1927, the Zeiss company founded the planetarium housing the small **Prater-Museum** ⊙. This traces the history of the Prater by means of a small exhibition of scale models and photographs. There is a scale model of the 1873 World Fair.

Fussball-Museum ⊙ (**CY**) – *Meiereistrasse 7. Closed until the end of 2002.* The Football Museum is located within the Ernst Happel Stadium. Entry to the stadium, which named after one of the most successful Austrian soccer trainers, is on the other side of the museum. The building by Otto Schweitzer dates from 1931, and since its last refurbishment in 1986 can accommodate 60 000 spectators.

EXCURSIONS AROUND THE PRATER

Coming from Praterstern, return along Praterstrasse for the town centre.

Just before the Johann Strauss Gedenkstätte, the Dogenhof *(No 70)* is worth noting, a pastiche of the Cá d'Oro on the Grand Canal in Venice. This neo-Gothic "Doge's palace" probably dates from the same era as the "little Viennese Venice" constructed in the 19C on the site of the Riesenrad during flow control projects on the Danube.

★ **Johann Strauss Gedenkstätte** ⊙ (**LP**) – *Praterstrasse 54. 1st floor. Underground: Nestroyplatz (U1); bus: Praterstrasse (5A).* It was in this apartment that Johann Strauss the Younger composed in 1867 *The Blue Danube,* an exceedingly famous waltz which seems to embody the long and eventful history of this type of music. The first public performance of this work took place on 15 February 1867, in the Diana Hall, to over a thousand spectators who had come to hear the Waltz King's latest composition. As often happened, he was conducting elsewhere that night. It was an immediate success. Eight months later, during a concert in London, there was such applause for the Waltz Opus 314 that Strauss had to play it four times in succession – a unique occurrence.

The museum – Numerous interesting objects and documents are on view here. Some attract attention more than others *(numbers in brackets correspond to the numbering of the*

ROGER-VIOLLET

Johann Strauss the Younger

exhibits): a xylograph depicting a masked ball in the Diana Hall where *The Blue Danube* was first performed *(9)*; several scores of this work *(22, 26, 27)*; the piece of furniture where the Strauss family kept their violins *(18)*; portraits of his parents, Maria Anna Strauss by JH Schramm (1835) *(42)* and Johann Strauss the Elder by J Kriehuber (1835) *(43)*; the invitation to the ball on 15 October 1844 *(see Outside the Ring, Hietzing, Insert "The Stormy Launch of Johann Strauss the Younger") (50)*; a letter from the son to his father, rejecting the latter's attempt at reconciliation following his liaison with a dressmaker *(51)*; his death mask by Kaspar von Zumbusch *(93)*. Finally, there are numerous portraits of Johann Strauss the Younger, including a bust by Tilgner *(81)* and an oil painting by August Eisenmenger *(83)*. Also of interest are the caricatures and silhouettes on display in the room where you can hear musical extracts *(earphones)*, particularly: *Schani*, on the first page of the Viennese newspaper *Der Floh* published on 21 February 1869 *(99)*, (*Johann Strauss als Vogel (Johann Strauss as a Bird, 102)* by Josef Beyer, or the famous **silhouette** of the composer by Hans Schliessmann *(121)*.

Augarten – *Main entrance: Obere Augartenstrasse. Tram: Heinestrasse (21, N), Obere Augartenstrasse (31, 32); bus: Obere Augartenstrasse (5A).* In 1650 trees covered this 52ha/128 acre park, which lies at the north end of the district. The Frenchman Jean Trehet, creator of Schönbrunn Park (1691), redesigned the Augarten in 1712, and in 1775 Joseph II opened this pleasure garden to the public, as he had the Prater in 1766.

Porzellanmanufaktur Augarten – After closure in 1864, the famous **Augarten porcelain manufacture** reopened in 1923. The former imperial factory was founded in 1718 and its "beehive" monogram is famous among connoisseurs of porcelain throughout the world, especially on its Du Paquier, Prince Eugène or Maria Theresa services. Nowadays, the most popular items represent Lipizzaner horses from the celebrated Spanish Riding School. These figurines which are great favourites today draw inspiration from models dating back to the era of Maria Theresa. Since reopening, the factory has been under the administration of the city authorities and occupies Leopold I's Alte Favorita. The Turks destroyed this small 1654 palace; but in 1705, during Joseph I's reign, it was rebuilt as a conservatory. Mozart, Beethoven and Johann

H. Wiesenhofer/ÖSTERREICH WERBUNG

Porcelain workshop in Augarten

Strauss the Elder performed concerts here which were very popular with the city's music lovers.

Augartenpalais – In the south corner of the park stands the garden palace. It was probably Johann Bernhard Fischer von Erlach who built it for a city councillor at the end of the 17C. Since 1948, this building has housed the *Wiener Sängerknaben* (Vienna Boys' Choir).

Strange concrete towers – On 9 September 1942, Hitler decreed that, like Berlin and Hamburg, Vienna should have some anti-aircraft towers. Six of them were built around the town centre, including two in Augarten park. Unfinished, they served only as air raid shelters, and could each accommodate up to 30 000 people. They had their own electricity and water supply, and the air was filtered. The upper platforms are all at the same height. These giant bunkers built in 1944 by Friedrich Tamms give the impression of being indestructible. One of them contains a museum *(see Outside the Ring, Mariahilf)*, while two are in military use and three are empty.

Wiener Kriminalmuseum ⊘ – *Grosse Sperlgasse 24. Tram: Obere Augartenstrasse (N, 21); continue by foot on the Taborstrasse; bus: Karmeliterplatz (5A).* **It is not recommended to bring children on a visit to this museum!** This museum presents the history of criminality in Vienna using some drastic cases as examples; among other things, the Viennese persecution of witches and the 1853 assassination attempt on Emperor Franz Josef are illustrated by means of historical objects and documents. The exhibition's main focus is the period from the 18C to the Second World War. Despite the very sober representation of these cases in the style of police reports and the shunning of sensationalism, some visitors may find the descriptions of the crimes and photographs of crime scenes of somewhat hard to stomach.

Among the nearest sights are the Fleischmarkt and Hoher Markt Districts (in the City Centre and the Ring section), and the Landstrasse, Donaustadt and Alsergrund Districts (found in the Outside the Ring section).

LIESING
23rd District
Local map page 10, **AZ**

Take the underground (line U4) and exit at "Hietzing" then take tram 60 and get off at "Maurer Hauptplatz" in Liesing; take the 60A bus and get off at "Kaserngasse". Walk down Maurer Lange Gasse on the right, then turn left to walk up Georgsgasse. By car, take Breitenfurter Strasse (Federal Highway 12) and turn right at Atzgersdorfer Platz into Levasseurgasse then left into Endresstrasse; follow the signs after Maurer Hauptplatz where there is a wine press dating from 1800.

Wotrubakirche ⊘ – *At the end of Rysergasse.* The church Zur Heiligsten Dreifaltigkeit (Most Holy Trinity) is pleasantly situated on St.-Georgenberg, at the edge of the Wienerwald (Vienna Woods). Consecrated in 1976, it owes its unofficial name to Fritz Wotruba (1907-75), a renowned Austrian sculptor who designed the model for the church and was also responsible for Arnold Schönberg's cubic gravestone *(see Outside the Ring, Zentralfriedhof).* Whether arriving from Rysergasse or Georgsgasse, visitors will be struck by the sudden sight of 152 octagonal concrete blocks displayed asymmetrically. This massive composition forming a sculpture 15.5m/50ft high does not conform to the traditional view of a religious centre. The church, with room for a congregation of 250, contains a replica of the cross made by Wotruba for the castle chapel of Bruchsal in Baden-Württemberg. Although it does not possess the remarkable spirituality of Notre-Dame-du-Haut church built by Le Corbusier in Ronchamp, France, Wotrubakirche is faintly reminiscent of the edifice created by the master of reinforced concrete. Both these works were built by atheists.

People travelling by car may choose to go on and visit Perchtoldsdorf (see the Further afield section).

The neighbouring districts (with the recommended sights described in this guide) are Hietzing and Favoriten (see Outside the Ring section).

MARIAHILF

6th District

Local map page 15, **EUV**

Underground: MuseumsQuartier (U2), Gumpendorferstrasse (U6), Neubaugasse (U3),
Westbahnhof (U6), Zieglerstrasse (U3)

Tram: Mariahilfergürtel (6, 18), Neubaugasse/Westbahnstrasse (49)

Bus: Neubaugasse (13A, 14A)

This district lies southwest of the city centre. Along its north side, it shares with Neubau District the long commercial thoroughfare of Mariahilfer Strasse. The Wien, which flows along the south side into the Danube Canal, gave the Austrian capital its name. Following the example of Döbling and the city centre, this district provided a home for Ludwig van Beethoven *(Laimgrubenstrasse 22)* from October 1822 to 17 May 1823. However, it was Joseph Haydn who left his mark on Mariahilf.

Walking along Mariahilfer Strasse, remember that the sights in Neubau District are not far away. Looking at our map of Vienna should make it easy to combine visits to both these quarters and their sights, depending on individual tastes and inclinations.

Mariahilfer Strasse – This busy street links Westbahnhof to Messepalast, which the identical buildings of the Naturhistorisches Museum and Kunsthistorisches Museum separate from the famous Ring. No 45 in this street was the birthplace of the playwright **Ferdinand Raimund** (1790-1836). This poet instilled new life into old Viennese folk tales and his plays formed part of the Burgtheater's repertory. He committed suicide after being bitten by a dog that he thought was suffering from rabies. A tragic mistake.

Mariahilferkirche ⊙ **(K²)** – *Mariahilfer Strasse 65.* This pilgrimage church (1686-1726) replaces an older church that the Turks destroyed in 1683. In front of it stands a monument to Haydn. The church houses a replica of the statue of the Mariahilfberg Virgin, which is said to work miracles. The original is in Passau, Bavaria. The architect of the church was probably Sebastiano Carlone. Inside, a Rococo organ console with a clock above it is noteworthy. The "Schustermichel", the second largest bell in Vienna after the "Pummerin" in the Stephansdom, hangs in the left tower

An adjoining chapel contains a crucifix from the "House of Ruffians" in Rauhensteingasse *(1st District)*, from where those condemned to death left for execution on Hoher Markt.

Walk around the church and down Barnabitengasse. Turn right for Esterházypark.

Haus des Meeres ⊙ **(M⁹)** – *Esterházypark 6. Underground: Neubaugasse (U3); bus:Haus des Meeres (13A, 14A, 57A).* The House of the Sea is in an enormous concrete tower (Flakturm) at the centre of the small *Esterházy* Park. This amazing structure was built by the Germans during the Second World War as an anti-aircraft tower *(also see Outside the Ring, Leopoldstadt, Augarten).*

The exhibition, which displays 2 500 animals from every continent, extends through four floors of the tower and a tropical house adjoining the outer façade that allows little monkeys and birds to move freely inside of it. On the ground floor, there is a 100 000-litre aquarium that is home to sharks. The reptile houses are on the 1st floor and additional aquariums on the two floors above. Although snakes and piranha fish are probably a major attraction, some visitors might also enjoy the quieter beauty of the vividly coloured tropical fish *(3rd floor).*

White-crested monkeys in the Haus des Meeres

Foltermuseum ⊙ – *The Foltermuseum is located in an underground former air-raid shelter in Esterházypark. Entrance from Schadekgasse.* This Museum of Torture illustrates the development of corporal punishment from antiquity until the beginning of the modern age. To do this, it uses exhibits that replicate the original methods. The various forms of torture are illustrated through scenes with dolls and detailed explanatory tablets, although not all of them were used in Vienna itself. The tour concludes with an exhibit by Amnesty International on torture in our present times.

A Quiet Departure

In spring 1809, Napoleon's troops entered Vienna. **Joseph Haydn** was seriously ill and the sound of cannonfire scarcely disturbed him. In protest, he would sit at his piano at midday playing *Gott erhalte*, the national anthem sung in every language of the Empire, including German, Hungarian, Italian, Polish, Romanian, Serbo-Croat, Slovakian, Czech and Ruthenian. While Napoleon moved into Schönbrunn, some French officers came to pay homage to the great composer. When one of them, a captain of hussars, hummed a tune from *The Creation*, Haydn was so moved that he embraced him. The composer's heart stopped beating five days later, on 31 May. When he heard the news, Napoleon ordered the posting of a guard of honour outside his house.

On 15 June, there was a memorial mass for Haydn in the Schottenkirche. Because of the French occupation of Vienna, hardly anyone attended it. One of the few who did was a certain Henri Beyle, better known as French writer Stendhal, then an official for Napoleon's army in Vienna.

Return to Mariahilfer Strasse keeping to the left side of the street and turn left again into Webgasse. Take the first street on the right, Schmalzhofgasse, then Haydngasse on the left.

★ **Haydn-Gedenkstätte** ⊘ (**M**[10]) – *Haydngasse 19. Underground: Westbahnhof (U6), Zieglergasse (U3); tram: Mariahilfergürtel (6, 18); bus: Brückengasse (57A).* "I like this house very much [...] I would like to buy it as a retreat for my old age, when I am a widow", Haydn's wife wrote in a letter to her husband. At the time he was in London, performing symphony concerts to much acclaim. He did not send the money to his wife, but he bought the house on his return to Vienna in 1793. It was in a new district called "Windmill", to be precise in Kleiner Steingasse, which in 1862 received the name of Haydngasse. He lived in this house from 1797 until the year of his death in 1809.

It was in this building that Prince Esterházy's musical director wrote his most famous oratorios *The Creation* (1798) and *The Seasons* (1801). Today it houses a Memorial Museum. The exhibits evoke mainly the people and places that had the greatest impact on Haydn's career. Besides musical excerpts *(earphones)*, there are also *(numbers in brackets correspond to the numbering of the exhibits)*: a facsimile *(1)* of the score of *Missa in tempora belli*; an engraving *(24)* from a watercolour by Balthasar Wigand depicting the performance on 27 March 1808 of *The Creation* at the Alte Universität in honour of the composer, who also attended; his last visiting card *(37)*, with one of his melodies printed on it; a facsimile of the composer's last letter regarding the purchase of a fortepiano *(41)*, written on 1 April 1809; his deathmask in a showcase (on 31 May 1809, Haydn died in the small room in which this mask is displayed); the composer's schedule, providing an insight into his everyday life (50); an interesting black pencil drawing of Haydn in profile (51) by George Dance dating from 1794, as well as a 1795 gouache portrait (52) by Johann Zitterer.

One of the rooms on the upper floor commemorates **Johannes Brahms**, who settled in Vienna in 1869. Since the building he lived in no longer exists, the memorial museum also includes personal objects and mementoes from the apartment of Brahms, who was a fervent Haydn admirer).

Also in the Mariahilf District are the Theater an der Wien and two buildings by Otto Wagner at 38 and 40 Linke Wienzeile. Their description is in the section on the Wieden District.

Sights in the area include the Kunsthistorisches Museum (see the City Centre and the Ring section), the MuseumsQuartier, as well as the districts of Neubau, Hietzing and Wieden (see the Outside the Ring section).

MUSEUMSQUARTIER★★
7th District
Local map page 13, **HS**
U-Bahn: MuseumsQuartier (U 2), Volkstheater (U 2, U 3)
tramway: Volkstheater (49)
Bus: MuseumsQuartier (2A), Volkstheater (48A)

Outside the Ring

The MuseumsQuartier, which lies in the axis of the Hofburg, the Kunsthistorisches Museum and the Naturhistorisches Museum, is one of the largest museum terrains in the world. It was built on the grounds of the former imperial stables, which were completed in 1725 by Johann Bernhard Fischer and his son Josef Emanuel on a commission from Emperor Karl VI. The complex of buildings was entirely renovated in the mid-19C by Leopold Mayer, and the Winterreitschule (Winter Riding School) was added. In 1921, it was once again rebuilt to serve as a trade fair venue: trade fairs and exhibitions were held here right up until 1995, when the Wiener Messe AG moved to the Prater.

The architect team Laurids and Manfred Ortner (of the architectural firm of Ortner & Ortner) were already contracted to rebuild the complex as a cultural forum in 1990. After redrawing their plans several times, they finally decided to add three new buildings altogether, creating a harmonious ensemble to house a cultural institution with room for all artistic genres. After only three years of construction, the new buildings were completed; in the meantime, all the museums have moved in – and what is even more surprising for a project of this dimension: besides remaining within the timeframe, it also remained within the limits of the original budget.

The MuseumsQuartier serves as a haven for painting, sculpture, music, dance and theatre. All the exhibitions are in fact independent institutions. Only the administrative services have been put in the care of an umbrella organisation.

MUSEUMSQUARTIER INSTALLATIONS

All entrances (Museumsplatz, Burggasse, Breite Gasse and Mariahilfer Strasse), the Ticket-Centre and the Visitor's Centre (Besucherzentrum) post overview maps of the MuseumsQuartier.

Ask at the Besucherzentrum or the Ticket-Centre for discounts for visiting more than one of the institutions (Kombi-Ticket). Information on tours through the MuseumsQuartier is also given there.

★**Leopold Museum** ⊙ – *Orientation map at the entrance. Audio-guides for a deposit with photo identification.* Ortner & Ortner chose the white Danube limestone as a building material for the museum, the same material used to construct the majestic buildings along the Ring. The building is oriented towards the Kunsthistorisches Museum. In other words, the entire building, material and orientation included, does justice to the Leopold Collection, which, in contrast to the collection of the MUMOK *(see below)* comprises works of art from the 19C and early 20C belonging to the traditional, generally accepted taste in art.

The collection of the Viennese doctor Rudolf Leopold was transferred to a private foundation in 1994, and now has proper exhibition space at its disposal in this new museum. The collection encompasses over 5 000 objects, including the single largest collection of Egon Schiele's works and other significant works from the modern period in Austria: Klimt, Egger-Lienz, Kubin and Kokoschka.

In the lower level 2 (Untergeschoss 2), you will find the graphic work (mainly Kubin, Schiele – represented by numerous self-portraits – Klimt), non-European and contemporary art. In the lower level 1 (Untergeschoss 1) are the works of 19C Austrian artists in the main. In his *Portrait of Frau Josefa Ernst* (1856), Ferdinand Georg Waldmüller depicted his elderly subject with ruthless realism. The *Portrait of Isabella Reisser* (1885) is a fascinating example of a quasi-Mannerist portrayal by Anton Romako. The ground floor displays the artists who worked under the aegis of the Wiener Werkstätte and the Secession. Gustav Klimt's outstanding skill is well demonstrated by the large format **Death and Life**★★ (1910/15) and the postcard-size, ultra-realistic miniature **Young Girl Seated**★ (1894). Koloman Moser is represented by, among other things, a life-sized sketch on paper of the Engelfenster (Angel's Window) from the Kirche am Steinhof. A café and shop welcome visitors on the first floor.

Upper level 2 (Obergeschoss 2) includes the tableaux by the Tyrolean artist Albin Egger-Lienz (1868-1926), who drew his inspiration from the meagre rural living conditions, and painting after 1945. Upper level 3 (Obergeschoss 3) focuses on Expressionism. Oskar Kokoschka is represented by his **Self-Portrait**★ (1918-19). What really captivates the viewer up here, however, are the works of **Egon Schiele**★★: His fascinating self-portraits still kindle debates as to his personality (the *Self-Portrait* with *Bowed Head*, 1912 – is taken up again in the mystical, dark composition with three figures painted in the same year, *Hermits*). It is well worth taking the time to examine the various aspects of Schiele's opus, such as his nudes (*Woman Lying*, 1917), landscapes (*Autumn Tree in Moving Air*, 1912– which almost appears as an abstract painting at first glance), or his many depictions of cityscapes and houses.

MUMOK (Museum moderner Kunst – Stiftung Ludwig Wien) ⊘ – *Audio-guides for a deposit with photo identification.* The Museum of Modern Art, panelled as it is in black basalt, is both a sequel and a counterpoint to the Leopold Museum. Like the Leopold, it has been situated in the inner courtyard of the MuseumsQuartier, but its dark façade is in sharp contrast to the brilliant white of its opposite. The collection, which was started in the year 1962, and which was enhanced considerably in 1981 after being integrated in the Austrian Ludwig-Stiftung (Foundation) today consists of around 6 000 items, some of which are displayed on a surface area of over 50 000sq ft. This overview of the most important movements of modern and contemporary art is displayed over nine different levels. It begins with Expressionism and Cubism and stretches all the way to the present. The collection's real strength lies in its broad range, but by the same token, some of the leading works of certain artistic movements are also to be found here, for example, the *Mouse Museum* (1965-77) by the Pop-Art artist Claes Oldenburg. The shorthand of the daily life of a "museum in a museum" corresponds to that of Disney's Mickey Mouse. **Wiener Aktionismus** is also well represented here. This Austria-specific variation on the theme of action art arose towards the end of the 1950s and is rooted in part in the theories of Freud and C G Jung. Please note, however, that some visitors might be adversely affected by some of the particularly harsh works by Nitsch, Mühl, Brus or Schwarzkogler.

J. Malburet/MICHELIN

The courtyard fronting the MuseumsQuartier

Kunsthalle Wien ⊘ – The Kunsthalle right behind the erstwhile Winterreithalle presents changing exhibitions concentrating on contemporary art (painting, sculpture, film, photos, performance, installations). Two exhibition halls are available, one with a surface area of 500m²/5 280sq ft, the other 1 000m²/10 670sq ft. The fact that the Kunsthalle sees its mission as not only providing exhibition space, but also as an area where art can be born, is obvious from the brick façade resembling a factory. It shares a foyer with the events venues E+G (for the Wiener Festival weeks, for example). Even if you are not interested in the exhibition, it is well worth having a look at the space here. The contrast between the Baroque imperial box of the Winterreithalle (now part of the MUMOK's café) and the steel panelling of the spectator stalls of hall E+G is very attractive.

Quartier 21 – Quartier 21 is the most explicit area when it comes to proving that the intention of the MuseumsQuartier is not only to exhibit art, but to produce it as well. Half-year stipends are granted to young artists for studios and apartments. In addition, media studios, an events arena and workshops offer the opportunity to engage in a cross-genre discussion with art in theory and practice.

Zoom Kindermuseum ⊘ – This Children's Museum is more a large playground than a museum. The areas of Research and Discovery *(Forschen und Entdecken)*, but above all for participation, have been arranged for children up to 12 years of age. And as opposed to the museums for adults, in this one running around and making noise is allowed. Children up to the age of 6 can go through a play world focusing on the topic of oceans accompanied by their parents. The older group can look at changing exhibitions or check out the multimedia lab. Special studio programmes are also available, where children of various age levels can express their creativity under the guidance of trained teachers.

Theaterhaus für Kinder – This children's theatre offers dance, musicals, puppet theatre and even experimental theatre especially for children between the ages of 4 and 13. The idea is to open them up to all forms of acting that go beyond traditional children's theatre.

Art Cult Center Tabakmuseum ⊘ – The history and culture of tobacco consumption from 1492, when Columbus brought tobacco back to Europe with him, until the present begins right at the entrance. The exhibits illustrate the various phases: clay pipes from the 16C, snuff boxes from the 18C, **meerschaum pipes★** from the 19C, cigarette accessories from the 20C. The actual significance of tobacco consumption in the modern age is well documented by the many often skilfully decorated items, such as the **Waldviertler Riesenpfeife★** (1906-10), a giant pipe from the Waldviertel region carved for Emperor Franz Joseph from a single piece of wood. The adjoining theatre is a venue for various events (concerts, readings, shows, exhibitions, etc).

Tanzquartier Wien – The Tanzquartier is a centre of contemporary dance and performance. Besides hosting its own stage and three studios it has a theory and information centre that offers a chance to learn more about the various forms of dance expression and gives artists and those interested in dance and performance the opportunity to share views. Own productions and guest performances are given, as well as workshops and lectures.

Architektur Zentrum Wien ⊘ – Present, discuss, publish, store are the topics guiding this institution's agenda. Every year it hosts the Vienna Architectural Congress as a forum to discuss international developments in architecture and urban planning. This already indicates the programme here: changing exhibitions (examination of works, architectural and cultural subjects, art installations) display aspects of international and Austrian art of the 20C. A special library of architecture at the Information Centre is open to the general public.

Among the neighbouring sights are the Kunsthistorisches Museum and the Hofburg (in the City Centre and the Ring section) as well as the districts of Mariahilf, Neubau and Josefstadt (in the Outside the Ring section).

NEUBAU
7th District
Local map page 13, **HRS**; page 15 **EU,**
Underground: MuseumsQuartier (U2), Neubaugasse (U3), Volkstheater (U2, U3)
Tram: Burgring (1, 2, D, J)
Bus: MuseumsQuartier (2A), Volkstheater (48A)

The Neubau District lies between Gürtel and the Ring, between the Josefstadt and Mariahilf Districts. It stretches along Mariahilfer Strasse, a busy commercial thoroughfare with a branch of the Dorotheum at No 88a *(see City Centre and the Ring, Kapuzinerkirche District)*. Croats and Hungarians once lived in this district now characterised by housing estates and residential houses.

Gustav Klimt lived here *(Westbahnhofstrasse 36)* and Josef Lanner, the famous composer of waltzes, was born here on 12 April 1801 *(Mechitaristengasse 5)*. The **MuseumsQuartier★★** *(see Outside the Ring)* was opened in this district in June of 2001.

While walking along Mariahilferstrasse, remember that the sights in Mariahilf District are nearby. A glance at our city map will make it easy to combine visits to both districts.

★**Kaiserliches Hofmobiliendepot** ⊘ (**EU M**[11]) – *Andreagasse 7. Underground: Neubaugasse (U3); Zieglergasse (U3); bus: Neubaugasse (13A, 14A).* This collection of court furniture gives a taste of how it once was "in the Emperor's home". Exhibits include several elegant and fascinating objects, which at least partially demonstrate the Habsburgs' liking for foreign and exotic cultures: **Egyptian Cabinet** *(at the entrance, to the right of the cashier)*; the **Habsburger Hall** (in which births and deaths, feasts, political events, religious and secular ceremonies are reflected in objects belonging to the dynasty or to individual family members); and the **Laxenburger Room** with its exquisite Renaissance furniture of German origin. The **Biedermeierkojen**, examples of the taste expressed by the solid middle class combined with court furniture in the 1920s, are found on the second floor. The second storey also houses a walk-in depot, illustrating one of the museum's important tasks: it continues to serve as a storage place for parts of the collection which are still used in exhibitions or government offices.

The imperial Hofmobiliendepot – Walk-in storage

M. Hertlein/MICHELIN

The Royal Furniture Depot

Transporting, caring for, and also storing furniture, carpets, drapes etc. to the various residences of the royal household was the task of the Hofmobilieninspection. Until the beginning of the 19C, only Vienna's Hofburg was permanently furnished, while the imperial summer residences and pleasure palaces were only equipped with furniture for the duration of their occupation by the court. On some occasions, furnishings for over 1 000 people had to be provided. Also, in the case of coronation or wedding trips (as far as Frankfurt, Florence or Venice), up to 100 heavily laden freight wagons preceded the court members, equipping their temporary residential and state rooms with furniture, tapestries, paintings and even lavatories. It wasn't until 1808 that Franz II issued an order which increasingly provided the temporarily used castles and residences with permanent furnishings.

Carry on along Mariahilfer Strasse and turn right into Zieglergasse.

Museum der Gold- und Silberschmiede ⊘ (**EU M¹²**) – *Zieglergasse 22. Underground: Zieglergasse (U3).* This small museum devotes itself to the history of silver- and goldsmithing of the last six centuries.

Go along Zieglergasse and bear right into Lerchenfelder Strasse. Turn into the 3rd street on the right, Döblergasse.

Wagnerhaus ⊘ (**EU M¹³**) – *Döblergasse 4. Tram: Strozzigasse (46); bus: Neubaugasse/Neustiftgasse (48A).* Otto Wagner completed Nos 2 and 4 in this small street in 1912. They contrast sharply with the two adjacent buildings he constructed on Linke Wienzeile *(see Outside the Ring, Wieden).* The later Döblerstrasse buildings are more geometrical and are typical of Wagner's second creative phase, when he favoured right angles and a certain restraint in his decoration.

Otto Wagner lived at No 4, where he died on 11 April 1918. Since 1985, it has housed the Otto Wagner archives from the Akademie der Bildenden Künste (Academy of Fine Arts).

Continue along Döblergasse and turn left into Neustiftgasse, then turn right just beyond Kellermanngasse.

St. Ulrichs-Platz (**EU**) – *Underground: Volkstheater (U2, U3); bus: St.-Ulrichs-Platz (48A).* This square and its church form a fine 18C Baroque ensemble. The most attractive façade belongs indisputably to No 2 (mid 18C), which features an elegant and aristocratic gate leading into a pretty interior courtyard.

Josef Reymund built the **Ulrichskirche** ⊘ between 1721 and 1724 on the site of two 13C chapels. It was the setting for the marriage of the German composer Christoph Willibald Gluck and the christening of Johann Strauss the Younger.

Near the chevet of the church, turn left into Burggasse. The Spittelberg quarter starts near Stiftgasse.

★**Spittelberg quarter** – *Underground: Volkstheater (U2, U3); tram: Stiftgasse (49); bus: St.-Ulrichs-Platz (48A).* Spittelberg, a rectangular area formed by the streets Burggasse, Stiftgasse, Siebensterngasse and Kirchberggasse, was once the artists' quarter. In the 1970s, it attracted people on the fringe of society and since then has experienced a revival. Aware of the charm of these few streets, the town of Vienna refurbished the area, restoring most of the buildings and turning it into a pedestrian precinct.

The past... – In 1683, the Turks decided to establish their artillery in this quarter, because it stands on a small hill. It was certainly a good strategic position, since Napoleon did the same at the beginning of the 19C when he directed his cannons against the town.

Spittelberg was always a working-class quarter, a centre for artists, actors and street singers. Spittelberggasse was once an alley where the army rabble came to forget the hardships and privations of barrack life by spending time with the prostitutes here. In 1787, even Emperor Joseph II had to hasten back to his unit in the Hofburg after being surprised in the company of a "most charming" lady.

... and the present – With its numerous shops, cafés and restaurants, the quarter now offers a wealth of cultural attractions. No 8 Stiftgasse (birthplace of the painter Friedrich Amerling) is a centre for musical or literary events, collective workshops for craft or restoration work, and exhibitions. Always lively, Spittelberg has remained a busy area: a craft market takes place here every Saturday from April to November; young people flock to the Christmas market, which is the most convivial in town.

Return to Burgasse and head towards the Ring.

Volkstheater – *Neustiftgasse 1. Underground: Volkstheater (U2, U3).* The popular theatre is the creation of two specialists in theatre architecture, Ferdinand Fellner and Hermann Helmer, who built it in 1889. This eclectic edifice offers an extensive repertoire, mainly made up of contemporary and avant-garde plays.

Turn left into Museumstrasse.

Palais Trautson – *Museumstrasse 7. Closed to the public.* Unfortunately this elegant Baroque palace is closed to the public. Johann Bernhard Fischer von Erlach designed it in 1710 and Christian Alexander Oedtl built it. Since 1961 it has housed the Ministry of Justice. The main body of the ornate façade is worthy of attention. At the top is a statue of Apollo playing the lyre. Beyond the twinned-column entrance, on the left, are telamones which the Italian sculptor Giovanni Giulani fashioned for the magnificent staircase leading to the ceremonial hall. Giulani had Georg Raphael Donner as a pupil.

The palace was built for Johann Leopold Trautson. Empress Maria Theresa bought it in 1760 and installed the Hungarian royal guard in it.

Go up Neustiftgasse and take the first street on the right. One of the houses is Josef Lanner's birthplace (Mechitaristengasse 5).

Besides the Kunsthistorisches Museum (see the City Centre and the Ring section) and MuseumsQuartier, Neubau is also close to the Mariahilf and Josefstadt (see the Outside the Ring section).

Spittelberg Quarter

PENZING★

14th District
Local map page 10, **AYZ**

Located west of Vienna, the Penzing District is to the north of Hietzing. It is for the most part a quiet residential quarter.

SIGHTS

★**Technisches Museum** ⊙ (**M²**) – *Underground: Schloss Schönbrunn (U4), Johnstrasse (U3); tram: Winckelmannstrasse (52, 58); bus: Linzerstrasse (10A). After extensive renovation, the Technical Museum of Craft and Industry, founded in 1909, was reopened in 1999. The present interactive exhibition offers a comprehensive overview of various facets of technology and industry: history of the natural sciences, instrument-making, communications, mining, process technology, heavy industry, energy, etc. The hands-on demonstration experiments for exploring technical phenomena are located on the mezzanine. They are fascinating for both children and adults.*

★★**Kirche am Steinhof** ⊙ – *Baumgartner Höhe 1. Bus: Psychiatr. Krankenhaus (48A). Enter the hospital precinct, turn left then immediately right to walk up the avenue. Guided tour only, in German (45min).* Otto **Wagner** designed St Leopold's church for the new psychiatric hospital of Lower Austria between 1904 and 1907. Symbolically, it occupies the highest position of a grassy hill (alt 310m/1 016ft) upon which the entire complex sprawls. It forms part of this development and faces north instead of the more usual east. It was Vienna's first modern church and is contemporaneous with the Postsparkasse, using the same method of construction *(see City Centre and the Ring, Fleischmarkt District.)*: its Carrara marble cladding lies on top of a simple brick construction. The enormous dome resting on a double tambour is a metal structure covered by copper tiles, which were originally gilded. The architect made use of these new technical devices to build a church, which in its form brilliantly echoes the Baroque creations of Bernini and Fischer von Erlach.

Interior – Wagner based his design for the interior on practical rather than aesthetic considerations: since this was intended as a church for the ill, the design of the stoups prevented any risk of infection, the floor sloping towards the altar allowed a better view, the pews had no sharp edges against which people might injure themselves and the staff could quickly intervene from any point in the church. The entrance doors made segregation of the sexes easy. However, the decoration is almost neo-Byzantine, the high altar, in particular, displays a gilded canopy that resembles a trellis of copper filigree. The angels adorning the canopy, after a design by Othmar Schimkowitz, were made in the Wiener Werkstätte studios. The huge picture adorning the high altar (84m²/860sq ft) shows the Saviour blessing the people, surrounded by the saints in Paradise. It was drawn by Remigius Geyling, and the mosaic atelier of Leopold Forstner carried out the work. Wagner himself designed all the liturgical fittings; he chose **Koloman Moser** to make the **stained-glass windows★** based on the iconographic theme of mercy. Above the entrance is a portrayal of Paradise Lost, which the saints in the side windows are seeking to regain; St John the Baptist leads those on the right, while Tobias conducts those on the left.

Kirche Am Steinhof – Window designed by Otto Wagner

208

★**Wagner Villas** – *Hüttelbergstrasse 26 and 28. Tram: Bergmillergasse (49)*. Otto Wagner built these two villas on a hillside that extends to the edge of the Vienna woods. Constructed in 1888, the first villa at No 26 has classical elegance, with its portico of Ionic columns. It looks as it has been transplanted from the Riviera. Wagner built this eclectic villa for his own use and lived in it until 1911. Originally, the wings were pergolas; they were altered and closed before the end of the century, diminishing their contrast with the central section. The present owner is the contemporary painter Ernst Fuchs, who created the colours of the façade. Today, the house contains the **Ernst Fuchs Private Museum** ⊘ with an exhibition of pictures, figures, objects and furniture by the Austrian artist.

A quarter of a century later, the architect built next to it a villa in a more austere style, which in its severity recalls the building in the Neubau District *(see Outside the Ring, Neubau, Wagnerhaus)*. Both date practically from the same period. Although it differs from the first villa in its more geometrical elegance, the second does not dispense altogether with decoration. In particular, it features a mosaic head of Medusa by Koloman Moser above the entrance.

The nearest sights are Schloss Schönbrunn and Hietzing District (see the Outside the Ring section).

Schloss SCHÖNBRUNN★★★

13th District
Local map page 10, **AZ**
Underground: Schloss Schönbrunn (U4), Hietzing (U4)
Tram: Hietzing (58, from Westbahnhof)

Schloss Schönbrunn station is less than 200m/218yd from Hofpavillon Hietzing (see Outside the Ring, Hietzing), which is in turn near the palace entrance.

Three centuries ago, immense forests covered Schönbrunn's present site, providing hunting grounds for the Habsburgs. A mill, the Katterburg, had been doing service here since the 14C , but it was destroyed by the Turks in 1529. Forty years later, Maximilian II bought the estate including the surrounding woodlands and reconstructed a hunting lodge cum seigneurial manor on it. Legend has it that the Emperor's brother Matthias discovered, at the beginning of the 17C, the *Schöner Brunnen*, literally "the lovely fountain", the spring which has given its name to the area. From it, there is a fine view over the vine-clad hills and the Kahlenberg to the west of the Viennese conurbation. The Katterburg, initially used for hunting purposes, was enlarged. Eleonora Gonzaga, wife of Ferdinand II, was given it as a widow's residence after Ferdinand's death, and initiated the construction of a small "Lustschloss" (leisure palace), which was completed in 1642/43. In 1683, the Turks totally destroyed the imposing pavilion for the second time. After the final victory over the Ottomans, there began a period of prosperity during which aristocrats built many magnificent palaces in Vienna. In 1693, Leopold I commissioned **Johann Bernhard Fischer von Erlach** to design a splendid hunting castle for his son Joseph. Fischer von Erlach had already attracted some attention with a monumental ideal design for an emperor's residence and he had made a name for himself although the work had not been meant to be realised. The Kaiser was suitably impressed and commissioned Fischer von Erlach with the construction of the hunting castle. In 1696 he began work building the work for the Crown Prince on the foundations of the old Gonzaga castle. Plans were changed in 1697, however, and Schönbrunn was now supposed to be a showcase residential palace for the future "Sun King" Joseph, a quite conscious indication of the rivalry with the French king Louis XIV.

The work begun during the reign of Joseph I and ended with his death. Karl VI was not particularly interested in Schönbrunn, preferring his "little Escorial" project *(see Further afield, Klosterneuburg)*. He made Schönbrunn into a summer residence for his daughter Maria Theresa who had married in 1736. This is why work resumed during her reign: she liked "her house". Wishing it to be more grandiose, she summoned **Nikolaus Pacassi** to complete, modify and enlarge the residence (from 1744 to 1749) on which she left her own mark, indicative of the brilliant, lively sovereign she became. The final result is a palace reminiscent of Versailles with its succession of major courtyards and its series of lavish state apartments. Architecturally, it was a huge success, a monumental edifice in classic Baroque style, although inside the Rococo style is dominant, representing a victory for French taste over the Italian taste prevalent until then. The decoration of the rooms dates from the reign of Maria Theresa who appreciated Rocaille style panelling, marquetry of rare hardwoods, floral embellishment and coloured chinoiserie, glowing damask and sinuous curlicues: an exuberantly decadent style typical of the Régence period in France.

A site steeped in history – Many historical memories are linked to the palace and the park. During Maria Theresa's reign, Schönbrunn was the summer residence of the Court. **Marie-Antoinette**, the future Queen of France, spent her childhood there. It was in the palace that Mozart played *(see Spiegelsaal or Hall of Mirrors below and inset "The Palace Theatre")*, amazing the empress and her court with his precocious talent.

The Duke of Reichstadt

On 20 March 1811, Napoleon II was born in the Tuileries palace in Paris. He was the son of Napoleon I and Marie Louise, the daughter of Emperor Franz I. Napoleon François, an imperial prince, King of Rome from 1811 to 1814, left Paris with his mother on 29 March 1814 for Blois then Austria shortly before his father was deposed. He was raised at the court of Franz I, but in 1817 was relieved of any claims to an inheritance. He was, however, given the Bohemian dukedom of Reichstadt in 1818. Schloss Reichstadt is a castle situated 65km/40mi from Prague; this duchy enabled the child to enjoy a position at the court among the archdukes. He died 22 July 1832 at Schönbrunn.

His coffin lay in the Capuchin crypt before being transferred to Paris to the Invalides on 15 December 1940 on Hitler's orders. His heart (Augustinerkirche) and his entrails (catacombs of St Stephen's Cathedral) are still in Vienna.

Here too, in 1805 and 1809, Napoleon I set up his headquarters, some years before the famous Congress of Vienna. After the fall of the French empire, Schönbrunn served as a home for Napoleon's son, the young King of Rome, placed under the guardianship of his grandfather, Emperor Franz who forbade him all contact with France *(see inset The Duke of Reichstadt)*. It was in Schönbrunn that Emperor Franz Josef was born and where he died. Here too, Karl I, last of the Habsburgs to reign, signed the Act of Abdication on 11 November 1918. In 1961, John F Kennedy and Nikita Khrushchev met here for the first time for a historical "summit conference" during the days of the Cold War.

THE PALACE COMPLEX

Ehrenhof – The gateway to this huge courtyard (24 000m²/28 703sq yd) is flanked by two obelisks surmounted by eagles. On the right is the sole remaining and oldest Baroque theatre in Vienna *(see inset)*. Ehrenhof, this immense courtyard, witnessed the parade of Napoleon's Grande Armée as well as the arrival of sovereign powers for the Congress of Vienna. It is bordered by the Cavalier wings and adorned by two fountains commissioned by Maria Theresa, allegories of rivers and kingdoms within the Austro-Hungarian empire.

The Ehrenhof gives a view of the 180m/590ft-long courtyard façade of the broad Corps de Logis which has rather excessively high entablatures and projecting corner wings. This lacks the fluidity characteristic of Viennese Baroque at its height, in the time of Johann Bernhard Fischer von Erlach. The green of the window frames emphasises the yellow ochre colour of the buildings which brings harmony to the whole construction.

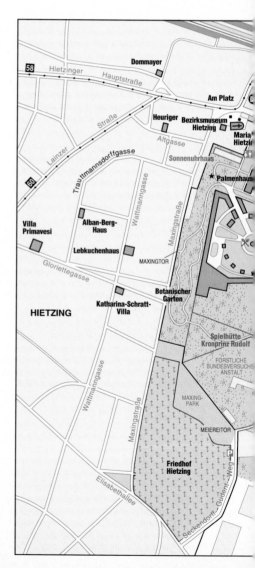

The ochre paint covering the exterior of the palace is also known as "Schönbrunn yellow". It dates back to the reign of Franz I. In Room VII of the Kunsthistorisches Museum *(see City Centre and the Ring)*, there is a painting by the Venetian Canaletto, dated 1758-61, showing a view of the pink walls and grey pilasters of the palace from the main courtyard.

The Palace Theatre

Maria Theresa wanted the palace to have a theatre, for her entertainment "in such a huge residence". The Schönbrunn palace theatre was built by Nikolaus Pacassi from 1741 to 1749. It was entirely remodelled about 20 years later as a French balcony theatre by Ferdinand Hetzendorf von Hohenberg.

Nowadays, the theatre is the summer setting for performances from the Wiener Kammeroper.

★★TOUR OF THE PALACE ⊘

Two tours are recommended: the **Imperial Tour** and the **Grand Tour**. The first comprises 22 rooms: the state apartments of the imperial couple Franz Josef and Elisabeth including reception rooms. The second comprises 40 rooms: the first tour plus the audience chambers of Maria Theresa and her husband François Étienne of Lorraine.

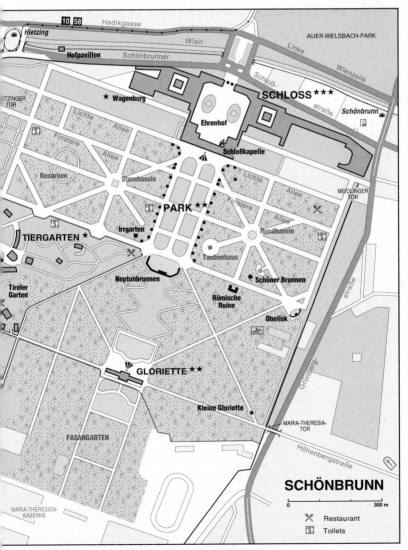

SCHÖNBRUNN

0   300 m

✕ Restaurant
🚻 Toilets

Façade of the Ehrenhof

Rich in historic memories, these apartments are a triumph of Rococo style, with their red, white and gold colour scheme, the delicate elegance of the stuccowork framing frescoes and ceilings with scrolled whorls, the outstanding luxury of crystal chandeliers, the faience stoves, tapestries and priceless furniture.

Imperial Tour – *About 30min. Tickets show the starting time for the tour. During busy periods, arrive at this time; there is no need to queue. "Audio-guides" are available on request (free and in several languages) after entering.*

Emperor Franz Josef's apartments – After the **Guard Room** and its portraits comes the **Billiard Room** with its Biedermeier billiard table, the waiting room for those to whom the emperor had granted an audience. Since petitioners might have to wait five hours, they had plenty of time to appreciate the paintings depicting the foundation of the Maria Theresa military Order in 1758, and the banquet over which Emperor Franz Josef presided in the *Grosse Galerie* (Great Gallery) for the centenary of the Order. The **Nusszimmer** served as an audience chamber and acquired its name because of its walnut panelling with the gilded Rocaille ornaments from the days of Maria Theresia; it displays busts of emperor Franz Josef, aged 23, and of his father Archduke Franz Karl. This opens into the **study,** (which is hung with portraits of the emperor at 33, his wife Elisabeth, the celebrated Sissi, and Crown Prince Rudolf). In a corner of the **Emperor's Bedroom** is the iron bed in which Franz Josef died on 21 November 1916. On an easel next to it is his funerary portrait painted the day after his death. A small chamber, the writing room of the empress Elisabeth and her bathroom lead to the **Imperial Couple's Bedchamber,** where the rosewood furniture contrasts with the blue cloth covering the walls; this room was only used during the first years of the marriage.

Empress's apartments – **Empress Elisabeth's Salon** displays the portraits of several of Maria Theresa's children; she had eleven girls and five boys. One of her daughters was Marie Antoinette who, at 15, married the dauphin of France, the future Louis XVI. After the **Empress's Grand Drawing Room**, which served as a dining room and has a dining table set in the original manner, the tour takes in the so-called **Children's Room**. This contains a fine escritoire which belonged to the last queen of France, depicted above it. The bathroom on the left was designed in 1917 for the imperial couple, Karl and Zita. The charming **Frühstückkabinet** (13) (Breakfast Room) leading off one corner of the drawing room is decorated with 26 framed yellow silk medallions. The embroidered flowers were made by Elisabeth Christine, Maria Theresa's mother. The **Yellow Salon** contains a clock, a gift from Napoleon to his father-in-law.

Reception rooms – In 1762, at the age of six, Mozart gave his first recital in the **Spiegelsaal** (Hall of Mirrors), with its white wood and gold leaf panelling. The three **Rosa Drawing Rooms** take their name from the Austrian painter Joseph Rosa who, between 1760 to 1769, decorated them with Swiss and Italian landscapes. The first panel on the left depicts the Habsburg ruins in the Aargau canton, between Basle and Zürich, which gave its name to the dynasty. The **Lanternzimmer** (Lantern Room) serves as an antechamber to the 40m/131ft long **Grosse Galerie★★★** (Great Gallery), a setting in the past for official banquets, balls and concerts (where from 1814 to 1815 delegates to the Congress of Vienna danced their time away; and where John F Kennedy and Nikita Khrushchev met in 1961). The allegorical ceiling frescoes (1760) by the Italian artist Gregorio Guglielmi represent the hereditary territories of the empire together with the Austrian nation as a major power for War or Peace. The **Kleine Galerie**, which was used for private family celebrations and was given its original polished while walls after restoration, is flanked by two superb **Chinese cabinets★** or chambers *(visible through the glass doors)* on either side of it. The first of these, which is circular, is magnificently decorated with lacquered panels, porcelain, gilded bronze chandeliers and Chinese porcelain vases (note the monkey sitting under the console table). Maria Theresa held meetings there with her chancellor, Count Kaunitz, who could reach it at any time via a secret staircase behind a concealed door. The room was equipped with a most ingenious device, a trap door in the centre through which a table of refreshments could be passed; to emphasise the secret nature of this chamber, it bore the name of "conspiracy table". The **Karusselzimmer** (Carousel Room) – named after the painting of the ladies' carousel at the Winter Riding School of the Hofburg, today's Spanish Riding School – opens into the **Zeremoniensaal** (Ceremonial Hall) which displays Maria Theresa's famous portrait by the court painter Martin van Meytens. The painting on the left depicts the marriage of the future Joseph II with Isabella of Parma in 1760. On the right of the portrait is a painting of a concert given in the **Redoutensaal** of the Hofburg; visitors can see *(using the magnifying glass)* a child said to be Mozart. The walls of the **Horse Room** *(visible through a glass door)* are decorated with portraits of horses painted on copper.

Grand Tour – *about 50min (including the previous rooms).*

Maria Theresa rooms – The walls of the **Blauer Chinesischer Salon★** (Blue Chinese Salon) are covered with hand-painted rice-paper wallpaper. This is where the last Austrian emperor, Karl I, signed his waiver to the throne, bringing to an end the reign of the Habsburgs, on 11 November 1918; thereafter, Schönbrunn was no longer an imperial residence. After her husband's death (posthumous portrait by Pompeo Battoni) in 1765, Maria Theresa had the magnificent **Vieux-Laque-Zimmer★** (old-lacquer room) redone as a memorial room; it is adorned with black Japanese lacquer framed in walnut and later served as a study for Napoleon during the periods of French occupation (1805 and 1809). It was in **Napoleon's Bedchamber** that his son, the King of Rome or Duke of Reichstadt, died at the age of 21 on 22 July 1832; the Brussels tapestries date from the 18C. Napoleon II's favourite companion was a crested lark (stuffed), with which he used to spend long lonely hours in Schloss Schönbrunn. The portrait shows him at the age of five, and the marble sculpture, that was made by Franz Klein using the death mask as a model, depicts him lying on his deathbed (the original is in Paris). Maria Theresa used the **Porcelain Room** – wood ornamentation painted blue and white in imitation of porcelain – as

The Great Gallery

a writing room. Next comes the **Millionenzimmer★** (Million Room), which is covered in rosewood panelling displaying Indo-Persian miniatures (painted on parchment after 16C and 17C originals) set in gilt Rocaille frames. 18C Brussels tapestries decorate the **Gobelinssalon** (Tapestry Drawing Room); the seats and backs of the six armchairs feature tapestries representing the months of the year. From here you walk into the former writing room of the Archduchess Sophie, with numerous family portraits depicting Franz Josef's mother. The **Red Drawing Room** is hung with the portraits of three emperors: Leopold II, Franz I and Ferdinand the Good. In the **Reichenzimmer** stands the only state beds of the imperial court – this one dates from 1736 and was probably made for Kaiser Karl VI. Originally, this splendid bed of precious velvet and gold thread embroidery, was in Maria Theresa's bedroom at the Hofburg. It has been at Schönbrunn since 1946. Franz Josef was born in this room on 18 August 1830. **Archduke Franz-Karl's study**, which is the next stop on the tour, contains an interesting family portrait by Meytens of François Étienne of Lorraine and his wife Maria Theresa: it is evident from the way in which they were represented which one exercised power and authority. To the left is a portrait of Countess Fuchs-Mollard, governess and confidante to Maria Theresa. The adjoining drawing room is visible through a glass door.

Schlosskapelle – *Enter through interior of palace; free.* Although the chapel was built in the late 17C, its architecture and decoration date from Maria Theresa's reign. The high altar by Franz Kohl is surmounted by Paul Troger's painting of the *Marriage of the Virgin to St Joseph*. Paintings on the side altars are by the Venetian artist Giovanni Battista Pittoni.

The future Joseph II married Isabella of Parma here, in 1760. When she died, he married Marie-Josephine of Bavaria, in 1765.

★**Wagenburg** ⊙ – The Carriage Museum has occupied the former Winter Riding School since 1922. It has a large display of coaches, carriages, sleighs and sedan chairs belonging to the imperial court, from 1690 to 1918.

In the first room is a collection of vehicles from the 18C, 19C and early 20C, including some especially valuable examples, such as Napoleon I's coronation coach (Paris, c 1790), which later became one of the most important gala coaches of the Viennese Court; Field marshal Schwarzenberg's parade coach (Vienna 1791) with neo-Gothic ornamentation; the "coronation landau" used by empress Karoline Auguste (Vienna, 1826); the two-seater gala carriage of Empress Elisabeth (Milan, 1857) and the four-seater gala carriage of her husband Franz Josef (Vienna, c 1865-70). Of historic interest is the small barouche (Vienna 1885) used by Empress Elisabeth in Geneva, before she was assassinated; the black funeral coach used to take the Habsburgs to their final resting place (1877); the coupé (1887) and state coach (1890) of Emperor Franz Josef I. What is very special is the collection of children's coaches, including **the King of Rome's phaeton★** (Paris 1811-12), a gift from Caroline Murat to her nephew, Napoleon's son.

The second room contains the most sumptuous exhibit in the collection, the **imperial carriage★★**, a heavily carved and gilded coach with painted panels by Wagenschön, which was pulled by eight white horses, being the highest ranking coach of the court; and the "mourning-homage coach" with panel paintings by Unterberger; and the wonderful carousel sleds and carriages used by Maria Theresa for court festivities.

The imperial carriage in the Wagenburg

The Palmenhaus

★★PARK ⊘

The park was laid out in the French style by Jean Trehet (who also designed the Schwarzenberg palace gardens) c 1691, and modified by Jean Jadot and Adrian Steckhoven from 1750-80. From the façade of the palace facing the park there is a splendid **view**★★ of the Gloriette.

These gardens, which cover an area of nearly 2km²/0.76sq mi, were already open to the public when Schönbrunn was an imperial residence, apart from the areas on either side of the palace – Kronprinzgarten and Kammergarten – reserved exclusively for the imperial family. Arbours, clusters of greenery and vast formal flowerbeds form a backdrop to graceful fountains and elegant groups of allegorical statues, most by Wilhelm Beyer von Gotha (c 1772). The park is one of the most popular tourist attractions in Austria (8 million visitors per year).

Irrgarten ⊘ – The **maze** originally consisted of four squares probably with a raised central pavilion overlooking the labyrinth of hedges. In the 19C it fell out of fashion and was cleared in c 1892. However, a few years ago it was replanted following the design of the original one, so that modern visitors are able to wander between the hedges in their turn.

Neptunbrunnen – This imposing white marble fountain lies at the foot of the mound on which the Gloriette stands. It is the creation of court architect Ferdinand Hetzendorf von Hohenberg (1780). The artist crowned the work with a scene from Greek mythology depicting Thetis kneeling to Poseidon (Neptune) entreating him to protect her son Achilles on his journey to Troy. Her prayer was answered, but only as far as Troy where the young hero was killed by an arrow which Paris aimed at the only vulnerable part of his body, his heel.

Schöner Brunnen – Emperor Matthias is said to have discovered this spring, after which the palace is named. Its waters are supposed to have had the power to preserve the beauty of anyone who drank them. In any event the spring water was highly prized by the imperial family, who even took it with them on their travels in lead casks.

Obelisk – Ferdinand Hetzendorf von Hohenberg designed this obelisk supported on four gilded turtles in 1777. Scenes carved on it trace the history of the Habsburgs until the reign of Maria Theresa.

Römische Ruine – The Roman ruins are a folly, conjuring up images of the destruction of Carthage by Rome. They, too, are the work of F Hetzendorf von Hohenberg (1778).

★**Palmenhaus** ⊘ – This, the largest glass and iron greenhouse on the European continent, was built between 1880 and 1882. About 4 000 plants from around the world are displayed in various, separated climatic areas, from Himalayan plants to vegetation normally found in the rain forest of the tropics. Wooden benches are conveniently placed for a pleasant and contemplative rest.

★**Tiergarten** ⊘ – The zoo was founded in 1752 by François Étienne of Lorraine, Maria Theresa's husband, and is the oldest in Europe. It is very popular with the Viennese. On fine Sundays, swarms of children come here to see the elephants, giraffes, monkeys, bears and penguins. An acrylic glass tunnel leads through the world of the Amazon in the **Aqua-Terrarien Haus**, with a large aquarium including a coral reef and the "ErlebnisWelt", where you can study the fauna and flora of the tropical forest and the steppes and desert.

In the middle of it all, the French architect Jean-Nicolas Jadot de Ville-Issey built the **emperor's breakfast pavilion**, which boasts precious wood panelling, gilded mirrors and oil paintings depicting 30 animals. It is now a café and restaurant. The vaulted rooms under the pavilion, where the kitchens have been situated, was once a laboratory where attempts were made to manufacture gold on the emperor's orders.

Tiroler Garten – To the west of the hill, Archduke Johann introduced an Alpine note to Schönbrunn Park by rebuilding two Tyrolean chalets and an Alpine garden towards 1800. Since May 1994, the park of the Tyrolean garden has given younger children an opportunity to get close to farm animals.

Botanischer Garten – Franz I, who was passionately interested in natural sciences, founded this botanical garden in 1753. World-wide expeditions to remote countries helped to endow it with rare plants.

Little Gloriette – East of the earlier Gloriette is this pavilion decorated with frescoes.

★★**Gloriette** ⊘ – Ferdinand Hetzendorf von Hohenberg built this elegant gallery with arcades in 1775 as a crowning glory for the Schönbrunn hillock, thereby pursuing an idea of Fischer von Erlach, namely to build a belvedere as the fitting focal point for the Baroque palace grounds. Outlined against the sky on top of its mound, the monument suggests a classical triumphal arch. It also heralds the start of the colder Empire style. A stairway in the eastern wing leads up to the lookout point, with an outstanding view extending as far as Kahlenberg and Leopoldsberg. Since 1996, the Gloriette has housed a café open during the summer months, where refreshment is a must after a climb on a hot summer day *(see picture in the Introduction, ABC of Architecture)*.

After Schloss Schönbrunn, you can visit the other sights of Hietzing (see the Outside the Ring section).

The Gloriette

WÄHRING

18th District

Local map page. 10/11, **ABXY**

Währing lies between the Döbling and Hernals Districts, northwest of the city centre, beyond the Josefstadt and Alsergrund Districts. It is a quiet residential area dotted with delightful Jugendstil houses.

SIGHTS

Schubertpark (ET) – *Währingerstrasse. Tram: Martinstrasse (40, 41).* A short distance from Volksoper *(see Outside the Ring. Alsergrund),* Schubert Park displays an unusual feature, visible to passers-by: several tombs and a cross, the remains of the former Währinger graveyard. Franz Schubert and Ludwig van Beethoven were buried here, next to the east wall. Their coffins were transferred to the Central Cemetery *(see Outside the Ring. Zentralfriedhof)* in 1888.

Türkenschanzpark – *Tram: Türkenschanzplatz (41); bus: Türkenschanzplatz (10A).* This park takes its name of Turks' fortifications from the encampment that Suleyman the Magnificent's janissaries created on its site, when retreating in the face of glorious resistance by Count Salm's army during the 1529 siege. Around 1880, this land covering 15ha/37 acres became a public park and Gustav Sennholz laid it out with a pond and avenues. With its pretty Jugendstil gate and lovely trees, the park was soon a focus of attraction for Viennese who enjoyed walking, notably Arthur Schnitzler, who especially enjoyed its small hills and dales.
South of the park, lovers of architecture will spot three houses from the early 20C: the first two are by Robert Oerley and the third by Hubert and Franz Gessner: Villa Paulick (1907, *Türkenschanzstrasse 23*), Villa Schmutzer (1910, *Sternwarte-strasse 62-64*), Villa Gessner (1907, *Sternwartestrasse 70*).

Villa Moller – *Starkfriedgasse 19. Closed to the public. Tram: Gersthoferstrasse/Scheibenbergstrasse (41).* Adolf Loos built this house in 1928 for Hans and Anny Moller. It was a major landmark in his career and its pure, stark geometric style shocks some, attracts others and never fails to elicit a response.

Geymüller-Schlössl ⊘ – *Pötzleinsdorfer Strasse 102.* The banker Heinrich Geymüller commissioned this mansion in 1808. It contains a collection of 17C to 19C antique wall clocks and grandfather clocks, ranging from the Baroque to the Biedermeier style. Visitors should pay as much attention to the decoration, furniture and ornaments in the seven rooms on view, as to the collection.

The nearest sights are in the Alsergrund, Josefstadt and Döbling Districts (see these sections in Outside the Ring).

WIEDEN★★

4th District

Local map pages 13/14, **HJKS**

Underground: Karlsplatz (U1, U2, U4)

Tram: Karlsplatz (62, 65)

Bus: Karlsplatz (4A, WLB)

The district of Wieden, so highly regarded by the Viennese, lies south of Innere Stadt, the inner city. Karlsplatz lies right at the intersection the two districts Wieden and Margareten (5th District) and is the centre of all of Wieden's tourist and cultural attractions. Three famous composers lived there: Johannes Brahms *(Karlsgasse 4),* Franz Schubert *(Kettenbrückengasse 6)* and Johann Strauss the Younger *(Johann-Straussgasse 4).* Like Mariahilf, Neubau, Josefstadt or Alsergrund, this is a pleasant district to explore, with interesting examples of domestic architecture in the city's older residential areas. The urbanisation of Wieden dates mainly from the second half of the 19C.

SIGHTS

Karlsplatz – The square named after St Charles Borromeo is an important junction for several underground and tram lines. In 1979, Sven Ingvar renovated this square bordered by large buildings. In the pleasantly shady Ressel Park stands **Johannes Brahms' statue** by Rudolf Weyr.

★**Wagner-Pavillons** – *Karlsplatz.* Facing each other, the two pavilions (1899) designed by Otto Wagner housed for a long time the entrances to the Vienna underground (one for each platform). In 1892, the architect was commissioned to design and build 36 stations for the 40km/24mi of underground railway. Wagner saw this project as being of major importance for the creation of a modern city. The pavilions, restored in 1979, formed the highlight of this scheme. Wagner was so successful in his project that the buildings now embody the Viennese Jugendstil in all its refinement, in contrast to the Historicism then prevailing on the Ring. They present a harmonious combination of dazzling white marble and green-painted pre-fabricated metalwork, a technique that was new at the time. The roof is made of copper oxidised to a brilliant verdigris. In keeping with the elegance of nearby Karlskirche, Wagner's buildings display delicate gold incrusted or embossed ornamentation (mainly sunflowers), which strike a Baroque note with their delicate floral motifs.

One of the pavilions serves as an exhibition centre, while the other is a café. From the terrace on the pavement there is an excellent view of the site.

Künstlerhaus – *Karlsplatz 5*. Founded in 1861 through the consolidation of two artists' associations, the "Artists' House" is today still the possession of the same artists' co-operative. Originally constructed in the style of a small Italian Renaissance *palazzo* in the era of the Ringstrasse, the building was considerably expanded in 1882, and since 1945 has been continually developed into a modern exhibition building. The focal points of the exhibition programming are architecture, interdisciplinary thematic exhibits and international co-operative projects, as well as members' exhibitions. The artists' union also operates a cinema (Künstlerhaus Kino), a theatre and a restaurant here.

Musikvereinsgebäude – *Dumbastrasse 3. Closed to the public.* Lovers of classical music will be familiar with the gilded decor of the Goldener Saal (Great Hall) in the Friends of Music Academy, since it is seen during the world-wide television broadcast of the New Year's Concert which takes place every year on 1 January at 11am. To attend this concert, not only is it necessary to apply a year in advance, but tickets for the seats are chosen by lots. This is always a festive event, and the public never fails to applaud in time to the rhythm of Johann Strauss the Elder's *Radetzky March* which traditionally closes the concert. The orchestra always performs, on these occasions, under the baton of a world-famous conductor. The building is the home of the Vienna Philharmonic Orchestra, which usually plays for the National Opera, but it also performs 18 annual concerts in the Great Hall (2 044 seats). The Great Hall and the Brahms Auditorium (600 seats) are home to two other orchestras: the Radio and Television Orchestra and the Vienna Symphony Orchestra. This institution's archives, the world's largest private collection, contain unique items, such as manuscripts of Ludwig van Beethoven's *Eroica*, Johannes Brahms' *Double Concerto*, Gustav Mahler's *Sixth Symphony*, and all Schubert's symphonies apart from the *Fifth*.

Founded in 1812, the Friends of Music Society commissioned Theophil Hansen in 1866 to build this neo-Renaissance temple (completed in 1869), recognisable from Karlsplatz by its red and yellow colour scheme. The building houses the famous piano-making firm, Bösendorfer, which still pays the same rent as in 1914!

★**Historisches Museum der Stadt Wien** ⊘ – *Karlsplatz 8*. The Historical Museum of the City of Vienna opened in 1887; in 1959 it moved from the City Hall to these new Karlplatz premises built by Oswald Haerdtl in honour of the President of the Republic Theodor Körner. Covering a surface area of 3 600m²/4 305sq yd, the exhibition traces the history of the city from Neolithic times to the 20C. For those

Karlsplatz – Wagner pavilions and Karlskirche

B. Kaufmann

P. Schramek/MUSIKVEREIN WIEN

Musikverein concert hall

without too much time, it is possible to make a rapid tour of the exhibits illustrating the landmarks in the history of Vienna, including remarkable pictures by Waldmüller, Klimt and Schiele.

Ground floor – On display are some precious architectural fragments evoking medieval Vienna, such as the three keystones from Minoritenkirche (early 14C), the *Beautiful Madonna* (c 1420) which used to adorn the south tower of the cathedral, the terracotta statue of St John (1430) from the cloister of St Dorothy, and a statue of St Michael (c 1440) from the west front of the cathedral. There are also stained-glass windows (c 1390) from the ducal chapel, which no longer exists, including the **portrait of Rudolf I**.

First floor – Among a series of engravings and paintings are a **circular plan of Vienna**★ by the Nuremberg artist Augustin Hirschvogel (1545 – *see illustration on p. 62*), Maximilian II's armour made in Augsburg c 1550, a facsimile of the Turkish map of Vienna discovered during the capture of Belgrade in 1688 and an attractive model of the old town dating from 1854, about 4 years before the razing of the fortifications. These objects are complemented by various etchings and paintings, including *The Battle to Lift the Siege of Vienna before the City Gates* (1683) by Franz Geffels; *View of the City* (1690) by Domenico Cetto; *Karl VI* (1716) by Johann Kupezky; *Franz I* (c 1740) and *Maria Theresa* (1744) by Martin van Meytens.

Second floor – This floor displays mementoes from the Napoleonic era, porcelain and glass exhibits from Viennese factories, a **Pompeian drawing room**★ (c 1800) from the Caprara-Geymüller palace *(Wallnerstrasse 8)* and an admirable picture collection: *Love*★ (1895), *Pallas Athena* (1898) by Gustav Klimt; *Lady in Yellow* (1899) by Max Kurzweil; *Landscape* (1901) by Adolf Boehm; *Arthur Roessler* (1910), *Self-Portrait with Outstretched Fingers*★★ (1911) and *The Blind Mother* (1914) by Egon Schiele; *Portrait of Peter Altenberg* (1909) by Gustav Jagerspacher, which used to hang in the American Bar *(see City Centre and the Ring, Stephansdom District)*. After the section on the 1848 revolution comes a collection of landscapes and portraits by Ferdinand Georg Waldmüller.

There is also a series of objects from the Wiener Werkstätte; there are also sculptures, including a bust of Gustav Mahler (1909) by Auguste Rodin and a bronze head of Adolf Loos by the Viennese artist Arthur Emanuel Löwental. Of equal interest are a reconstruction of the dining room in the architect's apartment *(Bösendorferstrasse 3)*, and of the flat of dramatist Franz Grillparzer *(Spiegelgasse 21)*.

★★ **Karlskirche** ⊘ – *Karlsplatz*. **Johann Bernhard Fischer von Erlach** was 60 when he started building this church dedicated to St Charles Borromeo, following a vow by Emperor Karl VI during the plague epidemic of 1713. Von Erlach's son would complete the building, which is undeniably the finest Baroque church in the capital.

Architecture – *See also Introduction, Architecture.* Legend has it that JB Fischer von Erlach had the unusual idea of combining Trajan's Column, the Roman portico of the Pantheon and St Peter's Dome, while standing on the Pincian hill in Rome. The façade used to stand in complete isolation near the slope of the old fortifications. At first sight this strange juxtaposition is startling, but visitors are soon taken in by the wonder of this unusual building.

Karlskirche

B. Kaufmann

On either side of the central staircase are two angels with outstretched wings, the one on the left represents the Old Testament and the one on right the New Testament. The stairs lead to a Corinthian *pronaos* over which is a triangular pediment decorated with a relief by Giovanni Stanetti, *The Cessation of the Plague*; above it is a sculpture of St Charles Borromeo by Lorenzo Mattielli. This central portico is flanked by two triumphal columns with spiral reliefs of the life of the saint, archbishop of Milan, who distinguished himself during an epidemic which devastated the capital of Lombardy in 1576. The left-hand column evokes the saint's steadfastness and the other his courage: *Constantia et Fortitudo*, Karl VI's motto. The presence of these columns in the façade was an idea that had been dear to Fischer von Erlach ever since his studies in Rome; he incorporated them in his first project for the entrance to Schönbrunn. Moreover, in Baroque art, columns do not usually support anything; there is no saint or emperor crowning these columns which end in a belvedere with a platform, faintly reminiscent of minarets.

Rising above a double-terraced attic, the dome of St Charles Borromeo evokes St Charles Church of the Four Fountains (a Romanesque church in Rome dedicated to the same saint); its lines are as elliptical though more graceful than those of Borromini's dome which predated Karlskirche by some 70 years. Between the eight windows are engaged columns and twinned pilasters bearing a projecting raised entablature. Above each opening is an elegant skylight with an angled pediment and consoles. Above the copper dome is a lantern turret with narrow windows; on top are a globe and a gold cross. At the sides, the surbased pavilions of the side entrances play an essential part in the illusion created by the architect: they widen the façade and counterbalance the vertical lines of the dome and columns. The **whole complex★★** makes a profound impact on the viewer.

Interior – While Rottmayr's fresco in the dome is being restored, scheduled from Easter 2002 until 2006, a panoramic lift takes you up to the cupola *(combined ticket with a tour of the church)*. This will give you a unique, limited opportunity to see the frescoes at close range. A stairway leads to the lantern turret, whose balcony offers a delightful view of the city.

KARLSKIRCHE

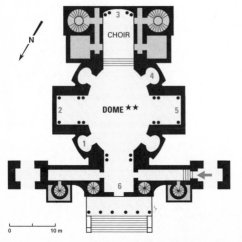

The plan of the building is a combination of an ellipse and an inverted Latin cross. In the absence of a nave and owing to the relative lack of decoration, all attention is normally drawn to the huge oval **dome★★** with frescoes by **Johann Michael Rottmayr**. They represent the apotheosis of St Charles Borromeo (on the left, there is an angel setting fire to Luther's Bible, which has been hurled to the ground).

Starting clockwise, visitors see: a baptistery with a vault decorated in *trompe-l'œil* style (**1**); an *Assumption* by Sebastiano Ricci (**2**); the high altar with sculptural decoration representing St Charles Borromeo's *Ascent into Heaven in the Company of Angels*, probably by Johann Bernhard Fischer von Erlach (**3**); *St Luke Painting the Virgin* by Jakob van Schuppen (**4**); *St Elizabeth of Thuringia* by Daniel Gran (**5**). Before leaving, make note of the frescoes above the organ loft (**6**), showing *St Cecilia among the Heavenly Choir* by Rottmayr.

The pool in front of the church is adorned with a sculpture by Henry Moore.

Technische Universität – *Karlsplatz 13. Closed to the public.* Johann Josef Prechtl founded the Technical University in 1815. Josef Schmerl von Leytenbach constructed the building from 1816 to 1818. It is an impressive neoclassical edifice, which acquired several additions during the 19C and in the early 20C. Sculptures in the centre of the main façade are by Josef Klieber and represent Austrian inventors; among them is Josef Ressel who invented the ship's propeller and who gave his name to the park on Karlsplatz.

The ceremonial hall of the Technical University is the work of Pietro Nobile, dating from between 1835 and 1842.

Go to the west corner of the square.

Kunsthalle wien Project Space – The architect Adolf Krischanitz fitted this 250m²/2 690 sq ft exhibition space with a glass shell, allowing the Kunsthalle the use of presentational forms ranging from installations to performance art. The exhibition room is complemented by a café.

Behind Kunsthalle, there is a view on the right of the Café Museum. Set at an angle to the left is the Secession Pavilion.

Café Museum – *Friedrichstrasse 6.* Belonging to the Viennese coffee-house tradition, this café is the work of Adolf Loos, but it has lost the original interior decoration. When it opened in 1899, Loos' contemporaries nicknamed it "Nihilism Café" because of its sober decor. Students and artists still frequent it.

The dome of the Karlskirche

B. Kaufmann

Close-up of Secessionsgebaüde

★★ **Secessionsgebäude** ⊙ – *Friedrichstrasse 12.* Two days after its completion on 10 November 1898, the Secession Pavilion opened for the second exhibition by the artists' group of the same name. This group, founded the previous year, was the creation of **Josef Maria Olbrich** and his friends, who repudiated academic Historicism, creating this building as a temple for their art.

"Mahdi's Tomb" – This is the strange appellation which the Viennese gave to Olbrich's pavilion. Owing to the proximity of the Naschmarkt *(see below)* and the gilded dome on top of the building, it was also nicknamed "the golden cabbage". (In the final analysis, the Viennese are rather sharp-tongued observers of the developments in their city).

The building now has a certain familiarity, but at the end of the 19C it was incredibly modern, a provocative assault from the avant-garde: Olbrich had designed a white cube – later he wrote that he had found inspiration in the unfinished sanctuary of Segesta in Sicily. This is particularly evident in this famous dome made of 3 000 gilded wrought-iron laurel leaves.

"Der Zeit ihre Kunst, der Kunst ihre Freiheit" – This motto ("To Each Century its Art, to Art its Freedom") features on the front of Olbrich's pavilion. It is an artistic declaration of war on the nearby Artists' Association *(see Künstlerhaus above)*. The pavilion is still an exhibition centre. The huge hall of this temple to art has zenithal lighting; it is functional in spirit, since the space can be modulated thanks to mobile partitions. The exhibition policies of the Secession are still enacted today, in accordance with the 1897 statutes of its founders. The democratic process is applied, with an exclusive reliance on artistic merit as determined by the association's board (which is elected every two years). As was also the case in the beginning, recent developments in contemporary Austrian and international art are showcased. The fundamental concerns of the Secession are openness toward new artistic trends, a love of experimentation, and the confrontation of native and international art. The **Beethovenfries**★★★ (Beethoven Frieze) by Gustav Klimt is in the basement to make sure it is kept in mint condition. The artist painted it on the theme of the *Ninth Symphony* for the 14th Secessionist exhibition (1902). Auguste Rodin came to see the frieze and declared it "tragic, divine and sumptuous". 34m/37yd long, it made its way through several private collections before the Österreichische Galerie bought it in 1975 and, thanks to the energetic Edelbert Köb *(see inset)*, put it back in the pavilion which was superbly refurbished and restored by Adolf Krischanitz in 1986. Those who have already been to the Burgtheater will appreciate the extent of the artist's evolution since the theatre frescoes. Left of the entrance, the project begins with *Longing for Happiness* which is dominated by swimming figures, and with the *Weak and Suffering Humanity* personified by a couple imploring a knight in armour (it is said to be a portrait of Mahler) with Ambition and Pity on either side of him; it continues opposite the entrance with a richly detailed panel displaying successively *The Three Gorgons*, *dominated by the feminine figures of Sickness, Madness and Death, The Giant Typheus, The Hostile Forces of Impurity, Unchastity and Excess, Nagging Worry and The Expectations of Mankind Flying over Hostile Forces*; it ends on the right again with *Longing for*

For or Against, but Never Indifferent

Despite the prevalence of received ideas, the **Secession** received a favourable welcome from the Viennese, who were probably somewhat weary of the grandiloquent excesses of Ringstrasse Historicism. The Viennese did not greet the Secession with indifference.

Resistance to change took root among intellectual circles, particularly at the University, where 87 professors signed a petition protesting against the works of Klimt. Recognition, on the other hand, came from the ranks of the bourgeoisie and captains of industry. Director of a steel cartel and a close friend of Gustav Mahler, Karl Wittgenstein (the father of Ludwig Wittgenstein) was the patron of the arts whom Klimt, Hoffmann, Olbrich and their disciples had been waiting for. There were others such as Ferdinand Boch-Bauer, August Lederer, Otto and Robert Primavesi, or the Belgian Adolphe Stoclet.

Although this is not generally known outside Vienna, the "Secession" association of visual artists is still alive and well. The movement's activities ceased in 1938, but it was never dissolved. A professor at the College of Fine Arts, **Edelbert Köb**, was responsible for its resurgence, with the assistance of a group of sponsors who created a foundation. It is thanks to this obstinate and generous man that it is possible today to admire Klimt's magnificent Beethoven Frieze.

Happiness flying over Poetry, the Arts with arms outstretched to a heavenly choir (Beethoven's *Ode to Joy*), and *The Fulfilment of Happiness*, an allegorical illustration of a sentence by Schiller: "This kiss is given to the whole world".

Go into Linke Wienzeile.

Linke Wienzeile – This thoroughfare links Karlsplatz to Schloss Schönbrunn. The left *(linke)* side of this row *(zeile)* of buildings borders the Wien and runs through Rudolfsheim-Fünfhaus (15th District) and Mariahilf (6th District). After leaving the Secession Pavilion, continue upstream along the river, which has flowed underground at this point ever since arches were built over it in 1912. On the right of the river is a group of buildings of special interest.

Theater an der Wien – *Linke Wienzeile 6.* In 1801, the librettist of *The Magic Flute*, Emanuel Schikaneder, founded this theatre, which four years later was the setting for the first public performance of Ludwig van Beethoven's *Fidelio*, which was very badly received. Towards the end of the century, the establishment became the home of Viennese operetta. People came here to listen to Johann Strauss the Younger's music or Franz Lehár's *Merry Widow*.

Naschmarkt – *Rechte Wienzeile.* Running between the Getreidemarkt and the Kettenbrückengasse, this fruit and vegetable market has the reputation of being solidly working-class, although its stalls display fresh, gourmet produce often from Central Europe (*naschen* means to taste things). As you approach the underground station Kettenbrückengasse, prices fall and the scene becomes increasingly lively. On Saturdays, the western end of the market is especially colourful, because it is the setting for a flea market.

Continue along Linke Wienzeile; Beethoven lived in a street at right angles to it, at No 22 Laimgrubengasse (from October 1822 to May 1823).

★**Two residential buildings by Otto Wagner** – *Linke Wienzeile 38 and 40. Closed to the public. Underground: Kettenbrückengasse (U4).* Wagner wished to turn this thoroughfare into a road fit for emperors. The project never came to fruition, but in 1899 the famous architect built two residential buildings embodying Jugendstil principles. Their façades are magnificent.

The actual entrance of No 38, the **Medallionhaus**, is at No 1 Köstlergasse. It displays two highly decorative corner façades. The golden stucco sparkles in the sunlight, sometimes impeding the view of Othmar Schimkowitz's *Criers* surmounting pilasters ringed with laurels, or of Koloman Moser's medallions, palm leaves and garlands. The building is in two horizontal sections, each with a different purpose, one for offices and shops, the other for apartments.

No 40, **Majolikahaus** *(see illustration, p. 1)* is of a similar structure to No 38. The building displays an architecturally austere façade covered in floral ceramic motifs, hence the name of the building. This façade is in the Jugendstil rather than the Secession style, since it is a spectacle in itself, with its polychrome rose spreading its branches between the regularly spaced windows.

Near the underground station, bear left into Kettenbrückengasse.

Schubert-Gedenkstätte Sterbezimmer ⊙ – *Kettenbrückengasse 6. Second floor. Underground: Kettenbrückengasse (U4); bus: Grosse Neugasse (59A).* From 1 September to 19 November 1828, Franz Schubert lived in the apartment of his brother Ferdinand, himself a composer. Franz moved there on the advice of his

© Österreichische Galerie Belvedere

Naschmarkt in Wien (1894) by Carl Moll

doctor, Ernst Rinner, to take advantage of the cleaner air in the inner suburbs. He did not intend to stay long. He had left all his manuscripts at the home of his friend, Franz von Schober, in the city centre where he had been living previously. He was right, his stay in Kettenbrückengasse was short – but fatal.

Here is Schubert's last letter, dated 12 November:

"Dear Schober,

I am ill. For eleven days, I have not eaten or drunk and I totter weakly to and fro between my chair and my bed. Rinna is taking care of me. Whenever I try to eat anything, I cannot keep it down. Would you be kind enough to help me in this desperate situation. Among Cooper's [James Fenimore Cooper] novels, I have read: The Last of the Mohicans, The Spy and the Pioneers. If you have any other novels by him, I implore you to leave them at the café, care of Bogner's wife. My brother, who is conscientiousness itself, will conscientiously bring them to me. Or anything else.

Your friend

Schubert".

Probably because he was worried about infection, Schober did not visit his friend, and Ferdinand was so "conscientious" that he claimed to be the composer of the Deutsches Requiem, which his brother had written for him to ensure that he acquired the status of composer.

Tour – Although the apartment has been extended and turned into a museum, it still stirs the emotions. The composer of *Erlkönig* died in the room directly past the hall on the street side.

Among documents and items of interest *(numbers in brackets correspond to the numbering of the exhibits)*, are: a lithography by Josef Kriehuber representing Ferdinand *(1)*; a reproduction of the watercolour and lead sketch by Josef Teltscher, *Franz Schubert in Teltscher's Studio (5)* (c 1827); an Elwerkember piano that belonged to Ferdinand *(4)*; Franz's last letter *(8, see above)*; a silver toothpick belonging to Franz *(11)*; facsimiles of his last works *(16)*, including *Tantum Ergo in E flat major*, D 960, and his last work, the *Lied Der Hirt auf dem Felsen*, D 965; a facsimile of the announcement of his death *(17)*; and a drawing of Augustinerkirche, in which funeral rites for Schubert were held on 23 December 1828 *(26)*.

The last sight in Wieden is at a distance from the preceding ones. It could be included in a visit to the Upper Belvedere.

Theresianum (FV) – *Favoritenstrasse 15. Closed to the public. Underground: Taubstummengasse (U1).* Empress Maria Theresa founded the College for Diplomats, which has occupied this building with its plain façade since 1946. It was first constructed between 1616 and 1625, commissioned by Emperor Matthias. After its destruction by the Turks during the 1683 siege, Lodovico Burnacini reconstructed it in 1690, turning it into a palace. Karl VI died there. His daughter, Maria Theresa, presented it to the Jesuits, instructing them to create a school for young penniless noblemen: the Collegium Theresianum.

The nearest sights are the Staatsoper District (found in the City Centre and the Ring section), as well as the Mariahilf, Favoriten and Landstrasse Districts (found in the Outside the Ring section).

ZENTRALFRIEDHOF

Simmering – 11th District
Local map page 12, **CZ**
Simmeringer Hauptstrasse 234
Tram: Zentralfriedhof 11, Tor (71)

According to one perhaps exaggerated view, Vienna is for many a city of the dead. The town and its suburbs comprise about fifty cemeteries, some of which have almost become tourist attractions, such as Hietzing, St Marxer Friedhof and to a lesser extent Grinzing. Kapuzinergruft *(see City Centre and the Ring, Kapuzinerkirche District)* where 138 members of the imperial family are buried is a standard part of any tour programme for visitors to Vienna. Several burial grounds such as the Stephansdom catacombs appeal to tourists because of their "special" atmosphere. As such, it is not so strange to see the Viennese adorning with flowers, on the first Sunday after All Saints' Day, the approximately one hundred tombs of the **Friedhof der Namenlosen** (cemetery of the nameless ones). This lies in Simmering on the banks of the Danube, and contains the remains of those washed up on the river bank.

Zentralfriedhof forms part of the traditional attractions of Vienna, containing the tombs of most Austrian celebrities from the political and artistic worlds.

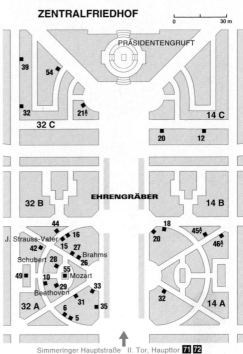

ZENTRALFRIEDHOF

Simmeringer Hauptstraße II. Tor, Haupttor **71 72**

An immense cemetery ⊘ – *A map of the cemetery is available at the main gate.* Zentralfriedhof was created in 1874 and contains nearly half a million tombs and monuments. It is the largest cemetery in Austria. The area covers 3.1km²/1sq mi (including the crematorium) and its boundary wall is 8km/5mi long, which is why some people drive through it by car.

The impressive main gate (1905) is the work of Max Hegele, who also built the church.

Dr.-Karl-Lueger-Kirche – This impressive Jugendstil church is dedicated to St Charles Borromeo and was named after the founder of the Christian-Socialist party, former mayor of Vienna. Max Hegele completed it in 1920. It occupies an area of 2 000m²/2 392sq yd and the cross above the dome is about 60m/200ft high.

V.I.P.'s – Foreign visitors to this cemetery will soon realise the extent to which Vienna attracted creative artists, particularly in the world of music.

Group 32A – No **5**: **Eduard van der Nüll**. Born in Vienna in 1812, died in Vienna in 1868. Architect of the Staatsoper. No **6**: **Johann Nestroy**. Born in Vienna in 1801, died in Graz in 1862. Actor, satirist, moralist and theatre director. No **10**: **Hugo Wolf**. Born in Windischgrätz in 1860, died in Vienna in 1903. Composer of *Lieder*, Kapellmeister (director of music) in Salzburg and music critic for the *Wiener Salonblatt* from 1884 to 1887. No **15**: **Johann Strauss the Elder**. Born in Vienna in 1804, died in Vienna in 1849. Composer and conductor who, with Josef Lanner, contributed to the world-wide triumph of the Viennese waltz. No **16**: **Josef Lanner**. Born in Vienna in 1801, died in Vienna in 1843. Composer. No **26**: **Johannes Brahms**. Born in Hamburg in 1833, died in Vienna in 1897. Composer who settled in the Austrian capital in 1862 where he wrote his four symphonies and the famous *Deutsches Requiem*. No **27**: **Johann Strauss the Younger**. Born in Vienna in 1825, died in Vienna in 1899. Composer who gave the waltz a symphonic structure and later wrote operettas; the graceful nymph on the tomb recalls *The Blue Danube*, while the bat alludes to the famous operetta. No **28**: **Franz Schubert**. Born in Vienna in 1797, died in Vienna in 1828. Composer of nine symphonies among other works. Tomb by Theophil Hansen. No **29**: **Ludwig van Beethoven**. Born in Bonn in 1770, died in Vienna in 1827.

225

Outside the Ring

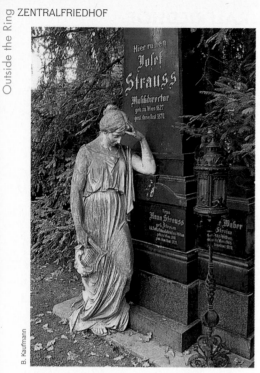

B. Kaufmann

Josef Strauss's grave, "Music Mourning",
in the Zentralfriedhof

This composer wrote most of his works in Vienna; his coffin was moved from Währing to Vienna in 1888. No **31**: **Franz von Suppé**. Born in Split in 1819, died in Vienna in 1895. Composer, conductor in the Theater An der Wien, composer of operettas which have become classics. No **33**: **Carl Freiherr von Hasenauer**. Born in Vienna in 1833, died in Vienna in 1894. Architect who built jointly with Gottfried Semper the Burgtheater and Neue Burg. The allegorical statue on his tomb represents Architecture. No **35**: **Karl Millöcker**. Born in Vienna in 1842, died in Baden in 1899. Composer of operettas. No **42**: **Eduard Strauss**. Born in Vienna in 1835, died in Vienna in 1916. Composer, brother of Johann and Joseph Strauss, whom he replaced as conductor of the Strauss orchestra. No **44**: **Joseph Strauss**. Born in Vienna in 1827, died in Vienna in 1870. Composer, conductor, brother of Johann and Eduard, composer of melancholy waltzes. No **49**: **Christoph Willibald Glück**. Born in Erasbach in 1714, died in Vienna in 1787. Composer of operas, imperial Kapellmeister. No **55**: **Wolfgang Amadeus Mozart**. Born in Salzburg in 1756, died in Vienna in 1791. Music's child prodigy was buried in a mass grave in the St. Marxer Friedhof. The monument is therefore a cenotaph and the statue holds the score of the *Requiem* in its right hand.

Group 32C – No **21A**: **Arnold Schönberg**. Born in Vienna in 1874, died in Los Angeles in 1951. Composer, inventor of atonal composition leading to serial music. Monument by Fritz Wotruba. No **32**: **Fritz Wotruba**. Born in Vienna in 1907, died in Vienna in 1975. Sculptor, pupil of Anton Hanak, creator of the Dreifaltigkeitskirche (Church of the Holy Trinity) in Liesing. No **39**: **Franz Werfel**. Born in Prague in 1890, died in Beverly Hills in 1945. Poet and man of letters who married Alma Mahler in 1929 and emigrated in 1938 to the United States via France. No **54**: **Curd Jürgens**. Born in Munich in 1915, died in Vienna in 1982. Theatre actor and film star who became famous in the Burgtheater from 1941 to 1953, then in numerous films.

Präsidentergruft – This crypt contains the graves of the presidents of the Austrian Republic. **Dr Karl Renner**. Born in Untertannowitz in 1870, died in Vienna in 1950. President from 1945 to 1950. **Dr Theodor Körner**. Born in Komárom in 1873, died in Vienna in 1957. President from 1951 to 1957. **Dr Adolf Schärf**. Born in Nikolsburg in 1890, died in Vienna in 1965. President from 1957 to 1965. **Dr Franz Jonas**. Born in Vienna in 1899, died in Vienna in 1974. President from 1965 to 1974.

Group 14C – No **20**: **Josef Hoffmann**. Born in Pirnitz in 1870, died in Vienna in 1956. Architect, pupil of Otto Wagner, co-founder of Wiener Werkstätte, founder of Austrian Werkbund.

Group 14A – No **18**: **Anton Dominik Fernkorn**. Born in Erfurt in 1813, died in Vienna in 1878. Sculptor, creator of the Aspern Lion and the equestrian statues on Heldenplatz. No **20**: **Theophil Hansen**. Born in Copenhagen in 1813, died in Vienna in 1891. Architect of several official buildings, including the Parliament. No **32**: **Hans Makart**. Born in Salzburg in 1840, died in Vienna in 1884. Painter of historical scenes and portraits, some of which are on view at the Oberes Belvedere (Upper Belvedere). No **45A**: **Joseph Kornhäusel**. Born in Vienna in 1782, died in Vienna in 1860. Biedermeier architect, whose principal works are in Baden. No **46A**: **Pietro Nobile**. Born in Campestra in 1773, died in Vienna in 1854. Architect, director of the Academy of Architecture, designer of the Äusseres Burgtor in the Hofburg.

Group 0 – No **54**: **Antonio Salieri**. Born in Legnano in 1750, died in Vienna in 1825. Composer who influenced Beethoven, Schubert and Meyerbeer, a rival of Mozart, imperial Kapellmeister from 1788 to 1790. No **84**: **Peter Altenberg**. Born in Vienna in 1859, died in Vienna in 1919. Poet, author, journalist, brilliant writer of aphorisms. Cross by Adolf Loos. No **112**: Count **Theodor Baillet-Latour**. Born in Linz in 1780, died in Vienna in 1848. The mob hanged this Minister of War during the 1848 revolution. No **195**: **Adolf Loos**. Born in Brünn (Brno) in 1870, died in Kalksburg in 1933. A great architect and pioneer notable for his functional style, active in Vienna and Paris.

Group 5A – No **R 1/33**: **Karl Kraus**. Born in Jisín in 1874, died in Vienna in 1936. Linguist, literary and theatre critic, journalist, satirist.

Group 24 – **R3**: corner crypt: **Victor Adler**. Born in Prague in 1852, died in Vienna in 1918. Doctor and politician, unifier of Social Democracy in Austria. **Otto Bauer**. Born in Vienna in 1881, died in Paris in 1938. Politician, leader of the Austro-Marxist movement in Austria during the 1920s.

Jewish section – *1. Tor*. Group 19, row 58: **Arthur Schnitzler**. Born in Vienna in 1862, died in Vienna in 1931. Doctor, author, and psychoanalytical poet. He is said to have asked to be stabbed in the heart to ensure he would not be buried alive … On the other side of Simmeringer Hauptstrasse is the crematorium, which Clemens Holzmeister built in 1922 *(Simmeringer Hauptstrasse 337)*.

Zentralfriedhof is not far from the sights in Favoriten and Landstrasse (to be found in the Outside the Ring section).

From here, people travelling by car can easily go to Petronell-Carnuntum or Neusiedler-See (found in the Further afield section).

Houses on stilts by the Neusiedler See

Further afield

Region around Vienna

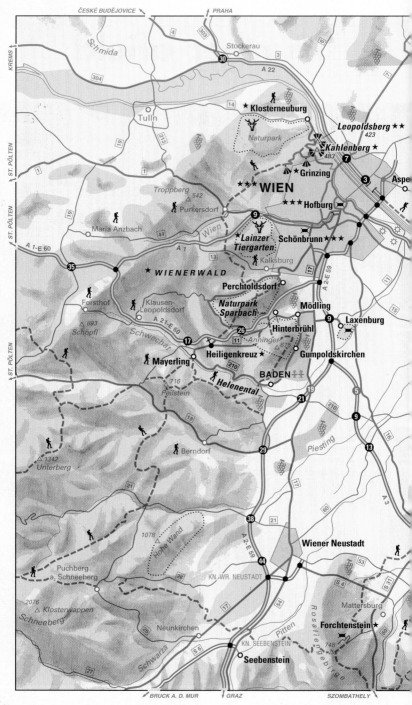

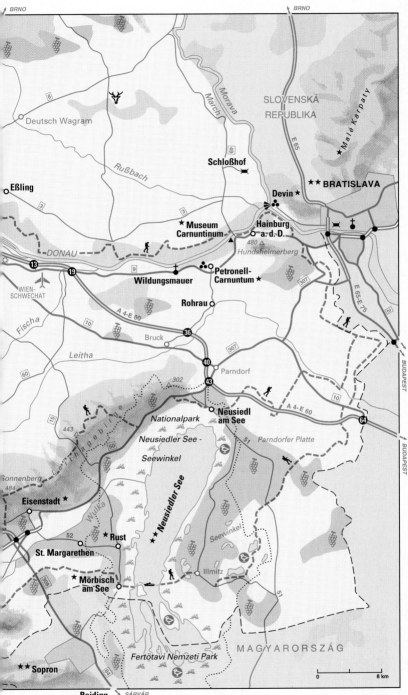

BRNO

BRNO

SLOVENSKÁ
REPUBLIKA

Malé Karpaty

Deutsch Wagram

Rußbach

Schloßhof

★★ BRATISLAVA

Eßling

Devin ★

★ Museum
Carnuntinum

Hainburg
a. d. D.

DONAU

480
Hundsheimerberg

WIEN-
SCHWECHAT

Wildungsmauer

Petronell-
Carnuntum ★

Fischa

Rohrau

A 4-E 60

Leitha

Bruck

Parndorf

302

BUDAPEST

Nationalpark
Neusiedler See -
Seewinkel

Neusiedl
am See

A 4-E 60

443

Parndorfer Platte

Sonnenberg
484

Eisenstadt ★

Neusiedler See

Seewinkel

St. Margarethen

Rust ★

Mörbisch
am See

Illmitz

BUDAPEST

MAGYARORSZÁG

★★ Sopron

Fertőtavi Nemzeti Park

0   8 km

Raiding   SÁRVÁR

BADEN♨♨

Niederösterreich
Population 23 900
Michelin map 926 fold 25 – 26km/16mi southwest of Vienna
Local map under Wienerwald

Near Vienna at the end of the Helenen Valley is the romantic town of Baden, idylli-cally located at the edge of the Vienna Woods. It is surrounded by vineyards yielding excellent wines. With its splendid Biedermeier architecture and magnificent houses, it deserves its reputation as a delightful resort offering a wide variety of pleasures: the ambience of an elegant spa, a picturesque townscape and entertainment provided by the casino, the modern Roman thermal springs and a renowned operetta theatre.

The resort – The beneficial effects of its sulphur springs were already known to the Romans and the emperor Marcus Aurelius mentions the *Aquae Pannoniae* situated "18 000 double paces south of Vindobona" (Vienna). Today the 15 springs yield over 4 million litres/880 000 gallons of water daily with a natural temperature of 36°C. The mineral waters are prescribed for the treatment of rheumatism and for strengthening the metabolism, the tissues of the joints and the vascular system. The spa had its golden age during the Biedermeier era and Emperor Franz I was a frequent summer visitor between 1803 and 1834; it regained popularity with the opening of the southern railway.

Famous guests – This idyllic setting attracted mainly musicians: Wolfgang Amadeus Mozart wrote his *Ave Verum* here, Franz Schubert stayed here as well as Ludwig van Beethoven who made five visits and finished his *Ninth Symphony* here during the winter of 1823-24. The writer Franz Grillparzer and the painter Moritz von Schwind were also visitors. Later, the town welcomed the kings of the waltz and the operetta: Johann Strauss, Joseph Lanner, Karl Millöcker, and Karl Zeller. From 1805, the guest list of people taking the waters reads like a *Who's Who* of European nobility. The Emperor Napoleon was particularly fascinated by the picturesque **Helenental** *(see Further afield, Wienerwald)* west of the city.

A Long theatrical tradition – For almost three centuries, Baden has enjoyed a rich cultural life all year round, including classical music concerts, plays and operettas, per-formed at the Jubiläumsstadttheater *(700 seats)* from October to March and at the Stadtische Arena *(see Kurpark below)* in summer.

SIGHTS

If going to Baden by local railway, get off at the final station: Josefsplatz, and turn into the Frauengasse towards the Hauptplatz. If arriving by car, it is easiest to park near the Casino.

A visit of the town reveals houses in the Classical or Biedermeier style, particularly on Kaiser-Franz-Ring *(near the Casino)*, Rainer-Ring *(between the Casino and Josefplatz)* and Breyerstrasse *(between Josefplatz and Wassergasse)*.

Hauptplatz – This pedestrianised square in the centre of town is recognizable by its *Dreifaltigkeitssäule*, a **Trinity Column** built in 1718 by Giovanni Stanetti (from a drawing by Martino Altomonte who was in the service of the Imperial family) after

View of the Spa Spring in Theresienbad by Johann Ziegler

Fotostudio Otto/Museen der Stadt Wien

Kurdirektion Baden

Baden – Stadttheater

the city had survived an outbreak of plague; the small fountain adjacent to it was added in 1833. The Town Hall *(Hauptplatz 1)* was designed in 1815 by Josef Kornhäusel who created a wealth of remarkable buildings for the city. The central entablature is adorned by four Ionic columns and a triangular gable; the three lunettes contain allegories of Intelligence and Justice.

The **Kaiserhaus** *(Hauptplatz 17)*, built in 1792, was for 30 years the summer residence of Emperor Franz I; the last Kaiser, Charles I, also stayed there between 1916 and 1918.

North of Hauptplatz, turn right into Pfarrgasse. On the left is the Stadttheater.

Stadtpkarrkirche Hl. Stephan – Nothing remains of the Romanesque building of 1312 except two truncated towers between which a Gothic bell-tower with an onion dome was added in 1697. Inside, the most interesting work is a *Stoning of St Stephen* by Paul Troger *(south wall of the chancel)*. Above the door leading to the organ *(facing the entrance)*, a plaque states that Wolfgang Amadeus Mozart wrote his *Ave Verum* in 1791 for his friend Anton Stoll who conducted the church choir. The fine organ designed in 1744 by Johann Genckl for the Dorotheerkirche was moved here in 1787.

Go along the west face of the church and turn left into Kaiser-Franz-Ring to enter the Kurpark.

★**Kurpark** – The spa park is a splendid place for a stroll. It runs up to the edge of the Vienna Woods *(there are two waymarked footpaths, see map at the park entrance)*. On the left stands the magnificent **Casino** (and Conference Centre) ⊘. This building occupies an historic site, since from the Roman well *(Römerquelle)* beneath its walls rose the oldest thermal spring. Just above, the **Stadtische Arena** (1906), a theatre, which is a blend of Jugendstil and Art Deco, forms a prestigious setting for the *Operettensommer*, thanks to its sliding glass roof that allows open-air performances.

Beyond the bandstand, where afternoon concerts are much appreciated by people taking the waters, the park is adorned by several memorials to famous musicians who visited the town: Lanner and Strauss, Mozart, Beethoven. The small oval pavilion dedicated to Beethoven is dominated by a circular viewing platform aptly named "Bellevue".

It is worth making the effort to climb a little further up the steep slope of the park to the Viennese forest, past enclosures where animals such as stags, deer, does, ponies, goats, etc graze peacefully.

Bear right after leaving the park, go along Kaiser-Franz-Ring and turn left opposite the Casino into Erzherzog-Rainer-Ring. Turn right for Brusattiplatz.

★**Spa architecture** – During the 1st half of the 19C, innumerable mock classical temples were constructed. Some of them still exist, even if most are put to a different use today. The **Leopoldsbad** *(Brusattiplatz)*, built in 1812, which now houses the Tourist Information Centre, was the dispatch point for mineral water; it was named after Margrave Leopold the Pious. To the right, partly concealed by a cluster of trees, is the **Römertherme**, the largest glass-roofed spa in Europe. The original building constructed by Eduard van der Nüll and August Siccard von Siccardsburg, the architects of Vienna's Staatsoper, has been preserved and combined with a modern spa environment that includes a whirlpool, active and resting pools, a children's paddling pool and two outdoor pools. On Josefsplatz nearby, the **Josefsbad** (1804) is a small rotunda reminiscent of a Vestal temple. It is now a restaurant. The **Frauenbad** (1821) by Charles de Moreau now houses art exhibitions. On the other bank of the Schwechat stands Joseph Kornhäusel's **Sauerhof** *(Weilburgstrasse 11-13)*, now converted into a grand hotel with a high-class restaurant.

Go down Frauengasse beside the Frauenbad.

Frauengasse – At No 10 is the Magdalenenhof, a Biedermeier house that accommodated Beethoven (autumn 1822) and Grillparzer (summers 1848 to 1850 and 1860). At No 5 is the Florastöckl, a building attributed to J Kornhäusel adorned above the cornice of its façade by a statue of the goddess Flora (Joseph Klieber); the Duke of Reichstadt, the son of Napoleon Bonaparte and Empress Marie-Louise, stayed here with his mother between 1818 and 1834. The Frauenkirche just before Hauptplatz was constructed in 1825 on the site of a church built towards 1260. Both churches were dedicated to the Virgin Mary.

Hauptplatz, turn left into Rathausgasse.

Beethoven Memorial Rooms ⊙ – *Rathausgasse 10*. It was here that the great composer stayed from 1821 to 1823 and wrote part of the *Missa Solemnis* and completed the *Ninth Symphony*. The house contains a small exhibition on his life and works, offering visitors the opportunity of viewing the composer's bedroom and workroom.

Return to Josefsplatz and turn right into Pergerstrasse. Continue straight on to Pelzgasse and enter the park opposite.

Doblhoffpark – The most interesting sight in this park is its *Rosarium*, an extremely well-maintained **rose garden**★ of 9ha/22 acres created in 1969. Rose enthusiasts will enjoy the wide range of specimens (25 000 roses, 600 varieties), such as the glowing red *Ruth Leuwerik* (1960), orange-tinted *Gloire de Dijon* (1853) or *Ave Maria* (1972), dazzling white *John F Kennedy* (1965), pink *Else Poulsen* (1924). In June, the *Badener Rosentage* with its luxuriance of flowers attracts many visitors.

Leave the park by the south and bear right into Helenenstrasse.

Thermalstrandbad – *Helenenstrasse. 19*. This public swimming pool was built in 1926 in the Art Deco style, which, despite being rare in Austria, does not jar in the birthplace of the Jugendstil and the Secession. There are in fact several open-air swimming pools (5 000m²/5 980sq yd) and a sandy beach; the architects hoped visitors would feel transported to the blue-tinged shores of the Adriatic.

EXCURSION

★**Wienerwald** – *See Further afield.*

BRATISLAVA★★

Slovakia
Population 450 000
Michelin map 926 fold 13 – 53km/32mi east of Vienna

EU members can enter with an identification card or passport. Swiss citizens will need a passport to cross the border.

On 1 January 1993, Bratislava became the capital of the Republic of Slovakia, a country with immense untapped potential for tourism. The former Pressburg lies on the banks of the Danube, at the western tip of the country, near the Austrian and Hungarian frontiers, between the Carpathians, the Danubian plain and Moravia. Owing to its strategic position, it became the capital of Hungary in the 16C under the name of Pozsony (until the 19C). It was the setting for the coronation of many Hungarian kings. In 1920, the city became part of Czechoslovakia following the division of the Austro-Hungarian Empire. Now it is a capital boasting numerous national, political and cultural institutions and a famous university.

A major road and railway intersection, Bratislava is a busy industrial city (chemical, electronics and engineering plants). Visitors arriving by car cannot fail to notice this. In the southwest, there is a major oil terminal at Slovnaff on the Danube. This is the most important processor of oil in Slovakia. There is a programme of waterway links to the Oder via the rivers Morava and Elbe, which includes the impressive Gabíkovo dam, completed in 1992 south of the city. It enables Slovakia to meet almost one-fifth of its energy needs, as well as canalising a stretch of the river.

GETTING THERE

Head eastwards out of Vienna, on the A 4-E60 motorway signposted Budapest. Leaving the motorway at exit No 19 (Fischamend), take road E 58 to Bratislava. After an early start, it is possible to combine a day in Bratislava with a visit to the Roman excavations at Petronell-Carnuntum (see Further afield).

ON THE DANUBE TO BRATISLAVA

From the beginning of April to the end of October, the DDSG Blue Danube Schiffahrt GmbH, Friedrichstrasse 7, 1010 Vienna, ☎ 01/58 88 00, www. ddsg-blue-danube.at, offers **rides in hydrofoil boats** from Vienna (embarkation at Handelskai 265, 2nd District) to Bratislava and back. Wed-Sun: departure from Vienna 9am or 9.30am (May to beginning of Sept), length of cruise 1hr 30min; return from Bratislava 5pm or 5.30pm (May to beginning of Sept), length of cruise 1hr 45min; single fare €17.44, round trip €26.89 . Bike transport possible (€5.09 single; €7.63 round trip). Check-in 1hr before departure.

It is also possible to book a **one-day cruise of "Historical Bratislava"** from Vienna, which includes the trip with the hydrofoil as well as a guided tour through the old town and a 4-course lunch in Bratislava (€43.24).

SIGHTS

There are three striking landmarks in the city: the **castle** with its four towers perched on a rock, the futurist **bridge of the Slovak National Uprising** *(SNP most)* and **Saint Martin's Cathedral** on the outskirts of the old town. Along the ancient fortifications, there are a series of bustling squares surrounding the historic heart of Bratislava. It seems small in comparison with the impressive but soulless suburbs and industrial areas that are now overrunning the banks of the Danube. Bratislava's charm lies in its old town, which can easily be explored on foot. It is a harmonious panorama of splendid Baroque palaces, beautiful churches and attractive squares.

★★**Hrad (Castle)** – The castle stands on the summit of the last promontory of the Carpathians, overlooking the Danube, which is much wider than in Vienna. Although it underwent several reconstructions, its rectangular structure dates from the Middle Ages. Empress Maria-Theresa commissioned the Baroque decoration in the 2nd half of the 18C. In 1811, a fire destroyed it and it was restored just a few years ago. It houses the historical collections of the **National Museum**.

From the castle ramparts as well as the terraces and gardens around **Parliament** nearby, there are unimpeded **views★★** over the city, the Danube, the plains to the horizon. The view also embraces the SNP bridge, which seems to be out of a science-fiction film, and the sprawling Petralka suburbs on the right bank of the river.

★★**Hlavné námestie (Market Square)** – This former market square was the centre of medieval Bratislava and features the Renaissance-style Roland fountain. At present, it has a strong 18C and 19C atmosphere. The café at No 5 is a masterpiece of Art Deco architecture, but the most impressive building is the old Town Hall (Stará Radnica) with its large tower. It is in a variety of styles from different periods, which all provide evidence of the city's long history.

Opposite the Town Hall, the French embassy and cultural centre occupy the Rococo style **Kutchersfeld palace**.

Franciscan square (Frantiÿskánske námestie) lies to the north, its trees forming an almost rustic setting for the Jesuit church. Further away is the Rococo **Mirbach palace★**, one of the finest of its type. Near it are the Franciscan church and monastery. In the palace, two **rooms★★** are curiously decorated with over 200 coloured 17C and 18C engravings, set into the wood panelling. Along the Municipal Museum (Metské), a narrow road links the main square (Hlavné námestie) with the Primatial square (Primaciálne námestie). The **Primatial palace** displays a delightful **façade★**, even lovelier when illuminated at night; it is notable for being the place where Napoléon and Emperor Franz I of Austria signed the Treaty of Pressburg in December 1805 after the battle of Austerlitz.

★**Michalská brána (St Michael's Gate)** – St Michael's is the only remaining gate in the city's medieval walls. After expansion, its original Gothic tower underwent refurbishments during the Baroque period. **St Michael's statue** surmounts it, soaring 51m/167ft above the ground. A fascinating Pharmaceutical Museum is nearby. The road to the south (Michalská extending into Ventúrska) is lined with exquisite houses and palaces from the Baroque and Renaissance periods, encircling the tiny Gothic Saint Catherine's chapel.

Bratislava – The Primate's Palace

★**Dóm sv. Martina** – The Gothic cathedral of St Martin stands on the southwest corner of old Bratislava. The road to SNP bridge separates it from the hill with its castle. The architects of St Stephen's cathedral (Stephansdom) in Vienna took part in the construction of St Martin's cathedral. Until 1580, it witnessed the coronations of Hungarian monarchs.

★**U Dobrého Pastiera** – This delightful Rococo house of **"The Good Shepherd"** now contains the Múzeum Bratislavskych Historickych Hodín (Museum of Historical Clocks), at the foot of the steep slope leading up to the castle. It evokes the charm of the old Jewish quarter that once stood there. The picturesque Jewish quarter extended between the castle and the cathedral. It had become insalubrious and the authorities tore it down to build the dual carriageway.

Hviezdoslavovo námestie – Many of the city's cultural institutions lie between the ramparts of the former town and the Danube. The 1886 National Theatre stands at the eastern end of the tree-lined **Hviezdoslav square**. It is one of the numerous buildings dating from the days of the Austro-Hungarian Empire by the Viennese architects, Fellner and Helmer. Near the river, the **Redoute** rises into view, a neo-classical building dating from 1912-13 that houses the Slovakian Philharmonic Orchestra. On the Danube waterfront itself is **Slovenské Narodná Galéria★★**, the Slovak National Gallery. The most interesting works are those dating from the late Middle Ages and the interwar period of the first Czechoslovakian Republic, including the bold and very colourful paintings of L'udovit Fulla and Martin Benka.

EXCURSIONS

★**Devin (Theben)** – *11km/6mi W*. From its rock, the old fortress of Devin overlooks the spot where the Morava meets the Danube. This medieval fortress is even more impressive than Bratislava castle. It served as a Celtic, Roman and Moravian stronghold and has been little more than a romantic ruin since the French invasion of 1809.

★**Malé Karpaty** – Vineyards spread to the foothills of the Little Carpathians from the gates of Bratislava. To the northeast there lies a string of wine-growing villages and small towns, including **Svätý Jur** (St. Georgen) with its famous early Renaissance **altarpiece**, **Pezinok** (Bösing) with its charming Little Carpathian Museum, and **Modra** (Modern), famous for its pottery and its wines.

EISENSTADT★

Eisenstadt has developed on the south slope of the Leithagebirge, forested like a huge park, the last outpost of the crystalline massifs of the eastern Alps. This marks the start of the great Central European plain. The mild climate makes it possible to grow vines, peaches, apricots and almonds.

The proximity of Vienna has checked the economic expansion of the town that, though small, is nevertheless the largest wine-trading community in the region. Since 1925, when Eisenstadt became the capital of Burgenland, its political and administrative role has imparted new life to the city. It is well situated about 15km/9mi from the shores of Lake Neusiedl, a major local tourist attraction.

The Austrian fief of the Esterházys – The Esterházys belong to one of the oldest noble Hungarian families. Good Catholics and loyal to the Habsburgs – which in Hungary was exceptional – they already owned the Eisenstadt and Forchtenstein domains in the mid 17C, as well as present-day Fertöd (formerly known as Esterháza) southeast of Lake Neusiedl, in Hungary.

Eisenstadt was the winter residence of this great family who made a major contribution to the establishment of Habsburg rule in Hungary. **Nicholas I** (1582-1645) ruled as Palatine and was made a Count by Ferdinand II; his son **Paul I** (1635-1713), also a Palatine, fought on the side of Leopold I who, in gratitude for his help during the Siege of Vienna by the Turks in 1683, made him a prince in 1697; despite this,

Nicholas I the Magnificent

Paul later opposed the Emperor by refusing to tax the Hungarian aristocracy; **Nicholas I the Magnificent** (1762-90) employed Haydn as musical director at Eisenstadt.

Haydn's town – Everything here calls to mind the brilliant composer who created the classical symphony and string quartet. For thirty years Joseph Haydn (1732-1809), born in Rohrau *(see Further afield, Petronell-Carnuntum)* divided his time between Eisenstadt and the Esterházy palace, nicknamed the "Hungarian Versailles", in the service of Prince Nicholas where he was the Court conductor and composer. Haydn's situation resembled that of a high-class prisoner in a golden cage, since he was not free and even had to don blue and gold livery before appearing before his patron and receiving his orders. Having an orchestra and a theatre at his disposal, Haydn worked without respite and achieved ever-growing fame. His remarkable works have made him one of the greatest composers in music history.

SIGHTS

★**Schloss Esterházy** (A) – *Esterházyplatz. Guided tours only (in German).*
Prince Paul Esterházy commissioned the Italian architect Carlo Martino Carlone to build him a palace appropriate to his rank. On the site of a medieval fortress built in the late 14C for the Kaniszai family, Carlone built a great quadrilateral structure between 1663 and 1672 around a main courtyard. At the time, an onion dome crowned each of the four corner towers.

From 1797 to 1805, the French architect Charles de Moreau updated the building in line with contemporary taste. The façade opposite the park acquired a neoclassical portico with Corinthian columns, and a terrace supported by Tuscan columns was built above the entrance gateway in the main façade. Terracotta busts portraying the ancestors of the Esterházy family and several kings of Hungary adorn this façade topped with a bell-tower and small onion dome.

Among other things, it is possible to purchase products of the royal Esterházy palace's vine-growing estate in the palace's boutique *(left in passageway to inner courtyard).* On the far side of the courtyard are the former royal stables, built in 1743.

Eisenstadt – Schloss Esterházy

Interior ⊘ – Visitors to the Esterházy exhibition will see numerous rooms with scenes devoted to the family (paintings, silver, furniture, library, etc.) The high point of the visit is undoubtedly the **Haydn Room**★, former ballroom and banqueting hall of the Esterházy princes; its marble floor was replaced by a wooden one in the 18C to improve the acoustics. In the noble setting of this huge hall decorated in the late 17C with stucco, *grisaille* (Kings of Hungary) and frescoes by Carpoforo Tencala (scenes from Greek mythology), Joseph Haydn conducted the orchestra of the princely court nearly every evening, often performing his own works. In terms of its acoustics, this hall is considered one of the best concert halls in the world. Among other events, it now serves as the site of the annual International Joseph Haydn Festival. The **Grand Tour Esterházy** also allows visitors to view the sumptuous rooms on the first floor and the palace chapel.

Anyone looking for a quiet spot of greenery after touring the palace should visit the Schlosspark with its romantic gardens around the **Leopoldinentempel**★ *(access through the Glorietteallee).*

CONCERTS AT SCHLOSS ESTERHÁZY

Between the end of April and the beginning of October, concert matinees (Haydn's works, as well as those by other important composers; sometimes presented in the historical costumes of the 18C) are presented in the Haydnsaal at Schloss Esterházy on Thursdays, Fridays and Saturdays. They start each day at 11am and last about 45min. Price €6.90.

Information and ticket reservations:
Schloss Esterházy Management Ges.mbH, Schloss Esterházy, A-7000 Eisenstadt; ☎ 0 26 82/7 19 30 00, Fax: 0 26 82/7 19 32 23, www.schloss-esterhazy.at

Haydn-Museum ⊘ (A) – *Haydngasse 21.* This is the building where the composer lived from 1766 to 1778. It now contains a small museum that depicts his life, his works, and his patrons. Exhibits include a copy of his death mask, his work piano (1780) and the console of the old organ from the Bergkirche *(see below)* on which Haydn and Beethoven played. Headphone installations, video presentations and PC stations give visitors the opportunity of also hearing Haydn's works.

Rathaus (B R) – *Hauptstrasse 35.* The Renaissance Town Hall acquired its current appearance in 17C. Its façade has a number of highly unusual features – pediments with cymas in counter-curves, three oriel windows, a semicircular gateway adorned by a boss with nail-head ornamentation and frescoes alternating with windows.

Domkirche (B) – This cathedral in late Gothic style was built in the 15C. It is dedicated to St Martin, patron saint of Burgenland. After renovation in 1960, only a splendid pulpit, the chancel and the organ are left of its late Baroque interior. There is a fine relief of the Mount of Olives (pre-1500) in the vestibule.

EISENSTADT

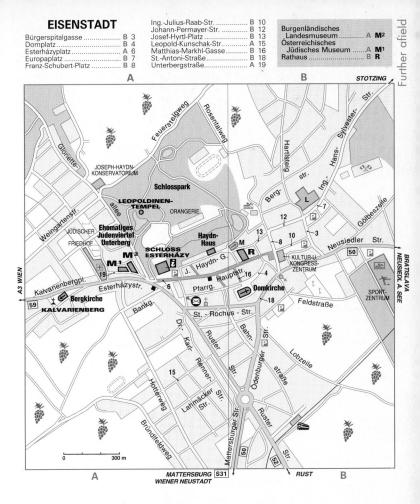

Unterberg: the old Jewish quarter (A) – Records state that there have been Jews in Eisenstadt since 1296. After Kaiser Leopold I had driven them from Vienna in 1671, many of them sought refuge in the Unterberg District, bounded by the Museumsgasse, Wolfgasse, Unterbergstrasse and Wertheimergasse. The ghetto still has the chain used to close off the streets, up until the end of the Jewish community in 1938, in order to maintain the peace of the Sabbath. It was once famous throughout the Empire for its Rabbinical School. Among the outstanding personalities who emerged from it were: Samson Wertheimer, who achieved great influence at the Habsburg Court as a financier, and Sandor Wolf, collector and patron of the arts.

An older Jewish cemetery with gravestones primarily from 17C and 18C in the Wertheimerstrasse is open to visitors. The newer Jewish cemetery (1875-1938) is located not far from it in the Carl-Moreau-Strasse. After the Second World War, mass graves opened here to receive the bodies of exhumed Jewish victims of forced labour.

"Court Jews"

Since medieval decrees forbade Christians to lend money at interest, several Jews ended up playing a major role in German and Austrian finances over the 17C and 18C. The Habsburgs appointed "Court Jews" who found themselves in a privileged position and who were given absolute freedom to trade as they wished. Among them was **Samuel Oppenheimer**, a banker from Speyer, who funded Prince Eugène of Savoy's campaigns against the Turks after being brought to Vienna by Charles of Lorraine. Another was Oppenheimer's son-in-law, **Samson Wertheimer**, who was a banker for Leopold, Joseph I and Karl VI. Although a number of Jews enjoyed commercial freedom, insecurity and oppression was more often the daily lot of the community as a whole.

OUR RECOMMENDATIONS FOR EISENSTADT

Parkhotel – *Joseph-Haydn-Gasse 38*, ☎ *0 26 82/75 32 50, Fax: 0 26 82/ 75 32 56, parkhotel.eisenstadt@utanet.at* Modern hotel close to the centre of the town. 28 rooms. Single rooms start at €43 .

Haydnbräu – *Pfarrgasse 22*, ☎ *0 26 82/6 15 61*, www.haydnbraeu.at House brewery with five locally brewed varieties of beer; also has regional cuisine. Guest garden adjoining the historic city wall. Main courses start at €6.90 .

Zum Eder – *Hauptstrasse 25*, ☎ *0 26 82/6 26 45*, www.zum-eder.at Inviting restaurant with a lovely winter garden. Fine selection of regional foods and wines. "Grüne Karte" (Green Menu) for vegetarians. Main courses start at €6 .

★**Österreichisches Jüdisches Museum** ⊙ (A M¹) – *Unterbergstr. 6*. The Jewish Museum is housed in Samson Wertheimer's charming old residence. The tour begins in the first storey with Wertheimer's former private **synagogue**, the current furnishings of which date back to the first half of the 19C. It is among the few synagogues in German-speaking regions that escaped destruction during the period of National Socialism. The exhibition includes Jewish ecclesiastical calendars portraying the individual stages in the life of devout Jews and the Jewish community of Eisenstadt. The conclusion of the tour is a memorial for Jews persecuted during the Third Reich. Interesting temporary exhibits are held here regularly on the ground floor.

Burgenländische Landesmuseum ⊙ (A M²) – *Museumsgasse 5*. This museum is devoted to the natural world, cultural history and folklore of Burgenland. One room commemorates **Franz Liszt**, who was born in Burgenland's Raiding *(see Further afield, Sopron, Excursions).* (Furnishings from Liszt's apartment in the Schottenhof are in Vienna.) In addition to the Wine Museum in the cellar, **Roman mosaics**★ (4C) from the Villa Rustica of Bruckneudorf *(north of Neusiedl)* can be viewed here.

★**Kalvarienberg and Bergkirche** ⊙ (A) – The peculiar architecture with the arched, concatenated roofs and the exposed position of the complex attracts attention from the distance. "Calvary Hill" was artificially created in the 18C to accommodate the **Way of the Cross**★. In a Baroque style, its 24 preserved Stations of the Cross, consisting of about 200 wood and stone figures, describe the Passion with great realism and drama. The **Gnadenkapelle** (Chapel of Grace), in which a statue of Maria has been venerated since 1711, is also part of this "Holy Mountain".

The **Bergkirche**, which was completed in 1803, contains the **Haydn Mausoleum**. After some errors – the skull was separated and only returned in 1954 – the composer's remains were laid to rest here.

Burg FORCHTENSTEIN★

Burgenland

Michelin map 926 fold 25

70km/44mi southeast of Vienna, via Wiener Neustadt and Mattersburg

The fortress of Forchtenstein, dominated by its massive 50m/164ft high keep, the oldest surviving part of the original construction, overlooks charming scenery from its site on a bluff in the Rosaliengebirge foothills.

The fortress was built at the beginning of the 14C by the counts of Mattersdorf, who had arrived from Spain in the 13C, and took on its present appearance in the 17C. The Esterházy family, owners of Forchtenstein since 1622, had the ring of bastions built because of the threat of Turkish invasion, and the living quarters converted into function rooms. After the early 18C the family moved to Schloß Eisenstadt and Forchtenstein was subsequently used as the family treasury, arsenal and archive.

TOUR ⊙

As part of the tour of the fortress, visitors view the **Fürstlich Esterházysche Sammlungen**★★, the extensive family collections which are particularly rich in 17C and 18C works. The majority of the items collected at Forchtenstein can still be seen in this setting, making the fortress with its 20 000 exhibits one of Europe's largest private collections open to the public.

Highlights of the collections include the **Schatzkammer** (the treasury, with art and precious objects, clocks and automata, silverware, chinoiseries, porcelain and library), an impressive testament to the Esterházys' passion for collecting things, with a number of magnificent and for the time very exotic items; the **Bildergalerie** (the picture gallery with family portraits and battle scenes); and **Waffenkammer** (the arsenal with Esterházy arms and armour, trophies from the wars against the French and the Prussians, and the "Turkish booty" from the field campaigns of Prince Paul Esterházy (between 1652 and 1713).

M. Hertlein/MICHELIN

Burg Forchtenstein

The Legend of Rosalia

Legend has it that a certain Giletus was the first lord of Forchtenstein. While he was away from home fighting in a war, his lady Rosalia imposed a harsh and cruel regime of discipline on the household. Upon his return, Giletus was informed of his wife's heavy hand by his confidants. He described them to his wife as if they had taken place elsewhere and asked her what her judgment would be on such a merciless mistress. Rosalia recommended a punishment to fit the crime and in accordance with this was thrown into the fortress dungeon, where she ended her days. Her restless spirit is said to have haunted the fortress until Giletus had the Rosalienkapelle built to appease it.

Follow the road further uphill from the fortress for about 4km/2.5mi to reach the **Rosalienkapelle** (1670), a chapel dedicated to Rosalia, curer of plagues, from where there is a good view as far as Eisenstadt and the Neusiedler See with the fortress of Forchtenstein in the foreground.

GUMPOLDSKIRCHEN
Niederösterreich
Population 3 266
Michelin map 926 fold 25 – 18km/11mi southwest of Vienna
Local map under Wienerwald

Amid the vineyards at the foot of the Anniger (alt 675m/2 217ft), this attractive village dating from the Middle Ages is famous for its white wines, which can be savoured in several *Heuriger*. Some of these taverns are in 16C houses. At the end of June and August, wonderful wine festivals are celebrated in the streets of Gumpoldskirchen. Surrounded by vineyards, the village stretches along Wiener Strasse. To appreciate its charm, go along the small Kirchengasse, signposted near the town hall.
At the top of the street beyond a pretty stone bridge is the "Gumpoldskirche", a hall-church (15C) dedicated to St Michael; its interior door is stamped with the cross of the Order of the Teutonic Knights, who had lived in the village since the mid-13C. The castle of the Order opposite the church now serves as a convent and meeting place.

A WALK THROUGH THE VINEYARDS

From Kirchenplatz, go along Kurzegasse below the castle. The path wanders through the vineyards and at regular intervals there are information panels about the origins and areas of cultivation of the various vines grown on this slope: Welschriesling (Austria, Hungary, Yugoslavia and Italy); Rheinriesling (Rhine Valley); Neuburger (Wachau, Burgenland and the spa region); Weisserburgunder (Burgundy); Rotgipfler (Gumpoldskirchen); Zierfandler or *Spätrot* (Gumpolds-kirchen); Blauerburgunder; Blauportugieser (Portugal and Austria).
At the top of Kalvarienberg is a chapel with a terrace. From here, there is a fine view of the plain.

Stift HEILIGENKREUZ★

Niederösterreich

Michelin map 426 fold 25 – 32km/19mi southwest of Vienna

Local map under Wienerwald

The Abbey of Heiligenkreuz was founded by Margrave Leopold III the Pious of Babenberg as a place of final rest for his dynasty. Under the influence of his son, Otto von Freising, who had joined the Cistercian Order, he invited twelve monks from Morimond, one of the subsidiaries of the Cîteaux monastery, to settle here. The foundation of the Stift Heiligenkreuz was laid on 11 September 1133. It was named for after a relic given to the Abbey by Duke Leopold V, a piece of the true cross.

This community of monks, actually the only Cistercian abbey that has existed without interruption since its foundation, is still very active to this day. It runs a seminary of theology and philosophy to train priests. It earns its income from agriculture and forestry and winemaking and tourism.

ABBEY TOUR ⊘

Although the abbey was founded in the 12C, most of the buildings date from the 17C, except the church (12C) and the cloister and adjoining buildings (13C). In the courtyard facing the church stands a **Trinity Pillar** by the Venetian artist Giovanni Giuliani (1663-1744) who was highly influential in Vienna and is buried in the church.

★**Church** – The west face is Romanesque. The three central windows and the absence of a tower on the façade are typically Cistercian; the doors were built later. The late-Romanesque nave was completed in 1187, while the Gothic chancel dates to about a century later. The furnishings were added in the 19C. The high altar in the chancel is a neo-Gothic construction. Behind it is a tabernacle containing the Holy Cross relic surmounted by a Greek-Orthodox cross. The rest of the decoration is Baroque: fine **stalls** by G Giuliani topped by carved saints of the order; paintings depicting Mary's reception in the heavens by Johann Michael Rottmayr.

Cloisters – The cloisters, on the south side of the sanctuary, date from the 13C. Their evolution may be traced by observing the Romanesque arches of the north wing and the Gothic arches of the south wing. Two sculptural ensembles by G Giuliani catch the eye here: *The Washing of Feet* and *The Sinner Anointing the Feet of Christ*. In front of the south wing is the **lavabo**, a small building (late 13C) containing a Renaissance fountain for washing which is both elegant and functional. The grey-black medieval **windows** depict members of the Babenberger dynasty.

St Anne's Chapel – This former library, which was used in the Middle Ages to keep the liturgical books, is now a chapel with an austere Baroque interior. The old library was called the *armarium* (arsenal), underlining the fact that the word was considered the most important means to spread the faith.

Chapter-house – This square room in which the abbot is elected, where novices take holy orders, and where the "chapters" of the Benedictine rule and regulations are read, houses the tombs of the Babenbergs. Mural paintings depict each member of the dynasty. The tomb with the most ornate cover is that of Frederick II the Belligerent. It was damaged by pillaging Turks.

The Cistercian Order

This reformed order of the Benedictines derives its name from the monastery of Cîteaux in France founded in 1098 by Robert de Molesmes. Under the leadership of Bernard de Clairvaux, the order spread its influence quickly – by the time of the saint's death in 1153, the order boasted 350 settlements throughout Europe. St Bernard forbade the levy of tithes, the acceptance or purchase of land and demanded strict compliance with Benedictine rules.

These severe principles are reflected in the stark architecture of the Cistercians, with unembellished churches (no bell-towers, just a ridge turret, no colourful stained-glass windows). On the other hand, even more effort was put into careful designing and building of edifices, whose beauty arises from the balance of their dimensions and the clarity of their lines. The strict artistic asceticism did not really hold out over the centuries, so nowadays one does find paintings and statues in Cistercian churches.

The *Carta caritatis* decreed in the year 1115 is still obeyed. Today the order boasts some 300 abbeys for priests and nuns around the world.

Chapel of the Dead – The erstwhile parlatorium, the only room in which the monks were allowed to speak, is now used to lay out the dead monks before burial. The decoration of the chapel is by Giuliani. The *Dancing Skeletons* may appear macabre to some, but they do represent the Christian hope that death is not the end and has therefore lost its power to instil fear.

Fraterie – The Fraterie was the monk's workshop during the Middle Ages. Some of the painting on the ashlars still dates to the 13C.

Sacristy – A small yard leads to the Sacristy. This prettily decorated room with an ancient lavabo niche, is executed in 18C style and shows all the typical features of the Rococo age. The wonderful **sacristy cupboards** with fine marquetry made in the early 19C display the considerable artistry of lay brothers. In the little churchyard in the village lies the tomb of

Heiligenkreuz Abbey

Maria Vetsera *(see Mayerling)*, with the words: *"Like a flower, man blossoms only to be cut down."* As suicide was mentioned in the death certificate, Vetsera had to be buried secretly by cover of night in the Heiligenkreuz cemetery.

KLOSTERNEUBURG★

Niederösterreich
Population 30 500
Michelin map 926 fold 12 – 13km/8mi north of Vienna

In 1113, after marrying Agnes, the Salian daughter of Emperor Henry IV, the Babenberg Margrave Leopold III transferred his residence from Melk to Neuenburg. He built his fortress on the heights of what probably had been a Roman settlement. He founded the Klosterneuburg Abbey there in 1114, which has been a monastery run by the Augustinian canons ever since 1133.
In 1296, Klosterneuburg acquired the status of a city. It prospered and gradually grew into the small modern bustling town of today.

ABBEY TOUR

Conducted tours of the abbey in German only (about 1hr). There is a separate tour of the Stiftsmuseum that is only guided when requested.

Stiftsplatz – This square gives access to the abbey and the Baroque wing. In the middle stands a Gothic Lichtsäule (Lantern Column) of 1381 featuring scenes from the Passion. Opposite the side entrance of the abbey church is Sebastianskapelle (St Sebastian's chapel) containing Albert II's altarpiece (1438), one of its panels showing the oldest view of Vienna cathedral. To the right is the chapter-house, and on the right again is the wine-tasting room *(Vinothek)* housing the famous *Tausendeimerfass* (thousand-bucket barrel) made in 1704 with a capacity of 56 000 litres. Every year on St Leopold's Day (15 Nov), it serves as a ramp for the traditional barrel-rolling competition. The Klosterneuburg Abbey wines (more than 100ha/250 acres of vineyards) are famous for their outstanding quality.

Stiftskirche – *For those not taking part in the guided tour, the interior is visible through the railings.* The three-aisled Romanesque abbey church was begun in 1114 and completed a few days before Leopold III's death in 1136. Over the centuries it underwent many alterations. Between 1634 and 1645, the Genoese

243

Klosterneuburg – Vaulting in the abbey church

B. Kaufmann

architect Giovanni Battista Carlone and Andrea de Retti refurbished it in the Baroque style. In 1879, Friedrich von Schmidt, architect of Vienna's Town Hall, restored its medieval appearance; both towers are now in the neo-Gothic style. The **interior★** of the church is almost entirely Baroque (1680-1702 and 1723-30). It conveys harmony and grandeur owing to the excellence of the artists involved. Georg Greiner painted the **frescoes** on the vault about 1689. They depict the Turks besieging Klosterneuburg, the Fathers of the Church, the Coronation of the Virgin Mary, and other scenes from the life of the Virgin Mary; portrayals of the Assumption (chancel and apse) are by Johann Michael Rottmayr. The Spaz brothers carved the decoration on the six side altars (early 18C). Matthias Steindl made the high altar (*Birth of the Virgin* by Johann Georg Schmidt), the copper sounding board above the marble pulpit and the magnificent **choir stalls** (1723) bearing 24 Habsburg coats of arms. The great Baroque organ dating from 1642 is famous for its original Baroque sound created by the exclusive use of tin pipes. Among other musicians, Anton Bruckner enjoyed playing it.

Kloster – Built in 13C and 14C, this is a fine example of early Gothic architecture with Burgundian influences. The former well-house contains a seven-branch bronze **candelabra**, which is worth viewing. This work from the first half of 12C comes from Verona and symbolizes the Tree of Jesse. However, according to the founding legend of the abbey in which Leopold came across his wife Agnes' lost bridal veil after nine years on an elderberry bush and then founded the abbey at that spot, this work of art is called *Sambucus* (Latin for elderberry). The Leopoldskapelle (St

Nicolas of Verdun

Nicolas of Verdun was a goldsmith and enameller from Lorraine. This is virtually all that is known about him. However, his name only appears on two objects: St Mary's reliquary in Tournai cathedral and this masterpiece in Klosterneuburg, which ranks among the finest achievements of medieval art. The long sides of the reliquary of the Three Wise Men in Cologne cathedral (1180-1230) are also attributed to him.

Leopold's chapel) is highlighted by the glowing colours of its 14C **stained-glass windows★**. It contains the tomb of Leopold III who was canonised in 1485. His relics rest in a reliquary that stands on the famous Verduner Altar (Verdun altarpiece) *(see below)*. The Freisingkapelle (Freising chapel) houses the recumbent figure of Berthold von Wehingen, Bishop of Freising who died in 1410.

★★**Verdun Altarpiece** – In 1181, Prior Wernher commissioned Nicolas to enamel the abbey lectern. The artist made 45 enamelled panels of gilded metal using the champlevé technique. In 1331 after a fire, the provost had the work turned into an altarpiece by adding six plaques and four painted panels as the reverse side *(see Stiftsmuseum below)*. The altarpiece comprises three levels depicting scenes from the Old Testament *(upper and lower levels)* and the New Testament *(middle level)*. Scenes from the New Testament are supplemented by events that took place *ante legem*, before enactment of Mosaic law, and after it *(sub legem)*. To the left of the central panel, for instance, one sees from the top downwards, *The Crossing of the Red Sea* (parable of baptism), *The Baptism of Christ* and *The Sea on the Back of 12 Oxen* (pool in King Solomon's temple). The centre panel of the altar shows *The Crucifixion*, symbolic of the Passion of Christ.

★**Baroque Wing** – After the loss of Spain through the Treaty of Utrecht (1713), Charles VI, Maria-Theresa's father, concentrated his efforts on Vienna, where he commissioned the construction of many representative buildings. In 17C and 18C central Europe, when the middle classes had not yet succeeded in making their presence felt as an autonomous social class, ostentation as an ideal was at its peak. In 1720, there were about 200 castles, palaces and belvederes on the outskirts of Vienna, and twice as many 20 years later! To represent the power of a centralising empire, Charles VI decided to turn the abbey into no less than an Austrian Escorial. This edifice, which was begun in 1730, would naturally symbolize temporal power as opposed to the abbey church embodying spiritual power; the dual nature of the architecture would express the alliance of the two powers, as in the Spanish *Escorial*. Josef Emmanuel Fischer von Erlach was in charge of the project. It was grandiose and included a number of wings surmounted by nine domes. However, the son of the great Johann Bernard Fischer von Erlach was working on other large-scale enterprises (the Hofburg Winter Riding School and the National Library, among others). The Milanese architect Donato Felice d'Allio was summoned and had to face numerous obstacles, mainly of a financial nature. The last difficulty, however, proved insurmountable: the emperor's death in 1740. Work was interrupted, and Maria-Theresa disliked the huge unfinished palace-monastery. In fact, it represents only a quarter of the original plan: a Baroque building with one courtyard and two domes (crowned by the Roman emperor's crown and the Austrian archducal crown) to which the architect Josef Kornhäusel added a wing around 1840 to close off the courtyard.

Kaiserzimmer – The imperial apartments are reached via the extraordinary Kaiserstiege (imperial staircase, 1723) left undecorated, apart from four angels playing music on the upper landing. Two of the rooms are especially interesting: the **Brussels Tapestry Room** (18C, scenes from the novel *Télémaque* by Fénelon) and the **Marble Hall** with frescoes by Daniel Gran representing the Glory of the House of Habsburg on the cupola.

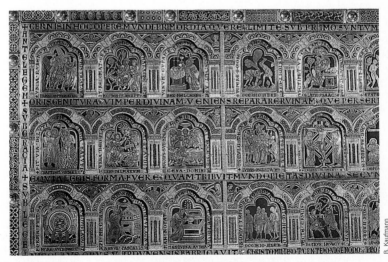

Klosterneuburg – Verdun altarpiece (detail)

B. Kaufmann

Bibliothek – Austria's largest private library possesses 200 000 books, 1 250 manuscripts and 850 incunabula.

★**Stiftsmuseum** ⊘ – The Abbey Museum is above the imperial apartments and displays some remarkable objects such as the **four panels**★ by Rueland Frueauf and the reverse side of the Verdun Altarpiece (1331), as well as a collection of Gothic panels. In addition, there are special exhibitions organised each year.

ADDITIONAL SIGHTS

Martinstrasse – North of Stadtplatz with the Trinity Column, this narrow rising street presents a picture of idyllic calm. It is lined by fine residential houses, such as the Martinschloss (No 34, now a hotel), and leads to **Martinskirche**, the oldest church in Klosterneuburg (first mentioned around 800), which contains fine Baroque decorations.

★**Sammlung Essl** ⊘ – *An der Donau-Au 1.* In 1999, the exhibition house designed by the Tyrolean architect Heinz Tesar for the collection of Mr and Mrs Essl opened its doors to the public. The building (depository, permanent exhibition and temporary exhibitions), which had been constructed especially for the collection of more than 4 000 works of art, attracts attention because of its varied architecture. Its changing exhibitions present post-1945 art with emphasis on Austrian painting. Created without the help of any public funds, this private museum provides a virtually complete, unique insight into Austrian post-war and contemporary art, as well as presenting it within an international context.

If arriving by car, it is possible and pleasant to return to Vienna via Leopoldsberg and Kahlenberg (see Outside the Ring, Döbling).

Schloss LAXENBURG
Niederösterreich
Michelin map 926 fold 25 – 15km/9mi south of Vienna
Local map under Wienerwald

A former imperial summer residence, Laxenburg estate lies near foothills of the Wienerwald, where Maximilian I hunted herons with a hawk. Initially, Albert II the Lame acquired the land in 1340. There, his son, Albert III, built a fortress, surrounded by water, where his wife, the beautiful Beatrix, liked to stay. Later, Laxenburg greatly appealed to Karl VI and court festivities soon replaced the delights of hunting. Today, the estate comprises three palaces and an immense park with trees hundreds of years old, where many Viennese families enjoy walking on Sundays.

CASTLE TOUR

Blauer Hof – *Schlossplatz.* The "blue palace" has yellow ochre roughcast walls, a colour known as "Schloss Schönbrunn yellow". It probably takes its name from its first architect, the Dutchman Sebastiaan Bloe. The architect Nikolaus Pacassi altered it, adding the main courtyard and a small theatre. The palace had its heyday in Maria Theresa's reign and Crown Prince Rudolf was born there on 21 August 1858. The back opens onto the park.

Pfarrkirche Laxenburg – *Schlossplatz.* Between 1693 and 1699, Christian Alexander Oedtl was commissioned by Leopold I to build this church on the site of an earlier sanctuary that had been destroyed by the Turks in 1683. Its towers date from 1722. Inside, there is a fine Baroque **pulpit** of gilded wood by Johann Baptist Straub. The frescoes on the dome are probably based on a drawing by Johann Michael Rottmayr; they depict Jerusalem the Celestial City.

Kaiserbahnhof – *Herzog-Albrecht-Strasse.* The Laxenburg imperial train station, built in 1847, is the only preserved Biedermeier station in the entire world. It is now used as a communications centre and event venue and houses a restaurant.

Park ⊘ – *Entrance through Hofstrasse. Car park opposite the entrance.* During a visit to his sister, Marie Antoinette, the future Joseph II visited Ermenonville park. On his return from France, he had this 250ha/617 acre park laid out in the English style. Franz I added a large lake, where pedalos and electric boats now glide through the water.
Bearing right after the entrance, you reach **Altes Schloss**, the old palace, where in 1713 Karl VI issued the Pragmatic Sanction that enabled his daughter Maria Theresa to succeed to the throne.
On the island *(passage: €0.44)* in the large lake stands the **Franzensburg**, an early 19C neo-Gothic fortress by Michael Riedl. Its romantic appeal has decreased since the opening of a café with a terrace displaying multicoloured sunshades that seem somewhat incongruous beneath a crenellated façade. 37 Habsburg busts are tucked away in niches in the interior courtyard.

MAYERLING

Lower Austria
Michelin map 426 fold 25 – 36km/22mi southwest of Vienna
Local map under Wienerwald

At the end of the 19C Vienna Mayerling became the scene of a tragedy that moved the whole world.

The death of the Crown Prince – The silence coming from the imperial court at the time about the events of January 1889 gave rise to a host of wild rumours. One representation of those events – albeit a controversial one – did become the officially accepted one:

In 1888, Archduke Rudolf, the only son of Franz Josef and Empress Elisabeth, and the successor to the throne of the Dual Monarchy, turned 30. The Austrian nobility shuddered at Rudolf's sympathies for the parliamentary opposition in Hungary and his liberal ideas. The Church attacked him for his lack of religious piety and for his less than harmonious marriage to Stephanie of Belgium. His somewhat unconventional private life also made him something of a noticeable personality. At the ball of the German Embassy, he met Mary Vetsera, fell in love with her, and that love was reciprocated.

When the Kaiser got wind of the affair, he decided to put an end to it. A violent argument took place on January 28, 1889, during which Franz Josef informed his son about Pope Leo XIII's refusal to annul Rudolf's marriage, adding that he himself did not agree with the idea of divorce. He also demanded that his son reveal the names of the Hungarian conspirators who were plotting against him, the Kaiser. The following day, Rudolf failed to show up for dinner at the Hofburg. Instead, he retired to the little hunting castle he had purchased in 1886 in Mayerling. With his mind made up not to divulge the names of his Hungarian friends, and tired of his life, which seemed to be a fabric of insurmountable problems, he chose suicide as the only way out. On 30 January the two lovers were found dead. Mary Vetsera had been the first to die. Before shooting himself with a revolver, Rudolf wrote a letter to his mother, one to his wife, and a third to a long-standing friend, Mizzie Caspar.

Archduke Rudolf

ROGER-VIOLLET

KRONPRINZ-RUDOLF-GEDENKSTÄTTE ⊙

Follow the signs for "Ehemaliges Jagdschloss – Karmel St. Josef":

After the death of Archduke Rudolf and Mary Vetsera, Kaiser Franz Josef had the former hunting lodge turned into a convent for the Barefooted Carmelite nuns. A church in neo-Gothic style now stands at the site of the shocking tragedy. The fresco on the altar represents St Joseph, patron saint of the imperial family, St Rudolf the martyr, name saint of the royal prince, St Elizabeth and St Leopold, patron saints of Austria. In the chapel, the altar from the Empress' palace at Corfu, the Emperor's prie-dieu and a *Mater Dolorosa* bearing the features of the Empress. The memorial rooms are adjacent to the church and contains some of the original furniture from the hunting lodge and an extensive documentation of the tragedy.

MÖDLING

Niederösterreich
Population 20 365
Michelin map 926 fold 25 – 12km/7mi southwest of Vienna
Local map under Wienerwald

Mödling was founded in the 10C. Although it suffered severe war damage during the Second World War, it is now a pleasantly restored small town. Three composers lived here and enjoyed its quiet ambiance: Ludwig van Beethoven *(Hauptstrasse 79, in 1818 and 1819; Achsenaugasse 6, in 1820)*, who worked there on the first pages of his *Missa Solemnis*, Arnold Schönberg *(Bernhardgasse 6)* and Anton von Webern *(Neusiedler Strasse 58)*.

SIGHTS

In addition to a traditional Pestsäule (Plague Column, *Freiheitsplatz*) in the form of a wreathed column, Mödling possesses a charming pedestrian precinct *(Fleischgasse and Elisabethstrasse)* that is a mixture of several architectural styles. The town contains some historic monuments such as the ruins of an 11C castle *(Brühlerstrasse)*, two 15C churches (St Othmar and St Aegyd) and a 16C town hall *(Schrannenplatz)*.

From Hauptstrasse, take Herzoggasse, which extends into Pfarrgasse.

Pfarrkirche St Othmar – Building began on this late Gothic style hall-church in 1454 and was completed in 1523. The church stands on a small hill overlooking the town. After suffering damage by the Turks in 1529 and 1683, the building acquired 12 columns to support its vault, symbolising the number of the apostles. On the left is the St John of Nepomuk altar with a painting by Brandl (1725).
Outside, the Pantaleon's chapel dates from the 2nd half of the 12C. This small Romanesque chapel has a charming portal and an apsis with 12C frescoes. Originally, the crypt served as a charnel-house for the chapel .

NEUSIEDLER SEE★★

Burgenland
Michelin map 926 fold 26 – 50km/31mi southeast of Vienna

Neusiedler Lake (alt 115m/376ft), which has shallow, cloudy, relatively warm, and slightly salty water, is the only example in Central Europe of a steppe lake and is one of the most interesting sights in Burgenland. The word "steppe" has a strange ring in a region so near Vienna. Yet the Hungarian puszta starts here, at the edge of the first foothills of the Alpine chain, the Leithagebirge. Of the area it covers, 320km²/121sq mi, more than half consists of the 2.5m/8ft to 3m/10ft girdle of reeds, which surrounds the lake. The southern end of the lake, which is extensively silted up, is in Hungary (about 1/5th of the total area). Its depth varies from 1m/3.28ft to 1.5m/5ft, never exceeding 2m/6.5ft. The lake has no permanent outflow; its only tributary, the Wulka in the northwest, is of negligible importance as the volume of evaporation is four times the quantity of water that flows in. Thus, it is fed mainly by rain and the melting of snow, as well as underground water tables. Very occasionally, the lake dries up completely only to reappear later as mysteriously as it vanished. Between 1855 and 1868, the lake even dried up completely for years.

THE LAKE AND ITS ENVIRONS

Although Neusiedler Lake is reminiscent of the Camargue or the Danube Delta, its shores are quite distinctive. On the eastern side is a plateau, Parndorfer Platte, and a steppe plain strewn with small lakes, the Seewinkel, which is gradually being taken over by orchards and crops, while to the west are two mountain chains, the Leithagebirge visible behind Donnerskirchen and Purbach, and the slopes of Ruster Höhenzug overlooking Rust and Oggau. At the foot of these uplands, vines, maize, fruit trees (even almonds), and market gardens flourish in the rich ochre soil and gentle climate.

A prized wine-growing area – The vineyards are terraced on the slopes or lie scattered throughout the plain. They enjoy plenty of sunshine and produce much-acclaimed vintages, the wines of Rust, Mörbisch, Gols and Illmitz being the most famous for their bouquet. This is why, in 1524, the wine-growers of Rust received royal recognition for the quality of their wine. By virtue of the royal warrant, they are entitled to display the arms of the town on the enormous vats in their vaulted cellars. In all the villages around the Austrian side of the lake, that is from Mörbisch to Apetlon, there are **Buschenschenken**. These are open-air cafés, embellished by lilacs in spring, where visitors may enjoy for the most part a fruity white wine.

Vienna's "seaside" – Apart from Podersdorf which is directly on the water, nearly every village by the lake has a small bathing beach, reached by a causeway through the rushes. For a closer look, excursion boats ply the lake's waters.

Owing to its proximity to Vienna, the Neusiedler See attracts in summer all those who care for water sports (sailing, windsurfing, rowing, swimming) and in winter those keen on ice sports, particularly windskating.

A NATIONAL PARK

Dating from 1992, the Neusiedler See-Seewinkel National Park straddles the border and is jointly administered by Austria and Hungary. It aims to preserve the fauna and flora typical of the Alpine and Eurasian areas.

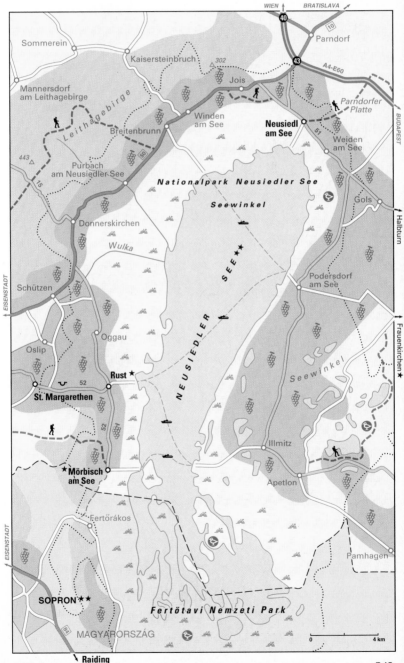

4Further afield

Nightingale

Bee-eater

Whinchat

Little ringed plover

Waterfowl

Grey partridge

Coot

Black-tailed godwit

Great white heron

250

Long-eared owl

Shrike

White-spotted
bluethroat

Common tern

Penduline tit

Avocet

Purple heron

Great bustard

M. Guillou/MICHELIN

An eldorado for botanists – With the first warmth of spring, myriad flowers start to open in this ancient, apparently arid Roman land of Pannonia. First to appear, towards February-March, is the spring-like yellow pheasant's-eye *(Adonis vernalis)* with its finely cut golden foliage. In season, there are displays of elegant dwarf irises *(Iris pumila)* no higher than 15cm/6in, hybrid lilies *(Iris spuria)* with their sword-shaped corolla, a tall mauve-tinted variety of clary *(Salvia nemorosa)*, slender purple mullein known as king's candle *(Verbascum phoenicium)*, luminous blue Austrian flax *(Linum ostriaca)*, superb salmon asters *(Aster canus)* indigenous to this region, and thousands of rosy stars *(Aster tripolium)* which in autumn carpet the sandy soil. Volumes would not suffice to list all the plant life on the lake shores.

A paradise for birds – In the dense thickets of reeds around Neusiedler See and the lakes at Seewinkel, there is an extraordinary variety of aquatic fauna ranging from Aesculapius' wild grass snake to the southern Russian tarantula. The region provides an exceptional natural habitat and breeding ground for migratory birds. The only breaks on this otherwise flat horizon are the observation posts for ornithologists watching for 250 species of birds. Thus, there is some chance of seing a purple heron, concealed in the midst of aquatic plants, a bee-eater with its multicoloured feathers, a little ringed plover, nesting on the ground, an elegant avocet, its beak slashing into the water as it looks for food, a little bluethroat, and even a great bustard moving in groups with its head up *(see double page illustration)*.

FROM NEUSIEDL TO MÖRBISCH

Go to Neusiedl by the A 4-E 60 motorway and leave by exit 43.

Neusiedl am See – The little town which gave its name to the lake has some interesting sights: a ruined 13C fortress, a 15C church near the Town Hall, and the **Pannonisches Heimatmuseum** *(Kalvarienbergstr. 40)* ⊙. This Pannonian Museum displays objects relating to the region's popular crafts and traditions.

Leave Neusiedl northwestwards on the Eisenstadt road. Bear left 2.5km/1.5mi after Donnerskirchen for Rust.

★**Rust** – This affluent and attractive town is famous for its storks' nests to which the birds return every year, and for its wine. The town has many interesting sights: delightful Renaissance and Rococo façades with corbelling and impressive carved doorways, pleasantly arcaded inner courtyards and partly preserved fortifications. Because of its considerable architectural heritage, the old town is classed as a historic monument.

Fischerkirche – *West side of Rathausplatz.* A wall surrounds the fortified Fishermen's Church with thirteen loopholes. It is an irregular building with remarkable 12C and 15C **frescoes★**. In the aisle, the three statues on the Magi Altar (early Baroque support, statues in Gothic style) are a major work. There is a fine 1705 organ. A causeway leads through the reeds to the **bathing resort** *(see Practical information)* and the curious lakeside dwellings. These *Pfahlbauten* are amazing wooden houses resting on piles, linked by pontoons. Tucked away in the reeds, their thatched roofs are not visible from a distance.

Rust is the ideal point of departure for a brief detour to St. Margarethen (9km/5.5mi round trip).

St. Margarethen – In summer, the old Roman quarries in this area are the natural setting for an open-air Passion Play held every five years since 1961 *(next performance is in 2006)*. It features hundreds of amateur performers. In addition, an Opera Festival has been held before this backdrop every summer since 1995 *(see Practical information, Calendar of events)*. St Margarethen's famous sandstone was used for the construction of renowned Viennese buildings: the Stephansdom, the Hofburg, the Karlskirche and Schloss Schönbrunn.

★**Mörbisch am See** – This is the last village on the western shore of the lake before the Hungarian border. It has great charm with its colourful and picturesque alleys running at right angles off the main street. The houses are whitewashed and nearly all have an outdoor staircase with a porch above it. They form a delightful and cheerful scene, with their brightly painted doors and shutters, bunches of maize hanging along the walls, flower-decked balconies and windows.

East of the village, the Seestrasse leads across marshes and reed-beds to a pier and a bathing resort on the lake, as well as to the site of the summer festival, with its floating stage *(see Practical information)*. It is the setting for performances of Viennese and Hungarian operettas *(see Practical information, Calendar of events)*.

By renting a bicycle and provided you have a passport, it is possible to visit the Hungarian side, in Nemzeti Park, by crossing the border at Fertörakos (see Practical information). It is also an excellent opportunity for visiting Sopron (formerly Ödenburg), a small Magyar community with a town centre dating from the 15C.

Between Austria and Hungary

The treaty of Saint-Germain-en-Laye turned parts of three counties in western Hungary over to Austria thus creating today's Burgenland. This explains that certain Magyar influence perceptible in Austria's youngest federal state. In Siegendorf, Trausdorf an der Wulka and **Apetlon** for instance, there are still *tamburizza* orchestras. (The tamburizza is a stringed instrument that recalls the Russian balalaika).

In fact, Burgenland still displays a mosaic of ethnic minorities: Hungarians, Rom and Sinté gypsies, people descended from Croats who fled the Turks, are all part of the social fabric here.

These minorities settled in Burgenland, particularly around the lake, because the region formed part of a defensive belt deliberately depopulated by Hungarian sovereigns who had bordered their kingdom by a no-man's-land.

PERCHTOLDSDORF
Niederösterreich
Population 14 159
Michelin map 926 fold 25 – 8km/5mi southwest of Vienna
Map under Wienerwald

The Marktplatz is worth discovering in the muffled silence of falling snow while drinking a warming *Glühwein* (mulled claret) from one of the miniature chalets open during the Advent and Christmas season. It is a typically Viennese winter scene. **Hugo Wolf** lived in this wine-growing village *(Brunnengasse 26)* and its centre has much to offer throughout the year.

SIGHTS

Marktplatz – At the centre of the square stands a fine **Pestsäule★** (1713) (Plague Column) decorated with eight sculptures by Johann Bernhard Fischer von Erlach. These columns, so numerous in the area, are a reminder that the plague once destroyed a major part of the European population. Vienna and its surroundings suffered four particularly disastrous epidemics in 1348, 1629, 1679 and 1714,

Close-up of the Plague Column on Marktplatz

causing over 30 000 deaths each time. People erected columns as votive monuments to thank God for having brought the plague to an end; the most famous of these is the votive Dreifaltigkeitsäule (Trinity Column) in Vienna's Graben. Johann Bernhard Fischer von Erlach built part of it. He had studied in Rome and greatly admired Francesco Borromini's work *(see City Centre and the Ring, Stephansdom District)*.

The town hall *(Marktplatz 10)* is in a late Gothic style (end of 15C) and houses three small museums.

On the north side, the Marktplatz is closed off by St Augustine's church and Perchtoldsdorfer Turm. This massive square tower, dating from between 1450 and 1521, has sides measuring about 13m/42ft and rises 59.5m/195ft from the ground.

Pfarrkirche zum Hl. Augustinus – St Augustine's hall-church, begun in 1435, contains some interesting works. The entrance is through the south porch, which displays *The Mount of Olives* (1511 polychrome relief). In the porch is **The Death of the Virgin★** (1449 polychrome relief). This work is noteworthy, because the Virgin is lying down, a typically Byzantine concept. Western art usually depicts the Virgin as dying with a candle in Her hand. A monumental Baroque high altar (c 1700) dominates the interior. On either side of the altarpiece, there are four statues of the patron saints of the imperial *Länder*, from left to right: Joseph (Styria), Domitian (Carinthia), Florian (Upper Austria) and Leopold (Lower Austria). To the left of the high altar, the cabinet dates from the 15C.

Outside, to the west, the remains of the Herzogsburg (dukes' palace) are visible. It dates from the 11C to the 15C and now houses a cultural centre. To the south is Martinikapelle, built between 1512 and 1520.

Almost opposite the church is Wienergasse.

Spitalskirche – *Wienergasse*. Duchess Beatrix von Zollern founded this church between 1406 and 1419.

PETRONELL-CARNUNTUM★

Niederösterreich
Population 1 200
Michelin map 926 fold 13 – 35km/22mi east of Vienna

On the site of this and the neighbouring town of **Bad Deutsch-Altenburg**, excavations have led to the discovery of numerous interesting remains from the garrison that the Romans established on the Danube during the 1C. At the beginning of the following century, this garrison became the seat of the governor of Upper Pannonia.

Origins – The ancient Illyrian-Celtic town of Carnuntum was built on the banks of the Danube during the 1C and was also on the amber route linking Italy to the Baltic. There is little doubt about the exact date of the Roman settlement on this site. The garrison is thought to date from the year 15 AD, when the Emperor Tiberius (14-37 AD) decided to send to the Danube his dreaded 15th *Apollinaris* legion to quell the Marcomani.

The capital of Upper Pannonia – Pannonia corresponded approximately to modern Hungary. Augustus conquered it after the rebellion of 16 BC. It became a Roman province starting in 9 BC. The camp quickly grew in size owing to the establishment of numerous veterans, who brought their families and attracted shopkeepers and traders. During the first decade of the 2C, Carnuntum became the capital of Upper Pannonia, the military, political and economic centre of the region. During the reign of Emperor Hadrian (117-138), it acquired the status of *municipium*, which meant that all its inhabitants became Roman citizens.

In 171 AD, Emperor **Marcus Aurelius** came to Carnuntum in person – according to tradition, this is where he wrote his *Meditations* – to drive back the Marcomani and the Quades, whom he eventually defeated in 174. Although it had suffered extensive damage from these military campaigns, the town was rebuilt and enjoyed a new period of prosperity. Septimus Severus was chosen to be emperor in 192, before which he had been commander-in-chief of Upper Pannonia, which is why Carnuntum immediately acquired the status of *colonia*. In 261, during a phase of complete military anarchy, the city, in a spirit of independence, even elected its commander as emperor, a man by the name of Caius Publius Regalianus. His soldiers killed him a short time later. Under the emperor Diocletian (284-305) the empire was divided into two sections (western and eastern). On 11 November 308, three years after Diocletian's abdication, the imperial conference for the preservation of the empire took place in Carnuntum. Licinius became augustus of the western section, while Galerius remained at the head of the eastern section. In 375, Emperor Valentinius I died. This marked the start of the great migratory invasions, in which the Goths – the Quades to be precise – and then the Huns plundered and finally destroyed the city in 407.

★ARCHÄOLOGISCHER PARK CARNUNTUM ⊙

Information Centre, Hauptstrasse 296 in Petronell-Carnuntum. An 18.5km/11.5mi "Roman culture path" called the **Via Carnuntina** *runs through the entire park (for hikers and cyclists).*

In this archaeological park, the Roman excavations extend over nearly 8km²/3sq mi and are contained in two open-air museums. They began in 1885, although the idea originated with Wolfgang Lazius who visited the area in the 16C. He was the author of the chronicle *Vienna Austriae* and had come to make an inventory of votive altars. His excavations brought to light the camp of the 15th legion (including its hospital).

In the **Petronell open-air museum**, the foundations of residential and merchants' dwellings, thermal baths and canals have been excavated; there is also a reconstruction of a temple to Diana, a reproduction of a Roman market stand, and a kitchen from that era. The visit can be rounded off with a look at an active excavation, a tent containing games, the "Roman café", a Roman construction crane, and an observation tower. The civilian town (or, more accurately, the colony) of Septimus Severus, which is thought to have numbered up to 50 000 inhabitants, contains the ruins of the "Great Thermal Bath". Also known as the "Palace Ruins", these remains are some of the largest remnants of ancient times so far discovered north of the Alps. They were altered in 308 to accommodate the imperial Roman conference; the rooms for changing and resting are easily identifiable, as are the small and large pools and the plumbing for the warm water supply. The Amphitheatre II, with a capacity of 13 000 spectators, is an elliptical building with two gateways. The southern gateway includes a basin, which is probably an early Christian baptistery. Much further to the south, the 20m/65ft **Heidentor** (Pagans' Gate), one of the original four Carnuntum city gates, has become the symbol of the excavation sites. The **Amphitheatre I open-air museum** contains the elliptical arena now known as Amphitheatre I; it measures 72m x 44m/78yd x 47yd and has rows of seating for 6 000 to 8 000 (in the centre there is a rectangular basin to which a canal supplies water for cleaning the arena).

Rundkapelle – *By No 173 Hauptstrasse in Petronell-Carnuntum. Entrance through the car park of Marcus Aurelius Hotel.* This circular chapel stands on the right of the road and is unusual for its pointed roof and semicircular chancel grafted on its east end. Outside, the building has a sober display of columns and arcades resting on ornamental brackets. The small carved **tympanum★** above the entrance represents the Baptism of Christ; this is perhaps an indication that the chapel was originally a baptistery. On the left, there is John the Baptist in his sheepskin; in the centre, Christ in a loincloth is surmounted by the dove of the Holy Ghost, the embodiment of divinity; on the right a winged Angel holds the chrismal cloth for covering the anointed part. Artists often depicted the Jordan as a person, but here it appears in the form of semicircular incisions; in accordance with the iconography of Christian art, it is almost dried up. The chapel is privately owned (containing the crypt of the Abensperg-Traun family), and can thus not be viewed from the inside.

Pfarrkirche der Hl. Petronilla – This church stands in the centre of the village, in the middle of the cemetery. Bishop Altmann of Passau founded it in 1078. Although the Turks damaged it in 1529, it still retains an attractive Romanesque chevet.

Go to Bad Deutsch-Altenburg; turn left just before the junction with route 9. Leave the car beside the park which borders the Danube.

★**Archäologisches Museum Carnuntinum** ⊙ – *Badgasse 40-46.* Emperor Franz Josef opened this building in 1904; magnificent restoration work was carried out here between 1988 and 1992.

The extent of the archaeological finds made here can be well imagined bearing in mind that the museum displays only 5% of the remains and objects recovered from the excavations of the Roman city. The items form an admirable collection in which the statuary is particularly noteworthy. The superb marble statuette, *Dancing Maenad of Carnuntum★* (2C, on the first floor), is one of the most important works here. Most of the items on the ground floor relate to the **cult of Mithra** and come from the mithraeum, a subterranean sanctuary found on the site. Mithra was a Persian divinity held in particular respect by Roman soldiers in border garrisons. This mystery religion had seven levels of initiation and attained world religion status in the first centuries of the Christian era under the protection of various Roman emperors. It provided strong competition for Christianity until the latter attained official recognition, at which point the cult of Mithra disappeared just as quickly as it had become popular.

EXCURSIONS

Wildungsmauer – *5km/3mi W of Petronell.* Despite restorations and additions (including a 19C porch and tower), the little church of St Nicholas has kept its essentially Romanesque character. This single-naved church originated from alterations to a fortified building, which took place before 1300.

Rohrau – *4km/2.5mi S of Petronell.* The 16C castle houses the **Harrach'sche Gemäldegallery★★** ⊙, the largest private collection of paintings in Austria. It dates from 1668 and until 1970 was located in the Harrach palace in Vienna. The museum displays works by 17C and 18C Spanish, Neapolitan, and Roman masters, and also by 16C and 17C Flemish and Dutch masters (Bruegel, Jordaens, Rubens, Ruisdael, van Dyck). *The Concert* is a graceful painting of half-length figures, presumably by a Dutch master, which enjoys special renown.

Museum Carnuntinum

The *Dancing Maenad of Carnuntum*

The **Geburtshaus Joseph Haydn** ⊙ is on the road through the village. The composer was born there on 31 March 1732. His mother was cook at the castle and his father was a wheelwright. On view are copies of the birth certificates of the Haydn brothers, Joseph and Michael, facsimiles of scores and some engravings. There is also a watercolour by Balthasar Wigand showing the concert of *The Creation* at Alte Universität in Vienna. The piano (1809) is from Érard Frères, Paris.

Hainburg – *9km/5.6mi NE of Petronell.* This town had a significant strategic role to play in the Middle Ages; today, at the foot of the fortress ruins, it has retained its circular wall and fortified gates.

If time permits, the Slovakian capital of Bratislava is only about 10km/6mi from Hainburg (see Further afield) and is well worth the detour.

Schlosshof ⊙ – *21km/13mi N of Petronell.* This splendid Baroque palace was built by Lukas von Hildebrandt (early 18C) for **Eugène of Savoy**, who was then a general in the service of the Austrian Emperor. The workforce for this project numbered no less than 800, including 300 gardeners. They created a magnificent landscape in the French style. With their sculptures, fountains, terraces, wrought-iron gates, the grounds represented a shining example of garden architecture (of which only a small portion remains today, viewable exclusively from the terrace). Empress Maria-Theresa bought the property in 1760, adding a storey and sumptuously decorating the interior of what was originally intended to be a hunting castle and pleasure palace. In the 20C, the palace served primarily as a military riding and driving school. Since 1987, it has been used as an exhibition and conference centre. In the context of annually alternating exhibitions, visitors can view the inside of the castle with its handsome series of rooms. The **Sala Terrena★** deserves particular attention, and opens to the terrace. The "Dokumentationszentrum für altösterreichische Pferderassen" *(entrance through the courtyard)* is devoted to the history of the famous breeds of horses in the Habsburg monarchy. It hosts exhibitions and horse shows.

SOPRON★★

Hungary
Population 55 000
Michelin map 926, fold 25 – 63km/39mi southeast of Vienna
See also the Green Guide BUDAPEST AND HUNGARY

EU nationals should take their identity cards or passports to cross the border. All others should carry their passports with them.

Formerly Ödenburg in the Austro-Hungarian empire, the town of Sopron is one of the few cities in central Europe whose old town centre has remained practically unchanged over the centuries. Its admirers have a man named **Endre Gatsk** to thank for the restoration of the buildings damaged here in the Second World War; Gatsk laboured half a century to restore and retain Sopron's architectural stock of treasures, which include medieval and Baroque buildings in equal part.

At weekends, the town attracts numerous Austrians who come to shop for bargains (clothes, wine, sausages and baked goods are less expensive here, but their quality is exceptionally high) or enjoy a relaxing weekend.

The wines of Sopron – 75% of the wines produced in the area are red wines; many of these are Cabernet-Sauvignon, several are Merlot. There are also Cabernet and a small number of Pinot Noir (blue Burgundies). The local red wines have a slightly sour taste and are rich in tannin. The Soproner Cabernet Sauvignon 1995 and the white Sauvignon of that year are especially recommendable.

Are toothaches and eye problems especially common in Sopron? – You might almost draw this conclusion, given the number of signs posted here for dentists, opthalmologists and opticians. Yet these indications are no cause for distress; the locals here are not under a particular curse in these departments. As in many other Hungarian cities, foreigners come to Sopron for medical examination and treatment, since these are cheaper than at home – despite the fact that the doctors are both excellent and equipped with modern instruments. It is sometimes said, though, that what is saved on the doctor bills is more than made up for by the hotel bills.

HISTORY

The first traces of a settlement in the area of the Neusiedler Lake are apparently of Illyric origin. The Celts followed in 3C BC, and then the Romans in 1C with the garrison of Scarbantia at what is today Sopron. Scarbantia soon acquired the status of *municipium*, a town whose people were granted Roman citizenship. Toward the end of the 3C, the settlement fell victim to attacks of mounted nomads from the east, but experienced a new heyday in the 4C under Constantine. Anticipating the great invasions, Emperor Valentinus reinforced the city (end of 4C); yet the Romans abandoned the settlement before the beginning of the migratory invasions, giving Pannonia to the Huns in 433. After the Huns came the Avars, the Bavarians and, finally, the Hungarians, who had the city walls built to such proportions (5m/16ft wide and 15m/49ft high) that the inhabitants were able to resist the roaming "crusaders" whom Peter of Amiens, called Peter the Hermit, took with him to Jerusalem in 1096.

In 1277, Sopron acquired the status of royal borough, a development which granted its citizens freedom of trade and protection from the despotism of neighbouring feudal lords. During this period the city's ramparts were outfitted with the equivalent of 34 peel towers, allowing Sopron's 20 000 inhabitants to prosper economically and culturally. The 150-year Turkish rule left Sopron almost untouched.

"Civitas Fidelissima", the Most Faithful of all Cities

Sopron received this title from Hungary's government after its citizens spoke up in December 1921 against the conditions of the treaty of Trianon, choosing to retain their allegiance to Hungary. Many municipalities in ethnic German areas of West Hungary voted to become part of Austria, and today belong to Burgenland. Internationally, Ödenburg's choice was subject to debate; on a map of the area, the border seems to make a loop just to keep the city at a 6km/3.7mi distance from Austria. Sopron's present residents still stand faithfully by the decision made by their forefathers.

TOUR OF THE CENTRE

The town centre is bordered by the Várkerület (Ring) in the east and north, the Színház utca and the Petöfi tér in the west, and by the Széchenyi tér in the south.

★★**Fő tér** – The main square is the only large open space in the town centre. In the middle of the square is a plague column, the Holy Trinity Column from the year 1701. The square is surrounded by splendid buildings, among which are several museums.

Sopron: The city tower

★**Várostorony or Tüztorony** ⊘ – This 61m/200ft tower is the city's highest structure and serves as its emblem. It is also known as the Fire Brigade's Tower, since
the alarm was spread from here in the case of fires and enemy advances in former
times. You can climb as far as the archers' gallery, which today offers a fine **view**★
of both the town and the surrounding area with its Alpine foothills. Resting upon
Roman foundation walls, the tower itself is a mix of highly divergent styles. The
square ground floor is built of 2m/6.5ft thick walls dating from the 12C, and the
cylindrical tower which it supports contains Renaissance arcades (16C), while the
onion turret crowning the structure (1680) is a purely Baroque addition.

Városháza – The City Hall was built at the end of the 19C in an eclectic style.
Besides the offices, the building is home to 15 000 volumes and 5 000 documents
from medieval times, including deeds, royal bulls, manuscript fragments etc which
have been collected here since 1381.

Storno-ház ⊘ – *Fö tér 8.* Built in the 15C, this house underwent several renovations in the late Renaissance and later acquired an arcaded courtyard and a late
Baroque façade. Its illustrious visitors included King Matthias in 1482, and Franz
Liszt in 1820 and 1881. The Municipal Museum is now housed here, with displays
on Sopron's history from the 16C to the present. In addition, the building is home
to remnants of the Storno family's assets, which reveal something of the manner
in which a wealthy merchant's family lived in the 19C.

Fabricius-ház ⊘ – *Fö tér 6.* Like most buildings in Sopron, this one consists of
Roman foundation walls and Roman or Gothic fragments, to which was added a
Baroque façade during the 18C. This edifice houses three museums. The first and
second floors are devoted to the story of the Amber Road on which Sopron lies.
The second museum concerns Sopron's everyday life in the 18C. The room, which

forms a foyer, is interesting in itself from an architectural standpoint, but the objects it contains are also worth seeing: these include sumptuous furniture, wooden trunks with items for a trousseau, tiled stoves. Among the kitchen appliances, a spit with variable rotating speeds is certainly a fascinating device.

★ **Roman Lapidarium** – The third museum in the Fabricius House is found in its splendid Gothic brick cellar vault. Funerary statuary from Roman times is on exhibit here, as are three monumental statues representing Jupiter, Minerva and Juno which were discovered during construction work for the city hall.

Patika Múzeum ⊙ – *Fö tér 2*. The **White Angel apothecary** was the city's first, in 1595 (or 1601). In 1623, a second one opened, the **Lion apothecary**. By the end of the 19C Sopron had eleven chemist's shops or one for every 6 000 inhabitants. Today there is still the **Lion apothecary** at No 29 in the Várkerület.

The White Angel apothecary now contains numerous objects dating from the time of its foundation: porcelain and blue-toned glass pots to protect salves, drops and other medicines from light; and drawers in which the various medicinal herbs were ordered alphabetically according to their Latin name and which also contain instruments, appliances and containers for the preparation of medicinal mixtures. The pots are marked with a lion or an angel, depending on which apothecary they belonged to.

From the Fö tér, turn right into the Templom utca (Church Street) to continue the tour of the old town centre.

Kecske Templom – *Templom utca 1*. The beautiful and purely Gothic Church of Mary is colloquially called the "Goats' Church". According to legend, the church was built with the gold which one shepherd's goats had scraped out of the earth with their hooves. A more plausible explanation may hinted at by the several sculptures which have a goat's head on them; this symbol is said to have been the heraldic animal of the church's founding family, whose name was presumably *Geissler* (a dialect word meaning goatherd).

The church was constructed by the Franciscans in the 13C and 14C; this order also was in charge of it until the end of the 18C. After that, the church entered the possession of the Benedictines, which is why it is sometimes also referred to as the Benedictine church. The **high altar painting** is by Stephan Dorffmeister, a local artist who was one of the great masters of Baroque painting and whose works are found in many Hungarian churches. Further noteworthy works here are the tabernacle and the pulpit, both of which date from the late 15C.

The **chapter-house** in the former Franciscan monastery is a beautiful Gothic hall with pointed arched vaults whose ribs extend as far as the pedestals of the pillars. During the Turkish occupation in the 17C the Imperial Diet convened five times here, and the coronations of two queens and one king were also held here.

Központi Bányászati Múzeum – *Templom utca 2*. Across from the Church of Mary, the Mining Industry Museum is housed in the Baroque palace of the **Esterházy Family**, whose emblem hangs above the entrance gateway. The western part of Hungary contains the country's oldest mines, which went into operation in the 18C. Old and new methods of mining are illustrated here, and huge movable models show how the gigantic coal mining machines operated.

In the City Palace next door (No 4), the representatives of the Entente Cordiale (the victors of the First World War) presided over the counting of the votes in the December 1921 referendum that the citizens of Ödenburg had demanded.

Evangélikus Templom – This Evangelical church was constructed 1782-83, yet was only allowed its tower 80 years later – since according to Emperor Joseph II's ingenious decree, only a ridge turret was allowed for Lutheran churches. On its three floors, the Evangelical church can welcome a total of 4 000 believers. The organ is one of the largest in Hungary and has three manuals, 52 registers and 1 860 pipes. The high altar, acquired at an auction in Vienna, is embellished with a woodcutting depicting God the Father, St Michael and six angels. Four large bells are found in the tower; the largest of these weighs 3 400kg/7 480lbs and bears an inscription commemorating the Protestant soldiers who died in the First World War. The second-largest, the bell of peace, is engraved with a picture of Martin Luther; the third, called the Our Father, is rung when the priest is saying the prayer of the same name; and the fourth, the "Bell of Loyalty", was rung when the results of the 1921 referendum were announced.

Proceed along the Templom utca, then turn left into the Fegyvertár utca.

★ **Orsolya tér** – Ursulines Square is home to **Church of Mary** and the arcaded Baroque **Lábasház** (House on Feet), which hosts special exhibitions. The fountain of Mary in the middle of the square dates from the 16C, but wasn't placed here until 1930.

★ **Zsinagóga** ⊙ – *Új utca (New Street) 22-24*. The former Jews' Street was named after the people who resided here from the 9C until they were driven out in 1526. The Old Synagogue which they had built in 1300 was then converted into a residential dwelling, and there was not one Jewish resident of Sopron from 1526 until the middle of the 19C. The building complex was painstakingly restored and has been a synagogue again since 1967; it is now very much worth seeing.

A commemorative plaque at No 28 informs visitors that Sopron's Jews were confined to a ghetto in this street in 1944, prior to their deportation.

Liszt Ferenc Kultúrház – The **Franz Liszt Cultural Centre** lies in the south of the old town centre; it contains the State foreign tourism agency Tourinform, a library and a multi-purpose room.

Gyüjtemény – *Deák tér 1.* This Municipal Ethnological Museum is still often called the **Franz Liszt Museum**, since his memory was honoured here until 1990. Today folkloric traditions are explored in this excellent collection, and handicrafts and music instruments are on view.

Franz Liszt in Sopron

Franz (Ferenc) Liszt was born in Raiding, only a few miles from Sopron; both these towns belonged to the same Hungarian province. The young Liszt first came to Sopron in 1820, at the age of nine, to give a concert, and returned frequently thereafter. The town is still moved by the memory of the composer of the *Hungarian Rhapsodies*, not least because he donated the proceeds from his concert performances to the city for charitable causes.

ENJOYING YOUR STAY IN SOPRON

Hungary's currency is the Forint (which is divided into 100 Filler); however, prices below are listed in Euros. Also, please bear in mind that the country code is included in the fax and telephone numbers listed here.

ACCOMMODATION

Sopron Hotel – *Fövényverem utca 7.* ☎ *0036/99/312 184. Fax 0036/99/311 090.* Total of 112 rooms, from about €22.50. Light, pleasant hotel, in spite of the rather cumbersome 1970s architecture. The rooms facing the old town centre offer a lovely panoramic view of the Lövér Hill. Outdoor pool, tennis, fitness room, restaurant, cafeteria and bar, and the old town centre is only a stone's throw away.

Palatinus Hotel – *Új utca 23.* ☎ *0036/99/311 395.* Total of 32 rooms, from about €40.90. The rooms are small. The hotel's most attractive feature is its central location in the middle of the old town centre.

Pannonia Med Hotel – *Várkerület 75.* ☎ *0036/99/312 180. Fax 0036/99/340 766.* Total of 60 rooms, from about €49. Located on the street that circles the old town centre. Very comfortably furnished, excellent cuisine at the hotel restaurant.

EATING OUT

Excellent restaurants are found in every nook and cranny throughout the city, in inner courtyards with a garden, passages with vaulted Gothic ceilings, or underneath shady trees, etc. For your sweet tooth, you can indulge in wonderful ice cream, cake and coffee at **Carpigiani** on *Szent György utca 12,* or the **Stefania patisserie** in the same street.

Pannonia Med Hotel – *Várkerület 75.* The hotel has a very refined restaurant with superb cooking. It is located in the old town centre at *Fö tér 3,* where everything from snacks to sumptuous meals are served on the terrace or inside the restaurant at all times of day.

Corvinus – *Fö tér 4.* Very hospitable; just the right place for a quick and simple meal.

Gyógygödör Borozó – Leaving Corvinus, steps lead down into a cellar in which this restaurant is found. Choice wines and local dishes.

Halászcárda – *Fövényverem utca 15.* ☎ *0036/99/338 403.* Attractive fish restaurant – the Danube and the Neusiedl Lake are nearby. Just a stone's throw from the city centre; below the Sopron Hotel, whose massive building in the north of the old town centre catches the eye. The prices are reasonable; it should be noted that the restaurant closes at 9pm.

Gabriel Étterem – *Elökapu 2-4.* ☎ *0036/99/340 311.* Simple and inexpensive. Mainly frequented by locals.

Cézár Pince – *Hátsókapu 2.* In the southeast of old town centre, near the Orsolya tér. A cellar in which you can sample the excellent beverages from the local vineyards.

EXCURSIONS

Raiding – *Leave Sopron on Route 84 (toward "Balaton", also called "Plattensee" in German) and turn right in the direction of Deutschkreuz to return to Austria. In Horitschon, turn left toward Raiding.*

Liszt's Birthplace ⊘ – The **Franz-Liszt Museum** is housed in a portion of what was once his father's servants' living-quarters. Liszt's father was bailiff for Prince Esterházy's shepherds in Raiding, and so it was here that the composer came into the world on 22 October 1811. Various items from the family's possessions are on exhibit here, for example photographs and documents illustrating the wunderkind's career. The small organ that Liszt liked to play was brought here from the old church.

★★**Fertő Lake** – *15km/9.3mi NE. Take the road toward Tómalón, and drive through Sopronköhida.*
This is the Hungarian part of the Neusiedler Lake. Stop in the village of **Fertőrákos** to visit the Roman **quarry**★. The view from the slope above the quarry is breathtaking. Concerts, operas and theatrical productions are also held here.

WIENER NEUSTADT
Niederösterreich
Population 35 050
Michelin map 926 fold 25 – 47km/29mi south of Vienna

As its name may suggest, this "new town" was created out of nothing – in 1194 by Leopold V of Babenberg. Aware of threats from the east, the duke wanted to protect the new duchy of Styria which he had acquired in 1192. The town acted as a frontier fortress against Magyar incursions from Hungary.

The ransom for Richard the Lionheart – According to tradition, during the Third Crusade, the King of England, Richard the Lionheart, quarrelled violently with the Duke of Austria, Leopold V. The Englishman had torn down the banner which the duke had just placed at the top of a tower during an attack on Akko. To regain his honour, Leopold of Babenberg had the naive Richard, returning from the Holy Land through his rival's territory, arrested in 1192 at Erdberg, now part of Vienna's 11th District. He had him imprisoned at Dürnstein in Lower Austria, then in the imperial castle of Trifels, in the Rhineland Palatinate.
Part of Richard the Lionheart's huge ransom paid for the construction of *nova civita*, later called *Niwenstat* then *Neustadt*: a quadrangular precinct with thick outer walls, strategically placed between the Leithagebirge and Hohe Wand mountains.

Imperial residence – After withstanding many attacks by the Mongols, the town became an imperial residence between 1440 and 1493, during the reign of Frederick III. He allowed the city to incorporate the double-headed eagle in its coat-of-arms. The Emperor Maximilian I was born there and buried there (although he died at Wels) far from his magnificent mausoleum in Innsbruck, a major legacy of German Renaissance sculpture.
The town achieved new splendour in Maria-Theresa's reign, and this continued until the 19C. The old town is now an elegant pedestrian precinct, which still displays the regular layout of the medieval streets.

SIGHTS

Ehemalige Burg – The central part of the former fortress dates from the 13C, but it has seen a series of extensions and alterations. In 1751, Maria Theresa established there a military academy for the training of elite officers; it is now considered the oldest in the world. It reopened in 1958, having been closed after the Second World War.

St. Georgskathedral ⊘ – The east façade overlooking the interior courtyard owes its name "Wappenwand" (heraldic wall) to the 107 carved coats of arms (15C) around the central window and Fredrick III's statue; some of the coats of arms are from the House of Habsburg, while others may be imaginary. Peter von Pusika built this church, then known as the Virgin's chapel, during Frederick III's reign. It was reconstructed after the Second World War. The Gothic hall-church houses a *Virgin with Cherries* (south altar); some stained-glass fragments (escutcheons) are the most outstanding remains of the original furnishings. Maximilian I's mortal remains rest beneath the steps of the high altar, in a red marble sarcophagus in the Apostles' chancel.

Neuklosterkirche – *Ungargasse, near Hauptplatz.* This Gothic building, in which the chancel (first half of the 14C) is higher than the nave, has Baroque furnishings and decoration.

THE WILD WEST AT VIENNA'S GATES

No Name City – *8km/5mi NW of Wiener Neustadt, on the national street B 21 near Wöllersdorf;* ☎ *0 26 22/4 34 00. www.NoNameCity.at* This wild-west theme city offers "cowboys and cowgirls" everything their hearts desire: a saloon, a gold panning camp, a bison corral, a horse ranch, etc. Stunt and western shows provide additional entertainment (the daily program is posted at the entrance or in the "Town Office"). The shows run 10am-7pm Thursday-Sunday and on holidays in April, May, September and October; daily June-August (Entrance fee €10, some attractions such as coach rides and canoe usage cost extra). The evenings' offerings go on until midnight (restaurants and some shops; admission free after 7pm).

Lodgings: Silver Star Hotel (single rooms from €40), in trappers' huts (up to 6 or 8 people for €55 or €70 per hut) or Indian tepees (€6 per person). You can even reserve a small island in the lake with a trapper's hut (up to 8 people, island and hut for €130). The lodging fees include entrance fees to the "city" for the next day. Breakfast €6 per person. Bring a sleeping bag for huts and tepees. Reservation definitely recommended. Bookings at ☎ 0 26 22/ 43 400 12.

In the apse, behind the high altar, there is the splendid **tombstone★** of Empress Eleanor of Portugal, wife of Frederick III, carved in 1467 by Niclaus Gerhaert von Leyden. Von Leyden was a German sculptor of Flemish origin who died in Vienna in 1473. He had also designed Frederick III's tomb *(see City Centre and the Ring, Stephansdom)*.

Hauptplatz – The Rathaus (Town Hall), built in 1488, stands south of this square, most of which is closed to traffic. In the 16C it acquired a rusticated stone tower, and, in 1834, was refurbished in neoclassical style. The *Mariensäule* dates from 1678. The fine houses to the north of the square are Gothic.

Go to Domplatz via Böheimgasse.

Dom – This late Romanesque basilica acquired a Gothic transverse nave and chancel in the 14C. The **Brauttor★** (Bride's Doorway), on the south side, is earlier than 1246 and displays diamond and zigzag patterns. Inside, the high ceiling is evidence of the interest Frederick III took in this church. The gallery in the courtyard bears his motto: "A.E.I.O.U." *(see City Centre and the Ring, Hofburg, Museums and Collections, inset)*. He probably donated the *Apostelchor*, 12 larger than life-sized statues of the apostles attached to the pillars by the sculptor Lorenz Luchsperger. The **high altar** with its six Corinthian columns of red marble is sumptuous. Above the **pulpit** (1609) by Johann Baptist Zelpi are statues of the Doctors of the Church: St Augustine, St Ambrose, St Gregory and St Jerome.

The **Propstei** housed the bishop's palace from 1469 to 1785 and lies north of Domplatz. It has a finely carved Baroque doorway bearing the arms of Bishop Franz Anton, Count Puchheim.

EXCURSION

Seebenstein – *17km/ 10.6mi S, on the A2 motorway toward Graz.* This community, located in the Pittental is indicated by two architectural structures which are visible from quite a distance on the motorway: the Burg Seebenstein and the Türkensturz, high above the valley.

Leaving the car at the car park by the Gemeindeamt (municipal office), follow the Schlossweg in a southerly direction. You reach a shaded forest path that leads to the Türkensturz; after about a 10min walk, a path branches off to the left to the Burg (fortress).

M. Hertlein/MICHELIN

Seebenstein – Türkensturz

Burg Seebenstein ⊙ – This proud fortress, dating back to the 11C, now stands guard over a private collection of medieval art. A *Madonna* by the Würzburg sculptor Tilman Riemenschneider (c 1460-1561) is especially worth mentioning here.

Return to the fork in the path, to continue about 45min uphill on the well-maintained Waldweg.

Türkensturz – Although the place name goes back to a legendary incident during the Turkish wars of the 16C, the edifice here was constructed in 1825-26 by Prince Johann I von Lichtenstein as a romantic ruin(!). The Türkensturz offers a picturesque view extending to the west as far as Raxalpe and to the impressive Schneeberg massif.

WIENERWALD★
Niederösterreich
Michelin map 926 folds 12 and 24

The Vienna woods might well be called the Vienna hills, since they form the eastern foothills of the Alps. This vast green belt stretches westward from the boundaries of the city, providing the heart of the city with an additional dose of charm and a breath of fresh air. Vienna is one of the few major capitals which within its walls has managed to retain the attractions of the villages of bygone times. Elsewhere, these villages have disappeared in the course of centuries, giving way to industrial cities full of iron and concrete.

In Vienna, the forest is a setting for vineyards and walks in the coolness of the woods during hot summers. However, it is more than this. The Wienerwald is also a tune on a zither emerging from a lonely inn, a scene painted musically in Beethoven's *6th Symphony*, "the Pastorale", and has been immortalised by a Strauss waltz. The Wienerwald is a vast and leafy rural area criss-crossed by attractive footpaths where holidaymakers still greet one another as they pass each other by.

Leave Vienna by route 12.

Perchtoldsdorf – *See Further afield.*

From Perchtoldsdorf, take route 13 at the corner of Spitalskirche (Donauwörtherstrasse then Hochstrasse) for Vienna. After 1.3km/0.8mi, turn left into Kaltenleutgebnerstrasse which becomes Hauptstrasse. After 11km/6mi, turn left for Sulz in Wienerwald. Cross Sittendorf and follow the sign for Naturpark Sparbach just before the motorway.

Naturpark Sparbach ⊙ – *If coming directly from Vienna by E 60/A 21 motorway, take exit 26 and turn right. Turn right again and carry on for 600m/654yd, following the signs. Large car park opposite the entrance.* This approximately 355ha/876-acre nature reserve, whose origins go back to the year 1812, has an enclosure with fallow deer and wild sheep. Boar, on the other hand, tend to run around freely in the park and can therefore be observed at close quarters on occasion. A wide network of footpaths leads to several romantic ruins, notably **Burg Johannstein** (12C), the Temple of Diana and the ruin of the Köhlerhaus (alt 567m/1 859ft). The idyllic Lenau Lake is well stocked with mandarin and mallard ducks. The park is a favourite destination in hot summer days because of its pleasant climate. But even during other seasons, it offers the opportunity for refreshing hikes.

Pass over the E 60/A 21 motorway and turn right into route 11 which runs through woods and vales to Gaaden and Heiligenkreuz Abbey.

Heiligenkreuz – *See Further afield.*

Continue along route 11 towards Alland. After 4km/2.5mi, turn left for Mayerling.

Mayerling – *See Further afield.*

Turn left into route 210 for Baden.

Helenental – The river Schwechat flows through this scenic valley lying between Mayerling and Baden. The valley includes 60km/37mi of waymarked paths, enabling visitors to explore it on foot, which is particularly pleasurable in autumn. Just before Baden are the ruins of two once great castles: Rauhenstein (12C) on the left and Rauheneck (11C) on the right.

‡‡**Baden** – *See Further afield.*

Leave from Baden town centre to take the Wine Road ("Weinstrasse") to Gumpoldskirchen and Mödling: take Kaiser-Franz-Joseph-Ring signposted to Gumpoldskirchen and Pfaffstätten. Continue under the railway bridge and turn left immediately beyond it (route 212). Follow the Gumpoldskirchen road.

Gumpoldskirchen – *See Further afield.*

The road rises through vineyards then winds down to Mödling. The bends in the road provide fine views of the town (as far as Kahlenberg on a clear day).

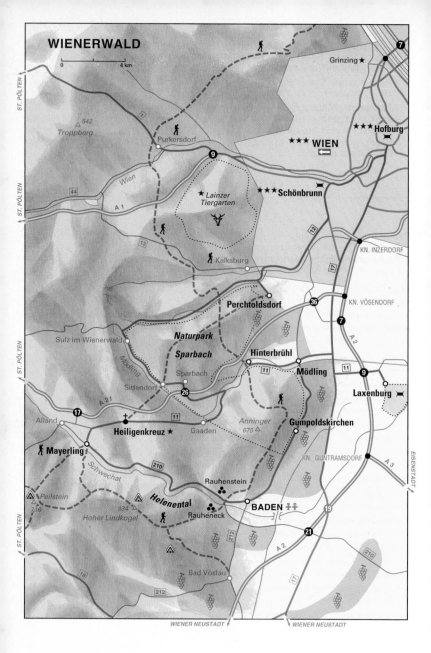

Mödling – *See Further afield.*

Go in the direction of Seegrotte to the west (signposted E 60/A 21) by Spitalmühlgasse which soon becomes Brühlerstrasse.

Hinterbrühl – Lying not too far west of Mödling, Hinterbrühl boasts a fascinating tourist attraction that draws visitors from around the world: the **Seegrotte★★** ⊘. It is the largest underground lake in Europe, covering over 6ha/14 acres. Visitors explore it by motorboat. The lake was formed in 1912 when an underground source was accidentally opened in the lower gallery of this former plaster mine.

Return to Mödling by route 11. Cross the town and rejoin route 11 via Triester Strasse, towards Schwechat. The road passes over the E 59/A 2 motorway. Follow the signs to Laxenburg.

Schloss Laxenburg – *See Further afield.*

Return to Vienna by the E 59/A 2 motorway.

RECOMMENDED HIKES

The Wienerwald extends far beyond the tour described above. For the benefit of keen walkers, we have listed a few waymarked footpaths, which are among the most attractive in the Vienna woods. These are only suggestions.

Anyone sufficiently interested should buy a detailed map. Maps of every kind are available at the travel guide bookshop Freytag & Berndt, 9 Kohlmarkt, 1st District. ☎ 01/53 38 68 50, www.freytagberndt.at

Klosterneuburg to Weidling – N of Vienna. Departure from Klosterneuburg station for Weidling via Leopoldsberg (alt 423m/1 387ft) *(2hr 45min)*.

Maria Anzbach – Between Vienna and St Pölten. Round trip via Kohlreitberg (alt 516m/1 692ft) *(2hr)*.

Böheimkirchen to Pottenbrunn – E of St Pölten. Departure from Böheimkirchen station for Pottenbrunn station, via Schildberg (alt 393m/1 289ft) *(1hr 15min)*.

Purkersdorf – On the W of Vienna. Round trip, departure from Unterpurkersdorf station *(2hr)*.

Kalksburg to Breitenfurt – W of Vienna. Departure from Kalksberg for Breitenfurt via Laabersteigberg (alt 530m/1 738ft) *(4hr 30min)*.

Klausen-Leopoldsdorf to Alland – NW of Mayerling *(3hr 30min)*.

The Schöpfl – W of Mayerling. Round trip, departure from Forsthof. Ascent and descent of the Schöpfl (alt 893m/2 929ft) *(about 2hr)*.

Mayerling to Bad Vöslau – This long and very pleasant tour leads to Bad Vöslau station *(6hr)*.

Berndorf to Pottenstein – SW of Baden. Departure from Berndorf station for Pottenstein station *(4hr)*.

A walk in the Vienna woods

H.A. Jahr/VIENNASLIDE

Admission times and charges

Every sight for which admission times and charges are listed is indicated by the symbol ⊙ in the alphabetical section of the guide. The information below is listed in the same order as the entries in the main body of the guide.

As admission times and charges are liable to alteration, the information below is given for guidance only. The information given applies to individual adults (not including special reductions for groups etc).

& denotes facilities for the disabled.

Following the introduction of the euro, prices communicated to us only in the local currency at the time of going to press have been converted by us and rounded to two decimal places.

If an Internet address was available at the time of editing, it has been listed. Otherwise e-mail addresses are listed.

City Centre and the Ring

FLEISCHMARKT District

Postsparkasse – & (side entrance). Main hall: Mon-Fri 8am-3pm (5.30pm Thur). ☎01/5 14 00 23 43.

Jesuitenkirche – & Mon-Sat 7am-7pm, Sun 8am-8pm. Free entry. ☎01/51 25 23 20.

Alte Schmiede – Call ahead of time for a tour. ☎ 01/5 12 83 29; www.alte-schmiede.at

Griechisch-orientalische Kirche zur Hl. Dreifaltigkeit – & Guided tour (45min): by appointment only. €1.45. ☎ 01/5 33 29 65.

Jesuitenkirche – *Trompe-l'œil* dome

FREYUNG District

Museum im Schottenstift – & Thur-Sat 10am-5pm, Sun 11-5pm. Closed: all public holidays. €4. ☎ 01/53 49 86 00; www.schottenstift.at

Palais Harrach – & For special exhibitions: 10am-6pm. €7.27. ☎ 01/5 32 12 30; www.khm.at

Kunstforum Bank Austria – & 16 Jan-3 Apr daily 10am-6pm (Wed until 9pm); 13 Apr-27 May daily 10am-7pm (Wed until 9pm). €8.72. ☎ 01/5 37 33 12; www.kunstforum-wien.at

Römische Baureste – (Roman ruins) Sat-Sun 11am-1pm. Closed: 1 Jan and 25 Dec. €1.82. ☎ 01/50 58 74 70; www.museum.vienna.at

Feuerwehrmuseum – Sun 9am-noon. Free entry. ☎ 01/53 19 95 14 44; gem@m68magwien.gv.at

Uhrenmuseum – Astronomical clocks

Museum Judenplatz – Mon-Thur and Sun 10am-6pm, Fri 10am-2pm. Closed: on the variable Jewish holidays Rosh Hashanah (2002: 7 and 8 Sept) and Yom Kippur (2002: 16 Sept). €3. ☏01/53 50 43 13 10; www.jmw.at

Uhrenmuseum – Tues-Sun 9am-4.30pm. Closed: 1 Jan, 1 May and 25 Dec €3.63 (Fri morning free entry). ☏ 01/5 33 22 65; www.museum.vienna.at

Puppen- & Spielzeug-Museum – Tues-Sun 10am-6pm. €4.60. ☏ 01/5 35 68 60; PuppenmuseumWien@everyday.com

Michaelerkirche – ♿ Exhibition in the church and the monastery: May-Nov Mon-Fri 11am-5pm. € 2.91. Church: daily 11am-5pm (closed Nov-May 1pm-3pm). ☏ 01/5 33 80 00

Minoritenkirche – Apr-Oct daily 8am-6pm; Nov-Mar daily 8am-5pm. Donation requested. ☏ 01/5 33 42 61

Pasqualatihaus – Tues-Sun 9am-12.15pm and 1pm-4.30pm. Closed: 1 Jan, 1 May and 25 Dec. €1.82 (Fri morning free entry). ☏ 01/5 35 89 05; post@m10 .magwien.gv.at

HOFBURG

Kaiserappartements – ♿ Daily 9am-5pm. €6.90. ☏ 01/5 33 75 70; www.schoenbrunn.at

Hofsilber- und Tafelkammer – ♿ Daily 9am-4.30pm. €6.90. ☏ 01/53 37 57 00.

Esperanto-Museum – Mon and Fri 10am-4pm, Wed 10am-6pm. Closed: 1-21 Sept, all public holidays. Free entry. ☏ 01/5 35 51 45; www.onb.ac.at/sammlgn/safr.htm

Hofburgkapelle – ♿ Mon-Thur 11am-3pm, Fri 11am-1pm. Closed: July and Aug. €1.45. ☏ 01/5 33 99 27; hofmusikkapelle@asu-wien.ac.at

Schatzkammer – ♿ Daily except Tues 10am-6pm. Closed: 1 Jan, 1 May and 25 Dec. €7.27 (26 Oct and 24 Dec free entry). ☏ 01/5 33 79 31; www.khm.at

Lipizzaner-Museum – Daily 9am-6pm. €5.09 (26 Oct free entry). www.lipizzaner.at

Österreichische Nationalbibliothek – ♿ May-Oct Mon-Wed, Fri and Sat 10am-4pm, Thur 10am-7pm, Sun 10am-2pm; Nov-Apr Mon-Sat10am-2pm. €4.36 (26 Oct free entry). ☏ 01/53 41 04 64; www.onb.ac.at

Globenmuseum der Österreichischen Nationalbibliothek – Mon-Wed and Fri 11am-noon, Thur 2pm-3pm. €2.18. ☏ 01/53 41 02 97; www.onb.ac.at/sammlungen/saglfr.htm

Albertina: Graphische Sammlung – Closed until Mar 2003. ☏ 01/5 34 83 49; www.albertina.at

Musiksammlung der Österreichischen Nationalbibliothek – Guided tours (1hr) by appointment only. ☎01/53 41 03 07; www.onb.ac.at

Schmetterlinghaus – Apr-Oct daily 10am-5pm; Nov-Mar daily 10am-4pm. €4.72. ☎ 01/5 33 85 70; www.schmetterlinghaus.at

Papyrusmuseum – ♿ Oct-June Mon and Wed-Fri 10am-5pm; July-Sept Mon and Wed-Fri 10am-3.45pm. Closed 1-21 Sept and all public holidays. €2.91 (26 Oct free entry). ☎ 01/53 41 03 23; www.onb.ac.at

Ephesos-Museum – Daily except Tues 10am-6pm. Closed: 1 Jan, Easter Tues, 1 May, Whit Tues and 25 Dec. €7.27 (26 Oct and 24 Dec free entry). ☎ 01/52 52 44 84; www.khm.at

Hofjagd- und Rüstkammer – ♿ Daily except Tues 10am-6pm. Closed 1 Jan, 1 May and 25 Dec. €7.27 (26 Oct and 24 Dec free entry). ☎ 01/52 52 44 84; www.khm.at

Sammlung alter Musikinstrumente – Daily except Tues 10am-6pm. Closed 1 Jan, 1 May and 25 Dec. €7.27 (26 Oct and 24 Dec free entry). ☎ 01/52 52 44 84; www.khm.at

Museum für Völkerkunde – Daily except Tues 10am-6pm. Closed 1 Jan, 1 Nov. €7.27 (26 Oct free entry). ☎ 01/53 43 00, www.ethno-museum.ac.at

HOHER MARKT District

Römische Ruinen (Roman ruins) – Tues-Sun 9am-12.15pm and 1pm-4.30pm. Closed 1 Jan and 25 Dec. €1.82 (Fri morning free entry). ☎ 01/5 35 56 06; www.museum.vienna.at

Neidhart-Fresken – Tues-Sun 9am-noon. Closed 1 Jan and 25 Dec. €1.82 (Fri morning free entry). ☎ 01/5 35 90 65; www.museum.vienna.at

Ausstellung der Österreichischen Freiheitskämpfe – Mon, Wed and Thur 9am-5pm. Free entry. ☎ 02 22/53 43 69 17 79; www.doew.at

Ruprechtskirche – ♿ Mon-Thur 9.30am-11.30am, Fri 9.30am-1pm. Closed all public holidays. Donation requested. ☎ 01/5 35 60 03; www.struprecht.freewebsites.com

KAPUZINERKIRCHE District

Salvador-Dalí-Ausstellung – Daily 10am-6pm. €6.54. ☎ 01/5 12 25 49; www.dali wien.at

Österreichisches Theatermuseum – Tues, Thur-Sun 10am-5pm, Wed 10am-8pm. Closed 1 May, 1 Nov, 31 Dec. €3.63 (26 Oct free entry). Ticket also valid for the Gedenkräume *(see Staatsoper District)*. ☎ 01/5 12 88 00 10; www.theatermuseum.at

Leopold I by Paul Strudel

Parliament building

Kapuzinergruft – Daily 9.30m-4pm. €3.60 (1 and 2 Nov free entry). ☎ 01/5 12 68 53.

Jüdisches Museum der Stadt Wien – ♿ Mon-Fri and Sun 10am-6pm (Thur to 8pm). €5 (26 Oct free entry). ☎ 01/53 50 43 10; www.jmw.at

KUNSTHISTORISCHES MUSEUM

♿ Tues-Sun 10am-6pm (Thur until 9pm). €7.27 (26 Oct and 24 Dec free entry). Closed 25 Dec. ☎ 01/52 52 40; www.khm.at

RATHAUS

Neues Rathaus – Guided tours (45min) Mon, Wed, Fri at 1pm. Closed all public holidays. Free entry. ☎01/4 00 08 13 60; www.wien.gv.at

The RING

Votivkirche – ♿ Church: Tues-Sat 9am-1pm and 4pm-6.30pm, Sun 9am-1pm. Free entry. Museum: Tues, Thur and Sat 10am-noon. €2.91. ☎ 01/4 06 11 92; votiv@vienna.at

Burgtheater – Guided tours (1hr): Tues, Thur and Fri at 9am and 3pm, Sat at 3pm, Sun at 11am and 3pm. Closed July and Aug, Good Fri, 24 Dec. €3.63. ☎01/5 14 44 41 40; www.burgtheater.at

Parlament – Guided tours (45min): July-mid Sept Mon-Fri at 9am, 10am, 11am, 1pm, 2pm and 3pm; mid Sept-end of June Mon-Thur at 11am and 3pm, Fri at 11am, 1pm, 2pm and 3pm. Closed 1 May, 24 Dec-6 Jan and during plenary sessions. €2.91. ☎ 01/4 01 10 25 79; www.parlament.gv.at

Naturhistorisches Museum – ♿ Daily except Tues 9am-6.30pm (Wed until 9pm). Closed 1 May, 1 Nov and 25 Dec. €3.63 (26 Oct and 24 Dec free entry). ☎ 01/52 17 73 35, www.nhm-wien.ac.at/nhm/aktuhell.htm

Akademie der bildenden Künste – Gemäldegalerie – ♿ (side entrance on Makartgasse, please advise the concierge or the ticket office). Tues-Sun 10am-4pm. €3.63. ☎ 01/58 81 62 25 (ticket office), 01 58 81 61 11 (concierge); www.akademiegalerie.at

MAK (Österreichisches Museum für angewandte Kunst) – ♿ Tues-Sun 10am-6pm (Tues until midnight). Closed 1 Jan, 1 May, 1 Nov and 25 Dec. €6.54. ☎ 01/7 12 80 00; www.mak.at

Urania Sternwarte – Closed for renovations. At the time of going to press, no date for reopening had been given. ☎ 01/7 29 54 94; www.urania-sternwarte.at

STAATSOPER District

Staatsoper – ♿ Guided tours by appointment (40min): July and Aug daily at 11am, 1pm, 2pm, 3pm and 4pm, Oct-Mar daily at 2pm and 3pm; Apr-June and Sept daily at 1pm, 2pm and 3pm. Closed Good Friday, 24, 25 and 31 Dec and during rehearsals (please call ahead of time). €4.36. ☎ 01/5 14 44 26 13; www.wiener-staatsoper.at

Gedenkräume des Österreichischen Theatermuseums – Tues-Fri 10am-noon and 1pm-4pm, Sat-Sun 1pm-4pm. Closed 1 Jan, 1 May, 1 Nov, 24, 25 and 31 Dec. €3.63 (26 Oct free entry), entrance ticket is also valid for the Österreichisches Theatermuseum *(see Kapuzinerkirche District)*. ☎ 01/5 12 24 27; www.theatermuseum.at

Haus der Musik – ♿ Daily 10am-10pm. €8.72. ☎ 01/5 16 48 51; www.haus-der-musik-wien.at

Sammlung Religiöse Volkskunst – Wed 10am-5pm, Sun 9am-1pm. Closed 1 Jan, 1 May, 1 Nov and 25 Dec. €1.82 (26 Oct free entry). ☎ 01/4 06 89 05.

STEPHANSDOM

The pulpit in Stephansdom (detail)

B. Kaufmann

♿ Mon-Sat 9am-11.30am and 1pm-4.30pm, Sun 1pm-4pm. €3.27. ☎ 01/5 15 52 37 67; www.st.stephan.at

Tower ascent – Ascent of the south tower: daily 9am-5.30pm. €2.54. ♿ North tower (lift to the Pummerin bell): Apr-Oct daily 8.30am-5.30pm (July and Aug until 6pm), Nov-Mar daily 8.30am-5pm. €3.27. ☎ 01/5 15 52 37 67; www.st.stephan.at

Catacombs – Guided tours (30min): Mon-Sat 10am-11.30am and 1.30pm-4.30pm every half hour, Sun 1.30pm-4.30pm, every half hour. Closed 1 and 2 Nov. €3.27. ☎ 01/5 15 52 37 67; www.st.stephan.at

STEPHANSDOM District

Peterskirche – daily 7am-6pm (Sat-Sun from 8am). Free entry. ☎ 01/5 33 64 33

Schatzkammer des Deutschen Ordens – Mon, Thur and Sat 10am-noon, Wed, Fri and Sat 3pm-5pm. €3.63. ☎ 01/5 12 10 65; www.dtorden.or.at

Mozart-Gedenkstätte "Figarohaus" – Tues-Sun 9am-6pm. Closed 1 Jan and 25 Dec. €1.820 (Fri morning free entry). ☎ 01/5 13 62 94; www.museum.vienna.at

Virgilkapelle – ♿ Tues-Sun 1.30pm-4.30pm. Closed 1 Jan, 1 May and 25 Dec. €1.82. ☎ 01/5 13 58 42; post@m10.magwien.gv.at

Dom- und Diözesanmuseum – Tues-Sat 10am-5pm. Closed all public holidays. 3.63 €. ☎ 01/5 15 52 36 89; dommuseum@edw.or.at

Outside the Ring

ALSERGRUND

Sigmund Freud-Museum – July-Sept daily 9am-6pm; Oct-June daily 9am-5pm. €4.36. ☎ 01/3 19 15 96; www.freud-museum.at

Bezirksmuseum Alsergrund – ♿ Wed 9am-11am, Sun 10am-noon; July and Aug by telephone appointment only. Closed all public holidays and school holidays. Free entry. ☎ 01/40 03 91 13; quox@gmx.at

Schubert-Gedenkstätte, "Geburtshaus" – Tues-Sun 9am-12.15pm and 1pm-4.30pm. Closed 1 Jan and 25 Dec. €1.82 (Fri morning free entry). ☎ 01/3 17 36 01; www.museum.vienna.at

Museum des Institutes für Geschichte der Medizin – ♿ Mon-Fri 9am-3pm. Closed all public holidays. €1.45. ☏ 01/4 27 76 34 01.

Pathologisch-Anatomisches Bundesmuseum – Wed 3pm-6pm, Thur 8am-11am and every 1st Sat of the month 10am-1pm. Closed all public holidays. Free entry. ☏ 01/4 06 86 72; www.pathomus.or.at

DÖBLING

Heiligenstadt: Beethoven-Gedenkstätte "Testamenthaus" – Mar-Dec Tues, Thur, Sat-Sun 10am-noon and 1pm-4.30pm. Closed 1 Jan, 1 May and 25 Dec. €1.09. ☏ 01/3 18 86 08

Oberdöbling: Weinbaumuseum – Sat 3.30m-6pm, Sun 10am-noon. Closed July and Aug and all public holidays. Donation requested. ☏ 01/3 68 65 46.

Oberdöbling: Beethoven-Gedenkstätte "Eroicahaus" – ♿ Tues-Sun 9am-12.15pm and 1pm-4.30pm. Closed: 1 Jan and 25 Dec. €1.82 (Fri morning free entry). ☏ 01/3 69 14 24; www.museum.vienna.at

DONAUSTADT

UNO-City – Guided tours (1 Std.): Mon-Fri at 11am and 2pm. €3.64. ☏ 01/2 60 60 33 28; www.unis.unvienna.org

FAVORITEN

Therme Oberlaa – Mon-Sat 8.45am-10pm, Sun 7.45pm-10pm. Closed 24 Dec. €9. ☏ 01/6 80 09; www.oberlaa.at

HIETZING

Bezirksmuseum Hietzing – ♿ Wed 9am-noon and 2pm-6pm, Sat 2pm-5pm, Sun 9.30am-noon. Closed July and Aug. Free entry. ☏ 01/8 77 76 88.

Otto Wagner-Hofpavillon Hietzing – ♿ Tues-Sun 1.30pm-4.30pm. Closed 1 Jan and 25 Dec. €1.82. ☏ 01/8 77 15 71; www.museum.vienna.at

Friedhof Hietzing – ♿ Mar-2 Nov 7am-6pm; 3 Nov-Feb 8am-5pm. Free entry. ☏ 01/8 77 31 07.

Lainzer Tiergarten – Mid Feb-mid Nov from 9am. Free entry. ☏ 01/8 04 13 15; mai@magwien.gv.at

Hermesvilla – Apr-Sept Tues-Sun 10am-6pm; Oct-Mar Tues-Sun 9am-4.30pm. €3.63 (Fri morning free entry). ☏ 01/8 04 13 24; www.museum.vienna.at

Excursions

Modesammlung – Mon-Fri 8am-4pm. Closed all public holidays. ☏ 01/8 04 04 68.

JOSEFSTADT

Piaristenkirche Basilika Maria Treu – ♿ July and Aug Mon-Sat 7am-9am (Tues, Thur and Sat also 6pm-7.30pm), Sun 7am-noon and 6pm-8pm; Sept-June Mon-Sat 7am-9am and 6pm-8pm, Sun 7am-noon and 6pm-8pm. Free entry, donation requested. ☏ 01/4 05 04 25 13; www.piaristen.at/MariaTreu

Alte Backstube – ♿ Café: Mon-Sat 11am-midnight, Sun 5pm-midnight. Closed mid July-mid-Aug. Free entry. ☏ 01/4 06 11 01; www.backstube.at

Österreichisches Museum für Volkskunde – ♿ Tues-Sun 10am-5pm. Closed 1 Jan, Easter Day, 1 May, 1 Nov and 25 Dec. €4.35 (26 Oct free entry). ☏ 01/4 06 89 05; www.volkskundemuseum.at

Dreifaltigkeitskirche – ♿ (side entrance). Mon-Sat 7.30am-noon, Sun 7.30am-12.30pm. Free entry. ☏ 01/4 05 72 25.

LANDSTRASSE

Arnold Schönberg Center – ♿ Mon-Fri 10am-5pm. €5.90. ☏ 01/7 12 18 88; www.schoenberg.at

Österreichische Galerie Belvedere (Barockmuseum, Museum mittelalterlicher Kunst, Sammlungen des 19. and 20. Jahrhunderts) – Tues-Sun 10am-6pm (5pm in winter). Closed: 1 Jan, 8-15 Jan, Tues after Easter and Whitsun, 24, 25 and 31 Dec. €7.27. ☏ 01/7 95 57-2 61; www.belvedere.at

Bundesgarten Belvedere – Apr-6 Aug 10am-6pm. €2.91 ☏ 01/7 98 31 49; www.bmlf.gv.at

Heeresgeschichtliches Museum – ♿ Daily except Fri 9am-5pm. Closed 1 Jan, Easter Day, 1 May, 1 Nov, 24, 25 and 31 Dec. €5.09 (26 Oct free entry). ☏ 01/79 56 16 00 02; www.bundesheer.gv.at/hgm

The Unteres Belvedere in Landstrasse

Wiener Straßenbahnmuseum – ♿ May-beginning of Oct Sat-Sun 9am-4pm. €1.45. ☎ 01/7 90 94 49 00.

Haus Wittgenstein – Mon-Fri 9am-5pm. €2.91. bki.wittgenstein@europe.com

KunstHaus Wien – ♿ Daily 10am-7pm. €6.90. ☎ 01/7 12 04 95; www.kunst hauswien.com

LEOPOLDSTADT

Riesenrad (Ferris Wheel) – ♿ May-Sept daily 9am-midnight; Mar, Apr and Oct-5 Nov daily 10am-10pm; 6 Nov-31 Dec daily 10am-6pm. Closed: 8 Jan-10 Feb, 24 Dec. €4.36. ☎ 01/7 29 54 30; www.wienerriesenrad.com

Planetarium – Guided tours (1hr) Sun at 3pm and 5pm. €3.63. ☎ 01/7 29 54 94; www.planetarium-wien.at

Prater-Museum – Tues-Fri 9am-12.15pm and 1pm-4.30pm, Sat 2pm-6.30pm. Closed: 1 Jan and 25 Dec. €1.82 (Fri morning free entry). ☎ 01/7 26 76 83; www.museum.vienna.at

Fussball-Museum – Closed until 31/12/2002.

Johann Strauss "Gedenkstätte" – Tues-Sun 9am-12.15pm and 1pm-4.30pm. Closed 1 Jan, 1 May and 25 Dec. €1.82 (Fri morning free entry). ☎ 01/2 14 01 21; www.museum.vienna.at

Wiener Kriminalmuseum – Thur-Sun10am-5pm. €4.36. ☎ 01/2 14 46 78.

LIESING

Wotrubakirche – Sat 2pm-8pm, Sun 9am-5pm. Closed 1 May, Corpus Christi and 26 Oct. Donation requested. ☎ 01/8 88 50 03.

MARIAHILF

Mariahilferkirche – ♿ Mon-Sat 7.45am-7pm, Sun 8.30am-7pm. Free entry. ☎ 01/5 87 87 53.

Haus des Meeres – ♿ Daily 9am-6pm. €6.90. ☎ 01/5 87 14 17; www. haus-des-meeres.at

Foltermuseum – Daily 10am-6pm. Closed 1 Jan, 25 and 26 Dec. €6.18. ☎ 01/5 85 71 85; www.folter.at

Haydn-Gedenkstätte – Tues-Sun 9am-12.15pm and 1pm-4.30pm. Closed 1 Jan, 1 May and 25 Dec. €1.89. ☎ 01/5 96 13 07; post@m10.magwien.gv.at

🛈 ☏ 01/5 23 58 81; www.mqw.at

Leopold Museum – ♿ Mon, Wed-Sun 11am-7pm (Fri 11am-9pm). Closed 24 and 31 Dec. €9. ☏ 01/52 57 00; www.leopoldmuseum.at

MUMOK (Museum moderner Kunst – Stiftung Ludwig Wien) – Tues-Sun 10am-6pm (Thur until 9pm). Closed 24 and 25 Dec. €6.58 (free entry on international museum day). ☏ 01/52 50 00; www.mumok.at

Kunsthalle Wien – ♿ Mon-Fri 10am-7pm (Thur until 10pm). €5.81. ☏ 01/5 21 89 33; www.kunsthallewien.at

Zoom Kindermuseum – ♿ We recommend you book for private (not group) visits. Up to 6 years old: Mon-Fri 9am-noon (duration of visit 1hr), Sat-Sun admission at 10am, noon, 2pm and 4pm (duration of visit 1hr). Workshop programme 3-6 years: Thur 2.30pm, Sat-Sun 2.30pm and 4pm (duration of visit 1hr). 7-12 years: Friday 3.30pm, Sat-Sun at 10am, noon, 2pm and 4pm (duration of visit 1hr 30min). Workshop programme for 7-12 years: Fri at 2pm and 4pm (duration of visit 1hr 30min). Zoomlab 7-14 years: Fri at 4pm, Sat-Sun at 2pm (duration of visit 1hr 30min). 3.50 €. Infoline: ☏ 01/5 24 79 08; www.kindermuseum.at

Art Cult Center Tabakmuseum – ♿ Tues-Fri 10am-5pm (Thur until 7pm), Sat-Sun 10am-2pm. Closed 1 Jan and 25 Dec. €3.63. ☏ 01/5 26 17 16; www.austria tabak.com

Architektur Zentrum Wien – ♿ Daily 10am-7pm. €3.63. ☏ 01/5 22 31 15; www.azw.at

Kaiserliches Hofmobiliendepot – ♿ Tues-Sun 9am-5pm. €6.54. ☏ 01/5 24 42 40.

Museum der Gold- and Silberschmiede – Guided tours (1hr): Wed 3pm-6pm. Closed July and Aug. ☏ 01/5 23 33 88.

Wagnerhaus – Guided tours (30min): by appointment, ☏ 01/5 23 22 33; a.sarnitz@akbild.ac.at

Ulrichskirche – ♿ Day chapel: workdays 6.30am-7pm, Sun and public holidays at religious services only. Guided tours of the church (30min) by appointment only. €3. ☏ 01/5 23 12 46; paulus.bergener@i-one.at

Kirche am Steinhof designed by Otto Wagner

PENZING

Technisches Museum – ♿ Mon-Sat 9am-6pm (Thur until 8pm), Sun 10am-6pm. Closed 1 Jan, 1 May, 1 Nov, 25 and 26 Dec. €7.27. ☎ 01/8 99 98 60 00; www.tmw.ac.at

Kirche am Steinhof – Guided tours (45min): Sat at 3pm. €4. ☎ 01/91 06 01 12 01; paul.keiblinger@ows.magwien.gv.at

Ernst-Fuchs-Privatmuseum – Mon-Fri 10am-5pm. www.ernstfuchs.privatstiftung @netwat.at

Schloß SCHÖNBRUNN

♿ Apr-Oct daily 8.30am-5pm (July and Aug until 7pm); Nov-Mar daily 8.30am-4.30pm. Imperial Tour 7.63 €, Grand Tour €9.81. ☎ 01/81 11 32 39; www. schoenbrunn.at

Wagenburg – ♿ 9 Apr-mid-Nov daily 9am-6pm; 1 Jan-8 Apr and mid-Nov-31 Dec Tues-Sun 10am-4pm. Closed 1 Jan, 1 May and 25 Dec. €4.36 (26 Oct and 24 Dec free entry). ☎ 01/52 52 44 11; www.khm.at

Schloßpark – ♿ Apr-Oct daily 6am till dusk (Nov-Mar from 6.30am). Free entry. ☎ 01/8 11 13-2 02; www.schoenbrunn.at

Irrgarten – ♿ Apr-June and Sept daily 9am-6pm; July and Aug daily 9am-7pm; Oct daily 9am-5pm. €2.18. ☎ 01/81 11 30; www.schoenbrunn.at

Palmenhaus – ♿ May-Sept daily 9.30m-6pm; Oct-Apr daily 9.30m-5pm. Closed 24 Dec. €3.27. ☎ 01/87 75 08 74 06; www.bmlf.gv.at

Tiergarten – ♿ Jan, Nov and Dec. daily 9am-4.30pm; Feb daily 9am-5pm; Mar and Oct daily 9am-5.30pm; Apr daily 9am-6pm; May-Sept daily 9am-6.30pm. €8.70. ☎ 01/87 79 29 40; www.zoovienna.at

Gloriette – Apr-Oct daily 9am-5pm €2.18.

WÄHRING

Geymüller-Schlößl – For visiting please make an appointment by phone at least a week in advance. ☎ 01/71 13 62 98; office@mak.at

WIEDEN

Historisches Museum der Stadt Wien – ♿ Tues-Sun 9am-6pm. Closed: 1 Jan and 25 Dec. €3.63 (Fri morning free entry). ☎ 01/50 58 74 70; www.museum.vienna.at

Karlskirche – Mon-Fri 7.30am-7pm, Sat 8.30am-7pm, Sun 9am-7pm (Maundy Thur and Good Fri from 10am). €2.91. ☎ 01/50 46 87 13; www.come.to/dekanat 4 u 5.

Secessionsgebäude – ♿ Tues-Sun 10am-6pm (Thur to 8pm). Closed 1 May, 1 Nov and 25 Dec. €4.36. ☎ 01/5 87 53 07; www.secession.at

Schubert-Gedenkstätte "Sterbewohnung" – Tues-Sun 1.30pm-4.30pm. Closed 1 Jan and 25 Dec. €1.82. ☎ 01/5 81 67 30; www.museum.vienna.at

ZENTRALFRIEDHOF

Mar, Apr, Sept-2 Nov daily 7am-6pm; May-Aug daily 7am-7pm; 3 Nov-Feb daily 8am-5pm. ☎ 01/7 60 41.

P. Koller/BILDAGENTUR BUENOS DIAS

Baden – Ladies' baths

Further afield

BADEN

Casino – ♿ Daily 3pm-3am ("Jackpot corner" from 1pm). Closed: 24 Dec. Photo ID and adulthood are requisites: Minimum playing sum chips valued at €21.80. ☎ 0 22 52/4 44 96; www.casinos.at

Beethoven-Gedenkstätte – Tues-Fri 4pm-6pm, Sat-Sun 9am-11am and 4pm-6pm. Closed 1 Jan, 24 and 31 Dec. €2.50. ☎ 0 22 52/86 80 02 30; www.baden-bei-wien.at

EISENSTADT

Schloß Esterházy – ♿ Guided tours (45min): Apr-Oct daily 9am-6pm; Nov-Mar Mon-Fri 9am-5pm. €4.50. ☎ 0 26 82/7 19 30 00; www.schloss-esterhazy.at

Haydn-Haus – Easter-end of Oct daily 9am-noon and 1pm-5pm. €2.18 (26 Oct free entry). ☎ 0 26 82/6 26 52 29; bgld.la@aon.at

Österreichisches Jüdisches Museum – 2 May-26 Oct Tues-Sun 10am-5pm. €3.60 (26 Oct free entry). ☎ 0 26 82/6 51 45; www.oejudmus.or.at

Burgenländisches Landesmuseum – ♿ Tues-Sun 9am-noon and 1pm-5pm. Closed: 1 Jan, 1 Nov, 25, 26 and 31 Dec. €2.91 (26 Oct free entry). ☎ 0 26 82/6 26 52; bgld.lm@aon.at

Kalvarienberg und Bergkirche – Palm Sunday-end Oct daily 9am-noon and 1pm-5pm. €2.18. ☎ 0 26 82/6 26 38.

Burg FORCHTENSTEIN

Guided tours (1hr 15min): Apr-Oct daily at 10am, 11am, noon, 1pm, 2pm and 3pm. €5.50. ☎ 0 26 26/81 21 20; www.burg-forchtenstein.at

Stift HEILIGENKREUZ

Guided tours by appointment (45min): Mon-Sat at 10am, 11am, 2pm, 3pm and 4pm, Sun at 11am, 2pm, 3pm and 4pm. Closed Good Friday and 24 Dec. €4.95. ☎ 0 22 58/87 03; www.stift-heiligenkreuz.at

View of Klosterneuburg

KLOSTERNEUBURG

Stift – Guided tours (1hr): daily 10am-5pm. Closed: 25 and 26 Dec. €5.10. ☎ 0 22 43/41 12 12; www.stift-klosterneuburg.at

Stiftsmuseum – ♿ May-15 Nov Tues-Sun 10am-5pm. €4.35. ☎ 0 22 43/41 11 54; www.stift-klosterneuburg.at

Sammlung Essl – ♿ Tues-Sun 10am-7pm (Wed until 9pm). Closed: 1 Jan, 24 and 25 Dec. €5.81 (Wed 7pm-9pm free entry). ☎ 0 22 43/37 05 01 50; www.samm-lung-essl.at

LAXENBURG

Park – ♿ Daily 24/24hr. €1.24. ☎ 0 22 36/71 22 60.

MAYERLING

Kronprinz-Rudolf-Gedenkstätte (Memorial – guided tours (30min): Mon-Sat 9am-12.30pm and 13.30pm-6pm (winter until 5pm). Closed Maundy Thursday to Holy Saturday. €1.50. ☎ 0 22 58/22 75.

NEUSIEDLER SEE

Neusiedl am See: Pannonisches Heimatmuseum – ♿ May-Oct Tues-Sun 2.30pm-6.30pm. Donation requested. ☎ 0 21 67/81 73.

PETRONELL-CARNUNTUM

Archäologischer Park Carnuntum – ♿ Petronell and Amphitheater I open-air museums: 31 Mar-4 Nov daily 9am-5pm. Petronell Museum: 3.63 €, Amphitheater I Museum: €2.18. Carnuntum pass (both open-air museums and the Carnuntinum Archaeological Museums) €7.63. ☎ 0 21 63/3 37 70; www.carnuntum.co.at

Archäologisches Museum Carnuntinum – 31 Mar-4 Nov Tues-Sun 10am-5pm; 13 Jan-30 Mar and 5 Nov-9 Dec Sat-Sun 10am-5pm. 4.36 € Carnuntum pass (both open-air museums and the Carnuntinum Archaeological Museums) €7.63. ☎ 0 21 63/3 37 70; www.carnuntum.co.at

Excursions

Rohrau: Harrach'sche Gemäldegalerie – Open Easter-1 Nov, Tues-Sun 10am-5pm. €4.72. ☎ 0 21 64/22 53 18; www.harrach.nwg.at

Rohrau: Geburtshaus Joseph Haydns – Open Tues-Sun 10am-4pm. Closed 1 Jan, 24-26, 31 Dec. €2 (free admission 26 Oct). ☎ 0 21 64/22 68.

Schloßhof: Schloß – Apr-Oct Tues-Sun 10am-5pm. €5.82. ☎ 0 22 85/65 80; www.schlosshof.at

SOPRON   100 Forint are worth about €0.40

Várostorony-Tüztorony – Mid-April to end of September Tues-Sun 10am-6pm. 120 Forint. ☎ 0036/99/31 13 27.

Storno-ház – May-Sept Tues-Sun 10am-6pm; Oct-Apr Tues-Sun 10am-2pm. 150 Forint. ☎ 0036/99/31 13 27.

Fabricius-ház – May-Aug Tues-Sun 10am-6pm; Sept Tues-Sun 10am-2pm. 80 Forint. ☎ 0036/99/31 13 27.

Patika Múzeum – May-end of Sept Tues-Sun 9am-12.30pm and 1.30pm-5pm. 60 Forint. ☎ 0036/99/31 13 27.

Ó-Zsinagóga – May-Aug daily except Tues 9am-5pm; Sept daily except Tues 10am-2pm. 100 Forint. ☎ 0036/99/31 13 27.

Excursions

Raiding: Liszts Geburtshaus – ♿ Palm Sunday-31 Oct daily 9am-noon and 1pm-5pm. €2.18. ☎ 0 26 19/72 20, bgld.lm@aon.at

WIENER NEUSTADT

St. Georgskathedrale – Guided tours (15min) Mon-Fri 10am-10.30am and 2pm-2.30pm, Sat 8am-4pm, Sun 11.30am-5pm. Free entry. ☎ 0 26 22/3 81 20 91.

Excursion

Burg Seebenstein – Guided tours (1hr): Easter-2nd Sun in Oct Sat-Sun at 10.30am, 2pm and 3pm. €4. ☎ 0 26 27/4 70 17.

WIENERWALD

Naturpark Sparbach – Apr-Oct daily 9am-6pm. Closed in bad weather. €1.45. ☎ 0 22 37/76 11.

Hinterbrühl: Seegrotte – Guided tours (45min): Apr-Oct Mon-Fri 9am-noon and 1pm-5pm; Nov-Mar Mon-Fri 9am-noon and 1pm-3pm; all year Sat-Sun 9am-noon and 1pm-3.30pm. €4.72. ☎ 0 22 36/2 63 64; www.tourist-net.co.at/seegr1.htm.

Index

Notes

Please write to us !
Your input will help us to improve our guides.

Please send this questionnaire to the following address:
**MICHELIN TRAVEL PUBLICATIONS, The Edward Hyde Building
Hannay House, 39 Clarendon Road Watford, Herts WD17 1JA**

1. Is this the first time you have purchased THE GREEN GUIDE? yes   no

2. Which title did you buy? :

3. What influenced your decision to purchase this guide?

	Not important at all	Somewhat important	Important	Very important
Cover				
Clear, attractive layout				
Structure				
Cultural information				
Practical information				
Maps and plans				
Michelin quality				
Loyalty to THE GREEN GUIDE collection				

Your comments :

4. How would you rate the following aspects of THE GREEN GUIDE?

	Poor	Average	Good	Excellent
Maps at the beginning of the guide				
Maps and plans throughout the guide				
Description of the sites (style, detail...)				
Depth of cultural information				
Amount of practical information				
Format				

Please comment if you have responded poor or average on any of the above:

5. What do you think about the establishments provided in the guide?

HOTELS:	Not Enough	Sufficient	Too many
All categories			
"Budget"			
"Moderate"			
"Expensive"			
RESTAURANTS:	Not Enough	Sufficient	Too many
All categories			
"Budget"			
"Moderate"			
"Expensive"			

Your comments:

6. On a scale of 1-20, please rate THE GREEN GUIDE (1 being the lowest, 20 being the highest):

How would you suggest we improve these guides?

1. Maps and Plans:

2. Sights:

3. Establishments:

4. Practical Information:

5. Other:

Demographic information: (optional)

Male ☐   Female ☐   Age

Name:

Address: